THE FATE OF THE ELEPHANT

THE FATE
OF THE
ELEPHANT

Douglas H. Chadwick

Sierra Club Books
San Francisco

The Sierra Club, founded in 1892 by John Muir, has devoted itself to the study and protection of the earth's scenic and ecological resources—mountains, wetlands, woodlands, wild shores and rivers, deserts and plains. The publishing program of the Sierra Club offers books to the public as a nonprofit educational service in the hope that they may enlarge the public's understanding of the Club's basic concerns. The point of view expressed in each book, however, does not necessarily represent that of the Club. The Sierra Club has some sixty chapters coast to coast, in Canada, Hawaii, and Alaska. For information about how you may participate in its programs to preserve wilderness and the quality of life, please address inquiries to Sierra Club, 730 Polk Street, San Francisco, CA 94109.

LIBRARY OF CONGRESS CATALOGING-IN-PUBLICATION DATA
Chadwick, Douglas H.
    The fate of the elephant / by Douglas H. Chadwick.
        p.   cm.
    Includes bibliographical references and index.
    ISBN 0-87156-635-4
        1. Elephants.   2. Poaching.   3. Wildlife conservation.   I. Title.
    QL737.P98C43   1992
    599.6'1—dc20   92-4520
                                                                    CIP

Production by Robin Rockey
Jacket design by Paul Bacon
Book design by Amy Evans
Printed on acid-free paper containing a minimum of 50% recovered waste paper of which at least 10% of the fiber content is post-consumer waste.
10   9   8   7   6   5   4   3   2   1

This is for Karen Reeves, whom I just love

CONTENTS

ACKNOWLEDGMENTS

To produce a story of this scope, I depended so much upon the generosity of so many around the globe that any attempt to properly acknowledge their help is bound to be inadequate. I have tried within the book to credit those who led me through elephant country and elephant society. A more complete list appears here. It includes people invaluable in opening doors within foreign lands and Byzantine bureaucracies, people who freely shared hard-won information and ideas, and people who helped keep me alive in the bush. It is anything but a polite phrase to say that without their assistance, this book would not contain nearly as much information. Without their kindness and knowledge, this book would not be.

In no particular order, I wish to thank: Diana McMeekin, Iain and Oria Douglas-Hamilton, Joyce Poole, John Lenhardt, Holly Dublin, David (Jonah) Western, Cynthia Moss, Dave Blasko, Ron Whitfield, Michael Fay, Maranosuke Okazaki, Jean Hromodka, Richard Carroll, Eric Dinerstein, Tom McShane, Bruce Bunting, Michael Schmidt, Lois (Betsy) Rasmussen, Richard Barnes, Karen Barnes, Simon Stuart, Raymond Mbitikon, Gustave Doungoube, Mbutu Clement, Widodo Ramono, Charles Santiapillai, Chris Wemmer, Mohammed Khan bin Momin Khan, Perez Olindo, Joe Kioko, Simon Trevor, Barbara Tayak, Tom Milliken, Chizuki Milliken, Sanet Thanapradit, Bhan Kanin, Choowit Mahamontri, Boran Gowda, N. Sivaganesan, Ajay A. Desai, Mark Butcher, Rowan Martin, Alan Sparrow, Norah Njiraini, Soila Sayialel, Venkatadri Ganapathy, Mohammed Shariff Daim, George Calef, Don Young, Mark Stanley Price, Ian Parker, Esmond Bradley Martin, Cyndee Martin, Daphne Sheldrick, Jorgen Thomsen, Richard Aylwood, Julian Trent, Adrian Read, Isaac Zhou, J. P. Mueleya, Joshua Munsaka, Buck DeVries, Penny DeVries, June Farquhar, Pat Carr-Hartley, Heather Carr-Hartley, Sojayi Mlambo, Kathy Martin, Mike Jones, Maxine Steffen, Rob Monroe, Alan Roocroft, Dick George, Tawny Carlson, Anita Schanberger, Doug Lee, Steve Johnson, Doug Seus, Lynne Seus, Hideomi Tokunaga, Katsuto-shi Saito, Junichi Yano, Shigeyoshi Araki, S. Sunamoto, Tam-otsu Ishibashi, Mikaail Kavanagh, Kageo Takaichi, Edmund Ho, Lee Chi, Meor Osman bin Imam Pinawa, Amy Lau Shuk Man, David Melville, Lee Chat, Jira Jintanugool, Satya Vrat Shastri, Pisit na Patalung, Siasp Kothavala, Zerene Kothavala, P. D. Gaonkar, C. D. Joseph, K. C. Panicker, V. Krishnamurthy, Manas Yaviraj, Constantius Mlay, M. L. Phiphatanachatr Dis-kul, Pranee Thanasamut, Jean Ngbodjourou, Alassan Garba, Ja-cob V. Cheeran, R. Kaimal, R. Seluakumar, A. J. T. Johnsingh, Jim Williams, Richard Lair, Robert Dobias, Niyom Vaewwong, Dee Chaona, Vo Quy, Preecha Phongkum, Sylvain Gerbet, Zaa-ba Zainol Abidin, Jasmi bin Abdul, Ahmad Zanudin bin Abdul Rahman, V. Thamilarasu Vaiyapuri, K. A. Belliappa, S. Ramesh Kumar, Ullas Karanth, Fred Koinange, Edward Barbier, Philip Camford, Tom Claytor, David Maitumo, James Ampany, Gid-eon Omyango Nyabola, James Ndegwa Nguniah, Bill Woodley, Ted Goss, Henry Malenya, Ram Munge, Hassan Idle, Fidelis Mwoki, Leonard M. Odhiambo, Peter Gitema Khsathi, Arthur Green, Anna Kretsinger, Quentin Epps, Henry Prankerd, Phi-lippe Vialette, Boby Jean-Baptiste, Mary Marshall, H. P. J. Pe-ters, Gloria Young, Jean Ndobale, Zaolo Casimir, Mesan Felice, David Fields, Alain LeFol, Martine Dietz, Andy Wilkinson, Alfred Momguenzi, Albert Essengamobe, James Deane, Teal Chadwick, and Russell Chadwick.

This will no sooner go to print than I will probably remember several other people who made important contributions. I apologize for any such omissions. Also, I must point out that despite the length of the list of those who assisted my efforts, I managed to make whatever mistakes this book contains all on my own. My special thanks to Bill Graves, Bill Thompson, John Echave, Robert Poole, Charles McCarry, Bill Garrett, Joseph Judge, Bob Caputo, Jonathan Tourtellot, Margaret Sedeen, Caroline Anderson,

Jan Thompson, and Michael Hopps of National Geographic and to that venerable Society as a whole for supporting the majority of my research. Special gratitude is also due Dr. R. Sukumar of the Indian Institute of Science, who reviewed the chapters on India, and Dr. Peter Hoch of the Missouri Botanical Garden, who took the time to check botanical information for the chapters on central Africa. Finally, I am most grateful to editors Jon Beckmann, Jim Cohee, and Linda Gunnarson of Sierra Club Books for their guidance, patience, and encouragement.

SIBERIA

ꆟꆟꆟꆟ THE NAME SIBERIA comes from *Sibir,* which means the Sleeping Land. Each summer in the far northern part of that region, as rivers cut deeper into their channels and waves from the Arctic Ocean break against the coast, freshly exposed sections of the frozen soil slump away, revealing troves of ivory. They are the tusks of wooly mammoths. Tens of thousands of years ago, these specialized second upper incisor teeth served the giants in defense, display, and dominance battles. Some are more than two-and-a-half times the length of a human. A few, permeated by copper compounds in the soil, are now blue. In places, they lie jumbled together by the hundreds.

Mammoth ivory—along with the rare spiraling tusk of a narwhal whale, often billed as unicorn horn—was the chief trade item from this permafrosted part of the world in ancient times and on through the Middle Ages, when the region was known as the Mongol Khanate of Sibir. The Russian Empire's own colonization of the sleeping land didn't begin until late in the sixteenth century. As Cossacks and other adventurers finally breached the wall of the Ural Mountains and began to explore northern Asia, the first treasures they sent back, even before gold and sable furs, were more tusks. Tales of those prehistoric lodes of ivory, passed along over time and great distances, may have evolved into the widespread legends of elephant graveyards.

I once stood within a mammoth graveyard at the cold sea's edge. Curved spires jutted everywhere from the earth with the midnight sun shining along one side of them. All else lay in fog and shadow. Hesitantly, I reached into the ground mist and picked up a fragment of tusk. Its musty-smelling surface was cracked and grey. Yet when I chipped away this rind, the core emerged white and lustrous, nearly perfectly preserved. Working more carefully now with my knife, I dug at the remaining patches of rot and age. As I did, a figure about the size of an egg took shape. It was a human head. I scraped off the last stains and strained to see the features more clearly. I recognized the face. It was my own.

The earliest known human portrait was one carved onto mammoth ivory 26,000 years ago. The one I saw was part of a dream I dreamed while on a boat rocking at anchor along the shore of Siberia's Lena River. Several days earlier, I had spent the morning watching Yakut carvers work fossil ivory at a native crafts collective. They used electric drills and lathes, and the final products were unremarkable figurines of humans and elephants. Still, with plumes of ivory dust ghosting through the air to give the workshop the unsettling odor of a tooth doctor's office, the scene managed to inscribe itself deep in my memory. That afternoon, I went on to the local science museum, where I remained for a long time before a tall, glass case that held the red-furred hind leg of a young wooly mammoth: more raw material for dreams.

The curator, paleontologist Svetlana Mochanov, guessed that the hindquarter had been cut off and cached in the permafrost by an Ice Age hunter who never returned for the meat. She listed several past discoveries of well-preserved mammoths. Often, it was camp dogs or sled dogs that led the way to an outcrop of prehistoric flesh in the tundra. And sometimes the only result was that the dogs' owner would dig down and extract more meat to feed his team for a while. A prospector claimed to have come upon a fully grown adult mammoth standing upright and completely intact within a block of clear ice squeezed out of a softening hillside.

In the stomachs of mammoth carcasses and in the crevices of their enormous molar teeth, scientists have found buttercups, sedges, dwarf willows—the same sort of plants common on the tundra today. In 1990, developers bulldozing an Ohio peat bog to make a golf course uncovered the remains of a mastodon. Paleontologists sampled what appeared to be the intestinal contents and from them isolated bacteria about 11,000 years old. These may be the oldest living organisms ever found, they announced. But there are more ways than one to define a living organism.

"In 1971," Svetlana related, "an expedition brought back tissues of a mammoth in which the frozen cells were still alive. They spoiled before they could be properly stored. However, if such a find were to be made now, it is quite possible that we could isolate the genetic material and preserve it intact. Given recent advances in microtechniques, it is even possible that the genes could be spliced into the egg of a living elephant. . . ." Surrounded by shelves where skulls of extinct bison rested alongside Stone Age spear tips and scrapers, she held her palms open and fixed me with a questioning look. I nodded to show that I understood: the offspring of elephants with such ancient DNA added to their own could be selectively bred over generations to recreate what would essentially be a living mammoth.

That would be a wonder. And a monument to irony. My trip through remote *Sibir* was a respite from daily news of the world. But before I had left the United States, reports about the slaughter of elephants by ivory poachers had been arriving in a torrent. As a biologist and natural history writer, I had paid close attention. I knew that whereas Africa held an estimated 5 to 10 million elephants—minimum—in the nineteenth century and perhaps 3 million as recently as 1970, it now held more like 600,000. Or less. Some wildlife protection groups felt that a guess of 400,000 might be high. At the rate these modern giants were being felled, experts predicted, they would be nearly extinct in the wild within another decade or two. Conservationists were drawing up a sort of triage strategy in which the limited money and manpower available to defend the giants would go toward reinforcing the most secure parks and preserves while other areas were essentially written off. It was hoped that 250,000 elephants might be saved this way, if the plan worked. Already, there was a move to place the African elephant on the endangered species list along with the last 35,000 to 55,000 wild Asian elephants.

Svetlana's husband, Yuri Mochanov, was instrumental in unearthing remains of the Diuktai culture of northeastern Siberia. The first bands of people to reach North America toward the end of the Ice Ages were probably Diuktai, and they were probably following mammoth herds. Like the carver of the first human portrait, these Late Paleolithic people preyed primarily upon mammoths, along with wooly rhinos, bison, and reindeer. Svetlana took me by boat to where she and Yuri had been working. Their excavations were on a hillside overlooking a bend of the Lena River and a tremendous expanse of low ridges and autumn-colored taiga that swept away to the north. I could make out the earth's curvature on the horizon. This was a good perch for watching lunar eclipses and northern lights, Svetlana said. She thought that might have been one reason the ancients chose the spot for burial ceremonies and, some of the evidence led her to think, ritual slayings.

I sat on the sacred ground and closed my eyes, feeling the upstream wind on my face. Beside me was a woman who spoke of reanimating mammoths while, far to the south, herd after herd of elephants collapsed in an explosion of screams and dust mixed with automatic rifle fire. Around us were the remains of people who sang to the stars and the northern lights while slitting throats on the ground. In what was still the Soviet Far East at the time, I had run into a Communist Party bureaucrat so obsessed with making sure that I wrote only good things about his region that he made my time there miserable. At one point he asked me about some people I had visited without his official permission. He demanded to know their names and what ideas they held. I told him that he needed a vacation. I have no doubt the unrepentant old Stalinist had sent more than his share of countrymen off to the gulag in shackles over the years. Was he merely the product of a modern totalitarian regime? Or was he, more in the tradition of the Diuktai, sacrificing lives to maintain his sense of order in the universe? Was there a difference? What is it in us that spawns and perpetuates such systems in the first place?

In my travels, there were days when I felt I was understanding more of the world in which I lived and days when I understood less and less. This was a less day. I had been blind-sided by several lately. Winter was on the way. It was getting to be time to turn home.

🔲🔲🔲🔲🔲🔲🔲🔲🔲🔲🔲🔲

I had been back in the United States a few weeks and was working around my house in Whitefish, Montana, when I got a telephone call from Charles McCarry in Washington, D.C. A former Central Intelligence Agency man, McCarry had turned to writing and produced, among other works, best-selling spy novels. He also happened to be the editor in charge of freelance writers for *National Geographic* magazine at that moment. In addition to producing chapters for several National Geographic books—my trip to Siberia was for a book on the fast-changing Soviet Union, which turned out to be changing even faster than we realized—I had written nine articles for the magazine. McCarry was calling to offer me number ten.

"Elephants," he said. "Elephants of the world."

"Of the world!"

"Right. We want to cover Asian elephants as well as African elephants, and everything from circuses to the ivory trade. We're talking about a lot of time and a lot of work. What do you think?"

During my first visit to Africa several years before, I had spent two months in Namibia's Etosha National Park. There were elephants chasing off lions at the waterholes, elephants rising above the low thorn scrub like landforms, elephants walking in the sky when the heat shimmering off the white salt pans formed mirages, elephants every day. Then there was the day I went along with a wildlife veterinarian as he felled two big bulls, or males, with a tranquilizer gun so that he could inoculate them against an anthrax epidemic sweeping the area. As the animals sank onto their sides, I began to explore their live geography with my hands. And it was as if I had never seen an elephant before. The veined ears, enormous leaves of flesh. Hillsides of skin, cracked and furrowed in honeycomb patterns like mud at a drying waterhole. A naked club of a tail with its fringe of stiff, black hairs. A penis nearly four feet long. And then the trunk, coiled upon the sand—the fleshy, fingerlike projection on the upper side of the tip bending slightly over twin nostrils and trembling with the rush of air in and out; miraculous organ, like a separate creature, animated by 50,000 muscles; taster, trumpet, periscope of smell, snorkel and showerhead, arm and hand. "With a single hand / He can pull two palm trees to the ground," a poem of West Africa's Yoruba people proclaims. "If he had two hands / He could tear the sky like an old rag." And when we found elephants dead of anthrax and burned their bodies to keep scavengers from spreading the disease, it took eleven dump trucks of wood for each one's funeral pyre. . . .

"Okay? Come back for a story meeting and we'll go over the details," McCarry was saying.

"Okay. Sure. I . . . Yes. Elephants. Yes!" As I replaced the phone, I realized that I had just decided what I would be doing for the next two to three years. I also realized that I was not going to have any second thoughts about it.

When I go out to observe an animal, I go with the expectation that I will do more than learn about it. I will learn *from* it, as a student from a teacher. Each successful species is a model of how to exist within a given environment. Each has arrived at a solution for living with its own kind and a solution to the problem of living among other species. Each perceives the world in a unique way, often through senses that I share but have not taken full advantage of, or through habits of awareness that I would do well to practice.

Now I would be dealing not only with the largest and most powerful creature that walks this planet but with one of the smartest. An inspirational teacher. The immediate question was how many might escape the ivory poachers' onslaught. If significant populations survived, the next question would be how animals that require such enormous amounts of food and space would coexist with a human population expected to shoot past 10 billion in the near future. It occurred to me that the fate of the last true land giants might teach all of us about what the future will be like, insofar as elephant conservation measures our willingness to protect large areas of the natural world. If we are not able to safeguard wildlands in sufficiently big tracts, then the processes and patterns that shaped existing biological communities can no longer operate as they have for millions of years. And that would mark the end of natural history. From there on, we would be pinwheeling into an unfathomable era with no reference point other than the shifting impulses and convictions of humankind.

The number of trees in the forest and fishes in the sea, the very color and transparency of the air, the temperature of the globe; these things did appear to be turning into extensions of human cultures and values. So tell me, as the future of virtually every species comes to depend upon the whim of just one, how does a person write meaningfully about natural history?

Here is what I had been doing: Typically, I would begin by recounting the special qualities of this wild creature or that one, move on to the grave problems confronting it, and conclude that it might not have much longer to go; that, at best, it might survive as a sort of precious artifact in some shard of its former range. This was not some formula I had settled upon. It was the essential situation in case after case. I was a half-step away from becoming a professional mourner. I could not bear the thought that the most I might aspire to now was to craft fine elegies in the Age of Extinction.

Were we really that close to a fundamental change in the nature of life on Earth? Or was I overly alarmed? Or was the change even more sweeping and farther along than I perceived? I would be off soon enough to elephant habitat in the tropics and subtropics, the biologically richest regions of the globe, to gauge the scale of transformation for myself. Right now, I just wanted to lay my hands on a live elephant, as I had in Namibia. It seemed important to make direct contact with the sheer physical wonder of these beings again and charge myself up for whatever was to come.

So I went to the zoo.

First Touch

᠎᠎᠎᠎ You don't get sniffed when you meet an elephant face to face in its compound. You get vacuumed. The giant looms before you, and its head alone is larger than any of the bears and gorillas you passed along the way. And from the head extends a tube of tissue as long and heavy as any man, and it pulls the scent off your body with a seemingly endless intake of breath. This probe—this colossal tentacle, this moist-nostriled, finger-headed python—is especially interested in your armpits and crotch, homing in like a great, rude, toothless dog to where the ripest essences collect. It also savors your feet, inhaling more details about you and where you have been lately and what you were up to there.

The elephant is treating you more or less as it would one of its own kind that it feels comfortable around. When such elephants greet each other, they reach out with their trunks and sniff tip to tip, or, more typically, extend the trunk tips into each other's mouths. The mutual gesture conveys information through smell, taste, and touch simultaneously. There is also a sort of mutual reassurance, as in a handshake, and the touch part of the greeting may expand into a rubbing of each other's tongue and gums.

That is what the elephant handlers at Marine World–Africa, U.S.A. in Vallejo, California, were doing while I met their charges: rubbing the animals' gums with their hands, reassuring them. And reassuring me, keeping things cool. Every now and again, a captive elephant is offended by someone or simply takes an instant dislike to a person and destroys him or her. The giant picks up the human creature and hurls it away, or flings it down and then tramples it, runs it through with a tusk, or does a head-stand on it, which is the handlers' term for dropping to one knee and plunging the weight of the forehead onto the victim. They say the headstand is a common technique when an elephant decides to nail somebody, which is not often but is less rare than generally supposed.

"You can go ahead and touch her," handler Dave Blasko said as a female Asian elephant named Margie inspected me. "They like it when you blow into their trunk." I cupped the probe now hovering in front of my face and gave it a sample of my breath and, as it stayed there expectantly, worked my hands up the trunk and felt them pricked by the short, stiff sensory hairs protruding from the skin along its length. Then I was touching the forehead and then the side of the head and finally stroking the curve of the jaw. I looked up into Margie's eye. It was a good eye, a gentle brown eye with long, long lashes. No tense movements in the lids. Not a lot of white showing around the iris. In many mammals, the eyes remain the single best indicator of an individual animal's mood and intentions, or at least the one we primates are best equipped to read. The feeling you get from an animal's eye is probably a better guide to what you ought to do next than any theories or general expectations you bring to the encounter. Margie opened her mouth. Dave nodded, and I began to rub her gums and the bulging pad of her tongue.

I did not hear her rumble of contentment—not exactly. I felt something resonate in my bones. Leaning slowly back to where I could see her forehead, I noticed that it was fluttering. I put my hand on the skin there, which covers a large sinus cavity in the front of the skull, and felt the vibrations more strongly. This was how researcher Katharine Payne discovered that elephants communicate with infrasound, or frequencies below the range of human hearing. In 1984, as Payne was watching Asian elephants at the Washington Park Zoo in Portland, Oregon, she felt the air around her throbbing. Having worked earlier with great whales and their songs, she was primed to recognize the possibility that giants of the land might also carry on conversations in wavelengths that humans can only sense, at best, as a kind of rolling, phantom thunder. (Actually, Georg von Bekesy had shown years earlier that the cochlea of the elephant's ear is designed to detect very low frequencies, and dolphin communication researcher John Lilly wrote in 1978 that "elephants apparently communicate in regions subsonic for humans.")

Of course, elephants also have a vocabulary of squeals, grunts, growls, roars, trumpet blasts, barks, putters, and rumbles that we can hear. In confinement, some amuse themselves by putting their trunks in their own mouths and blowing to create different sounds. Dave mentioned that Bandula, another Asian female, would put her trunk tip on the ground and step on it to squeeze high-pitched tones out of the passing air. In other words, Bandula had taught herself how to whistle. Meanwhile, many captive elephants respond to seventy to eighty different commands in the human language. Some understand a hundred.

Between twenty and thirty commands are necessary simply for care and maintenance. For example, an elephant's toenails grow at a rate suited to a beast that normally walks at least twenty to thirty miles each day in the wild. Without trimming, they can soon become ingrown, leading to painful infections. And once an elephant stops moving, it is highly susceptible to arthritis in the bones of its columnlike legs. In the old days, when zoo elephants were simply thrown into cages for a lifetime of solitary confinement, most became so crippled they could no longer have walked away even if set free. You can still find places, such as the zoo in Paris, where the elephant on display is expected to stand on ruined legs alone in a dim room until it dies. To keep a captive elephant in reasonable health, it should be exercised, socially stimulated by both its handlers and other elephants, and trained to, at the very least, lift one leg at a time in order to undergo nail-filing on an almost daily basis.

It should also be made manageable enough to submit to veterinary attention. If the vet has to knock out the animal with drugs every time he needs to treat some affliction, the risk of death becomes considerable. Accidental overdoses and allergic reactions are always threats, but the main problem has to do with the fact that elephants breathe differently than most mammals do. Instead of a diaphragm contracting and creating a vacuum in the pleural cavity to draw in air, their lungs depend upon the muscles that surround them to force air in and out. As a result, an elephant that falls unconscious onto its side is likely to develop serious breathing problems in a short time. If it collapses onto its knees with its head hanging down forward, the breathing passage becomes choked off and the animal will suffocate even more quickly.

The handlers were eager to present the training they did as a way of safeguarding the elephants' physical and mental health. The more tricks an elephant is taught to perform, the better various muscle groups are kept in tone and the more alert and active its mind remains. And the higher the status of the trainer within the close-knit fraternity of handlers, though they did not say that. Dave was working with a young Asian male named Roman. They made a nice pair as they strolled the grounds of Marine World greeting visitors: dark-haired Dave in his jeans and Western shirt, trim and athletic, with Roman, already the taller of the two at five years of age and 4000 pounds, freshly washed, his juvenile coat of long, reddish hairs standing out from his head and shoulders like mammoth fur. Roman gives rides and runs through a remarkably agile routine of stunts in an arena here. Sometimes, after playing a harmonica, the young male enacts a bedroom scene in which he wakes up, knocks an alarm clock off a table, pulls the blanket back over his head, then finally rises to shower and brush his teeth. Dave takes Roman to do Las Vegas shows, television appearances, parades, fairs, and the occasional Republican inauguration in Sacramento. A young, untrained, Asian elephant male sells for $30,000 and up. What is a well-trained one worth? Roman is insured for a million dollars.

"Some of the neatest tricks in their repertoire are ones they show you," Dave told me. "You just gain control over this thing they do bit by bit."

What elephants can train themselves to do is what I was most interested in, and this is what I heard. At any number of zoos, the elephants have figured out how to turn on water faucets. (They had in the bush of Namibia, too, cranking open the flow of water at windmill-powered wells within Etosha National Park and at livestock ponds around the reserve's borders. "It wouldn't be so bad if the big bastards would learn how to turn them off once they're done," one rancher told me.) They have also learned how to unfasten certain types of shackles put on their feet at night. "Once they see how you put them on, they'll know how to take them off," was the usual comment. A handler at the Phoenix Zoo accused one elephant of hastily putting on its fetters again so that they looked fastened when it saw someone coming, just as a human prisoner who had worked free of his bonds might do when the jailer arrives. On a day when I was visiting there, one of the handlers hosing down the elephant stall jokingly said to an onlooking African elephant, "Rafiki, you're in the way. Why don't you go outside and chain yourself?" Later on, the handlers could not find her until they looked in the yard. Rafiki had gone outside and chained herself.

꙳꙳꙳꙳꙳꙳꙳꙳꙳꙳꙳꙳

I was at the Phoenix Zoo to meet Ruby. Originally from Thailand, she was sixteen at the time and weighed 7800 pounds, and I was told not to mention the word *paint* aloud in her presence. Since she was present, walking beside me and trainers Anita Schanberger and Tawny Carlson, we spoke in code.

"I started teaching Ruby to engage in artistic endeavors as a form of enrichment—you know, something else fun to do for an animal stuck here in a compound," Tawny said. "We'd noticed all the elephants in the yard doodling with sticks on the sand or scratching the concrete walls with them, and Ruby was a pretty regular doodler. So we started off with a huge piece of cardboard as a canvas. At first, Ruby would P . . A . . I . . N . .T the canvas and the people holding the canvas, all with big, swinging strokes. Gradually, she got the idea of what she was supposed to do, and we cut down the size of the canvas to where she's working on eighteen-by-twenty-two-inch pieces now." That's like one of us painting on a cigarette paper, I thought.

"Anyway, Anita came up to me one day and asked, 'Can elephants see color?' I said, 'I dunno.' So Anita went all over

looking up information. Nothing. Everybody just assumed elephants were colorblind," Tawny continued. "Then the vet here
asked me one day, 'If Ruby can't see color, why does she always
pick the same ones?' So we did some crude tests with different-
colored objects and rewarded Ruby for picking certain colors.
She made the correct choice about 80 percent of the time."

When Anita started quantifying the pigments Ruby chose for
her canvases, it turned out that the elephant first selected either
blue or red from a full-spectrum palette about 80 percent of the
time. Equally interesting was the fact that if, say, an orange
truck parked close by in view, Ruby might choose orange instead. Or if a woman in a yellow dress came along with the handlers that day, then yellow was the first color on the canvas. A
zoo visitor was once taken ill while watching Ruby paint, and
paramedics were called to the scene. They wore blue suits. It
might have been a coincidence that after they left, Ruby painted
a blue blob surrounded by a swirl of red.

The day I watched this process, Tawny began by asking,
"Ruby, how would you like to *paint*?" Giant ears began flapping.
The elephant's eyes widened, the tail lifted and kinked, then the
trunk began flipping up and down. Ruby was rocking with excitement. The handlers brought out palette, brushes, and canvas. Ruby began with blue. She made very small dabs and loops
on the extreme lower right-hand corner of the canvas that she
towered above, concentrating the color in that one particular
section. This went on for several minutes. It looked to me like
Ruby was stuck there doodling, and I asked Anita what this had
to do with making a painting. Anita said, "That's where she
wants to paint right now. That's what she's working on. Okay.
Let's try something." Anita then rotated the canvas so that what
had been the lower right-hand corner was now the upper left-
hand corner. Ruby stood back a bit and studied the new arrangement for about ten seconds. Then she went right back to filling
in the part of the canvas that she had been working on, though
it was 180 degrees from where it had been before. Finally, when
she had finished that to her satisfaction, she went on to the heart
of the canvas with a new color and looser strokes.

Much later, traveling through Thailand, I heard that a painting made by an Asian elephant in an American zoo was shown to a Japanese Buddhist nun. The nun looked over the brush strokes, nodded, and said: Ah yes, that is the symbol for Buddha. Other stories floating around involve elephants that spelled out messages in the dirt or on paper. They are probably apocryphal, which is a polite way of saying they are bull, but I like them just the same. I like anything that makes us pause, however briefly, and ask: I wonder if an elephant really could do that. Naw; probably not. But I wonder how close. . . .

"Sometimes," Anita said, "we speak in complete sentences— for example, 'Ruby, hand me the brush, will you?'—and the brush suddenly shows up in your hand. I don't know what she understands exactly. It could just be she's so sensitive that she seems to anticipate what you might do next. Once, to make an entertainment system for her, I drilled a lot of holes in a log box and set up a complicated choice test with a food reward. Well, it was too tough. She tried it two or three times, then picked the whole thing up and just handed it to me, as if saying, 'What's the point here, Anita?' They know what they're doing at their level. We're asking them to make the link to our level, to understand how we look at things. That's asking a lot."

Ruby's artwork and Anita's research do not yet prove conclusively that elephants can see color. To satisfy scientific criteria for that, Anita first has to rule out the possibility that Ruby is responding to different tonalities of grey. This involves a bewildering series of experiments and tests of film emulsions and checks of actual wavelengths of light and checks of the checking instruments and the fact that different human cultures perceive different hues of red as true red, and so on. But color perception is not the revelation here. What we are learning is that a great many of the limitations we ascribe to such animals may have mainly to do with limitations in our viewpoint.

Ruby has now been painting for about four years with no waning of her interest. Nor has her original interest in playing with rocks and sticks to trace lines in the dirt diminished. Her paintings are in demand these days. Money raised from their sale has paid for her own artificial insemination, research on color discrimination, captive breeding facilities for black-footed ferrets and Mexican wolves, and an attempt to save the Pemba Island fruit bat in the wild. Still, the zoo, which at first let her paint for two years in private, is reluctant to have her face the palette and easel too often, lest she get bored. The whole affair still revolves around keeping this captive animal entertained and interested in her environment. In the meantime, Anita thinks, the African elephants in the yard have grown jealous of all the attention Ruby gets for her painting. They have taken to drawing on the retaining walls with the ends of logs, leaving designs for everyone to see.

Judy, an Asian female in her twenties living at Marine World, used to bunch up her chain and stand on it, then act as if she couldn't reach the meal of hay heaped near her. When a keeper moved in to push the hay pile closer, she would step off the chain, surge ahead, and whack the person with her trunk. She hurt three people with this trick before she was better trained.

Now and then, elephants simply remove the door to a cage by undoing nuts and bolts or pulling out nails or unscrewing screws. After staff at the Phoenix Zoo put steel plates over water valves in the yard to keep the elephants from turning them on, the elephants used rocks to break the nuts loose from the bolts holding the plates and turned the valves on anyway. Tava, a female at Marine World, once used a log in the yard as a lever to pry open a barred retaining wall. The handlers decided to use a strip of spikes on the ground as a barrier instead. The elephants got more logs and built a bridge across it. At another zoo, handlers found elephants throwing tires from their yard onto nearby trees, weighing down the branches to where the animals could grab them to eat. Initially, an elephant could have been merely tossing tires about to entertain itself when one landed in a tree and rewarded the animal with food. Only then, perhaps, did the animal make the connection between tire-tossing and food, and other elephants learned by watching it. The point is that it is not necessary to credit the first tire-tosser with forethought.

It doesn't matter how many crucial human inventions also

came about by happy accident—serendipitous diddling. As humans have set up the rules, anything an animal does is assumed to be fairly reflexive or, at best, simple-minded unless incontrovertible proof is offered to the contrary. During the first third of this century, Robert Yerkes of Yale University began exploring chimpanzee intelligence. When he showed that chimps were capable of using a stick to reach food beyond the grasp of their hands, and of piling several short boxes on top of one another in order to get to a reward overhead, this was considered a revelation. The implications are still being debated, for we have no solid framework for speaking about animal reasoning abilities. In his book *Apes, Men and Language*, Eugene Linden wonders whether this is because we honestly never imagined that animals could have such potentials or because we did not want to admit other life forms into a citadel we had reserved exclusively for ourselves—a citadel Linden calls the Temple of Reason.

Perhaps it is easier to let a few chimps in the door now that we have analyzed their DNA and discovered that 98.4 percent is identical to ours. Of the active part of the chromosomes, where the actual genetic instructions are sent forth, chimps and humans are 99.6 percent similar, which makes chimps and humans more closely related than chimps and gorillas. Most scientists now accept the chimpanzee technique of poking a twig into a termite mound and licking off the insects still clinging to the twig when it is withdrawn as a limited form of tool-using.

But what do we make of elephants that use sticks simply to scratch themselves? Is that tool-using? Nita, an Asian elephant at the San Diego Zoo, broke off one of her short female tusks, called a tush. Afterward, she seemed to be plagued by itching inside the empty socket left in her upper lip and would use a stick to reach into the cavity and scratch. She was also given to gripping the wrist of a trainer and guiding the man's hand up into the socket so that he could give her a more thorough scratching. Was that using a tool-user as a tool? And what of the zoo elephants that take sticks in their trunks and use them to draw in food otherwise too far to reach, just as Yerkes's chimps did? Or those that pile logs in their yard to use as steps to reach overhanging branches? A handler told me of watching more than one tethered elephant use its trunk like an air hose to blow an out-of-reach object against a wall so that it would bounce back within grasping distance. Isn't that good enough to win at least a day pass to the Temple of Reason?

Then there was Bertha, an Asian elephant who worked at the Nugget Casino in Reno, Nevada. As Dave described the situation to me, the showgirls there had to pass by Bertha on their way to the dressing room, and the elephant would sometimes try to get them to give her a treat from a nearby cabinet. The experienced ones had all been told to say no firmly. However, Bertha was able to spot women who had just been hired, and as a new employee hustled toward the dressing room, she would find her wrist suddenly in the grip of an elephant's trunk. Then Bertha would lead her toward the cabinet and hold her arm out toward a key dangling from a string beside the box. And there the arm would stay until the showgirl reasoned that she was to use the key and open the cabinet. Once she did, her arm was freed instantly. After all, Bertha was going to need her trunk to get at all those sugar cubes waiting inside the cabinet.

"It's almost like a chess game when you work with these animals. If you're not training them, they're training you," was Dave's assessment. I heard the same comment from other handlers, and I had heard it before from people who worked with dolphins, grizzlies, dogs, primates, and, of course, children. I think it means that the doors to the Temple are being chewed, tusked, rammed, pried, unscrewed, and unbolted, while a human hand, perhaps guided by an elephant trunk, hovers hesitantly before the lock.

A surprising number of handlers compared working with elephants to working with mentally handicapped people. At the San Diego Zoo, the director of the elephant program, Alan Roocroft, had hired handlers with a background in working with the handicapped. He also had a program that enabled mildly retarded and mute children to come and help out at the elephant compound. They performed basic chores and in return were allowed to touch and interact with the elephants. I noticed a boy with Down's syndrome there one day and was intrigued by the way he changed from withdrawn to buoyant in the elephants' presence. I had become aware that I, too, felt a powerful sense of opening up when I was around them.

My brother and sister are mentally retarded. Neither can speak in much more than calls and hooting exclamations. I learned from them that you work with what you have and that words are far less essential to real communication than we assume; in fact, they often conspire against it. Almost alone among the people I know, my brother and sister always mean exactly what they tell me they mean. Animals do the same. I have my brother and sister to thank for making me eager to listen.

Elephants in confinement, being regularly fed and frequently bored, will work considerably harder for a reward of play than for food. The trick in training them, then, is to combine learning with play. Game motivation, psychologists call it. Positive reinforcement. The old standbys of pain and fear work best when used sparingly. Some elephants will purposely act naughty to get the attention they crave. "A lot of training with these animals is just bluff," Dave added. "It's not the physical hurt you can give them; it's the mental punishment that finally controls them."

Yet some degree of physical pain is almost inevitably required. Here, the chief tool is the ankus, a short stick with a sharp metal hook at the tip. It is the same basic instrument used for millennia with domestic elephants in Asia, though some zoo people prefer to speak of it in modern behavioral terms as a surrogate tusk. Although pachyderm, meaning thick-skinned, is a synonym for elephant, the elephant's epidermis is thin in relation to the bulk of the body underneath and fairly easily scratched and torn. It is vulnerable to sunburn and remarkably sensitive to pricks as small as insect bites. Pluck a hair from the hide and the giant shudders. Tug on the loose folds of skin on the leg with an ankus, and the whole elephant moves forward. Make the ankus dig a bit into the nerve-packed base of the ear or the side of the face, and you'll have a recalcitrant animal's undivided attention.

When you've got an elephant acting especially ornery—about

half-tough, as Dave would say—you might have to use an electric cattle prod. Since one fully grown elephant is the size of a small band of cattle, a handler might hose down the giant with water, *then* put the prod to it if the animal is still acting balky. And sooner or later, a handler may have to just plain beat some elephant in a last-ditch effort to establish control before the animal kills someone or has to be destroyed itself.

That's how the handlers explained it to me, anyway. The reason everyone was doing so much explaining was that I arrived not long after several incidents involving battered trainers and battered elephants had made quite a stir in California. Staff at the San Francisco Zoo were so uptight about publicity that they wouldn't even grant me an interview. A female named Tinkerbelle had hurt a veterinary technician there, and the public, having heard reports of painful training practices, was blaming the situation on the handlers. The elephant, they assumed, was only lashing back at its tormentors. Earlier, the San Diego Zoo acquired a half-tough elephant named Dunda. Her previous training had been inconsistent, to put it nicely, and she reacted to her new social environment by threatening and injuring several people. One day, a crowd of tourists rattling merrily along on the little zoo train happened to roll by the elephant yard just as several trainers ganged up to work Dunda over with whatever was at hand, including shovels, and soon every newspaper reader in the state knew her name. The furor was loud and continued until California passed a law specifically prohibiting the abuse of elephants. Dunda went on to kill someone.

Most of the handlers I met did not think the public had any comprehension of what it takes to control a potentially aggressive beast of monstrous proportions. They saw the public as afflicted with what they referred to as the Dumbo syndrome, meaning that people ordinarily reluctant to approach a strange dog will tend to walk right up to begin petting a multiton zoo elephant, perceiving it as a gentle giant. The handlers get doubly irked by criticism of abuse because they view themselves as people who love elephants far more than most and, moreover, love them for what they really are.

I think they do. The handlers I met lived and breathed elephants. They were not zookeepers with twenty different species to tend to. They were elephant men, elephant women. They lived at the elephant house and in the elephant yard every day and thought about elephants and their personalities, and the relationships of each keeper and his or her personality to each elephant, and so on to the point of monomania. "Elephants are a religion with us. We don't care if we're in debt or don't have a decent car to drive or anything. We get to be with elephants," was how Jean Hromadka, the lead elephant keeper at the San Diego Zoo, put it.

"The term *humane* treatment of animals mystifies me," Dave Blasko told me one afternoon. "After all, what animal would want to be treated the way humans treat each other?"

Handlers tend to believe that it is crucial to become, in effect, the top elephant in the hierarchy and run a responsive herd. Some clearly relish the role, finding in it a perfect outlet for domineering urges that probably drew them to animal training in the first place. Others like the give and take more than the tight control and are mainly concerned with developing bonds with individual animals. In short, the spectrum of temperaments and motivations among elephant people is not much different than among horse people or dog people, people as a whole, and elephants as a whole.

In recent years, there has been a definite swing in the popular consciousness of Western society toward recognizing our commonality with intelligent mammals. This is largely because people have a good deal more information to go on. While scientific studies continue to reveal new aspects of animal behavior, media such as nature films bring the beasts into our living rooms every day of the week. Once we accept that those mammals have many of the same characteristics and needs that we do, it brings up the question of what sort of basic rights they deserve. Two centuries ago, no one spoke of racism. The practice was so ingrained that no one thought of it as a kind of prejudice. Now the word *speciesism* is beginning to appear in the political arena.

That trend-setting California was trying to legislate how hard you can sock an elephant didn't surprise me when I first heard the news. Coming at a time when wild elephants were being butchered for tusks and left to rot by the tens of thousands and Americans were still buying tons of ivory, the training method argument seemed slightly beside the point—or would have, were it not for the prospect that zoos might one day harbor the last living elephants.

Zoos have increasingly become reservoirs for endangered species, taking on the role of artificial breeding grounds, always in the hope that a surplus might one day be transplanted back into a protected segment of the species' original habitat. Lately, zookeepers have been working to standardize the commands used in elephant training so that animals shipped between facilities in the hope of building reproductive social groups can be more easily handled. Yet in all of North America there have been no successful births of African elephants and only fifty-odd births of Asian elephants. The breeding physiology and psychology of these animals is still not well enough defined.

I had assumed that people in Asia knew all about breeding elephants in captivity. Hadn't the giants been part of their cultures for thousands of years, hauling timber, plowing fields, transporting goods and royalty, and waging war as the prototype of tanks? Of course, the zoo people told me, but breeding a tame female would have meant taking her out of the work force for nearly five years at a stretch—twenty-two months of gestation followed by two to three years of nursing—and then having to wait several more years until the youngster was old enough to begin serious training. The Asians had always found it more expedient to capture subadult elephants from the wild and break them to harness. Besides, no one much wanted to have to deal with tame elephants thundering around in a courtship frenzy. And many Asians considered a wild-caught elephant to be ultimately less dangerous than an elephant raised among people, for the captive-raised animal would never have the wild one's innate fear of humans.

About 40 percent of the births of Asian elephants in North America have been at Portland's Washington Park Zoo, where chief veterinarian Mike Schmidt and researcher Lois Rasmussen have been analyzing the chemistry of blood and urine for many years to chart oestrous cycles. The female named Rosie has given birth to six calves here, a record for the Western Hemisphere. Shortly before one of those births, zoo handlers moved Rosie's best friend, an old female named Tuy Hoa, to another stall because she was nearing death and the handlers didn't want the public to see an elephant dying. Rosie delayed her calf's birth a half-hour, then an hour, then a day. Four days later, they put Tuy Hoa back with Rosie, and Rosie delivered within an hour.

Females are in heat for only a very short period—twenty-four to forty-eight hours out of every sixteen weeks. They tend to be fairly choosy about which male they will accept, and the whole affair can be easily disrupted by the presence of humans. Artificial insemination is an alternative. Males are held in a crush, a hydraulically powered metal version of the squeeze chute made of logs that is used in Asia to immobilize elephants, and then electroejaculated to collect sperm. One 13,000-pound Asian bull broke every metal door ever put on the crush, and no one has tried to put him in since. Another has been electroejaculated more than 130 times. Despite nearly a decade of efforts, however, successful impregnation of a female through such methods continues to elude Schmidt and his colleagues.

Meanwhile, in San Diego, Alan Roocroft gathers support for his dream of a compound stretching over many acres where people could build a facsimile of the elephants' natural habitat. Then, perhaps, the animals could rebuild their natural social structure and carry on with the creating and rearing of young the way elephants are supposed to. I know these are to be viewed as hopeful developments, but there remains in them something profoundly disheartening—something of an admission that an end to true wildness is possible, maybe even inevitable. I had started off my assignment by looking at what might be the future. Now, I began booking flights to such elephant country as remained in the present.

TWO

THE PAST

🔳🔳🔳🔳 THE DEMISE OF the dinosaurs marked the end of the Cretaceous period 65 million years ago and was followed by the Paleocene epoch, which lasted until 54 million years ago. The Paleocene is usually considered the beginning of the Age of Mammals. Yet it was barely under way when a different category of dinosaurs once again established a sort of rule. These were the ones whose scales had been modified into feathers. These were the birds, which taxonomists now lump together with dinosaurs as archosaurs. In existence as far back as the Jurassic period, they were well prepared to fill some of the niches that the reptiles had suddenly left vacant. Where fast, two-legged, sharp-toothed dinosaurs such as *Struthiomimus* had stalked, now huge, flightless, cruel-beaked birds such as *Diatryma*, the terror crane, lorded it over the scurrying little mammals.

The Paleocene had empty niches left for mammals as well, and it was therefore a time of unprecedented opportunity. Eventually, the existing groups of mammals began to develop forms large enough to withstand the terror birds and, in some cases, compete with them as predators. As the mammals continued to radiate into available niches, they produced entirely new taxonomic orders. Among them was one called the Proboscidae, after the Latin *proboscis*, meaning nose. In the distant future, it would include elephants. But from where or which creatures the first proboscideans came, no one is certain.

If we look among living animals for the species most closely related to elephants, we find ourselves off among the manatees and dugongs, commonly called sea cows. Highly streamlined for swimming, they are the sole truly aquatic herbivores among mammals. In common with elephants, they have thick, dense bones and a pattern of tooth succession in which new molars grow in at the rear of the jaw and migrate toward the front to replace old ones. And, like elephants, the females have noticeable mammary glands located on their chest, rather than on their abdomen as most mammals do. This is one reason manatees and dugongs are believed to have spawned legends of mermaids, soft-breasted sirens of the seas.

The only other living kin of elephants are furry scramblers that can just about fit into your coat pocket—the hyraxes, native to Africa and southwest Asia. Tree hyraxes sleep in holes in tree trunks by day and forage in the forest canopy at night. That is when campers new to such woods sit bolt upright every few minutes, sure that a leopard is going berserk on a branch just above their tent, for the little tree hyrax's territorial proclamation is an outrageous crescendo of growling croaks and shrieks that can be heard two miles away. Rock hyraxes tend to live in colonies on stony outcroppings anywhere from the plains to the mountaintops, grazing on surrounding vegetation during daylight hours. Both kinds of hyraxes display upper incisors that have developed into little tusks, and both have curiously elephantlike feet with padded bottoms and broad nails at the base of the toes. Still, the very largest among them are barely the size of a woodchuck.

The sea cows, order Sirenia, and hyraxes, order Hyracoidea, are classified together with the Proboscidae in the superorder Subungulata. But that doesn't really tell us much more than we knew before about what sort of beast the proboscideans actually came from. The best paleontologists can do is theorize a generalized marsh-dweller roughly the size of a pig. Fossil beds from the late Eocene epoch in North Africa have yielded a short-legged swamp inhabitant of that sort named *Moeritherium* that is often held up as an example of the earliest true proboscideans. Some taxonomists regard *Moeritherium* as atypical, pointing out that it appears more highly specialized for amphibious life in the manner of a hippopotamus than other proboscideans were. But then some taxonomists see this as all the more evidence of a common ancestry with early manatees and dugongs.

Later proboscideans appear to have remained strongly associated with swampy habitats. The trunk, formed by a fusion of the upper lip, palate, and nostrils, gradually lengthened over time. Possibly, this organ made it easier for the animal to gather submerged vegetation while moving along the shores of a marsh and through shallow water. In that respect, it could be viewed as a unique alternative to developing a longer neck—an alternative that enabled the animal to keep its head high enough to spot potential danger as it fed. But who is to say that the trunk didn't originally develop in part as a kind of snorkel and scent detector for animals that spent a lot of time in deeper water? The only other large mammals with trunks are the tapirs. Theirs is little more than a long snout by comparison, but it is a prehensile one, capable of grasping vegetation and drawing it into the mouth to be eaten. Although tapirs are not related to proboscideans, they frequent wet areas and are known to submerge completely at times to feed on aquatic plants. It may be that the proboscidean trunk originated because it offered some advantage in watery areas, then elongated for different reasons—such as the simple fact that the animals were also developing longer and longer tusks, which would have made it more difficult to eat directly with their mouths.

Whatever the case, the proboscideans' approach worked. They proliferated into almost two hundred species and spread to every continent except Antarctica and Australia. This spectrum of trunked and tusked creatures can be sorted into three distinct suborders. The first contains the deinotheres, better described as hoe-tuskers. Their tusks formed from their lower incisors and curved downward from the tip of the jaw. Paleontologists speculate that such specialized teeth were used to rake or dig food, a common-sense conclusion. But we can't rule out the possibility that the tusk shape developed primarily in association with fighting or courtship patterns instead.

The second suborder is that of the mastodonts. It includes true mastodons and another family called gomphotheres, described as shovel-tuskers because of their broad, flattened lower incisors. Again, common sense suggests that the shovels were used to scoop up aquatic plants in conjunction with an elongated lower jaw that was itself a sort of shovel. Certain of these species might have used their lower tusks more like spades to dig up nutritious tubers, or even like chisels to strip bark and branches from trees. Like some hoe-tuskers, some shovel-tuskers carried upper tusks as well. The true mastodons lacked lower tusks and were thought to have looked very similar to elephants. However, their great molar teeth had rows of rounded, conelike projections on the surface for chewing and grinding, whereas elephants and mammoths developed a maze of transverse ridges that were more efficient still in shredding mouthfuls of vegetation. You could grate carrots on an elephant molar. The ridges consist of alternating layers of enamel, dentine, and cement. As the softer material wears away more quickly, the hardest layer is left projecting as an even sharper cutting edge.

Elephants and mammoths are placed together in the family Elephantidae, which makes up the third and final suborder of proboscideans. Their ancestors apparently branched off from the mastodonts as early as the Miocene epoch, which lasted from 26 million years ago until 7 million years ago. The Pleistocene epoch began roughly 2 million years ago. It was then that true mammoths, in the genus *Mammuthus*, came into their own, flourishing while the various Ice Ages waxed and waned, covering a third of the planet's land surface with glaciers and snow for thousands upon thousands of years at a stretch.

Wooly mammoths, *Mammuthus primigenius*, were well adapted to the demands of the subarctic steppes of North America and Eurasia, where they made their home. Generally speaking, as mammals of a given type extend northward in range, their bodies increase in bulk while the total amount of exposed surface area is reduced, the better to conserve precious heat. Wooly mammoths fit this pattern, known as Bergmann's Rule. Compared to other elephant family members, their body was somewhat compressed from head to rump, and their trunk was slightly shorter. They had small ears and a tail not much longer than a deer's. They also had the same kind of double fur coat as found on large mammals in northern climes today: a dense, insulating, inner coat of fine wool covered by a long, shaggy coat of coarse guard hairs such as you might see blowing sideways on a musk ox or mountain goat in the northern wind. For extra insulation, wooly mammoths had a three-inch-thick fat layer under the skin, plus a reserve of fat stored in a hump above the shoulders. Judging from the way the tusks swept down to form a broad bow close to the ground, they might have been important in plowing snow away from food supplies. Then again, that possibility might make more sense to us than it did to the mammoths, which might not have needed or used such a plow.

Ice Age experts Dale and Mary Lee Guthrie have presented evidence that with so much available water locked up within the ice pack, much of the subarctic region not covered by glaciers was drier than it is today. As a result, its soils thawed to a greater depth and supported richer plant communities. They included a lot of nutritious grasses where only low, slower-growing, tougher tundra vegetation with bitter chemicals for defense against grazing are found today. According to the Guthries, the greater variety and nutrition offered by steppe habitats during the Pleistocene go a long way toward explaining how grazing mammals could attain such great size and abundance in subarctic pastures.

The word *mammoth* is synonymous with *colossal*, and a few, such as North America's imperial mammoth, were very big indeed—close to fifteen feet high at the shoulder by some estimates. But most mammoths, including the wooly mammoth, were close to modern-day elephants in size. During interglacial periods, when melting ice sheets caused sea levels to rise and cut off certain outlying areas from the mainland, some populations stranded with a restricted food supply and a limited gene pool evolved into pygmy races. This was the case for mammoths isolated on California's Santa Rosa Island, just a few miles across the channel from the huge mammoths of the mainland; one specimen of pygmy mammoth found there had an arrowhead embedded in the bone. The same downsizing process transformed primitive elephants called *Palaeoloxodon* on the islands of Crete, Cyprus, and Malta in the Mediterranean, creating dwarf species no more than three or four feet high at the shoulder. The remains of other pygmy elephants have been uncovered on islands in the Philippines and on Indonesian isles such as Java.

Mastodonts were still thriving during the Pleistocene. While mammoths grazed the tundra and steppe, the mastodonts browsed the woodlands, generally occupying habitats farther south. A gomphothere called *Cuvieronius*, with shovellike lower tusks and spiraling upper tusks, dwelled in South America until the end of the last Ice Age, at which time all mastodonts and mammoths alike are thought to have died out. When European explorers invaded North America, they heard Indians from different tribes claim that their great-grandfathers hunted creatures as tall as trees. Possibly they did. For all anyone knows, true mastodons may have survived in North America in a few pockets until relatively recent centuries.

True elephants were also around during the Pleistocene. The dominant form in Africa was the genus *Elephas*, which is thought to have arisen there and spread to Europe and Asia, eventually giving rise to the modern Asian elephant, *Elephas maximus*. Meanwhile, another true elephant genus, *Loxodonta*, had been evolving in Africa's rainforests for at least 2 million years. Half a million years ago, it produced the modern African elephant, *Loxodonta africana*. Africa's savannas and dry woodlands held a species called *Elephas iolensis* until about 40,000 years ago. When it disappeared, *Loxodonta africana*, the modern African elephant, spread from the rainforests to claim the rest of the continent as well.

Proboscideans were not the largest land mammals this planet has produced. Some of the giant ground sloths and early rhinoceros-type titans matched the elephant line in size and occasionally exceeded it in any given age. During the Eocene and early Oligocene, there was even a minor order of hooved animals that scientists label pseudomastodonts because they evolved bodies of elephantine size along with the kind of thick, straight, columnlike legs typical of big proboscideans, plus tusks, mastodontlike molars, and, judging from the structure of the skull's nasal area, a fairly substantial trunk. The biggest land mammals discovered to date were *Indricotherium* and *Baluchitherium*, rhinoceros relatives eighteen feet high at the shoulder and thirty-five to thirty-seven feet long.

Still, when taken as a group, the proboscideans were the most durable group of warm-blooded giants in history, consistently larger than any other order of terrestrial mammals through a longer period of time. This may be because they represented the best combination of great bulk and great intelligence. Whatever the reason, they dominated faunal communities through a major portion of Earth's history since the passing of the dinosaurs. And now, of the many scores of different proboscideans that came into being, of all the truly gigantic beasts that have walked this planet since the very first amphibian wriggled out of the water onto a muddy Paleozoic shore, just two species remain.

卐卐卐卐卐卐卐卐卐卐卐卐

Elephas maximus, the Asian elephant, has an arched back, an enormous, domed head with relatively small ears, and a single protuberance, or "finger," at the tip of its trunk. The front feet have five toes and the back feet have four. As a rule, only the males carry tusks; females have tushes—short second incisors that barely protrude past the upper lip—though an occasional female is found with longer tusks. A large bull may weigh some six tons and stand a bit more than ten feet high at the shoulder. Adult females are about half the size of the largest males. The gestation period is between nineteen and twenty-two months, with male infants possibly requiring a slightly longer term than females.

Loxodonta africana, the African elephant, has a straight back, a tapering head with enormous ears shaped like the African continent, and two trunk "fingers." The species is named for the lozenge-shaped ridges on its molar teeth. The ridges are fewer and coarser than those of Asian elephants. The African elephant has one less toe on each foot—four on the front feet and three on the back feet—but one more vertebra in the lumbar section of the spine. Both sexes carry tusks, and both are larger than their Asian counterparts. The biggest African bull on record weighed nine tons and stood more than twelve feet high at the shoulder. In the British Museum are a pair of African male tusks with a combined weight of more than five hundred pounds. Females average about half the size of the largest males when fully grown. Gestation may be slightly longer than in the Asian elephant.

Asian elephants inhabit India as well as Southeast Asia today. The species used to extend much farther northward and was still a resident of north-central China's Honan province in 1500 B.C., during the time of the Shang, or Yin, Dynasty. Pakistan and Afghanistan also held populations in historical times. So did the Middle East region that takes in Syria, Iraq, and Iran, the focus of the Persian Empire. It was inhabited by *Elephas maximus asurus*, the largest Asian subspecies of all. During the sixteenth century B.C., an excursion into Syria by Thutmose III of Egypt was recorded by a loyal officer named Amenemhab: "Again I beheld another excellent deed which the Lord of Two Lands did in Niy. He hunted 120 elephants for the sake of their tusks. I engaged the largest among them, which fought against his majesty; I cut off his hand [trunk] while he was alive before his majesty, while I stood in the water between two rocks. Then my lord rewarded me with gold."

Asian elephants have been tamed for use in work and war since at least 3000 B.C. From India to Burma and Thailand, dynasties rose and fell on the backs of elephants. When Westerners think of war elephants, however, they are more likely to envision Hannibal, leader of the Carthaginians, crossing the Alps with elephants to invade Italy in the third century B.C.

Part of the popular tale holds that although Hannibal had precious few elephants—he started off with thirty-eight and lost around thirty of those before he even met the Roman forces—the sight of the huge, trumpeting beasts filled his enemies with panic, giving him a rare advantage. That was probably not the case (though the sight would have panicked their horses). Elephants were not really unheard of in that part of the world. Alexander the Great had met elephant armies as he swept eastward to India in the fourth century B.C., and some of the captured giants marched on with his columns as spoils of war. Then came Pyrrhus, the Greek who won notable victories against both Macedonians and Romans, though with such heavy losses among his own forces that people still use the term Pyrrhic victory to describe an excessively costly gain. Pyrrhus employed elephants in his campaigns. They may have been part of his problems. One chronicle of the time claims that Pyrrhus was soundly thrashing the Romans when an elephant calf left behind while its mother carried troops into battle began squealing and bleating. The mother broke ranks to dash back for her calf. All the other female elephants followed and ended up busting a path through Pyrrhus's legions rather than those of the Romans.

If elephants were the prototype of tanks, they rather quickly spawned the development of anti-tank weapons: fire arrows; huge, wagon-mounted bows; battering rams with spiked tips; rows of spikes set in the ground; and cataphracts—warriors dressed in suits of armor studded with metal spikes to keep elephants from seizing them.

The interesting thing is that no one yet knows for sure what species of elephants Pyrrhus or Hannibal had under his command. The usual assumption is that they must have been Asian elephants. Trained Asian elephants were probably available from Persia and certainly from points farther east, and Carthage was the seat of a large trading empire. Besides, it is often said that African elephants can't really be domesticated. On the other hand, Carthage was located in what is now Tunisia, and North Africa held plenty of herds of wild elephants, for the African elephant was once distributed throughout virtually the entire continent. It is quite possible that the Carthaginians or the people of one of their subject states learned to train those animals. Or perhaps Asian elephant handlers were brought in to teach the techniques. That's what the Belgians did in Zaire several decades ago: they imported Burmese handlers, who succeeded in training a small group of African elephants for logging work. Of course, quite a few other African elephants have been trained in modern times to perform in zoos and circuses.

Why weren't African elephants ever domesticated on a larger scale, then? The answer takes us back to the differences between the two species. Almost all elephant people at zoos describe African elephants as being a bit more temperamental than Asian elephants—a bit wilder-eyed and "trunkier," meaning that they are more exploratory and more likely to test you and everything else in their environment. Put another way, an African elephant might perform upon command perfectly nine times in a row; the tenth time, you might blink, or a door might slam shut nearby, or the animal may simply decide the elephant equivalent of "The hell with this trick; let's see what *you* can do"—and you're suddenly in the middle of an elephant rodeo. With younger animals and certain females, handlers may be able to maintain a degree of control, but the sheer size of grown African bulls makes them simply too much to deal with, given this species's extra measure of unpredictability.

If those were African elephants the Carthaginians used, it may have had something to do with the fact that the North African subspecies was smaller than the typical African elephant. Whatever the subspecies's other characteristics were, they are no more; North Africa's last elephants vanished around the second century A.D., primarily because of the Roman Empire's insatiable demand for ivory tusks.

Not that the Romans didn't think highly of elephants. They believed the giants worshipped the sun, moon, and stars. The Romans even minted a coin showing an elephant with its head uplifted toward the heavens. Aristotle, tutor of Alexander the Great, had earlier described the elephant as "the beast that passeth all others in wit and mind. . . . and by its intelligence, it makes as near an approach to man as matter can approach spirit." The great Roman natural historian Pliny the Elder devoted the first and longest chapter in his survey of the animal kingdom to the elephant. Why? In an essay entitled "Man, the Sky and the Elephant: On Pliny's *Natural History*," Italo Calvino says, "Because it is the largest of the animals, certainly, but also and above all because it is the animal [Pliny calls] 'closest to man'! . . . In fact, the elephant—[Pliny] explains immediately afterward—recognizes the language of his homeland, obeys orders, remembers what he learns, knows the passion of love and the ambition of glory, practices virtues 'rare even among men,' such as probity, prudence, and equity. . . . The rites and customs of elephant society are represented as those of a people with a culture different from ours, but nonetheless worthy of respect and understanding."

Nevertheless, wealthy Romans used ivory perhaps to a greater extent than any major civilization had before. In addition to collecting decorative ivory items from combs to scroll-holders, they used thin sheets of ivory for inlay and veneer on furniture of all kinds. They also used ivory for a type of statuary known as chryselephantine, in which the ivory represented the flesh of a figure while the clothing was done in gold. Chryselephantine was common in earlier empires of the Fertile Crescent, Egypt, and Crete. The Greeks were especially fond of this form of sculpture and often covered immense temple figures with ivory veneer, one of them being the famed forty-foot-tall statue of Athena made by Phidias for the Parthenon. (The Roman poet Ovid's tale of a sculptor who fell in love with his own creation— a perfect rendering of a woman, done in ivory—was reworked by the English playwright George Bernard Shaw. The result, *Pygmalion*, in turn formed the basis of the popular Broadway musical, *My Fair Lady*.) A few Roman nobles had entire rooms constructed of ivory tiles. Ivory even served as currency in portions of the empire.

Another use of ivory in ancient empires had to do with the belief that it could detect or, some believed, neutralize poison. Ornamental items such as a dagger with an ivory handle served a double purpose, since they could be dipped into suspect drinks or food. Ivory was also believed to have healing powers and a particular ability to cleanse the blood. Narwhal tusks and hippo teeth were valued for preventing poisoning and for healing in many parts of the ancient world before elephant ivory became more widely available and more popular. In all likelihood, the

Roman market for ivory played a key part in eliminating Asian elephants from the eastern parts of their original range as well as in wiping out African elephants in the northern third of their range.

"Recently . . . even the bones have begun to be cut into layers," Pliny wrote, "inasmuch as an ample supply of tusks is now rarely obtained except from India, all the rest in our world having succumbed to luxury."

Is it so surprising that the Romans could hold a beast in such high esteem and still drive it to extinction in one area after another? They fashioned art that glorified the human form, and they created literature that gave a new nobility to the human spirit. Yet their empire's growth was predicated on the subjugation of other civilizations, and its labor force consisted largely of slaves. Audiences at the circus in Rome watched lions, bears, and elephants perform. They watched gladiators fight each other. And they also watched bears and lions and elephants fight each other, or fight the gladiators, or slaughter runaway slaves and Christian dissidents. Like lions, elephants were often used as public executioners.

Though it would be fascinating to explore the Romans' attitudes toward animal and human life in depth, it is hardly necessary in order to explain why they drove populations of the elephants they so admired to extinction. They thought ivory was a thing of splendor, wanted it, got it. They gave no more thought to where it came from than consumers in recent decades have. Compared to modern societies, the Romans had little information about how wildlife in distant lands was faring. While elephants were disappearing due to ivory exploitation, Pliny was writing that the main natural enemies of elephants were known to be dragons.

The order Primates came into being in the late Cretaceous days of the dinosaurs, long before the first proboscideans. The genus *Homo* appears to have been around for at least 2 million years, about as long as either *Elephas* or *Loxodonta*. And modern humans, *Homo sapiens*, emerged at roughly the same time in the Pleistocene that the modern Asian and African elephant species did. The relationships between early humans and proboscideans are unknown, but the remains of elephants in Stone Age human sites in Africa indicate that elephants were a prey item. We already know that mammoth meat played a key role in sustaining the Stone Age cultures of Eurasia, while carved mammoth ivory stands as a sort of fossil record of their spirit. The Paleo-Indians who invaded the New World from Asia toward the end of the last Ice Age brought their mammoth-hunting traditions to a fauna that had never seen humans before.

A great many large mammals vanished rather suddenly as the Pleistocene came to a close. Climatic change probably explains most of the losses among the megafauna. Yet many of the species that vanished had survived through earlier interglacial periods with temperatures as warm as those today. The pertinent question, then, is: Would some of the species undergoing declines and struggling to readjust to shifting habitats have made it through this warming trend, too, had they not been subjected to intense hunting pressure from an expanding human population?

By the time the Roman Empire flourished 10,000 years later, a microtick on the geologic clock, *Homo sapiens* had become a force of entirely new magnitude. It was as predatory as ever, but it no longer hunted just to obtain protein for migratory groups. Traditional hunting had been joined by commercial hunting to supply large, settled, agrarian-based populations with consumer goods. Populations had become highly concentrated in places and so had political power, spiritual authority, and capital. The highly stratified societies contained entire classes of people who paid others to acquire things for them. They used their wealth to accumulate goods that signified their wealth—luxury items, which in turn symbolized their power and prestige.

The more highly prized a product derived from a wild species became, the scarcer the species itself became. This made the product still more costly, which made it more desirable to the elite, further increasing the pressure upon the species's populations. The trade connections of the Roman Empire in its glory extended to Ethiopia and beyond in Africa and across Asia to China through Indian intermediaries. Thus, the demand for ivory by affluent consumers in urban hubs such as Rome, Alexandria, and other major cities throughout the empire affected the lives of elephants thousands of miles distant. Here was a story that would recur many times in many places over the centuries to come.

However, it was probably not ivory consumption alone that squeezed the largest of all native inhabitants out of the Middle East and northern Africa. Most likely, it was overhunting combined with destruction of forests and the degradation of other habitat, a relationship seen throughout elephant range today.

A good deal of the greater Mediterranean region, from Turkey to Algeria and Morocco, supported robust stands of cedar, oak, and other large trees. These contributed to the rise of the great early civilizations there and provided the raw material for the ocean-going fleets that spurred trade and the spread of cultural advances. But the timberlands were soon being overcut to supply more ships, more pillars and beams, and more fuel, and to make room for more grazing and agriculture. The Roman empire placed further demands on the dwindling forests of vassal states and trading partners. Elephants found themselves with less and less good cover in which to take refuge from pursuers, and less and less suitably productive acreage in which they could recover their numbers if hunting pressure eased a bit. In the end, landscapes that once supported giants often became hard-pressed to support goats—or, for that matter, humans. And although many a dusty veil hides the details of history from our eyes, we can look directly at sub-Saharan Africa—Mali, Niger, Chad, Sudan, Ethiopia, Somalia—and see the latter stages of a very similar process of desertification underway at the moment—complete with the impoverishment of, first, native wildlife and, then, our own species.

THREE

East Africa: Amboseli

🔲🔲🔲🔲 WHEN PEOPLE FROM other continents envision African wildlife, they usually call to mind pageants of beasts making their way across tallgrass savannas dotted with thorn trees. Whether they know it or not, they are envisioning habitats typical of East Africa. More specifically still, they are envisioning scenes from the nature reserves of Kenya and Tanzania. That is where most of the films and photographs of African wildlife have come from and where most of the safari tours go. A disproportionate amount of scientific research on African wildlife has come from these areas as well. This is not to say that equally rich wildlife communities cannot be found in other parts of the continent—only that Kenya and Tanzania are preferred.

For good reason. Visibility on the high, open plains along the Rift Valley is ideal for naturalists and photographers. The weather is more than cooperative—generally dry and sunny, yet pleasantly cool from evening through the early morning hours —and the green highland slopes where sunbirds sing from flowering flame trees are paradisiacal. Both Kenya and Tanzania are reasonably stable and fairly easy to get around in. English is still widely spoken in these former British colonies. Things such as telephones, petrol stations, permit offices, and hospitals are operative, which is the last thing you can count on in a number of other African countries.

Tanzania had a brief fling with Marxist economics in recent years, and for a while things there did not work so well. Some feared that this country might follow the path of Uganda, whose once exemplary complex of East African parklands has been disintegrating along with the rest of the nation's infrastructure through years of political and economic chaos. But Tanzania has lately loosened its centralized planning schemes, begun to encourage private enterprise, and pushed hard to win back lost tourism. Kenya meanwhile consolidated its position as the main focus of people interested in African wildlife. Tourism there generates more than half a billion U.S. dollars in foreign exchange annually, making it Kenya's single most important source of outside income, with coffee exports from its highlands a distant second. The capital, Nairobi, serves as the hub of an international community of scientists and conservationists.

I got off the airplane in Nairobi close to midnight, at once dopey with jet lag and wired with the slightly paranoid energy that comes from entering someone else's sovereign territory, no matter how often I do it. It was late February of 1989. I had come through here a couple of years earlier to climb Mount Kenya, or, rather, to climb the lowest and easiest of the three summits of Mount Kenya. At that time, a photographer I got to know on the flight over had to pay $800 in bribes before the customs people let all his equipment through. His documents were all in order, and he probably could have demanded to go through the official procedure of paying duty instead and saved some money. But they would have made sure that he lost several days in the process. He could pay them or pay to stay in a hotel while he drove himself crazy trying to deal with mysteriously sluggish paperwork. That was the game. They knew it, and he knew it. So he paid.

This time, I was carrying quite a bit of camera gear myself and trying to get straight in my mind how to play things if someone put the touch on me when a platoon of soldiers in full battle dress raced into the building. They swarmed up the stairs to take positions all along the balcony of the second floor, with weapons—semiautomatic G-3 rifles, from the look of them—partially raised and ready. Ready for what? A major smuggling bust? A hijacking? An attempted coup? Maybe it was just that a

Big Man was about to catch a flight out. No one on the floor other than a few tourists seemed overly concerned, so I humped my bags toward customs and pushed unhesitatingly up to the counter as if I had nothing else on my mind but a hotel bed, which wasn't hard to fake.

Customs was a piece of cake. The hundreds of us who had spilled out of the jumbo jet were ready to exchange a bit of currency and depart for the city. Midnight arrived just then, and all but one of the currency exchange booths closed. I queued with everyone else at the remaining booth to get at least enough Kenya shillings for cab fare and spent the better part of the next hour taking little steps toward the counter and making proprietary nudges with my elbows while the troops stared down from the balcony and signaled to one another, gun muzzles wagging in the fluorescent lights. Someone outside was yelling in Swahili. A Japanese couple in American T-shirts were trying to calculate the exchange rate with the help of a Muslim businessman in a traditional robe and lace cap. A young American clad from headband to toe in camouflage chic, ready to meet the wild kingdom, was being hauled off toward a back room, having violated a Kenya law forbidding civilians to dress up like soldiers. Montana was a long way on the other side of the turnstiles and immigration barriers now. Right. Here we go: elephants.

〰〰〰〰〰〰〰〰〰〰〰

The central fact about elephants at the time of my visit was that they were dying at a rate of three hundred per day in Africa. The reasons were myriad and complex, but could be distilled to one basic, familiar driving force spelled M-O-N-E-Y. Easy M-O-N-E-Y. Almost unimaginable amounts of M-O-N-E-Y. Ivory, which sold for a few U.S. dollars a kilo back in the early 1970s, was going for $200 a kilo and up. Prize tusks weighing twenty kilos or more apiece fetched $300 a kilo and up; had the animals borne tusks of solid silver instead, such teeth would have been worth considerably less, figuring silver at its current price of $5 to $6 an ounce.

Those were the retail prices for ivory. The poachers got only a percentage, but it was as much as $20 to $50 a kilo. In a part of the world where the average annual income is a couple of hundred dollars a year—the combined per capita income from all of Africa south of the Sahara is roughly equal to the combined per capita income of Belgium—this was more than enough incentive to drop whatever else you were doing and rush out to begin looting the countryside of its elephants. Even a half-grown animal's tusks could be worth a couple of years' wages. It was as if the moose in North America were suddenly worth $25,000 minimum, with the biggest ones fetching more than a quarter of a million dollars. I wonder how long they would last.

Many of the Westerners to whom I spoke before leaving for Africa were under the impression that most of the elephant killing had to do with small farmers protecting their crops and huts and hungry tribesmen trying to bring in some meat. "It's a shame about the elephants, but you can't blame those people," they'd say. "They're only trying to feed their families." These same Westerners tended to think of rural Africa in terms of scenes from East Africa's wildlife reserves. They imagined islands of human settlement surrounded by a sea of wildlife.

The reality is that by the 1950s, Africa's human population was already soaring. Somewhere around the 1960s it reached critical mass, and it has been increasing exponentially ever since, causing more and more wildlife habitat to be converted to cropland and livestock pastures ever closer to existing reserves. The result is modern-day Africa, where islands of natural communities lie surrounded by a sea of humanity. Having quadrupled since the turn of the century, this continent's population is on its way toward doubling within the next two decades. There are no longer many more wild creatures roaming between protected areas in most nations than you would expect to find in rural landscapes of the United States or Europe. For example, Rwanda, where the mountain gorillas studied by Dian Fossey live among the mist-shrouded Virunga Volcanoes, has a population density of 670 people per square mile, a higher figure than for India. By comparison, France has about 270 people per square mile. Although outsiders continue to cherish a different vision, Africans, too, have to go to parks and zoos to see African wildlife these days.

During the early part of this transformation, a lot of elephants did die in conflicts over food and living space; some still do. Small-scale poaching for meat was common; it still is in some places. A fair amount of ivory found its way into the tourist trinket market. And tourism was growing rapidly, in part because modern jet airplanes had made international travel so much faster and easier. Efficient air transport was also making it easier for goods such as ivory to reach international markets. Ivory became more widely available and more heavily purchased, and the price began to increase in a simple expression of the law of supply and demand. Smalltime meat poachers started paying more attention to the tusks. The commercial poaching networks that dealt in rhino horn and spotted-cat skins had already started to move in when two other multipliers entered the price equation.

One was the worldwide rise in commodity prices during the 1970s, led by oil and accompanied by the onset of widespread economic uncertainty. Traders in nations trying to cope with alternating bouts of recession and inflation noted that ivory continued to hold its price or increase. Suddenly elephant incisor teeth became more than an object of beauty. They became a full-fledged commodity themselves, a hedge against future hard times. Increasingly, people began to buy, sell, and speculate in raw ivory as they would with corn futures or real estate.

The second multiplier was the growing affluence of Asian nations that were emerging as economic powerhouses. Their demand for ivory both as a luxury item and as a commodity was huge. Added to the existing demand from the Western world, it soon sent the price of ivory skyrocketing into the rarefied realm where the likes of gold, rhinoceros horn, diamonds, and hard drugs mingle with potent human fantasies and cravings. Elephants would start to undergo drastic declines, but with the law of supply and demand still in full force, scarcity only increased the price of ivory and the pressure on the surviving animals.

Regulations on ivory trading existed through CITES, the Convention for International Trade in Endangered Species, established under U.N. auspices during the 1970s. Since 1986, each country has been allowed to export only a given quota of tusks based upon what officials believed could be taken without harming existing populations. In practice, the wildlife inspection and customs paperwork was easy to subvert, especially since bribery was already standard procedure in many places. With a little extra under-the-table money, poached elephants could be listed as having been shot as crop raiders, or a false figure could be given for the total number of tusks. Or the tusks could be smuggled into a country with a higher export quota.

For example, the small nation of Burundi, with a population density of about 490 people per square mile, has not had one wild elephant living within its borders for years. Everyone knew it, but no one had bothered to prove it beyond a doubt. So Burundi applied to CITES for high export quotas, was granted them, and proceeded to ship out thousands upon thousands of tusks from elephants shot in neighboring nations. On the receiving end, importers employed the same combination of payoffs and doctored papers to hide the fact that they received far more tusks from certain sources than could be legitimately accounted for. Or they simply slipped them through in packages labeled as museum specimens, bones, minerals, native African village craftwork, and a hundred other things.

Several different attempts were made by CITES officials to tighten controls on the ivory trade. Each time, the dealers managed to quickly circumvent them. If they couldn't get around the restrictions where they were doing business, they moved to someplace where they could, shifting ivory factories, carvers, dummy corporations, and retail outlets from Hong Kong to Macao to Singapore to Taiwan to portions of the Philippines and Thailand, always one step ahead of the undercover investigators from conservation groups, two thoughts more clever than the bureaucrats, and richer than everyone.

CITES decided to clamp down on the export of raw tusks by permitting only worked ivory—the finished products of artists or artisans—to flow along certain routes. Within weeks, the same volume of ivory was traveling along the same routes as before, except that now the tusks had a couple of rings or cross-hatch patterns scratched onto one end. They were officially worked ivory—an expression of craftsmanship. The United Arab Emirates (UAE) withdrew from CITES, meaning that it no longer agreed to abide by international regulations on wildlife products. CITES could issue new edicts until it grew hoarse; they didn't apply there. Almost overnight, there were Hong Kong ivory factories staffed with itinerant workers from throughout the Far East in the heart of the UAE city of Dubai, carving elephant teeth while praises to Allah rang out from mosque towers toward the desert sands.

Eventually, ivory turned into an international underground currency, outlaw capital, spawning webs of corruption from remote rural villages to urban centers throughout the globe. The parallel to the drug business was striking, from the outrageous profit margins to the level of violence involved. In Asia, ivory was being smuggled out of Burma along with heroin and opium. Many African poachers resembled the field forces of drug operations in the Golden Triangle and Colombia: they traveled in large, well-armed, paramilitary gangs supported by vehicles, radios, an occasional spotting plane, and a network of informants that sometimes reached to the highest levels of government. Their weapon of choice was the semiautomatic rifle or machine gun. Few ever stopped to take so much as one steak from the tons of meat left lying to rot after the tusks were hacked out of the animals with an axe or chain saw.

Some poachers were more than paramilitary. They were the military themselves—or the police, or, not uncommonly, the wildlife rangers and wardens in a given area. In quite a few regions of quite a few nations, the only risk a local poacher faced from those in authority came if he failed to give them their cut of the profits.

🜲🜲🜲🜲🜲🜲🜲🜲🜲🜲🜲🜲

The situation in East Africa when I visited was this: Tanzania's elephants had dropped from nearly 250,000 in the early 1970s to

55,000; Uganda's from 20,000 to barely 1000, headed fast toward zero. Kenya, home to 140,000 elephants in 1970, held perhaps 16,000, and there was what amounted to a small-scale war over elephants under way in the country.

At first, Kenya's park rangers had tried to deal with elephant poaching as part of their overall duties. When that proved hopeless, the government created antipoaching units (APUs) from the best qualified among the ranger ranks and gave them special training. This proved no match for the scale of illegal elephant killing either. Kenya then assigned government service units (GSUs) from its military and police forces to the task as well and gave them more and better equipment. They were also given the discretion to gun down suspected poachers on sight.

The main result of the shoot–to–kill directive was to make the poachers less likely than ever to give up without a fight. Kenya's daily newspapers were full of reports of running gun battles between government forces and poachers, human body counts, elephant body counts, raids, arrests, and trials. Politicians traded charges and countercharges, accusing one another of incompetency or outright involvement in the underground ivory business. Even with the upbeat tone the papers tended to use when chronicling the government's latest antipoaching efforts, it was clear that this war's outcome was very much in doubt. At one point, I learned, a GSU patrol was advancing through part of the hard–hit Tsavo National Park area when a man in a ranger uniform burst into view ahead of them, waving frantically to them to follow. They did. But he was a poacher, and it was an ambush. Badly shot up, the GSU radioed for back-up. An APU squad raced to the rescue. As they arrived, the poachers dissolved into the bush, and the GSU troops began firing into the APU squad, thinking that more poachers in uniform were attacking.

As I began making my rounds in Nairobi to introduce myself to people directly involved with elephant conservation, the crisis atmosphere grew palpable each time I crossed the threshold into an office. These people, too, considered themselves locked in combat. Many of them had been dug in there battling and losing, chewing on rage and sorrow, in relative isolation for years. Although they had not been able to slow down the pace of illicit ivory trading, they had at least succeeded in awakening the world to the scale of the slaughter. All at once, everyone seemed to be looking at Africa—which meant, in large part, looking at Kenya—to see what the elephant's fate would be. I discovered that I was one of scores of magazine and television journalists traipsing through the same office bunkers.

Elephants were prime time. They were hot. But they were still dying. Because people kept buying ivory. Of every hundred dead elephants, ivory sales to Japan ultimately accounted for forty. And what of the West, so fond of wild creatures? The European Community took twenty-five of that same hundred, and the U.S. demand for ivory claimed fifteen, for a total of forty between them. Among conservationists, there was a sense that the situation was so desperate and so shameful that it could not continue, and a sense of confoundment that it was continuing anyway. Month after month, the news feed kept going out, the world stayed tuned, the poachers went on killing elephants, and the illegal traders kept shipping unprecedented quantities of tusks all around the globe.

If ivory was traded like drugs and made fortunes like drugs, was it going to prove as resistant to all efforts at control as drugs? Rhino horn had. Used for ceremonial dagger handles in various Arab nations, notably Yemen, and ground into an aphrodisiac powder in the Far East, it had risen in value until it sold by the ounce on a par with cocaine. And in defiance of every protective measure, poachers went on to wipe out both black rhinos and white rhinos from one country after another, reducing a population of hundreds of thousands to, at most, 5000. Outside southern Africa, where nearly all of the survivors remained, both species had become ecologically extinct—too few and scattered to play their normal role in wildlife communities. Only handfuls could be found here and there, most of them huddled within specially fenced and guarded enclosures. Even that was not always enough to ensure their safety. Shortly before my visit, an East African poaching gang had surrounded one such enclosure and held the guards at gunpoint while systematically executing every last rhino.

Understandably, the wildlife and conservation people in Nairobi were completely absorbed in the current stage of their struggle, which they saw as being waged against not only poachers but ineffective bureaucracies, crooked wildlife officials—and biologists and conservationists within their own ranks who promoted unworkable solutions. That is what they wanted to talk about. I wanted to talk about it, too, but not just yet. Before I jumped into a whirlpool of events and opinions, I wanted some time alone with the beasts in the bush, for much the same reason I had wanted to start off this project by getting my hands on live elephants in zoos. I did not yet feel that I understood enough about the animals' nature and potential to comprehend what was really being lost, much less to choose sides in the ongoing debates. I was in Nairobi to make some key contacts, set up the logistics for later trips, and then get out—out among free-roaming herds of elephants to learn what I could directly from them before I picked up anyone else's prejudices or expectations.

I had a particular group of wild elephants in mind: those of the Amboseli Reserve, where southern Kenya borders Tanzania. These herds had been more intensively studied than any others on the continent. Luckily—most luckily, from the standpoint of understanding these animals—they were also among the few whose social structure and traditions had not yet been disrupted by rampant illegal killing.

Cynthia Moss, an American and former Nairobi-based journalist, began studying elephant society in Amboseli during the 1970s. Over the years, she built a history for each family unit, chronicling new generations, the passing of the old, and changes in relationships within and between kin groups. This is similar to the way an anthropologist might study a tribe of people, and it is how some of the most revealing studies of other mammals are accomplished.

I met with Cynthia while I was still in Nairobi. We made polite introductory conversation and discussed her recently published book *Elephant Memories*, a popular account of the behavior and ecology of Amboseli's giants. Throughout its pages, she had avoided emotional interpretations and maintained the tone of an objective scientist, but it was plain between the lines that she was in love with her subjects. I asked how it had been for her to watch and wait through Kenya's debacle, and she suddenly caught her breath. I looked at her more closely and realized that she was struggling to keep back the tears welling up in her eyes.

After taking a moment to compose herself, Cynthia said, "I've been deeply depressed for about a year. I thought it was only a matter of time until Amboseli got hit. Massacred. Amboseli has about a million dollars' worth of ivory—retail. If it weren't for the heavy tourist traffic and for the presence of us researchers, who are there even in the off-season, I'm not sure we would have elephants in Amboseli now. The scarcer elephants become everywhere else, the harder the poachers are going to be eyeing this place. You start to wonder about every person you see coming through the countryside: Is he sizing up the place for an assault? I struck rock bottom in November."

Cynthia's mentor in the early period of her research was Iain Douglas-Hamilton. Iain and his wife, Oria, carried out the first in-depth research on elephant social behavior, working in Tanzania's Manyara National Park during the 1960s. The Douglas-Hamiltons finally gave up their ground-breaking investigations in order to devote their considerable energies to saving elephants because they had seen what they thought was a drastic decline in numbers in many regions. They undertook the first continent-wide surveys of elephant populations in order to lay a solid foundation for conservation action. They have been counting elephants and trying to rally support for the animals ever since.

And now Cynthia was phasing out her own investigations to become a full-time spokesperson for the elephants, she informed me. The Amboseli project would be carried on by her long-time colleague Joyce Poole, though for how long was difficult to say. Joyce was contemplating leaving Amboseli to survey the ruins of elephant populations elsewhere in an effort to help salvage them.

I was on the verge of becoming as gloomy about the future of elephants as everyone else seemed to be before I had gotten beyond my first hotel in my first country on this story. I called Joyce at a lodge in Amboseli, and it was refreshing to hear her trumpet, "Oh, the elephants are so happy. There's green grass everywhere after the rains. The elephants are just fat and sassy. They're playful, and I see mating going on all over the place. Hurry down. It's wonderful." I did, and it was.

The rains Joyce spoke of were harbingers of the long rains that would begin in March and last until May, soaking the ground with a succession of rolling storms. After the lushness, after the flowerings, would come six to eight months of heat and ever drier, dustier landscapes that would check up on each plant-eating animal's survival strengths. In good years, the grip of dry weather would be broken by the short rains, or little rains, that fall as light showers between late autumn and early winter.

Much of Amboseli is almost perfectly flat and open, for it is the bed of an old alkaline lake grown up into savanna with salt-tolerant grasses and brush. Distant hills, some so low they can scarcely be seen except at dawn and sunset, mark the ancient lake's shores on several sides. On the southwest side, just across the border in Tanzania, rises Mount Kilimanjaro, 19,340 feet tall. Its glacier-covered summit is the first and last thing lit by the sun, shining forth above the indistinct, blue-distant slopes as if it were hovering there unsupported and giving birth to the world below anew each day. By midmorning, the first clouds in a clear sky will have begun to coalesce around the upper reaches of this volcano and stream off to create weather across the rest of the land.

After adding East Africa to his Abyssinian Empire, King Menelik I, the conquering son of the Hebrew King Solomon and Queen Sheba, is said to have rested on the saddle between two of Kilimanjaro's main peaks, Mawenzi and Kibo, where the gods dwell. He found himself weary beyond tiredness and knew that death was approaching; so he gathered his slaves and loaded them with all the treasures he had gained. Then he led them into the crater of Kibo, and there in the exhalations of hot, sulfurous mist they all vanished together. One day, the legend adds, a successor to Menelik's line will recover the hoard from Kibo and in it will find the seal ring of Solomon. Slipping it onto his finger, he will feel the wisdom of his great ancestor upon his own brow and the power of his heritage surging through his limbs, and he will emerge to restore Ethiopia to its former glory.

A substance equally precious—water, from Kilimanjaro's glaciers and snowfields—percolates down through the volcanic ash and cinder to resurface as springs at the foot of the mountain on the Kenya side. Around the springs have formed swamps of tall, papyruslike reeds and succulent grasses, oases in the rainshadow of the highest mountain in Africa. They are the heart of Amboseli.

Even the sunburned alkali pans, where the dust devils whirl their short lives away, had a glaze of green as I drove into the reserve. The taller grasses hid hours-old wildebeest, born in anticipation of the long rains that would bring forth real lushness from the land by the time they stopped suckling regularly. Thompson's gazelles looked up from their feeding as zebra stallions chased one another at the edge of a herd, striped flanks zithering in the sunlight.

These three—wildebeest, zebras, and Thompson's gazelles—keep regular company on East Africa's broad plains. The zebras mow down the coarse upper stalks of the grasses, their digestive systems being designed to process forage in bulk. Then the wildebeest select the more palatable lower grass blades that have been exposed, their four-chambered ruminant stomachs enabling them to extract greater nourishment from less fodder. Finally, the small Thompson's gazelles snip new grass shoots as they reappear in closely cropped areas. When the grasses cease sprouting, the "tommies" can browse low shrubs and dig for roots, being the only one of the three adapted for feeding on a mixture of plant parts.

Bands of somewhat larger Grant's gazelles grazed with the three companion species, keeping slightly toward the periphery.

Behind them, giraffes rocked slowly along with the grace of schooners, their heads swiveling in the sky, and ostriches raced across the driest part of the pan past a group of oryx with horns like a phalanx of Masai spears.

I continued on toward a large marsh named Ol Tukai and watched a pair of crowned cranes float overhead. Kilimanjaro floated behind them. I imagined the angel-winged birds that dwell up there—the Mackinder's owls, Verraux's eagles, lammergeier vultures—soaring through cloudbanks and blizzards, past crags and curtains of sunlight. . . . All at once I was among elephants. A herd of them was making its way toward the marshes with me.

Towering like landforms, like moving biomes, they raised a light cloud of white alkali dust even in this green time. It made the air shine beneath their bellies. A haze of swallows wove through the air above, catching insects flushed from the trembling ground. Stalking beside the elephants' pillar legs and riding perched on their backs were egrets white as Kilimanjaro's crown. The giants' heads alone were the size of the zebra and wildebeest that had seemed so grand and strong to me a few moments earlier. Thick mud and dirt caked the elephants' baggy, wrinkle-patterned skin. When a gust of wind struck the herd from behind, the huge ears snapped taut like sails, and puffs of dust cracked loose to join the surrounding haze. And I kept thinking: Look what has come from the African soil. Look what our earth can do.

That night, I slept—off and on—in one of the inexpensive bandas, or huts, set at the marsh's edge. Gecko lizards rustled in the roof thatch while the crickets and big spiders they hunted dropped onto my mosquito net and elephants trumpeted just outside. In the predawn there were still elephants just outside. Their hulking shapes seemed no more than a thickening in the greyness around them until Kilimanjaro began to glow and the world grew solid again and I could make out a large herd of black Cape buffalo grazing on either side of the giants. This freshest part of the day would be the most active time for many creatures, before the air heated up. I grabbed a water bottle and drove out to see what I could see along some little road trails that wound through a woodland of wild date palms and yellow-barked acacias called fever trees.

Fever trees got their name because they were once thought to somehow harbor malaria. That was close; the type of moist, periodically flooded ground where *Acacia xanthophloea* flourish makes good breeding areas for *Anopheles* mosquitoes, the vectors of malaria. Rounding a corner, I found a young bull elephant feeding on the long-thorned acacias. He would break off a branch and use his trunk to pull it slowly sideways through his mouth, bending down the arriving thorns with his lips and then milling them between his molars along with the nutritious sprigs of little acacia leaves. All this was closely observed by both myself and a fiscal shrike perched just above the elephant. The shrike impales prey such as large insects and small lizards on acacia thorns, the better to hold them while it dines, since its talons are too weak to be of much help in grasping and dismembering prey.

The elephant moved into a thicket of date palms to munch on the fronds. I followed. A litter of baby wart hogs flushed from the grass. Vervet monkeys and a half-dozen turkey-size ground hornbills picked insects from elephant droppings nearby. In the shadows beneath the palms, impalas turned to watch me pass, then resumed their skittish feeding; I had noticed fresh leopard pug marks in the road dust not far back. A branch cracked, and I looked behind me. The young bull and the rest of his family were emerging from the palms, and my car was surrounded by giants. Had I reached out the window, I could almost have touched the closest one.

The day warmed quickly as I rambled along with the family. Before long, they had taught me that it was alright for them to approach in my direction but not for me to steer the car too abruptly or directly toward them. They considered such a move enough of a threat that one of the females, usually a younger one, would threaten back, giving me an ear-flapping shake of her head as she suddenly turned in my direction. The group's leader, the largest female, generally ignored me but kept a close watch on her baby whenever it strayed from her side. I was taken by how much contact there was between the family members, how often they reached out to brush one another with their trunks, how they fed shoulder to shoulder when all the woodland was their undisputed domain.

In what seemed a very short while, it was straight up noon and the family had wandered beneath the shade of several large acacias. They moved indolently, essentially resting. From time to time, one would shower itself with dust. Another might twist a bunch of grass stalks together with its trunk, pull them taut, then mow them off at the base by scuffing the ground with one nail-edged foot. If too many roots pulled loose with the stalks, the animal would whack them against the ground or its ankle to shake loose the clinging soil before finally reaching its trunk up to stuff the grass in its mouth. It reminded me of Ruby, the elephantine painter at the Phoenix Zoo, using her drinking pool to wash the dirt off bunches of carrots that her keepers gave her.

Baboons trooped by the elephants. A chase between two young baboons attracted the attention of the baby elephant, and it made a quick-shuffle run at them, its trunk raised and ears spread full. As soon as the baboons scattered up trees, the baby slowed and changed its gait to a sort of prancing shimmy. Quite pleased with itself—that's the phrase I want to add here. However, to avoid anthropomorphism, I am not supposed to use it, because I do not *know* that this baby was quite pleased with itself. I could instead say something like: the juvenile's heightened level of aggression spilled over to activate nonspecific play activity patterns. They included picking up a stick and racing back and forth between some slightly older members of its family, waggling its head. Then several baboons edged back down the tree they were in and started shrieking what I would call abuse if I were being anthropomorphic but will call high-pitched, grating hoots. And the baby charged again. The baboons scampered up the tree again, more casually this time, then returned more quickly to heap high-pitched, grating hoots upon the baby while its mother placidly scratched her side against another tree. Eventually, the baby tired of making rushes and settled for throwing its trunk in the baboons' direction now and then, along with a short, high trumpet blast, just enough to force a reaction. The baboons' reaction was sometimes to fling an arm back in the elephant's direction along with more hoots. Anthropotranslation:

"Yo, Hose-nose."

"Hey, just because you drink water with your *face*, Monkeypunk."

"Oh, yeah? I oughta come over there and . . ."

"And what? Maybe I'll come over there and . . ."

Droppings and a few bones of various kinds lay scattered across the ground, and an elephant skull lay like a white boulder at the base of a palm a ways off. The air smelled of dust and dung, urine, sweet musks, rotting carcasses, torn and fragrant leaves—the way I remembered that wild places in Africa smell when they are full of life. In the afternoon, I trailed the family members as they moved toward the swamps of Ol Tukai. Once among the tall grasses and reeds, they joined more than two hundred other elephants, feeding, drinking, bathing, playing, and sorting out social relationships in this plush oasis before heading back toward the woodlands for the night.

As before, a few elephants remained through the evening by the swamps in what was more or less the front yard of my hut. By dark, the afternoon clouds over Kilimanjaro had blossomed into thunderheads with lightning running through them, while the rest of the sky produced an infinite eruption of stars. I sat with my back against a pole on the porch, looking from the strange array of flying insects that collected around my candlelight to the flashes of lightning that would reveal, frozen in a single frame, silhouettes of the great mountain above and the great beasts just beyond my small door.

Each day, I watched different families of giants. And each night, dry lightning spewed over Kilimanjaro and more elephants, until the old, good feeling of being in the regular company of beasts came back. With so many species imperiled and the prospects of saving them so grim, I sometimes felt that what I did for a living was worry and explain problems. I tended to forget that there had been a time when everything I learned about the natural world enthralled me and I had chosen my career because I thought that learning more about natural history would only make me happier. But now I was remembering. I shook my head and smacked my hands together and did a little shuffle on the porch. I had definitely come to the right place. I started chanting my smug journalist mantra—always a good sign when I am on assignment. It goes: I can't believe I'm getting paid to be here; I can't believe I'm getting paid to do this. An elephant observing me might have thought: The human appears to be, well, to put it proboscideomorphically, feeling quite pleased with himself.

Perhaps the most important feeling I had was simply one of growing to like these wild elephants tremendously. It was hard not to. They were overwhelmingly sociable, expressive, and emotional—qualities that humans readily relate to. Because of their great, pulverizing size, each care-giving gesture seemed all the more tender; each deliberate manipulation of some little object all the more delicate. They reacted to surprisingly small things—pausing to let a mongoose scurry by, cautiously circling a paper wrapper left by a tourist. I had a very strong sense of a mind behind each elephant's actions—a sense of information being processed in interesting and highly individual ways in the pause between stimulus and response.

Although I've been joking about anthropomorphism, my real opinion—as a former wildlife biologist—is that we make mistakes using it to interpret an animal's behavior. But we can also make mistakes going out of our way to avoid it when dealing with creatures that clearly have a great deal in common with us. We need every tool we can muster for understanding other beings while we still have time to do so.

Once I lay down beneath my mosquito net to sleep that night, the questions suspended by the magic of the lightning show lay down beside me: Could it all be razed by poachers tomorrow, this generous, embracing elephant domain? Lives like these? Was it really possible that elephants themselves could be all but gone from the earth within another couple of decades? How could things have come to this? No wonder Cynthia Moss had been slowly going half-crazy with worry.

My next order of business was to pester Joyce Poole, who was trying to carry out vital field work each day at Amboseli while also writing up technical papers and assembling census data from surveys she had recently made elsewhere *and* being polite and helpful to the passing parade of journalists doing stories, news reports, and documentary films about the elephant crisis. Everyone picked on the Cynthia Moss–Joyce Poole project— not only because it was the longest-running and most detailed investigation into the nature of elephant society, but because there were not many others from which to choose. Given the popularity of elephants and the dimensions of the crisis affecting them, I was surprised at how few researchers were actually working full time to gather information about these animals' behavior in the field.

I drove out among the elephants with Joyce and her colleagues Soila Sayialel and Norah Njiraini, "two of the top six people in the world as far as understanding what elephants are doing," in Joyce's estimation. Soila was in her twenties and was one of eleven children from a traditional Masai cattle-herding family based in the nearby village of Loitokitok. Norah, one of eight children, was also in her twenties and from Loitokitok. But she was Kikuyu. Like many Kikuyu families, hers had left their traditional home in the increasingly overcrowded highlands of central Kenya. They had settled here because the Masai were beginning to realize the potential profit that lay in selling off some of their traditional grazing pastures to land-hungry farmers. Over most of the Masai's vast holdings, water was a limiting factor, but there was enough of it around the base of Kilimanjaro to sustain crops. Norah's brother had married Soila's sister. So, of the top six observers of elephant behavior in the world, one third were sisters-in-law and, counting Joyce, one-half were bouncing along in the car with me.

As time allowed over the next several days, the three women introduced me to elephant society properly. Most of my time was spent with Norah and Soila, who pointed out the various families, their members, and the animals' histories. Like Joyce, both of them could identify all 715 or so elephants using Amboseli at the time, and the women seldom needed more than a few moments to recognize any one of them.

Here, then, was Karen, age forty to forty-five, leader of the KA family. And her sister Kiera, twenty-four. And Kerry, the mother in the KA group with a calf less than three weeks old. Typically for a baby that age, the calf was still learning exactly how the miracle organ in the center of its face operated. It had trouble making the trunk go where it was intended to go and sometimes just stood around twirling the thing or swinging it in a figure eight. And sometimes the baby tripped over it, especially when climbing or getting up from a rest. An older baby in the group, like the one I had seen earlier, was given to chasing whatever it could get a reaction from: monkeys, birds, even wildebeest and zebras. Other members of the family came over, intrigued by the baby's efforts: first Katrinka, then Kristie. . . .

If any doubt arose as to an elephant's identity, Norah and Soila could flip through a card file containing sketches, photos, and a list of each animal's usual companions. The key identification marks had to do with the ears, which usually bore a unique pattern of holes and tatters along the outer edge. The general length and shape of the tusks offered further clues. On a finer scale, each elephant generally favored one tusk or the other for such activities as digging and prying away bark, and this resulted in one tusk being noticeably more worn at the tip. Moreover, each elephant had a favored side for drawing branches and roots into its mouth, and this often wore a distinct groove across the upper surface of that tusk. Scars and various abnormalities, from limps to crossed tusks, made certain individuals and their family groups easy for even a newcomer such as me to pick out.

So that would be Wart Ear over there, age forty to fifty, leader of the ΛΛ family. Near her in this group were Allison and Agatha, each with babies less than a year old that were mounting each other and wrestling. One kept trying to trip the other by grabbing a hind leg with its trunk.

Looking on, Norah commented, "I never tire of studying elephants. I forget they are animals. It is just like studying people.

When one dies, it is terrible for me. If this study ended, I would go on and work with other animals."

Like us, elephants reach puberty at age thirteen or fourteen, occasionally younger. They continue to breed until around age fifty and, again like us, may live seventy years or more. A cow produces a single calf or, rarely, twins. The interval between births is two-and-a-half to four years, due primarily to the long gestation period. Even so, a female may ultimately have ten to twelve births over her long reproductive lifetime. Many of her offspring will also have several births while she is still fertile.

As a rule, an elephant family is led by an older female, or matriarch, and consists of her female offspring and their young. It may take in one of the matriarch's sisters and her descendants as well. Accordingly, a basic family unit for elephants throughout much of the African bush contains at least six to twelve animals, and families of twelve to twenty are quite common. Sooner or later, part of the group is likely to split off and form a new family. How much sooner or later seems to depend upon how well the particular individuals within the family happen to be getting along and how much food is available. When a matriarch dies, one of the elder offspring often takes her place in a smooth transition, but the family may split on this occasion as well. Males gradually grow more independent as they approach puberty, spending more and more time on the periphery of the group. Eventually, they leave the family to attach themselves to bands of other males. Such bull bands vary in size from two or three to more temporary groupings of as many as twenty or even thirty, with the average falling well toward the lower end of this scale.

The female groups are the enduring social units. Even when they split up, they frequently remain in close association, traveling together throughout the range. Related families form what Cynthia and Joyce term bond groups. Related bond groups sometimes associate in turn to form still larger units the researchers call clans. As with families, the size and stability of these groupings varies somewhat with the food supply, abundant forage naturally making it easier for elephant kin to remain near one another. During times of severe drought, even relatively small, tightly knit families may split up, at least until better times return. These days, group size also reflects the fact that a number of surviving populations are unnaturally crowded within relatively small sanctuaries—a situation true of Amboseli to some extent. Elephants also tend to congregate in larger than normal groups as a response to harassment and shooting.

The KA and AA families were a good example of a bond group; they often traveled side by side, Norah and Soila told me. The two groups had been close together when we first arrived, then fed in different directions until they were roughly two hundred yards apart. Now they turned back and began running to reunite. You might have thought they had been lost to each other for years. The meeting was a detonation of trumpets, screams, and rumbles, thundering feet, flapping ears, and extended waving trunks that met and enwrapped and moved on to caress heads and mouths. The animals' temporal glands—modified sweat glands that form a bulge on each side of the head several inches behind the eye—had clear liquid flowing from them, a common sign of excitement or stress among females.

As we approached many families for the first time on a particular day, they responded by approaching us in turn and commencing a toned-down version of the same expressive greeting celebration. They plainly recognized the research vehicles, and it seemed to me that they recognized the women within them, at least by their scent. Joyce was particularly given to calling out each animal's name, alternately talking to it in a crooning voice and cupping her hands around her mouth to make a slow motorboat sound with her lips—her approximation of an elephant greeting rumble. Soon, we would be encircled by giants scuffing the dust, lifting their trunks toward our car, and rumbling out messages of their own.

One afternoon, Norah, Soila, Joyce, and I came alongside a bond group consisting of three related families. They were on their way back from the swamps, moving along through a dry plain and snatching mouthfuls of salt-tolerant *Sporobolus* grass. By evening they would reach the woodlands near the reserve's border, and there they would spend the night.

"That's Jezebel," Soila said, pointing to a large female with two large lumps from an old wound or infection on the right side of her abdomen. She was standing quietly amid several other females. "She is the matriarch of the JA family. When all three families are together, Jezebel usually leads the entire bond group. She is about sixty years old."

After reaching adulthood, females seem to elongate as they grow older, and they end up with a sort of stretched out, sagging body. The skin over the massive skull takes on a sunken look as well, notably around the temple and jaw. Jezebel had that appearance, as if gravity were finally beginning to get the upper hand in her lifelong endeavor to keep so much heaviness active so high above the ground. As her kin spread out around the car, Jezebel stayed in place, resting her trunk across one of her long tusks. Now and then, a tired-looking elephant will hold its trunk in its mouth. I even saw one tusker lift a log, rest it on its tusks, then rest its trunk upon the log.

With Jezebel was her son, seven years old. He looked as though he was still trying to suckle. Could that be? Yes, said Joyce. A female with no new progeny may allow a juvenile to continue nursing for several years, and this young male may well have been the last offspring Jezebel was able to conceive. Nearby was a two-year-old just beginning to show its tusks and a weeks-old baby scratching its rump by rubbing up against its mother's leg.

Joyce Poole was busy rumbling greetings to another grown female. "That elephant's name is Joyce," Soila said. "She is the number-two-ranking female in the JA family, after Jezebel."

"Joyce has a ten-year-old son named Joshua—that one there," Norah added, indicating an alert-looking bull nearly the size of the smaller elephant mothers.

Joyce Poole just said, "Watch this," and she threw a chip of dried buffalo dung halfway to Joshua. He walked toward our car, picked up the dung, and very accurately chucked it straight back to Joyce. Joyce laughed and turned away to explain something about this family's history. In short order, she was bonked on the head with a tossed wildebeest bone; ten-year-old male elephants don't drop a game that easily. Joyce then took off one of her rubber sandals and threw it to Joshua. He stared at it a moment, walked up, put it in his mouth, looked at Joyce, and chewed on the sandal a little. Then he threw it over his shoulder away from her, kinking his tail and shaking his head with a hint of challenge. As that failed to draw a reaction from Joyce, he walked back, picked up the sandal, and threw it part way to Joyce, still head-waggling a bit. Then he walked up and tossed it the rest of the way. Joyce tossed it back. And so it went, two species playing catch on the shimmering plains beneath the snows of Kilimanjaro.

Eventually, Joshua grabbed the sandal and threw it over his shoulder again. Then a younger male named Jocelyn took over, tossing the sandal into the air and kicking at it with a foot when it fell. Joshua, now more intrigued with us than with the plaything, edged closer and closer to the car while Jocelyn rubbed the sandal across his chest and behind his ear, then tossed it into the air once more.

I couldn't say what Joshua's intentions were. My impression is that males of that age, on the verge of becoming independent, have a general tendency to push encounters a bit to see what will come of them. They do this with one another, frequently shoving and sparring their way across the savanna while the females feed, and they do it with other species, carrying on the tendency of juvenile elephants to try to bluff various animals out of their path. I noticed that as they become older and larger, the males move on from baboons and antelope to bigger animals: buffalo, for instance, which do not yield their ground readily. And rhino, where there are some still around.

Two days later, Joyce and I encountered the JA family again. The females seemed as comfortable around Joyce as ever. But without any sandal-tossing or other prompting on our part, Joshua jogged up to test us again, slinging dust and mud whenever Joyce moved the car, seeing if he couldn't force us to back off. His actions still had elements of a game, but it was a more aggressive one this time—more like a taunt, an invitation to spar. Joyce dismissed him as being in "a pissy mood." So it seemed. Joshua even tried to kick one of the ubiquitous egrets feeding around the JA family. The kick was fairly high and unexpectedly quick, with the rear leg shooting out to the side and slightly backward. After watching this kung-fu move several more times in wild African elephants, I kept it in mind, and that saved me from a couple of serious knocks later on among working Asian elephants.

There are a few elephants that Joyce can do more with than play catch. There are those she can touch and be touched by in the wild. The Douglas-Hamiltons had some elephant companions of that sort in Manyara. Yet a couple of Joyce's are unusual in that they are huge, fully grown males. I met one in a seldom-visited corner of the reserve as he walked over to reach in the car window and greet Joyce. Like all experienced animal people, Joyce moved with slow, confident motions whenever she was close to elephants, and her crooning voice sent out a consistent signal of reassurance as this bull greeted her with a trunk-tip touch, then quietly turned and went on his way.

Joyce discouraged me from asking many questions about the extent of her direct contact with the animals. She worried that if she made much of it, visitors might try the same thing and get whacked. There might also be criticism from colleagues about influencing the natural behavior of the animals she was studying. I understood her concern but found it ironic. Tiny Amboseli was hardly a natural situation in many respects. Barely 150 square miles in size, it was more like a large, open-air zoo where tourist vans were a major part of the environment. Officially, the drivers were supposed to avoid interfering with the animals' activities and stay on the roads in order to keep from tearing up the grasslands. In practice, urged on by passengers brandishing cameras, binoculars, and money for tips, the drivers would barge in as close as possible to animals along the main routes and go bounding cross-country whenever anyone spotted something extraordinary. At times, half a dozen vans would end up converging on lions and rhinos like scavengers on a carcass. Amboseli had only about half a dozen rhinos left. Lions were also scarce, several prides having been poisoned by Masai herders. Because of political pressure from cattle grazers, the reserve itself was shooting another key predator—the African wild dog—on sight. And the elephants were exceptionally concentrated, in part because they had learned that they were safe from shooting here.

Which brings up the question of where in all the savannas of Africa one might find a "natural" elephant population. A few herds remained fully protected in parks such as Amboseli, only to be affected by the constant presence of visitors to the point where they were both unnaturally disturbed by people and unnaturally tolerant of human presence. Nearly every other herd had experienced high enough levels of poaching to make the animals unusually intolerant of human presence. Joyce had just returned from trying to census herds in a heavily shot-up region, and she told me that they began racing away in panic when her vehicle was still half a mile off. I wondered how that felt to someone used to greeting elephants by name with an occasional touch as she made her rounds in Amboseli?

Joyce Poole grew up in Kenya and decided at age eleven that she would one day study elephants. That decision came, she told me, when she went to hear chimpanzee researcher Jane Goodall speak at the National Museum in Nairobi. In 1976, at the age of nineteen, Joyce made good on her promise to herself, and she has been living with elephants ever since. "I've had a tent as my only home until last year, when I got a house in Nairobi," she mentioned as we wound through thickets of palm and fever trees to her current campsite in the reserve. This camp consisted of several large canvas tents with awnings and a cook shack built of sticks and scrap lumber, all clustered within a small, grassy clearing. The grass, I noticed, had been mowed to make a small yard. I thought it might be to keep down ticks and make snakes easier to detect. I learned that it was partly to do that, but mainly to keep down elephants.

Joyce pointed to grey shapes moving among the palms.

Those, she said, were the Tuskless family, which also used this particular area as a sort of home base. In earlier years, they and other elephants often tromped through camp, snagging guy lines and knocking down tents. They also raided the cook shack, which had to be rebuilt and resupplied any number of times. Now, the mowed grass served as a sort of perimeter—a human territory marker for the elephants to recognize. To cross it was to set humans in motion yelling and clanging on pots. The elephants quickly learned this and, by and large, accepted the arrangement. Just the same, a second line of defense in the form of an electric wire enclosed the cook shack to deter the occasional midnight snacker. On the other hand, elephants were also drawn by the strains of guitar music issuing from camp some evenings, and no one bothered to run them off then. "They seem to like the harmonics," Joyce surmised. "They enjoy being sung to as well."

As the Tuskless family emerged from the foliage, I could see that the matriarch did indeed lack ivory and had passed this trait on to the younger females in her group. There was another female near them, an intruder from a different clan. She was in heat and being pursued by a bull, which helped explain why she was temporarily separated from her own group. The presence of the courting pair in the Tusklesses' usual haunts made the family restless, and as Joyce and I sat in the clearing to go over details of her work, there was a good deal of trumpeting, branch-breaking, and general elephant commotion on all sides. At times, I could scarcely make out her words. When Joyce had said that she was living among elephants all those years, she meant it literally.

Later, the Tuskless family moved off, and another family appeared. A twenty-year-old female from this group was soon racing around camp, trumpeting, head-shaking, ear-flapping, and snarfing, which is Joyce's description for a peculiar nasal trumpet. What had inspired all this? Joyce replied, "She's just feeling playful. So much expenditure of energy in such a massive animal to no apparent purpose—I find it wonderful. One of these outbursts a week would be enough to keep me watching elephants.

Any other animal . . . I'd have quit during the tough times, and there have been some real tough times."

To the inevitable difficulties of carrying out field research and obtaining funding, add interminable delays due to bureaucratic bungling and red tape, squabbling and jealousies within the conservation and research community, management problems within the Amboseli Reserve, poaching of study animals, years of harsh drought, illnesses among researchers, a physical assault on Joyce by two men in the hills around Nairobi, and petty but persistent annoyances such as resentment of Norah and Soila by some tribespeople envious of the fact that these women drove cars. A car represented wealth and status, and driving one was a privilege seldom available even to leaders in the local male-dominated community.

Beneath Joyce's efficient and determined exterior lay a few hollows of quiet despair. Perhaps that was why she reveled in the elephants' quality of being what she often called funny or silly. "Whether sad, angry, distressed, eager, or playful, elephants are this in a *big* way," she told me as we drank tea by the cook shack. "And it's not only their size but the intensity. You've seen them greeting each other at 160 decibels fifteen feet away when they've been separated less than half an hour. Also, I love the family structure. If a baby so much as makes a tiny complaint that doesn't deserve attention, the entire family rumbles and goes over to touch and caress it, to worry about what could be wrong. They have so many qualities that we do and such a definite sense of themselves. They are a large, funny animal, and they seem to know when they are being funny, the same way they act embarrassed when they have done something dumb. They convey a sense of knowing how they fit into the world."

"I'm with you, but I'm having trouble thinking of the particulars. I haven't watched elephants that much yet," I said.

"Have you ever watched one relate to a blacksmith plover defending its nest?" she asked.

I had. All around the waterholes of Etosha Park in Namibia, I had seen giants back away when confronted by a shrieking bird with raised wings that did not quite reach up to an elephant's ankle. Sometimes the elephants pranced and waggled their heads as they retreated, as if laughing to themselves, the "laughter" perhaps serving to release tension, as it does for us. Sometimes they retreated with great solemnity and gave the bird a wide, dignified berth. Do the words *laughter*, *solemnity*, and *dignity* sound excessive? Then forget them. This much is indisputable: what I had observed between bird and elephant was a message plainly sent, plainly received, plainly respected. And I had been watching the same behavior in Amboseli. Which, I now found myself thinking, was why I had been so surprised when the young bull Joshua had kicked at the egrets around his feet; it was totally out of character for a large elephant. And that said quite a lot about the character of large elephants, I suddenly realized. "Yes," I answered. "Yes, I've seen that."

"So gently done," Joyce mused. "So sensitive not to hurt the displaying bird. But happy to interact with it. Tom comes to mind as another example. Tom, the young male elephant, who was about to mess with a garbage can here at camp. He was waggling his head as if to say, 'I'm going to do something silly.' He was so *pleased* with himself."

I laughed and told Joyce how many times that expression had come to mind while I was watching elephants.

"Or I'll be winding up a string used to mark out a vegetation study plot," she continued. "Well, the elephants come. No indifference or fear or shying. Instead, it's 'Omigod! There's a *string* in the environment.' So everyone has to trumpet and scream and race around. Then they all have to talk about it. And then pretty soon one is winding the string up around its trunk. Then one whirls and winds it around all four legs. Then off they go into the bush, playing, hauling off all my string along with them. Nearly any other animal would have sniffed once at the string and gone on its way.

"They start playing by trumpeting. I once had fifteen elephants going mad around the car. One tusk through a window. Feet on my fenders. They would step down on the fender, but ever so lightly—enough to bounce but not to crush anything. Another elephant had a tin can it was playing with stuck on the

end of its trunk and was trying to act wild and rolling its eyes—
trying to make it into a big deal. That's how they are. One animal
can amuse itself for two hours beating up a bush or just goofing
around with a stick."

I had read several of Joyce's scientific publications and knew
that she was perfectly capable of couching any description of elephant behavior in neutral scientific jargon to avoid the taint of
anthropomorphism. She did not really write about such qualities in the first place, confining her papers to specific aspects of
elephant biology and social relationships. She knew that I was
aware of this. We both understood that we were talking freely
about impressions and ignoring the chore of qualifying everything to make it sound less subjective. At the same time, I believe we both keenly felt that there ought to be a better way of
speaking about such matters.

Our subject was the things elephants do and feel—and, more,
why they do them and how they feel about them. These are
things that bridge the gap between what science accepts and
what intuition suggests. Yet we have almost no equivalent language to bridge the gap between rigorous scientific terminology
and the drama of thoughts and feelings that animates the human
sphere. We have no words to hold and make real the in-between.
And, lacking words, we lack ways of thinking coherently about
animal consciousness, for things become real to us only after we
have named them.

Science shuns all but the most conservative interpretations of
animal motives, states of awareness, sensitivities, and yearn-
ings, thereby safeguarding its objectivity but doing the creatures
a genuine disservice. Their capacities clearly exceed the effec-
tiveness of our current scientific method to discover and define
what exists. To my mind, that gap constitutes an exciting challenge. Here is the epitome of a proper scientific frontier. But it
is more confusing than others, since we define animals in relation to ourselves and vice versa. Consequently, many scientists
continue to shy away, warning about the dangers of anthropomorphism when what they are really concerned about are the
dangers of breaking through into new and uncertain ground.
This amounts to the same old fear of upsetting established ways

of looking at the world that has always stymied the practitioners of science.

They can see the edges of the box that holds the words *person* and *human* becoming blurred, dissolving, melting down from the top of the pyramid of life, where we have placed the box, to merge into the supporting layers below. They can see the realms of morality and philosophy hovering closer than they would like. What is harder for them to see is the extent to which morality and philosophy have already shaped, and continue to shape, the perceptions of science. It is cultural prejudice, not logic, that makes it so difficult for us to comprehend the meaning of the things our fellow creatures do and feel. It is cultural prejudice, not logic, that limits our understanding of their true nature and, thus, of our own. For example, I am convinced that elephants experience delight, and I do not think it would take any observer of them long to reach the same conclusion. Scientists working with elephants know this quality in the animals but forbid themselves from speaking and writing about it in their formal work. I do not see how even their most detailed investigations can yield a true understanding of the nature of these beasts as long as their results hew to a framework in which humans are allowed to experience delight and sorrow while elephants are not.

So much for my cant. Joyce had a somewhat different view. She expanded upon it after I commented that the Amboseli elephant research team—an all-female group consisting of Cynthia Moss, Joyce, Norah, and Soila—seemed a match for the matriarchal structure of elephant society. "Men," she said, "have a hard time dealing with truly tough animal behavior problems, which involve intuiting creatures and working with emotions. I would suggest that men don't do particularly well with other people either. Human males tend to be more interested in imposing schemes, or, I could say, fitting things into a system. It's part of the dominance games that intrigue them—games that extend to the whole biosphere. It's so much easier to 'take charge,' even if you don't know what you're doing, than to speak of emotions in animals."

We talked for a while of the differences between the sexes: of the female tendency toward nurturing and empathy, as opposed to the male predisposition toward, not to say obsession with, taking control. Of the puffing of chests and the drive to make others submit, whether they be people or ideas. Of territoriality and testosterone. It wasn't anything original. But I was intrigued when Joyce mentioned that the attitudes of men often turned around once they visited the Amboseli project and got to know individual elephants. The guys gentled down, she said; they got less hard-nosed about scientific wildlife management and more in the spirit of being among the elephants and listening to what the giants had to say.

"Finally, I link elephants and freedom," Joyce told me. "Freedom of speech. No, freedom of expression. All their vocalizations—and we're just beginning to scratch the surface of their language—all their body language communication. Greeting ceremonies among bond groups forty-five animals strong. When they're so expressive, it makes me feel free. Liberated. Especially when I'm working alone here." Especially during those times when they become my closest companions, she seemed to be saying. I felt something similar. How else to explain why the sight of elephants together had begun to give me such a burst of pleasure? Maybe the sense of liberation I experienced had more to do with a feeling that if lives as great as these could exist, then anything was possible.

Implicit in Joyce's talk of expressiveness was a degree of understanding of elephant communication abilities shared by only a handful of other people in the world at the time. She and Cynthia had long been in the forefront of research along this line. They had already defined a variety of vocalizations and the behaviors associated with them when, in 1984, Katharine Payne discovered the ability of elephants to communicate in subsonic frequencies. Over portions of the next two years, Payne and her Cornell University colleagues William Langbauer and Elizabeth Thomas visited the Amboseli project and worked with Cynthia and Joyce to explore the use of subsonic, or infrasound, communication in the wild. The Cornell team moved on to pursue further experiments in Namibia's Etosha National Park, while Joyce carried out similar work at Amboseli, recording various rumbles on tape and then playing them back through loudspeakers and observing the reactions of elephants in the area.

For many years, scientists had remarked on the strange ability of elephant groups some distance apart from one another to coordinate their activities. For instance, an observer perched on a hilltop might notice several families spread out across the plain below all turn more or less at once and begin walking in the same direction. No sound would have been heard; yet no wind could have carried scent from one group to the next quickly enough to account for such a simultaneous reaction either. "I was greatly relieved to learn about the discovery of infrasound," Iain Douglas-Hamilton had remarked when I met him in Nairobi. "You see, when we got together with other scientists, we'd end up comparing notes on this remarkably synchronous behavior in widely separated elephant groups, and not one of us could come up with a reasonable explanation. We didn't mention ESP openly, but I can tell you that some of us were ready to entertain the idea that these animals were sending bloody mind waves to each other."

To date, Joyce has identified a minimum of thirty-four distinct elephant vocalizations. Among them are an assortment of trumpeting sounds, from outright blasts to a type of groan that a male uses to indicate that he has had enough of a jousting session with another male. Elephants also issue various kinds of screams, including expressions of social excitement and a particular pulsating bellow given by a female being chased by a suitor she wants nothing to do with. Babies scream as well, mainly when they want milk. "They scream louder and louder if they don't get any," Joyce informed me. "Actually, they always get milk in the end. I have never seen a young baby denied by its mother. One sister got very upset when her younger brother was not getting milk, and she came over and rumbled at mom about it." (Both elephants and humans regularly suckle their offspring for a relatively long time—two or even three years. Human milk is the second sweetest among mammals, judging by the concentration of lactose, or milk sugar. Only elephant milk is sweeter.)

Rumbles comprise the majority of vocalizations, and they are used for a wide range of occasions. When an elephant is surprised by something altogether new in its path, it gives off a trumpet. When it encounters something new yet somehow familiar, the result is a snort-rumble instead. There are rumbles of reassurance, rumbles to say "Let's go," rumbles to maintain contact once going, and rumbles to cry "I'm lost"; rumbles involved with dominance and with courtship and mating; and a humming rumble sent forth by mothers to newborn calves.

About fifteen of the known rumbles have an infrasound component. These low frequencies are what permit elephants to maintain contact over long distances. Higher-frequency waves —the ones we can hear—dissipate more quickly as they travel. In some cases, the infrasound may serve to alert elephants to stop what they are doing and listen carefully for faint sounds at higher frequencies that are carrying more detailed information. The elephants respond to certain rumbles by "freezing"—becoming motionless and alert. That was another anomaly that caused observers to contemplate the possibility of ESP not so long ago— widely dispersed elephants all freezing at the same time. Tests with recordings show that rumbles carry well for at least two to three miles, and circumstantial evidence suggests that the range may be double that.

"Playing back recordings of elephant calls is a very powerful tool," Joyce told me. "It is our way of asking elephants questions, of seeing how they view their social world." She readily admits that translations of known elephant vocalizations are still rudimentary at best and that many more calls and variations on them may yet be uncovered. Imagine falling in with an unknown tribe of humans and trying to translate their language from scratch, understanding only the grossest of shouts, grunts, and coos. But at least the extended family structure of bond groups and clans makes more sense now that researchers can envision how the animals maintain contact while traveling throughout their range.

Joyce has a hunch that certain rumbles serve to coordinate activities within a given group when its members are preparing to begin a dominance battle with another group, which is part of the process of dividing up available habitats and the resources contained within them into social territories. Joyce also sees clues that mothers have a reassembly rumble to draw together younger members of the family. Beyond that, she suspects that they may even have a different rumble to address each different member of their family. She also thinks that one purely subsonic rumble may reflect the fact that humans and elephants have evolved together in the same environments for many tens of thousands of years. She thinks, but cannot yet prove, that this rumble may mean, in effect, "Take care; people are near."

While Joyce had lately focused much of her attention on making an inventory of vocalizations, the chief subject of her research had always been the behavior of bulls.

"Musth male," Joyce proclaimed, nodding toward a fairly distant bull that was coming our way late one morning. "You can tell just by the way he walks. Look at how he carries his head." He carried it high. There was the same suggestion of tension and excitement in his gait. He was a titan—one of those that, when he entered a group of females and young, would seem to belong to a different race. He moved with such a direct, purposeful stride that I could not at the moment imagine anything short of a cement wall deterring him. As soon as he was within a hundred yards, I could smell him. He reeked of musty male scents, filling the savanna with his rankness. A dark stain ran from his temporal gland down to his mouth. His penis, thick as my thigh, was partially extended and dribbling urine. When he drew nearer still, I saw that this normally pinkish grey organ had taken on a strange, greenish color, which Joyce pointed out but could not explain. She guessed that it might have something to do with bacteria flourishing in the dampness.

The musth bull drew near a family and went from one female to another, probing between their legs with his trunk. The cow elephant's vagina is unlike that of typical mammals. It runs ventrally, along the underside of the abdomen, then curves upward toward the center of the body cavity. The male's penis, extended to its full three-and-a-half- to four-foot length, bends to match the course of the female's uterus, taking on an S shape, with the last foot or two moving up and down and from side to side almost independently. With his penis hard, crooked, and mobile at the end as the head and neck of a separate creature, the musth male reared on two legs, a sky-high colossus, and mounted a female that was little more than a third his size.

The Masai call the elephant *ol tome* or *olenkaina*, meaning he with the hand. They often snicker when they say this, for it may also be taken to mean he with the long, active penis. I had seen bulls courting and mounting females some distance away in earlier days, but I had never seen anything remotely like a sixty-plus-pound articulated penis in action up close. My whole impression of this beast shifted onto a mythic plane. He became one of the ancient earth gods, the generative phallic force incarnate, fashioned from mud and mucus and overpowering crotch perfumes: Mighty Bull Elephant, lord of creation, bent upon sowing his seed across the land and filling it with his indomitable life force. For the moment, he was my totem.

Musth is a word derived from Sanskrit. It means intoxicated. Indian mahouts have long used it to describe a state that mature elephant bulls enter once, occasionally twice, each year. This period may last two months or more in an Asian bull in prime condition, whereas one in poor condition may not come into this state at all. During musth, the male's temporal gland produces a copious, dark, oily or waxy secretion. Yet for a week or two before this is visible, the onset of musth is evident in the bull's behavior. He grows steadily more restless, irritable, and aggressive, in large part because his testosterone level is shooting up to several dozen times normal.

This is when a lot of mahouts—and handlers at zoos, circuses, and so forth—get killed, and the killer is often an otherwise tractable bull with whom they have worked closely for years. It is a little like dealing with a bad human drunk: you can see with your own eyes that your old friend has turned half-crazy and belligerent as hell, but you can't quite bring yourself to believe that he is really going to lash out at you. Many mahouts tie such a bull to a stout tree or post at the first sign of musth and starve him, which brings this period to a close sooner. Some try to hasten the end—and ease the bull's fury—by feeding him tobacco, hashish, or opium balls.

Musth is very similar to the rutting, or mating, period during which males of various hooved species fight and pursue females to the virtual exclusion of all other activities. Certain male African antelopes, for example, become too busy defending territories and the females within them to snatch a bite of food for days on end. In the Northern Hemisphere, rutting bull moose, intoxicated with hormones, have been known to attack passing cars and even trains. Yet while musth might be called rutlike, it is not confined to any particular season as it is with most hooved animals. Nor does it coincide with a peak of female receptivity, for cow elephants do not come into heat, or oestrus, in any one season either.

Female African elephants secrete fluid from the temporal gland during greeting ceremonies but do not show an increase in secretions during oestrus, and female Asian elephants apparently produce temporal secretions only rarely, if at all. Even among males, the correlation between temporal gland secretions, aggression, and testosterone levels is not always direct, and there may be key differences between the Asian and African species in this respect as well. Perhaps secretions from the temporal gland play as yet undiscovered roles in scent communication.

Although musth has been known and its outward signs described in detail for millennia in the East, its actual function in wild Asian elephant populations remains unclear, largely for want of good data from the field. And until Joyce Poole joined Cynthia Moss and began to specialize in studying male behavior at Amboseli, it was widely held that African elephants did not experience musth at all. They do, and this condition doubtless goes a long way toward explaining generations of tales about confrontations with enraged "rogue" elephants. But it still doesn't clear up the mystery of exactly what musth is or what purpose it serves.

As Cynthia and Joyce have pieced the puzzle together so far, the breeding behavior of African elephants works as follows. Cow elephants periodically come into heat and attract suitors from the surrounding area. These may include males that are not in musth. They, too, are quite capable of impregnating females. However, under natural conditions, enough males will come courting that one or more of them are likely to be in a state of musth. Musth males are more actively roaming between family groups in the first place, testing the females for signs of oestrus. A male does this by sniffing a female's urine, which contains pheromones—chemical compounds that act as sexual attractants—when the female is in heat. Actually, the male does more than sniff; he samples the urine with his trunk tip and places that sample in a pit on the roof of his mouth that contains the vomeronasal organ, a highly developed chemical detector. Exactly what makes up the pheromone is an open question—one that has kept biochemist Lois Rasmussen busy for years in her laboratory at the Oregon Graduate Center for Study and Research, located in Beaverton. So far, the main thing she knows, she told me, is that this chemical compound appears to be unlike any other yet found in the animal kingdom.

Elephant cows in heat are choosy about which males they mate with. They prefer large, dominant males to lesser ones, and males in musth to those not in musth, and they will go to great lengths to keep away from suitors that do not appeal to them. Meanwhile, the various males drawn to an oestrous female will compete for the right to attend her. Most such contests involve little more than threats and are settled after a brief chase or two. But pitched battles do occur, and it goes almost without saying that a head-to-head clash between tusk-bearing heavyweights of this order can result in serious injuries.

Musth males have an advantage in mating rivalries due to their increased level of aggression. This is one time when a smaller male may supplant a larger one, for if the smaller one is caught up in the intensity of musth, he is not easily intimidated. Nevertheless, nature has found a way to ensure that the victor is still likely to be a fairly large and dominant male whose survival abilities—whose genetic fitness, in other words—have been tested over a number of years. Although bulls may be capable of breeding in their early teens, they do not begin regularly coming into musth until they are at least twenty-five years old and usually closer to thirty. Moreover, the length of musth for those young males is only a week or less, considerably shorter than in older bulls. Only between the ages of thirty-five and forty or so do males begin regularly coming into full-length musth. So when this factor is combined with competition among rival males plus the female's say in the matter of who she will be mounted by, the likelihood is that she will end up being fertilized by the largest musth male in the vicinity. Overall, musth males probably impregnate 90 percent of the females in Amboseli. The three top-ranking bulls, all older than forty, are thought to be responsible for 15 to 20 percent of the breeding.

It is to the female's advantage to attract as many rival suitors as possible in order to increase the probability that a top-ranking bull will emerge from the testing ground of competition to breed with her. Joyce was not surprised to discover that an oestrous female sends out not only pheromones to announce her condition but a long-distance infrasound call. Nor was she surprised that males are especially attuned to respond to it, moving almost immediately in the direction of the sender. What Joyce had not expected was a reaction to the oestrous call among females. There are two kinds of reactions, really: unfamiliar groups tend to leave the vicinity, whereas familiar ones—the immediate and extended family—approach the sender, showing excitement. This hints strongly at a previously unguessed mechanism for reinforcing social territories.

After the female has been mounted and mated, she sends out a great call, and all her family members come racing over, agitated and trumpeting. Joyce termed this mating pandemonium. "Biologically, you could say that mating pandemonium serves to attract still more males to the oestrous female, increasing the chances that a still more dominant bull will come and drive off the one guarding her and end up being the one to actually fertilize her. I happen to think mating pandemonium is more than that, but whether it has to do with social territories, some type of emotional support for the female in heat, or something else altogether, I couldn't say."

Elephants do not maintain any sort of rigid boundaries to their social territories. Their system appears to be one in which various groups favor certain areas within seasonal ranges and maintain primacy there over intruding groups. Is a particular area selected by a group out of a tradition passed down from one generation to the next? Or does each group occupy the best habitat it can defend, with the highest-ranking groups claiming the choicest sections, subject to occasional challenges? The answer is: probably both.

Compared to any number of other species, elephants appear to have evolved a smoothly functioning, harmonious society that incorporates a strong measure of altruism. Still, like all life forms, elephants ultimately compete with one another for resources and for success in producing offspring. Predictably, the Amboseli researchers found better reproduction among elephants occupying the center of the reserve than among those toward the periphery, where habitats offered less abundant food and less security from conflicts with humans.

Since members of a bond group generally defend social territories together, it is greatly to the advantage of a low-ranking family to associate with a high-ranking one. Consider a mother and her offspring recently split off from a large family. Alone, this new family might find itself subordinate to most other groups in the area and prevented from using many portions of the range. But so long as the new family remains associated with the original group and joins it in defense of social territory, the family members continue to enjoy much the same access to resources that they had before. They continue to be represented by the highest-ranking female in the bond group—usually the matriarch of the original family or one of her elder offspring.

Only two families in Amboseli were not part of a bond group, and only rarely did bond groups form between unrelated families. This being the case, joint defense of social territory is to the advantage of the higher-ranking family as well as to the rest of the bond group. By helping to ensure the success of individuals related to them, members of the dominant family are working to increase the degree to which their own genes are represented in the population as a whole. And that's what the game is all about in the end. To some extent, the same general principles could be used to help explain the organization of human society into extended families, clans, castes, tribes, and so forth.

Of course, other species have found success through quite different social arrangements, ranging from a largely solitary existence to life in a crowded hive. Why should humans and elephants, who belong to two widely divergent mammalian families, have developed such similar social strategies? To begin with, both invest a great amount of time and energy in the care of young. In fact, humans and elephants are together at the extreme end of the scale in terms of the number of years during which offspring are carefully tended by their parents. Both have young that mature only in their early teens, and both continue to care for them until that time. This derives from another basic shared quality: we are both unusually long-lived as mammals go. Such lengthy nurturing also presupposes a good deal of intelligence.

For societies to operate at the bond group and clan level, each individual must be able to maintain preferentially close bonds with a large number of other individuals over an extended period of time. To do this without squandering a lot of effort in rituals and displays designed to sort out friend from rival and good intentions from harmful ones, it helps to have a good memory for purposes of recognition, combined with good communication skills. And the key to fast, efficient communication is the ability to use a fairly sophisticated language. All of these are characteristics both humans and elephants possess. They again relate to a more general shared quality, which is a high degree of intelligence. In terms of learning abilities, we and elephants are once more together at the extreme end of the scale.

Most mammals' brains at birth are about 90 percent of their adult weight. The majority of what the animals need to know to survive is already built in—hard-wired, largely instinctual. By contrast, in a human infant, the brain is only 23 percent of its adult weight; for elephants, the figure is 35 percent. Like humans, elephants are designed to learn most of what they need to know. The extended period of nurturing is part of that process, and they continue learning throughout their long lives. Their brain is highly convoluted—another measure of intelligence, which they share with humans, the great apes, and dolphins. And they have the largest brain of all land mammals. It weighs four times as much as ours.

During the second week of March, storms brought wind and rain to the Amboseli plains and fresh snow to the crown of Kilimanjaro. The air was cool and moist. Small, fast-evaporating puddles patterned the game trails. Here and there among the grasses, the extra water spurred insect hatches, marked by congregations of hundreds of crowned cranes, glossy ibis, and sacred ibis, with a host of swallows scything the air just above them. The elephants continued their pattern of gathering each day in the central marshes, and each day I roamed among them, harvesting notes while they took grasses, sedges, and reeds.

Joyce thought it possible that nearly all the elephants in the heart of Amboseli knew one another. Certainly, it looked as if each of the more than two hundred giants using the marsh where I spent most of my time had a firm sense of its place within the family and of its family's status relative to every other group. The large herd went about its affairs with only occasional disputes, quickly settled when the elephants talked things over with a combination of subtle body language and vocalizations. In all, the animals got along so well that it was difficult for an inexperienced observer such as myself to sort out the existing social hierarchy at all.

Late one afternoon, as maroon thunderheads blossomed from every horizon to meet toward the top of the sky, a stiff wind began to sweep across the swamps. It felt ionized, as if the electrically charged air that heralds a rainstorm was condensed and streaming past in a current. Suddenly, all the zebras and wildebeest in sight seemed prone to outbreaks of playing, fighting, and racing about. The baby wildebeest had been gamboling and leaping skyward all day, as young animals will. Now the adults that they scampered by would turn and take up chases of their own. The elephants appeared caught up in the general restlessness. Virtually every subadult bull was locked in a vigorous trunk-wrestling contest with another. Subadult females went trotting past with upraised tails, frolicking like two-ton kittens. Three young elephants between two and four years of age simultaneously raised branches in the air with their trunks and ran to and fro among their elders. A fourth animal, slightly older than the others, broke off a branch and flourished it overhead while making a mock charge at my vehicle.

A volley of trumpet blasts heralded a dominance contest grown out of a meeting between two families. The matriarchs, who were probably long familiar with one another, resolved matters in fairly short order. Each time the dominant female approached, the subordinate one backed away until, finally, she lowered her head and turned aside to feed while moving off slowly. As is often the case, it was the younger males and females in each family that prolonged the contest. Their social status continues to change as they grow, and they are not so certain of where they stand relative to members of different families if they have not interacted with them for a while.

Two mature females, each between fifteen and twenty years of age, met and faced off with outstretched ears. A horizontal crease appeared across each ear, causing the upper third or so to fold backward—a sign of serious aggressive intentions. One charged with a clarion trumpet call. The other broke and fled, but she wound up circling back at a trot to confront her pursuer. The two then trotted back and forth, sounding high-pitched trumpet blares. Several more charges led to the same female racing away but then returning. Even after their families moved farther apart and all the other members resumed feeding, these two kept a wary eye on each other and slowly drifted back to within sparring distance. The next chase resulted in the pursuer closing in fast with her tusks aimed at the other female's rump.

The fleeing female bellowed loudly just before she was about to be struck. Elephants in such situations often give out such a call, a last-ditch effort to avoid harm, and it may cause the pursuer to pull up short or at least soften its blow. But not this pursuer. She delivered a solid poke before she slowed her pace.

The other female slowed farther on, stood rocking slightly for a while, and then shook her head once and turned to feeding. Even then, though, she lagged behind her family and continued watching her rival, who was in turn still slightly apart from her own family, also watching. I missed the beginning of the final chase but turned to see the two already running full out. This time, the fleeing female stumbled in her rush and fell to her knees. Her pursuer, close behind, drove one tusk a good foot deep into her flank. I could not say how much of the force of that thrust was intentional and how much was the result of the pursuer being unable to break her momentum. The injured female screamed, and the younger members of her family quickly ran to her side, followed by two older females, who inspected the wound with their trunks. When they turned to walk away, one older female was on each side of the injured one, and I could see blood gushing down her flank. Joyce had told me of seeing a female walking around with a broken-off tusk sticking out of her side.

⌙⌙⌙⌙⌙⌙⌙⌙⌙⌙⌙⌙

When not at the swamps, I patrolled the nearby woodlands, noting ground hornbills, mongoose families, and troops of baboons and vervet monkeys picking through elephant dung for seeds and insects. The jackrabbit–size antelope called dik-dik fed on the leaves and buds of branches broken off at higher levels by elephants. Impala grazed young grasses growing where elephants had created clearings within the woodlands by pushing over acacias and palms, browsing shrubs, and generally trampling around acting like giants.

Elephants browse trees and shrubs throughout the year. Because the bark and leaves of woody plants contain the best stores of nutrients during the dry months, elephants increasingly turn to them once the grasses cease growing and become brown and brittle after the rainy season. Elephants not only smash down tree limbs and shrubs in the process of foraging but can kill even the largest trees by stripping away enough bark to girdle the trunk. Their overall effect is to open up stands of forest. Where densely populated, the giants tend to transform woodlands into savannas. Elephants have been having this effect on the savanna-woodland balance for eons. Many ecologists believe that, together with fire and drought, these giants helped mold the very look and feel of Africa.

All would agree that elephants fit the definition of a keystone species, whose activities can affect the niches and population levels of a variety of less dominant life forms. Certain starfish are keystone species in the intertidal zone along sea coasts; as they plunder thick beds of mussels and barnacles, they shift the structure of the community and open up opportunities for countless species of colonists. In similar fashion, elephants can increase habitat for an array of grazing animals while decreasing habitat for arboreal, or tree-dependent, species. Once the elephants move on, the grasses in the elephant-made openings are succeeded by brush, temporarily favoring an assortment of browsing animals such as eland and kudu, until the forest reestablishes itself and the cycle is ready to begin anew.

The corollary is that an absence of elephants or a serious reduction in their numbers can lead to grasslands being replaced over wide areas by increasingly thick scrub while existing forests grow more dense and expand, all to the detriment of the grazing community and the benefit of browsers and arboreal animals. In desert areas, and during times of drought elsewhere, elephants keep shrinking water supplies available by deepening and enlarging springs and seeps, excavating with their tusks and trunks. Animals from ostriches and oryx to hyenas and foxes endure with the help of these elephant-maintained wells. Without them, the delicate balance can tip away from life toward the rule of sand and dust.

Just as northern latitude forests are adapted to periodic wildfire, Africa's semiarid ecosystems may depend upon a certain amount of flux to maintain their vitality. No one has carried out detailed studies over a sufficiently long time to know the full extent of the elephant's role in this respect. It is not as simple as elephants being living bulldozers, for at the same time that the giants open up woodlands, they help trees disperse into new areas by spreading the seeds around in fertile heaps of dung. Scavengers from wart hogs to various antelopes and primates come in to glean nuts, pods, and fruit on the ground below trees that have been shaken and rattled by feeding elephants. Some of these animals, too, go on to spread the seeds around in their own dung.

This much is certain: the richest wildlife communities in Africa are found neither in pure woodlands nor in pure savannas but in areas where the two general types of habitat meet and become interspersed with each other. Elephants are one of the most important agents influencing the dynamics of that mixture, and their activities generally increase the overall biological diversity of a region. Conserving elephants, then, becomes much more than an issue about how to protect a single great species. It is about protecting one of the forces that shapes ecosystems and helps sustain the wealth of wildlife found across much of the continent. It is about saving the creative power of nature.

<hr />

So far, I have all but ignored another major component of the Amboseli ecosystem: indigenous people. Until about four hundred years ago, this region was inhabited by the Ilogalala, or People of the Hard Teeth, a cattle-based pastoralist culture. They were replaced by other nomadic pastoralists, the Masai, a Nilotic group that spread along the Great Rift Valley in Kenya and Tanzania. Renowned as warriors, they were successful herders of their own cattle and raiders of everyone else's. They believed that the gods had given them all the world's cattle, so they were perfectly within their rights taking them back. They proved powerful enough to resist slavers, British colonialists, and early commercial ivory hunters alike until epidemics of smallpox spread from the colonialists, sharply reducing Masai numbers, while an outbreak of rinderpest—bovine typhus—decimated their cattle. Taking advantage of their weakness, British administrators began moving groups of Masai off traditional grazing grounds. The Masai and their herds have since rebounded in numbers, but their distribution remains in good part an artifact of arbitrary colonial policies.

The Masai of Amboseli follow much the same migratory pattern as the resident wildlife. During the long rains, they move out across the surrounding plains flush with new grass growth. Then, as waterholes dry up one by one, they withdraw toward the reserve, with its permanent springs and the lush vegetation of the swamps. The reserve itself is Masai territory set aside by a cooperative agreement between these people and the government. The Masai have the right to drive their livestock into the swamps to obtain water, but they are not supposed to let the animals graze extensively until they are back outside the boundaries, lest they deplete the limited forage available for wildlife in the small reserve. In return, the Masai receive a percentage of park fees along with rent from the hotel concessions within the park.

When the reserve staff, who are rangers from Kenya's national park system, come down hard on the Masai for grazing too much along the allocated routes to water, the Masai sometimes respond by sticking a few elephants and an occasional rhino with spears. And every so often, members of the Masai's young warrior groups, known as *moran*, spear a few elephants and rhinos simply to prove their courage, just as they maintain the tradition of spearing a lion to validate their entry into full manhood. The elephants know where they stand with the Masai. They tend to give passing herders and their cattle a wide berth, often fleeing the vicinity altogether, whereas the same elephant families will stroll within arm's length of tourist vans. Elephants everywhere seem to have a fairly precise sense of exactly how safe they are in a given set of surroundings, and it is not surprising given their learning abilities. (A natural-history tour guide told me of ele-

phants in the Aberdares, a mountain range in the Kenyan highlands, racing for cover during thunderstorms. They were much
more panicky than typical elephants in such conditions, he said.
But then some of these animals still carried shrapnel as well as
memories from the days when British forces were bombing
rebel Mau Mau strongholds in those hills.)

All things considered, the elephants' brushes with the Masai
were a minor trouble. The Masai have always been pure pastoralists; they have no tradition of hunting wildlife for meat. Their
migratory patterns are well integrated with those of native grazing animals. As a result, they view wild creatures as a normal,
fully acceptable dimension of their environment.

Heavy cattle grazing encourages encroachment by brush, because cattle avoid the woody plants while selectively mowing
down their competitors—the grasses and succulent herbs. Once
a pasture has grown up into scrubland, the land simply cannot
support as many grazing animals, wild or domestic. At the same
time, tsetse flies, *Glossina*, flourish where brush is abundant, and
they carry the blood parasite *Trypanosoma*, which causes lethal
infections in livestock and sleeping sickness among humans. So
by browsing and trampling back brush, elephant herds can benefit pastoralists in more ways than one.

The us-versus-them frame of mind concerning wildlife seems
to develop most strongly in agrarian cultures. Once people have
settled and planted crops, all kinds of native animals become
pests, vermin, thieves, and enemies, no longer part and parcel of
the perceived natural order of things. Especially elephants. They
are adapted to seek out the highest-quality vegetation within
their domain in any given season, and crops are exactly that:
modified cereal grasses, starch-rich tuberous plants, and fruits.
Incomparable elephant chow. These creatures are smart enough
to remember where the best food supplies are and strong enough
to plow through fences, barricades, and storehouses to get at the
stuff. Conflict between elephants and most types of indigenous
agriculture is almost inevitable.

With that in mind, the Masai's relative tolerance of elephants
takes on special significance. Unfortunately, so does the recent

trend of these people to become more sedentary, develop agricultural schemes to help feed their now burgeoning population, and sell parcels of former grazing territory to land-hungry farmers from ethnic groups indigenous to other parts of the country. During the wet season, virtually the entire Amboseli elephant population disperses beyond this little sanctuary's boundaries. Even in the dry season, when the population has contracted toward the swamps at the heart of the reserve, nearly two-thirds of the families retire to woodlands outside the sanctuary to pass the night. By itself, the reserve could support only a small fraction of the current number of elephants year-round. The future of Amboseli's giants clearly hinges upon the attitudes and land use practices of the people surrounding the reserve.

I discussed the problem with David Western, an ecologist who has investigated this area for more than two decades, and his Masai associate David Maitumo. We flew over Amboseli in Western's light plane, counting elephants and buffalo. We tallied 713 elephants in and around the swamps. Western pointed out that as many as 1000 more elephants inhabited the forested slopes of neighboring Mount Kilimanjaro, an area vastly larger than the reserve. The Kilimanjaro elephants appear to represent a different ecotype. On the rare occasions when a group of them visits the swamps, they can be distinguished easily by their comparatively smaller heads and narrower, straighter tusks. I had also noticed that they seemed much warier.

"Indeed," Western agreed. "Enough rain falls at higher elevations on the mountainside to grow excellent crops along with coffee and tea. The elephants raid the *shambas* [small farms] up there, and I suspect that they are shot at rather often. As far as I know, very little interchange occurs between the Kilimanjaro and Amboseli herds. Now that herds in every other direction have been shot out, the Amboseli group is basically on its own. Do you realize that just two decades ago, elephant populations were continuous from here across to the east coast and southward into the Serengeti?"

The Masai do not take kindly to trespassers on their territory and thus tend to discourage invasion by poachers. Before the

1970s, though, they weren't as quick to turn in the poachers they did encounter to government authorities as they are today. The change was symptomatic of an effort facilitated by David Western to make sure that the Masai gained a direct financial boon from the protection of wildlife in Amboseli—namely, the revenue-sharing from park gate fees and hotel leases. At the time, this was a revolutionary concept in African wildlife conservation. Up to that point, parks and preserves typically operated on much the same principles as a colonial estate. The idea was, in effect, to lock out the local people and make the resources available to white folks half a world away.

"I saw Amboseli as a chance to break away from the humans-as-the-enemy tradition. Two-thirds of the income of the Masai county council for this area now comes from Amboseli," said Western, who heads the Nairobi office of Wildlife Conservation International, an outgrowth of the New York Zoological Society. "This is a vast improvement over earlier conservation plans, but I'm not sure that it will see us through current changes. Part of the original agreement was to build a school and medical facilities for the Masai at the reserve, to show the direct rewards of having the reserve in their midst. We got those going. Then bore holes were to be drilled to provide water for Masai outside the reserve, to compensate them for restrictions on using the central swamps."

"The bore holes went in, but they do not produce water any longer," David Maitumo observed. He and Western proceeded to discuss this in Masai before turning back to include me.

"The government reneged on its agreement to maintain these wells," Western said. "The Masai are also supposed to receive grazing compensation for the amount of forage taken by wildlife. But, you see, it's rather like the programs to compensate them for direct damage to crops and for depredation by predators on livestock: the people wait and wait and are paid late or not at all. We also have the problem that most of the funds that go to the county council end up with the greater Masai government in Nairobi. They end up being distributed to other projects in other Masai homelands. The Masai here—the local people who have to put up with problems caused by the wildlife around them—get very little, and those who do are unclear that it comes from wildlife conservation."

It seemed another case of good intentions being unable to alter the physics of money, which tends to float to the top rather than filter down to the grass roots. Throughout my travels, I would discover that putting conservation revenues directly into the pockets of local people affected by wildlife was the best idea around—a straightforward, effective, democratic idea—and almost impossible to put into practice. For that simple concept threatened the entire bureaucratic structure and all the inefficiency—not to say graft—built into it. An enormous amount had already been invested in systems based upon power and prestige, designed to reward people at the upper levels at the expense of the general populace. Every minor functionary and Big Man alike within that system would work to sabotage what he (occasionally she) saw as a potential loss of influence.

This is a universal problem, and, universally, conservationists hesitate to scream too loudly for fear of losing such influence as they have with the governments involved and such hopes as they might entertain of encouraging more common-sense policies. In many developing countries, after all, conservation concern and conservation expertise are in large part the province of outsiders, who are vulnerable to charges of meddling in a nation's way of doing business. Besides, many experts are still just coming around to accept the idea of true grass-roots involvement in conservation projects themselves. Think how much easier it can be to go directly to the top and dictate policy from there down. Conservationists might not be as keen on the grass-roots approach as they are these days had they not learned in one developing country after another about the peril of throwing in solely with the government and ignoring the locals. The peril is that when a government topples—and, sooner or later, most do—the preserves and wildlife almost immediately follow if the residents have no stake in the resources protected there. For that matter, so long as people view those resources as an extension of an unpopular or repressive regime, they will work all the harder to loot them.

A lack of attention to the local situation also affected the national park operations at Amboseli. Apart from the percentage of gate fees due the Masai council, revenues generated by the reserve went directly to the coffers of the national government. And in return? In return, barely 5 percent of all the revenues earned by Kenya's system of parks and reserves went back into parks and reserves. This could be called starving the goose that laid the golden egg. Kenya's major source of foreign revenue was tourism. And the majority of those tourists came to view wildlife.

Amboseli, one of the most popular and crowded wildlife meccas, had only two working vehicles when I visited. The rest of the reserve's fleet of jeeps and trucks were idled for want of parts costing pennies and lack of gasoline to run them if they ever were repaired. Rangers hitchhiked with me and anyone else they could flag down to get from one post to another. Their wages were not far above subsistence level; their morale, lower yet; their guns, outmoded World War I British Enfield bolt-action .303s. These were the men who would be called upon to risk their lives defending the elephants of Amboseli if and when the poachers arrived with their AK-47s.

Until the 1970s, the park service had been semi-independent of the government, free to disburse its revenues as it saw fit. David Western told me of plans afoot to return to that arrangement in hopes of reversing the deterioration of Kenya's system of parks and reserves. As for the problem of getting wildlife dollars more directly to local Masai, Western saw a partial solution in promoting more direct ownership of tourist facilities in and around the reserve. At the moment, the main lodges were owned by outside individuals and corporations. They earned terrific sums, charging tourists more than a hundred dollars a day, yet contributed practically nothing to the area other than the cost of their leases. David Western thought the Masai could develop lodges and souvenir shops of their own and upgrade the dusty, cattle-trampled campgrounds that a few of them operated along the periphery of Amboseli. They had already set up a concession to sell land to tour companies for the development of more camps, and the contract guaranteed the Masai a substantial income each year.

I asked the idealist's question: Wasn't this commercial emphasis further undercutting the traditional Masai way of life? And I
got a realist's reply: The proper question is, do the Masai themselves want to be traditional Masai? The world is changing faster
and faster, and the Masai are changing with it. Some of the
younger generation are classroom-educated and increasingly familiar with the gadgets and lifestyles of outside cultures. They
may not necessarily want to spend their days following behind a
bunch of cows and their flies. Soila Sayialel could have been one
of a Masai herder's several wives. She may yet be, one day. Or
she may choose not to. Right now, she has chosen to study
elephants.

"Tourists always like the Masai," David Maitumo said.
"They like the spears and the red powder on the hair. The necklaces the women make. The houses of cattle dung. All that." He
patted his factory-made trousers and white shirt, shrugged, and
went back to writing up notes on our aerial census.

⌘⌘⌘⌘⌘⌘⌘⌘⌘⌘⌘⌘

Several days later, I was in the 1470-square-mile Kenyan reserve
known as Masai Mara, or just the Mara, for short. Located west
of Amboseli, the Mara protects a portion of the northern end of
the 15,440-square-mile Serengeti ecosystem, most of which lies
in Tanzania. Like Amboseli, the Mara is formed from Masai territory, with a share of revenues from gate fees and leases to tourist lodges going to the Masai council, and the reserve is bordered
by traditional Masai pastoralists. It is no accident, then, that Masai Mara still holds one of Kenya's least disturbed elephant populations outside of Amboseli.

Commercial ivory poachers had been obliterating the Serengeti's elephants on the Tanzanian side of the border. They had hit
the Mara herds as well, but Kenya's APUs had successfully
knocked the gangs back. Such poaching as continued here was
more the work of Tanzanian villagers who slipped across the
border to take buffalo, eland, and the like for meat. Along the
way, they had killed a couple of tourists and robbed a few others
in remote sections of the reserve. Still, in comparison with other

parts of the country, things were basically under control. The Mara was the core of an elephant population estimated at about 1500 and probably even increasing. Part of that increase was due to the wrong reason—habitat compression; elephants were moving in from lands lost to cultivation or rife with poachers. But once within the Mara region, they could still roam more or less freely between the reserve and Masai grazing territory, just as at Amboseli.

At the time of my visit, nearly half the herds were outside the sanctuary's official borders. It was then mid-March. The wet season was on its way. Roads through the western part of the reserve, running through the fine volcanic soils known as black cotton dirt, were rapidly turning into quagmires of slick gumbo mud. The thunderstorms came each evening, rolling off a side wall of the Great Rift Valley escarpment to pour their water onto the plains below. The little rains had been so generous that the grass already stood shoulder-tall to a wildebeest: *Themeda*, red oat grass; *Pennisetum*; and others I didn't recognize. Thick, sweet-smelling, wind-rippled, wild grain—green seas of it rolled beyond the horizon to join the rest of the Serengeti. The smooth prairie cloak was broken only by scattered acacias, giraffes, and little, bare hillocks formed by weathered termite mounds. Standing sentinel on them were male topi, antelope with coats of burnished purple, scanning their surroundings for rival males and prides of lions—black-maned lions, characteristic of the Mara. By June, hundreds of thousands of wildebeest would be arriving, sweeping along the northern arc of their annual circuit through the Serengeti. This ecosystem holds more than a million of them all told. It is the greatest single mass of wild hooved animals left on the planet.

For the first week I was at the Mara, I kept staring out across those plains and thinking of the native American savanna. I found myself conjuring up plains grizzlies the color of cured grasses, plains wolves, the grazing complex of plains elk, mule deer, antelope . . . and sixty times more bison than the Serengeti has wildebeest. *That* was the greatest single mass of wild hooved animals on the planet. So little remained, so pitifully little. Had

I not come to the Mara, I would never have been able to even sense what such a community might have been like. Sometimes I wished I hadn't. The Mara plains made the loss too achingly real.

Some two hundred elephants were spending their days in the woodlands along the Mara River. They left a perfect browse line there, pruning all the branches below about fifteen to eighteen feet, which is the height to which large bulls can reach with their trunks. Each afternoon, the giants emerged from the trees to begin grazing across marshes not far from the river, joining waterbuck and mud-coated buffalo. As the afternoon merged into evening, storm light would stream through gaps in the clouds and cast rainbows over the boundless savanna. Then, as the rainbows dissolved into a topi-colored sunset, the elephants would march off in long files northward across the plains to spend the night in the open country, feeding on fresh grass growth. And I would return to camp with memories of the sky full of fire and the earth full of great beasts, as if I were returning through time from the Age of Mammals. At the first light of dawn, I was there to see the giants file back across the plains through veils of rising mist and vanish into the woodlands lining the river, where the eyes of hippos and crocodiles glided along the water's brown surface.

Elephants are so *big*. The realization struck me afresh every day. From deep within the forest came the clacking of tusks from young males jousting, the snapping of branches, rumbles like the thrumming of an unseen waterfall. I could hear one of the giants scratching its side against a tree trunk hundreds of feet away. Yet their feet are cushioned with thick pads of fibrous tissue to support their great weight, and if they choose, elephants can walk up on you as silently as cats. Abruptly, one would emerge from the trees beside me. I would turn at a faint scuffling sound and find myself looking across at the belly of a big bull, then up and up at a huge head, and start back-pedaling, trying to act calm, promising myself to do a better job of heeding the park rule requiring visitors to stay in their vehicles.

When I was chased off, it was almost always by the teenage

females and young mothers in family groups. The bull bands more or less ignored me. Though not quite in my vehicle, I was at least on the roof when an enormous male appeared close by and began tusking at the bark of a thick combretum tree. He reached high to do this and finally worked a piece loose. He tore it off with his trunk, dropped it to the ground, and then moved on. I was about to go over and see what it smelled like when a second bull showed up and went over to sniff at the piece of bark himself. He then probed up the tree trunk until he found the place the first bull had gouged. The newcomer proceeded to reach as high as he could with his own tusks and tried to work another piece loose at the same spot. He managed to rake off a chunk just slightly lower, dropped it, and left. A third bull followed and repeated the whole procedure, also leaving a tusk mark on the trunk. Last came a male little more than half the size of the lead bull. This young one got his trunk on the freshly torn part of the tree but could not get close with his tusks, not even when he reared up and placed his forelegs against the tree. He settled for prying off a piece as high as he could, then followed the others out into the marshes.

I was left with the distinct impression that this was not so much an attempt to get at a tasty section of bark as some sort of dominance-related male affair—perhaps like grizzly bears leaving scratch marks as high as possible on tree trunks, though the significance of that is not really understood either. The most interesting thing about the scene was the drongo perched on a slim branch of the first tree limb above the tusked section. The bird had just captured a large cicada and settled onto the branch with its prize when the first elephant began shaking the tree with its tusking. Clutching the cicada while being whipped sharply back and forth, the drongo rode out the entire elephant storm, watching the giants with intense interest. When it was finally over, the bird methodically began picking apart the insect.

After I caught up with the bulls in the marshes, I could no longer tell which they were, for seven different males were milling around a single female. When one tried to mount her, two others ran up and butted the suitor off her. A fight erupted, with mud and dust exploding off the colliding heads of the rivals. The female ran back into the trees, immediately followed by three of the males. I could no longer see them clearly, but, following a tremendous roar and more sound of heads clashing, I noticed the drongo flying off to another copse of trees carrying the remains of its meal in its bill.

With a young Masai named Tim Kapeen, I went north of the Mara to wander through Masai grazing lands for a while. I was sick of viewing wildlife from my car. I understood the reserve's rules but was, as ever, constitutionally unable and unwilling to see the world while sitting on my rump. I felt drugged relating to the African bush in such a passive mode, as if I were watching an endless television special. After all, one of the greatest resources of this continent to someone from an overdeveloped nation is the opportunity to experience what it feels like to be just one more creature out there immersed in an environment that shaped our species. It has to do with appreciating at a gut level how many of those fellow creatures can strike you, stomp you flat, or rip your limbs off. It has to do with adrenaline and humility, knowing what it is like to feel occasionally like a predator and occasionally like prey.

That was one reason I went with Tim—to walk. The other was that I wanted to see which routes the elephants took when they headed north for the night. Besides, more wildlife of certain types could be found at that moment outside the reserve than inside it, and the ecological explanation was interesting. Until the wildebeest arrived with the onset of summer to mow down with sheer numbers the tall grass of the Mara reserve, the areas cropped by cattle outside the borders offered more young, sprouting grasses, which were both tastier and more nutritious as far as animals such as the hartebeest, topi, Thompson's gazelle, impala, and zebra were concerned.

The elephants I encountered were much warier than those inside the reserve—warier and, at the same time, more aggressive if pressed. This was a pattern I would see repeated many times in the wild throughout Africa and Asia. I think it again shows how well the giants remember their encounters with people. For what it's worth, my conclusion is that bad experiences can make them more shy in general but more prone to attack when surprised or seriously harassed.

Tim was not yet twenty, but he was a veteran of raids into the Tanzanian border region to recover Masai cattle stolen by villagers there. Once the spear fights were finished and the cattle recovered, the danger was not over. He still had to drive the cattle back through the reserve past park service wardens who could shoot him on sight as a suspected poacher. So he had to travel by night and hide in the brush with his herd as soon as it grew light. I found it ironic that a Masai within the reserve had to become perhaps even warier than an elephant traveling through Masai land outside the reserve.

Tim was a treat to spend time with. He was a natural tutor: "Do you see the buffalo? There. Three bulls. . . . Ummm. Who made these droppings? Yes, hyena. And this digging? Honey badger. And look where the topi have been grazing. Just here. . . . Ummm. Do you remember the buffalo? Do you know where those buffalo are now? See those bushes you are walking straight toward? If it was one alone, he might have charged by now. They are not so bad together."

Tim pointed out a tree called *osokonoi* in Masai—*Warburgia ugandensis*, the East African greenheart—with bark that resembled an elephant's wrinkled hide. The Masai eat its fruit when it is ripe and sweet and use it for stomach medicine when it is still green and bitter. The elephants, he said, take the fruit when bitter, and it makes them crazy. The fruit has a very hot, spicy taste, and various observers claim to have noticed both elephants and baboons become unusually aggressive after feeding on it. Africa is full of tales of elephants getting drunk on the overripe, fermented nuts of the doum palm, *Hyphaene coriacea*. They may be exaggerations, inspired by the fact that people commonly make wine from the starchy heart of this widespread palm. I was more inclined to believe the many stories I heard of elephants raiding storehouses of fermenting grain and breaking into stills and proceeding to get roaring drunk.

Tim said the elephants' main enemies here were lions, wild dogs, and cobras, and that the wild dogs, which attack elephant babies, would defecate on the carcass to keep the family from lingering by it; otherwise they would stay around for as many as five days. He had seen elephants form a defensive circle around sick or injured companions and stay with them for at least that long. He pointed out that they will surround a sleeping companion the same way. He knew they would support a wounded companion while traveling by positioning themselves on each side and pressing against it, and would attempt to lift the animal with their trunks and tusks if it stumbled.

Earlier, I had gone on patrol in the reserve with a nine-year veteran ranger, James Ampany, who told me he had seen bull elephants carry tender young branches as food to an old bull lying on its side, too weak to forage on its own. I knew that this kind of care had been documented by others as well. But when James also said he had seen mother elephants pick up newborn babies with their trunk and run with them to avoid danger, I was skeptical. I had never heard of this in the wild. Ordinarily, elephant families bunch together when threatened. The infants run to stand directly under their mothers, usually toward the center of the group, leaving any would-be invader facing a solid fortress of elephant bodies. If the group flees, the babies stay beneath their mothers' shuffling feet unless the group is running flat out, in which case the babies are better off racing at their mothers' heels.

No researcher I met could confirm the behavior of mothers lifting their babies. Yet farther along in my journeys in both Africa and Asia, I would speak with villagers who said they had seen elephant mothers lift their young over fences, and somewhere along the way I recalled an elephant keeper at a zoo telling me of a mother lifting her baby up to get at a store of food. Many centuries ago, Pliny wrote: "The females in a herd often aid a youngster by pushing it up a bank or helping it out of a mud hole or river bed and even carry them at need." On the other hand, Pliny passed on a lot of dubious information. Then I found this passage in the writings of Colonel J. H. "Elephant Bill" Williams, who oversaw hundreds of working Asian elephants for the Bombay-Burma Trading Company in the early 1900s: "I believe that if she is disturbed, the mother elephant will carry her calf during its first month, holding it wrapped in her trunk. I have seen a mother pick up her calf this way."

It is difficult to know where the facts give way to fables in the case of a creature with the learning abilities of an elephant. For example, James and others mentioned seeing bulls break off heavy branches and use them as clubs in battles with other bulls. More likely, what they saw was an aggressive display—a big male's version of the brandishing of branches I had seen among juvenile elephants. But then again, chroniclers in ancient times wrote of war elephants specifically trained to swing heavy objects and throw missiles in combat. The trainers were building upon behaviors elephants naturally perform in a less directed way. Who is to say that a few elephants have not learned to channel such behavior on their own? Elephants caught in a trap in the wild will throw whatever they can reach at someone who approaches and swing wildly at their tormentors with a handy branch or root. I know, because I had to dodge them.

My most remarkable experience in Tim's company had nothing to do with elephants except that we were looking for them at the time. Instead, we came upon a young male lion with two lionesses. They were working their way toward a Masai and his herd of cattle. As they drew closer, they began to belly along through the grass, then crouched to eye the cattle. The young male started growling. His tail switched with excitement. He half-rose to coil for a running start several times.

"We'd better help that man," I said.

"No," Tim said firmly. "He knows the lions are there. This is for him to do. He would not want us to interfere."

The herder stood staring straight at the cats and slowly raised his spear to a throwing position without once moving his gaze away. From a distance, other herders who had noticed the man's posture drew nearer to watch the stand-off, but not too near.

They, too, thought that this was for him to do. This was what he had been trained for as a *moran*. Each time the male lion growled and poised itself, the man would shake his spear and spread his stance a bit. Each time the cat was still, the man was still, matching the animal's steadfast, golden-eyed stare. The stand-off continued for a quarter of an hour. At last, the lions crouched away into a line of thornscrub. Had the herder communicated the slightest hesitation or fear, I think they would have gone for his cattle in a flash. If these youngish lions hadn't known much about the Masai when they started, they knew something now, and it might help them survive among people in the future.

Although the Masai have plenty of traditional tales about mighty lions, the heroes of their folk tales tend to be the little fellows—a mongoose or a hare. As for the elephant, Masai fables regard the great beast more for its sagacity—its elephantine wisdom—than for its size and strength.

Among many Masai, it is considered the greatest good fortune to find the afterbirth of an elephant, I learned from David Round-Turner, one of the original wardens of Masai Mara. Only a single family in the Narok district, which takes in the Mara, was known to have discovered one. They were now very wealthy. Upon finding an afterbirth, tradition called for the herder to construct a rough *boma* (corral) with as many doors as he has wives (or, in the case of a bachelor, as he wishes to have wives), then spend the night inside with no fear of harm befalling him. Soon, the herder and his family would find themselves accumulating large herds of healthy, fertile cattle. A related belief holds that a small piece of dried elephant ear ground into powder and ingested would relieve the suffering of a woman with a retained afterbirth.

Since they did not traditionally hunt elephants, the Masai presumably collected material from carcasses found in the countryside. From the tail hairs, they braided bracelets and necklaces, and from the tusks, they made more bracelets and the *rungus*, or staff of authority, carried by chiefs.

At a meeting in a lodge along the Mara River, I met several

Masai chiefs carrying staffs of authority. A couple were dressed in traditional red robes, the others in suits. They represented Masai group ranches. Also present were hoteliers from Nairobi and high-ranking officers from the APU in Narok dressed in camouflage gear. The meeting concerned future development plans for the Mara. Before it began, I cornered one of the APU officers, Franco Kamanja, to ask about poaching in the area. He had been in dozens of firefights, he said, and described a few. But he soon grew bored with providing what amounted to the usual fodder for eager journalists and turned the discussion around by asking me a series of far more penetrating questions.

"I understand that many states in your country do not believe in capital punishment," Franco noted. "Tell me, what do Americans think of killing a man for killing an animal? What about a poacher who is just hunting meat for food? Under our new directive, we are to treat him the same as a commercial poacher. What state are you from? Do you shoot poachers in Montana? Do your conservationists approve of shooting trespassers in your national parks?"

The inequity of foreigners with genteel sensibilities supporting shoot-to-kill measures to protect African wildlife goes hand in hand with First World attitudes about what it is pleased to call the Third World and white attitudes about blacks—is that what he wanted me to say? No, he just wanted to make me think hard about it. He succeeded. I was stumped. Embarrassed. Admiring. He grilled me a while longer and then, as if he were privy to my innermost thoughts, inquired, "And what of your Great Plains? Didn't it once have even more wildlife than Kenya? Where are your animals?"

"Geez, Franco, give me a break."

He smiled and said, "We have learned from your mistakes, perhaps."

On that note, the meeting began, punctuated by hippo grunts from the river. The main speaker was Dr. Perez Olindo, director of Kenya's Wildlife Service. He had a twofold purpose. One involved increased tourism. The Masai leaders already supported it. A step beyond Amboseli, everyone was already gung-ho to put in more lodges, roads, and other facilities for visitors all over the place. That was the problem: haphazard development. "There is a way of promoting tourism, and there is a way of killing it," Olindo said. "We must do this with the least change to the scenery and wildlife people come to see."

Olindo's second purpose was to announce that big money, serious money, was being made available through a special package from the World Wildlife Fund (WWF), European Economic Community (EEC), and World Bank. The funds were earmarked for community improvement—schools, hospitals, transportation services, veterinary work, and so on. But Olindo wanted to make it clear that they would be linked to Masai efforts to practice conservation of the greater Mara ecosystem. In other words, the cash was intended as a reward for leaving room for wildlife.

"We want to get money not to a few pockets but directly to villagers, and in proportion to each villager's habitat requirements," is how Olindo phrased it for me later. "The threat is that the Masai here are converting extensive areas of plains in the northern extension of the Mara to agriculture. No, not regular crops; they require too much water. But the same conditions that cause tall grasses to flourish can support wheat. There are plans to go to wheat farming on a massive scale, promoted by our Kenyan agricultural agencies, the FAO [Food and Agriculture Organization, a branch of the United Nations], and American advisors. Those areas are rich in wildlife and vital to the whole ecosystem.

"Yes, yes, Kenya needs to feed its rapidly growing population. But not with the Mara, because what can sustain millions of animals will not yield agriculture over the long run. The soil will be exhausted within three to five years, if drought does not ruin the crops first. This scheme is for dryland farming, utterly dependent upon rainfall. People have already tried farming in the very upper end of the Mara ecosystem. It ends up being shifting cultivation on a massive scale as they go from one worked-out area to another. The encouragement to convert pastures to farmland comes solely from subsidies and from the quick money people can make selling off their grazing land. We must talk about what can be sustained over the long run. I tell them that the Mara, developed properly, is something that makes money even while they sleep. Tourism—you don't have to dip it for ticks, nor inoculate it, nor herd it, nor plow it and cut it and store it.

"Wisdom is not confined to people who have been in a classroom," Perez continued. "These people, the Masai, have survived because they understand their environment. They understand very well when I talk about bringing their land up to its natural potential, to use the grasses and the soils the best way possible—and that is to grow animals. Cattle, if they wish. Wildlife most definitely. Nothing else is so efficient. Over the years, this approach will be the best way for them to improve their lifestyle. People cannot easily see that far ahead. They want money now. Well, with this new program, we can offer them that."

Several days afterward, Holly Dublin, a conservation biologist specializing in the Mara, filled in some details for me. "Right now, 70 percent of the funds for projects in the Masai's Narok district come from the Mara reserve. Less than 1 percent goes to people immediately adjoining the reserve—the ones most affected by wildlife. That is the inequality conservationists are trying to rectify with the WWF/EEC/World Bank money. People lump the Masai together, but there are a number of subgroups. The Il-Purko subgroup is not native. They were transplanted here by the Brits from the Laikipia Hills. They've done well for themselves with revenues from the Mara, but they aren't especially inclined to share it with different subgroups. They distribute the money to other Purkos and their projects, especially this wheat-growing business. Funds also get fiddled and filtered off to God knows where. Individuals have become millionaires off the Mara through owning lodges, yet they have little or nothing to do personally with conservation.

"We've already got elephants raiding new fields up north," Holly continued, "and it's going to get messier. But the scary part of wheat farming isn't just the conversion of habitat. It's the conversion of ownership. The land used to be controlled by a few private people—tribal leaders, mainly—but grazed as a commons. In the sixties, following independence, these holdings became group ranches, literally owned by groups of people. If the group approves, a ranch can be broken down now into small, individual properties that may be sold or leased independently. And I mean small. People are selling off one-acre plots. Some Masai want to divide up the Koyaki group ranch just north of the Mara. It's a key wildlife area, and it's a wildebeest calving ground for the entire Serengeti. Imagine it subdivided. In ecosystem matters here, we've been dealing with maybe half a dozen individuals representing the group ranches. Some may be tough, some may be even corrupt, or at least less scrupulous than you'd like. But it's a heckuva lot easier than dealing with 4000 individual landowners after subdivision. Besides, they'll wind up fencing it all and stopping movement through the ecosystem anyway."

Having invested the better part of his career in wildlife conservation at the Mara, David Round-Turner put it this way for me: "So far, we don't really manage wildlife in the reserve. We don't have to impose heavy-handed human manipulation—culling, artificial waterholes, predator control, the divine right sort of stuff. We manage people and let the ecosystem run itself. But ultimately, all this will be fenced and heavily, intensively managed. With this specter of burgeoning population"—adding immigration of farmers from other ethnic groups to an already high birth rate, the Mara was undergoing an 11.5 percent annual increase in people—"human needs will be paramount. The best we can do, our only real achievement, is to slow down the deterioration of wildlife."

FOUR

EAST AFRICA:
TSAVO

🔲🔲🔲🔲 BACK IN NAIROBI, elephants were much in the news, and the news was truly international. In Angola, where Cuban communist troops guarded American oil company wells from American-supported rebels, the rebels were still financing their weapons with poached ivory laundered by Afrikaner military people, who sent the ivory on through their Hong Kong connections labeled as tusks from legal culling operations in South Africa. When a plane full of smuggled tusks bound from Angola to South Africa crashed en route, one of the passengers was revealed to be the son of the president of Portugal, Angola's former colonial master. In Tanzania, the Indonesian ambassador was busted trying to leave the country with trunks full of tusks. Two Germans and an Austrian were arrested after two Tanzanian *dhows* (traditional Arab sailing vessels) were intercepted on their way to Dubai in the United Arab Emirates loaded with seventy tons of poached ivory ultimately destined for France, where it would be made into bijouterie and piano keys. Sometimes, East African tusks that were successfully smuggled by *dhow* to Dubai were then flown to Zaire, where they were given forged certificates identifying them as legal ivory, then reexported, often to Belgium and France. French diplomatic papers were known to have been doctored along the way to make the going smoother. The Republic of Congo alone had exported 130 tons of ivory to Paris in 1984. And yet some of the Parisian outlets, along with the Zairean dealers, were ultimately associated with the same Hong Kong ivory syndicates sucking Angolan ivory out through South Africa. The Hong Kong network had established dummy corporations and retail outlets in nations throughout the globe.

For all its sophisticated international convolutions, the ivory trade still began with the dirty business of blasting elephants in the field and hacking out their tusks. In Amboseli and Masai Mara, I had been in what were probably the two best places in East Africa to ignore that business. But just forty miles east of Amboseli began the killing fields of Tsavo National Park. At least forty elephants and one ranger had been shot to death in Tsavo during the last week I was in Masai Mara. GSU troops killed a thirteen-year-old boy herding cattle in the area. There were daily reports of new elephant carcasses being discovered. . . .

"The Kenya government is strenuously avoiding publicity over the shooting of several hundred elephants now taking place in Tsavo National Park. . . . Because wildlife is a major source of income, the government doesn't want to draw attention to the shooting," read one newspaper article. It was from 1968.

Tsavo's 7720 square miles were set aside by the British colonial administration in 1947, protecting an immense expanse of scrubland dominated by thorny *Commiphora* shrubs. One native life form not protected was the indigenous Wata tribe, also called the Wakamba. Traditional elephant hunters, they used a long-bow more powerful than any carried in medieval Europe and arrows dipped in a poison potent enough to stop a huge heart within minutes after the elephant was shot, usually in the soft underbelly. By merely continuing to do what their clans had always done, the nomadic Wakamba abruptly became trespassers and poachers. Park wardens waged a low-level battle against them for years.

By the time the most notorious, which is to say skilled, Wakamba giant-slayers had been rounded up, the whole contest had become irrelevant. Poaching and settlement around the park were driving elephants into Tsavo's wild stretches in unprecedented numbers. Depending upon drought cycles, the parklands might ordinarily hold anywhere from 10,000 to, at most, 20,000 elephants. By the late 1960s, the population, swollen with refugees and increasingly cut off from traditional migratory routes, was approaching an estimated 42,000. They were trampling the countryside into dust, degrading the range used by other wildlife along with their own.

Various authorities called for a culling program to reduce their numbers. Another faction, led by chief park warden David Sheldrick, urged forbearance. Let nature take its course, they said. Our task is not to impose some preconceived notion of a proper balance on Tsavo but, rather, to wait and see what happens and learn from it. Isn't that what parks are for? We won't learn about nature, countered the culling proponents, because this is not a natural situation to begin with. Humans wrought the habitat changes that forced so many elephants to seek refuge in Tsavo; humans must repair it before the park habitat is destroyed as well.

A philosophical Great Rift has always split the conservation community, and I cannot think of how to define it other than in somewhat simplistic fashion. On the one side are people drawn to animals because they intrinsically care for them. Their concern is an extension of emotional drives, foremost among them the human capacity for sympathy. They tend to believe that nature knows best, that animals have every right to exist for their own sake, and that they should be set aside unmolested in wildlands to be observed and enjoyed.

On the other side are people who envision wildlife as a resource that we have a right to direct as we see fit. Their concern is an extension of the human drive to improve and master. They are inclined to believe that, without our guidance, nature can be somewhat messy and inefficient and that it benefits from more intensive management. For many in their ranks, the goal of manipulating wildlife populations and habitats is primarily consumptive—to produce a supply of meat, fur, hides, hunting opportunities, and trophies.

To risk simplifying things even further, the one side believes that people should stop doing so many things to wildlife, whereas the other believes the answer to saving wildlife is to do more things to it. Hand off versus hands on. At times, the reverence-for-nature school can grade into righteousness, escaping from the flood of everyday realities and politics to moral high ground. Conversely, the more pragmatic, utilitarian approach can grade into what Joyce Poole described as the male-oriented imperative to "take charge, even if you don't know what you're doing."

There was the rub. Neither side really knew enough about either elephants or the long-term dynamics of African ecosystems to set forth a compelling argument. That in itself was seen by some as a good reason to leave matters in Tsavo alone. The argument was still raging when drought struck. Between 1970 and 1972 alone, some 6000 elephants died of starvation and thirst. You see? cried the culling advocates: a disaster. See what? replied the others. Is it somehow better to die from a bullet?

They were still arguing when poachers in unprecedented numbers began to slip in, lured by the tusks strewn across the countryside—and by the more than 35,000 elephants that had survived. The majority of the illegal hunters were no longer local ethnic groups but Somalis, themselves victims of drought, which had displaced subsistence farmers and herders across much of Somalia. In the process, it had also exacerbated political conflicts. That, in turn, had led to an influx of weapons. Here, then, came poachers who were not only tough and bush-savvy but well armed and unafraid of battle. Fellow Muslims, who made up the majority of eastern Kenya's population, provided a network of food supplies, transportation, hide-outs, and caches for weapons and tusks. Continuing economic failure and civil unrest in Somalia produced a steady supply of new poaching recruits and AK-47s, along with vehicles and communication gear.

People called them *shifta*—bandits, outlaws. But Kenyan antipoaching forces had arrested more than a few regular Somali soldiers, in uniform, among them. In fact, it appeared that the impoverished Somali government was encouraging the raid on Kenya's ivory troves, having exhausted its own supply. I sensed a powerful undercurrent of political tension about this aspect of poaching. Many Kenyans saw it as an unofficial invasion by a neighbor feared to have grander designs beyond its borders on the Muslim-dominated territory that was once part of Somaliland.

Like Amboseli, Tsavo had seen its infrastructure and staff morale steadily erode since the national parks department was absorbed into the government and subjected to a continuing drought of funds. Through most of the 1970s and 1980s, illegal grazers drove herds almost at will through the parklands while poaching gangs essentially controlled large portions of Tsavo's backcountry. By the time I reached Kenya, special military forces had been stationed in the park and joined with APU units to clear out much of the livestock. But barely 5000 elephants remained. And still the killing went on.

I flew into Tsavo in a light plane. Oria Douglas-Hamilton sat in one seat, and her husband, Iain, was at the controls. As we crossed over the Tsavo boundary, a spectacular terrain of iron-red rock outcroppings thrust upward from sandy plains of the same color. Termite mounds stood scattered like more hills in miniature. Waterholes took on the appearance of ganglia in skeins of game trails across the scrub. *Ipomoea*, a morning glory–like vine with white blossoms, lit up clusters of bushes, and doum palms lined the edges of rivers. Nowhere, however, did I see an elephant until, well into the park, Oria finally pointed below and said, "There!"

A section of scrub several acres in size lay surrounded by a fence. Inside were several elephants the fired-brick color of Tsavo's soil. With them were a handful of black rhinos. They were the last of the 5000 rhinos that had inhabited Tsavo two decades earlier, representing Africa's largest population. As with elephants, drought had taken some, poachers the rest. These surviving Tsavo rhinos were enclosed by an electric fence and under round-the-clock guard in their little sanctuary within a sanctuary. The elephants, Oria told me, came in by themselves, because they knew that this little plot was safe. The big ones stepped over the electric wires. Those with young held the wires down for them with thick-padded feet or insulating tusks.

Farther on, Iain spotted a family at a waterhole and began to exclaim, "Ah ha, look at them! This is lovely. This is how Tsavo used to be everywhere. It was an elephant world." He was grinning to himself. Iain was playing hooky; he was supposed to be back in a Nairobi office, wearing a suit and writing up reports for the World Wildlife Fund, not chasing elephants in Tsavo.

A short distance beyond the family, vultures flapped away from a treetop. Iain strained to look out the side window and said, "Oh *!#@%, here we go." Circling down, we saw an elephant, red like the other ones, lying by a reddish-brown pool of dried blood. It had no face. That had been cut off to get at the tusks. Four lions appeared a moment later, moving in the direction of the carcass. More miles brought more carcasses, and then we landed alongside the Tsavo River near the tent camp of Ted Goss, a long-time Kenya wildlife manager currently working for the World Wildlife Fund.

We had not been there fifteen minutes exchanging news before the ranger in charge of the rhino sanctuary ran up with the news that a tourist had been shot in the stomach by bandits. "That's just what we feared. With all the poachers and guns in this place and fewer elephants for them to find, we've been waiting for this to happen," Iain said as we raced back to the plane. Ted roared off in his Cessna Super Cub. We were airborne just behind him, with Iain muttering, "This will really put the fat in the fire. By God, I'd like to catch those bastards!"

We tried. I had wondered how the trip would turn out ever since I noticed back in Nairobi that Iain had thrown a flak jacket in with the rest of his gear. The reports on the park radio channel were confusing, but we established that a tourist van had been ambushed just a mile or two beyond the park's western boundary on the road to Amboseli. Eventually, we reached the road, then a van with people beside it and what looked like bullet holes on its side as we roared by. The tourist—a German woman—had been taken off with bullet wounds in her stomach and leg. A second tourist, a man, had suffered minor injuries. No sign of the bandits so far, said the voices on the radio.

Iain began to sweep over the nearest hills. He was plainly galvanized. In his consuming role as a leader of the struggle to save

Africa's elephants, he had found it neccessary to devote ever
more of his time to office-bound meetings and administrative
duties. But this was a man known for standing his ground in the
face of a full-blown elephant charge while swinging a survey tripod wildly over his head. During a stint with the game department of Uganda, he hunted down poachers by airplane as his
daily routine. He would probably not have paid much attention
to a bullet or two perforating his wings now. I had the impression that he would have preferred it to returning to his desk.

The plane's stall light and buzzer were on the whole time as
we circled tightly over canyons and boulder fields that could
have hidden the gunmen. We made out giraffes among the trees
and hartebeests and zebras watching us from the shade of
bushes. But it was futile to hope that we would catch a glimpse
of the bandits, unless they were incredibly stupid, for the terrain
had become a maze of geologically fresh, ropy lava flows,
twisted gullies, and volcanic rubble too coarse to hold a set of
tracks.

We flew back and landed next to park headquarters at Voi,
where the tents of a paramilitary GSU encampment rose not far
from a luxury safari lodge. The day before, we learned, bandits
had robbed a lodge in the Taita Hills, between Tsavo East and
Tsavo West. Not long before that, they had held up a private
ranch bordering the park on the east. At about the same time,
tourists in Tsavo were watching in horror as elephants with
blood pouring from fresh bullet wounds staggered in to the
drinking hole below the lodge. Several elephant families remained close to the lodge and headquarters, probably recognizing that they were more secure there than farther afield. And yet
when the chief ranger, Joe Kioko, had left headquarters for a
meeting in Nairobi, elephants were shot awfully close to Voi. It
looked like an inside job. Someone had opened the gate to a park
road that led to the elephants and locked it shut behind them.
Everyone was suspect, from the local rangers to the elite GSU
troops. Some whispered that Joe himself was in on it, despite the
fact that he had won honors for leading the long and desperate
fight against poaching here. Whoever the real poachers were, it
paid to keep things confused this way.

I found Joe Kioko at the safari lodge bar, nursing a badly needed beer. He looked more than exhausted. He looked beaten. He had been flying his own light plane almost nonstop looking for poachers, landing after dark on an unlit field, sometimes with bullet holes in the fuselage. "We've shot something like seventeen or eighteen poachers in the last four or five months. You think you're winning a little, and then there is an eruption of elephant killings like we have now," he sighed. "I'm flying nine-and-a-half hours a day. I have a crook in my neck from constantly looking out the window. I'm tired; I'm understaffed. You literally have no time for yourself. We work flat out. We didn't know what Christmas was. We need more men and equipment to close off certain corridors. We have to abandon the northern part of Tsavo East for tourist use. We have no control there. . . ." He sounded like a besieged commandant in the midst of a war, which is essentially what he was.

"In some ways," he continued, "the poaching was worse in the 1970s. It involved a lot of big shots in the country." Notably the family of then-president Jomo Kenyatta, he might have added but didn't. "Now it is mostly mercenaries from outside. These Somali guys fight back. Every time. They never throw down their guns. Always a shootout." I bought us another round, and he resumed. "I keep telling myself, what we do isn't just for Kenya. It is for the whole world. Then I wonder: Is it fair to ask a poorer country like Kenya to solve everything? Man, we have to have money for education, for roads, for food. These tusks are not ending up in Kenya, you know. Sometimes I get discouraged seeing countries—rich countries like your United States—continuing to buy ivory while we have to go after the Somalis out here."

Over the days that followed, I looked hard for elephants and found mostly dead ones. I learned to locate them the same way scavenging lions find carcasses, by watching the sky for vultures. Once I found the first of a group, the stench would lead me to the rest of the family. Four bodies here, six there, another two across the gully, whitewashed with vulture droppings, putrefying under the sun until the flesh liquefied and oozed out onto the sandy ground, leaving a great, deflated-looking envelope of hide. Always, the bodies were faceless. After four or five days under the African sun, an elephant corpse is soft enough for a man to pull the tusks loose. Before that, they must be chopped free. The severed trunk might lie somewhere nearby, like the carcass of a strange and separate organism. The tough pads of the feet would rot off and rest on the ground like grey saucers.

Iain said, "You're seeing the real end of the game now—the final part of the story."

I stayed briefly with Simon Trevor, a former Tsavo warden who had turned to making wildlife films. An honorary warden still, he occupied a house within the park near Voi and there kept company with an assortment of beasts, including a ground hornbill, various tame owls, and a honey badger, or ratel. A member of the mustelid, or weasel, family, the ratel closely resembles North America's wolverine, both in physical appearance and in its reputation for ferocity. Like the wolverine, the long-clawed ratel will attack animals many times its size. Stories of how it supposedly kills large bull antelopes by rushing up and raking off their testicles linger in the mind. Which explains why my first few meetings with these predators resulted in a 180-pound man stampeding away from a little beast that weighed less than twenty pounds. Simon's ratel was friendly as could be.

The ratel was another species partly dependent upon the elephant's presence in the ecosystem, Simon informed me. More than a hundred kinds of dung beetles could be found in this region. The insects lay their eggs in manure, which serves as a food source for the developing larvae. First, however, the adults may pack the manure into a ball and roll it away to a relatively safe place. Some roll it along the ground, others push it up to be attached to the stems of shrubs. Many burrow directly under the manure pile and pack the droppings into underground storage chambers, where the grubs feed and metamorphose toward adulthood. After rain softens the soil, they emerge and go on to mate and repeat the life cycle.

At night, the largest of Tsavo's dung beetles, *Heliocopris*, would sometimes fly into the illuminated porch where I sat listening to the lions of Tsavo proclaim their territory. To have one of these beetles hit something and fall onto your shoulder or lap can be startling, because some of them are four inches long. I had seen them rolling spheres of wet dung nearly the size of soccer balls across the plains, and now, in the lamplight, I understood how. Even when I squeezed hard to hold them in my hand, these animals could pry my grip loose by pushing with their hind legs. In the field, the beetle used those powerful legs to roll the dung ball while pressing the ridged forward edge of its thoracic shell into the ground to anchor its body while it shoved. It had definite intentions about which way that ball was to go. If I stopped a beetle's progress and rolled the ball a short way along a different tack—quintessential human behavior; hmmm, let's screw up this bug's plans and see what it does—the beast would climb atop its ball, taking a bearing, presumably from the sun, climb down, and resume rolling along in the same direction as before. Upon reaching its chosen destination, *Heliocopris* still had the chore of burying the ball, and it buried the thing three to four feet deep.

An adult African elephant typically consumes between 250 and 500 pounds of forage daily and excretes 90 percent of it as feces. Simon estimated that at its peak in Tsavo, the elephant population was producing up to 10 million pounds of manure every day. Dung beetle paradise. As for the ratels, the earth beneath their feet was a larder of plump grubs. Prowling along with its nose low to the ground, a ratel is able to scent the dung balls through several feet of soil and dig them up. Dung beetle larvae form an important source of protein in the ratel's diet, and *Heliocopris* are its favorite.

On the ground, I searched in vain for live elephants in the backcountry. I spent an entire day marching double time across the bush following Danny Woodley, the son of former Tsavo warden Bill Woodley, archenemy of poachers in the days of the Wakamba. Danny was on one of his surveys for black rhino sign, hoping to find at least a few of these animals somewhere beyond the little pasture ringed by electric fencing. With us were several rangers and Elui Chthenge, a Wakamba elephant poacher arrested by Bill Woodley four decades earlier and employed by him as a tracker ever since. Elui turned up the fire pits and camp-sites of poaching gangs but no rhino tracks. Nor had Danny found any in the hundreds of miles he had covered earlier. That night, we heard that President Daniel Arap Moi had responded to the shooting of the two tourists at Tsavo. Moi announced that the future of Tsavo and other Kenya parks and reserves was to ring them all with electric fences. This, he proclaimed, would keep livestock out and wildlife in and gain better control over park boundaries in general—by implication, better control over the incursion of poachers. To me, it implied an end to migration, natural dispersal, long-term adjustment to weather patterns, and gene flow.

The next day, I saw only one cluster of elephants—leaderless subadults and babies. They raced away in terror before I was even close enough to guess their ages. Simon told me he regu-larly saw groups of four to six motherless young off by them-selves, and it depressed him to know that half of them would never make it on their own. Actually, the prospects are worse than that. Joyce Poole had told me that virtually every elephant calf orphaned under the age of two dies. Those orphaned be-tween ages three and five have just a 30 percent chance of sur-vival. Only those between the ages of six and ten have a 50 percent chance, but no more than that.

A related study by Phyllis Lee, who worked with the Am-boseli team, concerned allomothers—the immature females who help take care of older females' babies within the family. As early as age three, females begin looking after their little broth-ers, sisters, or cousins, keeping the infants out of trouble and alerting the mother if serious danger develops. Lee found that this type of care has a significant effect on the survival of calves. Those with more than four allomothers enjoyed a survival rate of more than 84 percent; those with three or four allomothers, 81 percent; one or two allomothers, 79 percent; and those infants with no allomothers, just a 68 percent chance of survival. This, remember, is when the mother is around. The baby of many a young adult female may suckle its mother but actually spend more time in the company of an older female—an aunt or grandmother. Besides providing additional care and attention to its needs, the elder female offers the youngster extra learning, passing on her store of experience and home range knowledge.

Thus, the quality of care a young elephant receives depends not only upon the presence of its mother but upon the presence of both older and younger females within the family. As any one of these social supports is removed by poaching, infant survival decreases. When Joyce surveyed Tsavo, shortly before I met her, she found that 45 percent of the young elephants were either orphans or in groups missing most of the adults. She also found that adult males were scarce throughout the park. Tsavo West had only thirteen males of any age for every hundred females.

In this part of Africa, male tusks become noticeably larger and heavier than those of females by about age seventeen, sometimes earlier. By the age of sixty, a bull carries six times the weight of ivory that a female does. Poachers have always sought out the big males first, followed by the medium-size bulls. In the absence of dominant males, breeding behavior can become more chaotic. Then the poachers begin to turn to the females—the mothers and grandmothers with the longest ivory. The matriarchs are often the very first to fall anyway, for they are among the first to defend their families from attack, and a matriarch's death makes it easier to bring down the others. "Bang!" exclaimed Iain. "There goes the reproducing part of the population—and its learned traditions involving migratory routes, dry-season water sources, salt licks, and so on. The whole society begins to collapse." There goes the culture, the accumulated wisdom of generations about how to use the land and its resources. Boom! The females fall faster as ivory grows more scarce. Crack! There go the allomothers. And not long afterward, with a whimper and the soft scrape of flesh on earth, there go the orphans. They get lost, starve, trap themselves in mudholes and crevices from which an adult would ordinarily have pulled them, and succumb to predators undefended. Cynthia Moss, Joyce Poole, Iain, Oria, Simon, and many others I was still to meet told me they believed elephants could also literally die of grief.

I took to the air with Iain once more, and we located what may have been the largest single elephant group left in the park, perhaps six hundred of them crossing the Ndara Plains of Tsavo East. This being the wet season with abundant new vegetation, the elephants normally formed larger groups than at other times of year. Yet Iain thought one of this size might also reflect the tendency of harassed elephants to bunch into big, terrified herds. The next day, I tried to locate the same herd by car, eager to watch their behavior. I found fresh sign from the herd and followed it through the green scrub to the edge of a river; but the tracks led across, and I had to give them up as lost for the day.

I looked over the massive trunks of baobab trees deeply gouged by elephants that had been seeking the moist tissues inside almost two decades earlier during the bad drought. I could see fresh, red mud rubbed off against the trunks of younger trees by the passing herd. In one tree perched a pair of fire-fronted bishops, a type of finch. Close by, three long-necked gerenuk reared on their hind legs to feed on the new leaves of shrubby commiphora.

Granted, it was the rainy season—a good rainy season—and the country looked exceptionally lush. Yet even without new foliage, the impressive height and density of the trees and shrubs told a story of how quickly this land had renewed itself since the time of too many elephants and too little rain. Photographs taken in Tsavo in the 1970s showed a sere, blasted, mineral landscape that looked like the day after the end of the world. The thick vegetation around me now didn't prove that the advocates of culling were entirely wrong—only that this land was perhaps more resilient than they realized. Portions of it were already turning into bush and young forest almost too thick to push through. The sad thing was that we still hadn't learned much about the healthy, long-term relationship of elephants and their habitat—only how prolific the habitat could be when elephants were all but wiped out of it.

Then I heard a trumpet and the sounds of splashing. I crept through the shrubs toward the river. They were there, scores upon scores of them, churning the water and wallowing in the mud along shore. Two new calves tried to spray themselves. Still uncertain about the operation of their trunks, they missed as often as they hit. I made out juveniles crawling on their knees to play with smaller ones, mothers worrying over babies slipping back from the mud into the water, banded mongooses picking insects from dung piles—all the things to which I had become accustomed among the giants. The wind turned. An elderly female wheeled toward me and blared. Dozens of trunks periscoped my way. A younger cow began to trot in my direction with creased ears and an upraised trunk. I didn't think she'd seen me yet, but I was looking for an escape path when the whole group—some 3 million pounds of beast—suddenly wheeled, tore apart the water with plunging feet, and went screaming away into the distance. All because of one 180-pound man who would have backed off from a single ratel.

One ashamed and angry man, left to return to his doomsday safari among vultures massed in acacia trees, the droning fly swarms, the foul miasma of dissolving flesh. Damn it. So much death among animals with such a keen sense of things that they were even known to cover over the dead of other species. The poachers had robbed Tsavo, robbed tourists, and now robbed me of any chance to be near elephants without adding to their stress and misery.

I was still in a dark mood when I visited Simon Trevor's house and learned that his daughter and a friend were missing. They had gone out to film wildlife and failed to return at the appointed time. No one wanted to raise false alarms, but several more freshly killed elephants had turned up fairly close by the day before. The proximity of poachers was on everyone's mind, all the more so since the tourists had been shot. We were fairly sure that the women were merely mired in the mud somewhere, but they were getting more and more overdue. Worse, they had failed to tell anyone exactly where they were going. Joe Kioko returned from an airplane patrol for poachers, learned of the problem, rubbed his eyes, and took off again to look for the women's car. Iain, Oria, and Simon did the same in the Douglas-Hamiltons' plane. The women were found, stuck in the mud as we were almost sure they would be. We made nervous jokes about the whole affair and split up to go our separate ways.

I went to see the hippos and crocs that share the crystalline waters of Mzima Springs the following day. My route took me by the road leading out of Tsavo toward Amboseli. From a hillside, I could make out the stretch of road where the tour van had been ambushed and the ropy lava flows the Douglas-Hamiltons and I had flown over that first day. The volcanic terrain had looked so beautifully chaotic and intriguing from the air, I was tempted to go hike around it. But I lingered where I was, my attention focused on a nearby trio of giraffes among flowering *Bauhinia*. A van came speeding up the road from the direction of the volcanic hills and screeched to a stop beside me. Several passengers started shouting to me at once: "Robbers, back there. . . . Turn around! . . . People hurt. . . . shooting."

I waited a while, wandered off on another road, and then went on to the Kiligoni Lodge nearby. It presented the usual scene: enormous buffets spread before ample tourists in brand-new safari uniforms, with black waiters in starched, white uniforms hustling back and forth past walls hung with Masai shields and crossed spears. But in a room off the side of the main lodge I found David Kariuki Nyoike, the driver of one of the two vans of German tourists that had been attacked. He lay with a bloody leg propped up on a pillow and breathed through clenched teeth. He was clear-headed, though, and able to describe the assailants: "Two Somalis—*shifta*, young, with G-3s." Sold by Germany, used on German tourists, I couldn't help thinking. "No, just one had a gun. The other . . . I think an axe. Maybe a *panga* [machete]. They fired when I tried to back up. The tires were blown . . . car rolled. They ran up demanding money. Young guys. They were nervous. I handed it over. 'No! No!' they say. 'No Kenya shillings! Dollars!'"

A second van arrived at the scene as the tourists in the first van were still handing over their money. More *shifta* appeared. They ran for the vehicle and shot it up as it tried to back away. From David's description, the entire ambush was virtually a repeat of the one the week before and in almost precisely the same spot.

Three tourists were hurt this time, none seriously. I helped one of them out the door and toward a car that would carry him to an incoming plane at the airstrip. He was wounded in the leg by a bullet and metal shards from the van. At one point, he stumbled and drew a sharp breath.

"You okay?" I asked.

"I'll live," he grunted. Not long after I left Kenya, bandits shot up yet another van full of German tourists in Tsavo, and that time they killed some.

Back at the Kiligoni Lodge, tourists were wandering between overflowing buffet offerings and the bar, some of them grumbling about the lack of protection by rangers. These people were paying up to U.S. $200 a night to stay here; one lodge in Masai Mara charged more than $400 a night. The average ranger was being paid $80 a month to protect them. No extra pay for high-risk duty, nor hardship pay for being camped in the field for long stretches away from his family. He had no decent boots for patrolling, no mosquito netting to protect him when he slept, no antimalarial drugs available when he fell ill. As at Amboseli, he was short on transportation due to lack of park funds for spare parts, and his weapon was likely to be a vintage single-shot rifle with the rifling blown out. Some rangers poured in new metal to make a truer bore, but in so doing, they reduced the caliber to little more than a .22, good for something the size of, say, a rat.

I knew this because all the personnel I talked with complained of the same shortages. I heard it from both ordinary rangers and some of the APUs. What of the GSUs, I asked—surely these quasimilitary units were well supplied? They were, and it made the others jealous. That might explain why many spoke so disparagingly of the GSUs' abilities. The GSU guys might be good in a firefight, but these were men from the army and police, used to being stationed in towns and cities. They were poor help in the bush when it came to tracking and outguessing the *shifta*. And it seemed that when the poachers struck, the GSU guys were always back at their big camps, drilling, eating their rations, and cleaning their guns.

Once again, I returned from the field to Nairobi to find

elephants in the news and dominating the affairs of the conservation community there. These groups covered the whole spectrum, from local to international, from radical to bureaucratic and bland. Their members ranged from those often labeled bleeding hearts or humane-iacs to those who promoted safari hunting and game ranching. The level of bickering, infighting, and competition for funds and influence with the government in the capital city was already rather intense when a proposal came along that made the philosophical Great Rift seem wider and deeper than it had ever been during the controversy over culling in Tsavo.

The proposal was to change the official status of the African elephant as determined by CITES, from threatened to endangered. Keeping the elephant in the threatened category (Appendix II of the Endangered Species List) meant a continuation of existing approaches, such as trade restrictions, intended to help the species. The methods might be expanded and intensified but not overhauled. This amounted to agreeing that the elephants' situation was not yet so dire as to call for drastic measures. A shift to endangered status (Appendix I) meant an outright worldwide ban on trade in ivory, along with any and all other products derived from elephants at the cost of their lives. It amounted to an admission that existing approaches had failed and the elephants' prospects of survival had slipped to a dangerously low point. Appendix I or Appendix II; you were either on one side of the Rift or the other.

Worldwide, the Appendix II camp was led by Zimbabwe and South Africa, with support from Botswana. All three countries had stable or increasing elephant populations. This southern African contingent believed strongly in using trophy hunting of elephants and culling as management tools and claimed that an Appendix I listing would deprive their wildlife programs of crucial funds raised through the sale of legally taken ivory tusks. Their allies were a handful of other nations, such as China and the Republic of Congo, which had a stake in the ivory trade, and of course the ivory dealers themselves, particularly the consortiums from Hong Kong and Japan. One of their strongest arguments was that declaring the elephant endangered would make ivory more valuable and accelerate the rate of poaching as had happened with rhinoceroses and their horns.

In the other camp, favoring an Appendix I listing, was perhaps the bulk of world opinion, shaped by the news reports streaming out of Africa about the wholesale slaughter of elephants for their tusks. However, most nations, including opinion leaders and major ivory consumers such as the United States and members of the European Economic Community, had yet to take an official position. For that matter, the biggest and, arguably, most influential conservation group, the World Wildlife Fund, was now wavering after having first supported keeping the elephant on Appendix II. Campaigns to win the minds and hearts of the undecided made the furor over elephants within the conservation community all the louder and, at times, embarrassingly mean-spirited.

Continent-wide, the giants were being depleted at a rate of more than 10 percent annually. East Africa was losing its elephants at a rate of 14.2 percent per year. West Africa, which once hosted at least a million elephants, was now left with only isolated groups numbering, at most, 19,000 and declining at the rate of 17.8 percent a year. There was not much nature left between the few little nature reserves, not much "out there" left out there anymore. As a prime example, the Ivory Coast (Cote d'Ivoire) had so few elephants of its own left that the president was reportedly going to have to buy some from outside sources to stock a presidential hunting reserve. The country named for ivory still had some ivory for sale in its markets, but it consisted primarily of illegal tusks brought in from neighboring nations. Officially, the Ivory Coast claimed to have some 3000 elephants. In reality, it had more like a few hundred. The average population size of the scattered groups was less than 50, which put it more or less in the same category as Guinea Bissau, Mauritania, Niger, Senegal, Sierra Leone, and Togo.

Statistics like these plainly show a species on a toboggan ride toward absolute zero. Drastic measures certainly seemed in order. A newcomer to the controversy might be puzzled as to why a proposal to list the elephant as endangered should be controversial among conservationists. I was puzzled as well. The explanation goes back almost three decades to the days when Iain and Oria Douglas-Hamilton began publicly warning of rapid declines in elephant populations. From the start, they were branded as alarmists—not only by bureaucrats with a congenital dislike of boat-rockers but by a number of colleagues in the scientific world who felt that the Douglas-Hamiltons lacked sufficient information.

The compilation of hard data about the largest of land mammals was indeed slim. Whole sections of the continent remained blank spots when it came to the number and distribution of elephants. This was due to the difficulty of travel within those areas and to economic and political instability. Which is a neutral way of saying that there were a lot of places where it was a nightmare trying to get around, almost nothing worked, and the last thing anyone bothered with was keeping track of elephants. The criticism concerning lack of information was therefore valid. Yet it was not exactly fair, since such information as was available—spotty studies, second-hand reports, and rumors— nearly always suggested that elephants were in serious trouble.

In any case, Iain and Oria took on the challenge of trying to survey Africa's elephants and encourage additional surveys and studies by others. As more numbers came in, they seemed to confirm fears of a rapid decline in the species. Nevertheless, some individuals took every opportunity to find fault with the data and cast the results in a more positive light. Personal differences had begun to get in the way, as they often do. For one thing, a certain amount of jealousy was generated by the Douglas-Hamiltons' popular writing and growing reputation as *the* elephant people. In addition, it was not too difficult to portray Iain as an outsider to the wildlife management establishment. Here was a wild, long-haired Englishman who flew airplanes like a stunt man and his gorgeous free spirit of a wife, who took their children out to greet wild elephants hand to trunk tip. In their writings, they portrayed elephants as individual personalities, and it was from the Douglas-Hamiltons that the press had picked up and sensationalized the phenomenon of elephants sometimes mourning and burying their dead—lingering by deceased family members and covering them with branches and debris. Could you trust these *subjective* observers—these flakes!—to dictate future management policies for the beasts?

A number of the Douglas-Hamiltons' opponents saw a "save the elephants" campaign as part of an unwarranted trend toward total protection of wildlife in reserves. When Kenya and Tanzania banned all big-game hunting, beginning in the late 1960s, some supporters of traditional game management and safari shooting never quite got over it. Many of them genuinely felt that the money, meat, hides, and other products generated by cropping wild animals provided a more reliable incentive for Africans to protect their wildlife resources. For others, it was more a case of feeling personally threatened. People hesitate to speak of this openly because the hunting/antihunting controversy is universally such a bitter, emotionally charged disagreement. Nevertheless, the elephant issue in good part came down to the new sensitivity against the old sporting ethic.

Publicly, the arguments were mostly about technical and scientific matters, but the forces driving those squabbles often sprang from intense private feelings and deeply held beliefs—in other words, from things about which a professor I knew used to say, "You're wasting your time trying to argue them out of people's heads through logical discussion, because they didn't get in that way."

Elephants are magnificent beings worthy of being accorded many of the rights we extend to our fellow humans; I cannot put into words the thrill and sense of meaning I experience in the company of these intelligent, expressive beasts. No. Elephants are magnificent prey; I cannot express the thrill and sense of meaning I experience in the chase and the shooting and the whole camaraderie of a hunting camp. Or, make that: the sense of empowerment given me by actively managing wildlife for the use of people. Elephant as friend; elephant as worthy adversary. Elephant as fellow being; elephant as harvestable commodity. Human as seeker of animal companionship; human as controller of animal destiny. These may not be easy things to discuss, but they are worth every effort, because they are at the heart of our relationship with nature.

ᚌᚌᚌᚌᚌᚌᚌᚌᚌᚌᚌ

From desert sands to lush rainforests and lowland swamps to subalpine meadows, elephants occupied a broader assortment of habitats than almost any other large mammal on the African continent besides humans not long ago. People on the island of Lamu, more than a mile off the coast of Kenya, used to ornament their doors with spikes. Although the big, metal thorns probably symbolized resistance to invaders in general, I was told that they were to keep elephants from hammering down the door. Elephants were once common on the island and sometimes could be seen snorkeling across the open sea between Lamu and the mainland, where herds use to range through the humid forests along the coast. At the same time, elephant carcasses have been found 16,000 feet high on Mount Kenya, just below the glaciers. On an earlier visit, I had seen where groups crossing between valleys had munched on giant groundsel along talus slopes at 14,000 feet.

After the hot plains of Tsavo, I had an urge to see elephants in the mountains once more. My first choice was Meru National Park. However, poachers had harassed tourists so badly there—robbing many and killing a couple—that the lodges had closed and the park was all but shut down. Its main occupants other than poachers were now illegal livestock grazers. Similar problems, combined with political pressure from overcrowded subsistence farmers and grazers, had led Kenya to degazette—unmake—another park farther north.

I settled on Mount Elgon National Park instead. I had read of its caves, where generations of elephants had gone to tusk away salty, mineral-rich earth from the walls, steadily making the caverns ever deeper and wider. Their activities had been studied by Ian Redmond, who was among the first to propose listing the

African elephant on Appendix I of the Endangered Species List. Redmond had documented a sharp decline in the number of elephants using the caves in recent years, and I wanted to see this rare phenomenon while it still existed.

Like Mount Kenya and Mount Kilimanjaro, Mount Elgon is a towering, isolated volcano, one of a series of such cones formed along the edge of the Great Rift Valley by the hot, subterranean forces pushing the earth's crust apart here. And like the parks on Mount Kenya and Mount Kilimanjaro, Mount Elgon National Park takes in only the upper elevations of the peak. In fact, it includes only the high slopes on the Kenyan side; the eastern half of the mountain and its outlying ridges lie in Uganda. The lower half of the volcano has been transformed from rainforest to cropland, and new fields march ever farther up the slopes every year. Some of the woodlands that remain at higher altitudes are part of a forest reserve, but selective logging, grazing, and cultivation are permitted within these lands. Only the least productive life zones—bamboo, heath, subalpine, and alpine—with the lowest diversity of species are fully protected as a national park.

At least these park habitats are scenic—spectacularly so. After checking on the caves, I planned to explore the high country. Cautiously. Poachers, mostly from Uganda, had been robbing trekkers. Sometimes the thieves would be satisfied with taking your lunch, just as they raided the farms here for food. The Ugandans were hungry. They had shot out most of the game on their side of the mountain and now came here to shoot meat. They had already taken most of the elephants on both sides for ivory.

Because poachers were so prevalent, I was not permitted to travel alone. I set out in the company of two rangers, Hassan Idle and Fidelis Mwoki, along a winding dirt track to the caves. Fidelis told me that in earlier years it was hard to get anywhere along these roads; so many elephants used them as convenient routes across the steep-sided terrain that they often blocked the way. I saw only one old dropping on the road. Nor did we turn up fresh sign along the hiking trail to the caves. What we found were dozens of spent rifle cartridges. Once at the caves, we heard bats chirruping in the darkness and located the tracks of one small female elephant and a subadult on the dusty cavern floor, where scores of the animals used to walk. That was it.

It was early morning of the next day when we drove up a different road toward the subalpine zone to begin our hike. Part way there, we noticed smoke rising from a valley. At first we thought the fire might have been set by slash-and-burn cultivators or was coming from honey-gatherers smoking out bee hives. But as we drew nearer, we saw that it was a wildfire burning above the forest zone in the heath. Poachers had set it, Hassan said.

"To drive game?" I asked.

"No, to keep us busy. A distraction. They know we have only one or two vehicles that run and not many men. If we go out to fight the fire, who will be left to bother them? They can hunt as they wish."

When we reached the fire, it was midmorning. Many of the bushes that formed the heath contain volatile oils, and the sun had nearly dried the last branches of dew. The flames were beginning to race through them. We used green branches to beat down fingers of the blaze, trying to keep them from creeping upslope, but our efforts were useless. It would take a brigade to put out this fire, and there was no brigade. We could only hope it would burn itself out on the ridges. Shots echoed lower on the slopes. Shots had been reported to the rangers the day before. Fidelis and Hassan shook their heads, and we went on to start hiking. The charred residue of poachers' campfires rested here and there among the rocks. Hassan pointed out that eyes might well be watching us cross the open highlands. I scanned the outcrops with my binoculars but eventually gave it up. Deciding that I wasn't going to let the outlaws ruin this place for me too, I turned my attention to the remarkable adaptations of the life forms around me.

Giant lobelias stood out like shaggy pillars among the grasses, and I swung my binoculars from one to the next, searching for a certain species of bird. Besides being beautiful, it bears one of my favorite names for things in this world: the scarlet-breasted malachite sunbird. I had found two of my other favorites—the joyful bulbul, a thrushlike eater of fruit, and its close relative, the yellow-throated leaflove—in a remnant of Kenya's lowland forest. I watched sunbirds, found a chameleon with jewellike green coloring tucked between a lobelia's hairy, insulating leaves, hiked some ridges, and circled back to the car in the afternoon.

Driving down the track, we had to race to escape a wall of flames burning up the mountainside toward us. As we came around a blind corner at high speed, we practically slammed into a Toyota Land Cruiser stalled in the middle of the road. Its radiator had boiled over, and some of the electrical wiring had shorted out. Rangers in uniform stood around it. One poured in water and another frantically scraped wires while others fought flames at the side of the road. We got the engine going and gunned both vehicles downslope, then stopped and introduced ourselves. The man in charge of these rangers and the beat-up, balky car was Ram Munge, the number-two man in charge of the nation's APU forces. He had come from Nairobi on an inspection tour. He described the battle against poaching the same way I would describe his means of transport: it might work, but you couldn't trust that it would; there wasn't enough money at hand to ever really get the thing fixed right.

🔲🔲🔲🔲🔲🔲🔲🔲🔲🔲🔲🔲

The day I arrived at Mount Elgon National Park, I had presented my letter of introduction from the park service director, Perez Olindo, to the ranger sitting in the shade at the gate house. He smiled and said, "But Mr. Olindo is no longer the director, as of this morning. Did you know this?"

The new director was Richard Leakey, who until recently had served as the head of Kenya's National Museum. A paleontologist widely acclaimed for his work on the origins of humans, he had continued the pattern of discovery begun by his parents, Louis and Mary Leakey, at Olduvai Gorge. Richard Leakey had been highly critical of the Kenya antipoaching campaign and ridiculed official claims that the country still held large numbers of elephants. Correctly pointing out that the true number was barely 16,000, he claimed that responsibility for the debacle lay directly with corrupt individuals at high levels of government. Yes, it would be nice to have more money to fight the poachers, he agreed, but where had earlier funds gone? How could so many people be accomplishing so little unless those in charge had something to gain on the side from the failure to stem the tide of ivory poaching?

For such comments, he was labeled "cheeky Leakey" by the minister of tourism, who oversaw the parks department. Cheeky Leakey was very nearly expelled from the country. And now, abruptly, he was being invited by President Moi to run the parks department and solve its problems—problems such as the shooting of tourists in Tsavo. It seemed the back-to-back incidents that took place while I was there really had "put the fat in the fire," as Iain had phrased it. A few more shoot-ups like that, and tourists by the plane-full were going to drop Kenya from their itineraries. The backbone of the country's economy was at stake. Leakey was being given a directive to clean house and, in effect, bring back the heads of poachers to show the world.

With Leakey's appointment, the ivory war in Kenya appeared to have taken a turn for the better. But poaching was only one threat to the survival of elephants here. It could be dealt with far more handily than the more ominous one awaiting the giants— the one seldom mentioned in all the news coverage of the crisis or any of the "save the elephants" pleas issued by conservation groups. That threat is the multiplication of humans.

Elephant populations had already been displaced and fragmented by the burgeoning populace of Kenya. Most of the existing parks and reserves were no longer connected by habitats the animals could use. If those preserves were to be fenced, as the president's plans called for, the isolation of herds would become truly unavoidable. Then inbreeding, genetic drift, and vulnerability to random disasters such as fires, floods, disease epidemics, and so on would become problems. Meanwhile, a problem of far greater magnitude would continue building outside the fence.

The average woman in Kenya bears six or seven children in her lifetime. The population is increasing at 4.2 percent annually—twice the average for the developing world and eight times that of the developed world. At the start of 1970, Kenya had just over 11 million people. It now has 25 million, of which three-quarters are under thirty years of age. By 2025 the total could be nearly 80 million.

More than 75 percent of Kenya's land is too dry to support crops. Of the remaining 25 percent, less than a quarter is very productive, and that figure is going to be very difficult to increase, again for want of water. By 2025, when the current population of Kenyans has tripled, who will oppose converting Masai land from open range to wheat farms? Who will oppose degazetting more parklands with precious timber, water, and good soils? Political pressures to use every available resource will become a juggernaut. There has been considerable agitation lately to oust the Moi government. Will a government trying to satisfy the needs of a populace three times as large and farther out of balance with its support system be more stable? A sanctuary filled with natural bounty surrounded by a crush of people in need is not a recipe for long-term survival of any wild plant or animal. It might last years, decades, maybe even a century. Then, in a few weeks of political upheaval, it will be gone.

Kenya was one of those places where people would ask how many children I had and shake their heads and cluck sadly when I told them I had two. They were sorry for me that I had failed to do better. The terms *population explosion* and *population bomb* are more than figurative in this nation. Children beyond counting careen in all directions along the street, through the villages, among the fields. Clouds of smoke and dust rise from towns and cities teeming with people forced out of traditional homelands for want of living room. Their families' fields have been divided and divided again among the children until nothing was left for the next generation. Nairobi is gaining a sprawl of slums to match those of Rio de Janeiro and Mexico City. In the end, it isn't just wildlife that is being displaced by unchecked human multiplication.

The average Somali poacher in Tsavo or Ugandan poacher in

Mount Elgon is not a goon or thug by nature. He is a young man—perhaps more ambitious than most—with few prospects back home on the overcrowded, overused lands of his forefathers. How I wished I could believe that they were the bad guys and that once the good guys finally thrashed them, the elephants' future would once again look bright. Instead, I was beginning to glimpse the potential catastrophe awaiting all efforts to secure wildlife preserves. In the absence of equally forceful efforts by governments to encourage family planning, the odds are overwhelming that every conservation plan, every meeting, every dollar contributed, every scientist's years of careful observations, and every ranger's life lost in a fight against poachers will one day prove to have been for naught.

🙢🙢🙢🙢🙢🙢🙢🙢🙢🙢🙢

I forgot to mention the one elephant group I was able to stay close to in Tsavo. I had returned from a drive to check on some carcasses not far from Voi when I saw a huge, red female in plain view not far from the airstrip. She showed no signs of nervousness. She scarcely paid attention to any of the human activity nearby. Ah, I remembered: Eleanor. Orphaned in Tsavo at an early age, she had been raised by the chief warden at the time, David Sheldrick, and his wife, Daphne. Since then, David Sheldrick had passed away, and Daphne was living near Nairobi at the edge of Nairobi National Park, where she operated a wild animal orphanage. Most of her wards were very young elephants.

After years of frustration and failure, Daphne had finally developed a system that would keep nursing orphaned infants alive. The first trick had been to come up with a formula that provided enough nourishment without causing diarrhea. She had also learned that the babies needed to be fed every few hours, both night and day. To give them the companionship they craved almost as strongly, she kept a sheep that would tag along with the newest arrivals. She also had a staff of nine or ten men that kept an eye on the elephants by day, washed them, gave them mud baths, held their bottles (while standing behind a tarp that loomed over a youngster like the grey side of a grown female), and slept in a shed with them at night. Almost all the youngsters were survivors of poaching. They came in suffering from dehydration and, having no adult to shade them, serious sunburn. And psychological trauma. They had watched their families slaughtered, seen men axe or chain-saw the tusks from their relatives' faces. Sometimes they woke up screaming from their dreams at night, Daphne said.

Daphne Sheldrick is a mush-heart and makes no apologies for it. She cooed and baby-talked constantly to the tiny elephants racing around her yard and, like any number of people given to talking to their pets, she told me she is sure they understand everything she says. I am sure they do not, though I believe they understand and thrive on the warmth and good intentions sent their way. At the orphanage, I had noticed one baby that was missing the lower part of its trunk. Caught in a snare, I assumed. Daphne shook her head and explained that the baby had made the mistake of greeting a fellow orphan, a young rhinoceros named Amboseli, by placing its trunk in the rhino's mouth. Amboseli, not known for his social skills, bit the trunk off.

Once the elephants were weaned from the bottle, the next step was to let them begin exploring parts of Nairobi National Park under the supervision of her staff so they would become familiar with the scents and sounds of the bush. Sometime after the age of three, they would be loaded into a truck and taken south to Tsavo to be released into the care of Eleanor, who would be accompanied by some of her earlier charges plus three men who walked with them through the bush around Voi all day. Each evening, of her own accord, Eleanor led the way back to a compound where she and her adopted family could rest safely during the night.

Eleanor was thirty years old by the time we met and had served as foster mother for quite a few orphans. Not all of them came to her in fine fettle from Daphne's Nairobi operation. Some were brought in straight from the bush, and Eleanor had seen enough of these die that she grew edgy each time even the healthiest youngster lay down still on the ground to rest. When Chuma, a baby in her care, rolled in the mud at a pool, Eleanor thundered over to pull it away from the water. Too many weak ones had been unable to climb out of mudholes by themselves.

Job Mbindyo, one of Eleanor's keepers at Tsavo, said, "Last month, a baby is stuck in a mudhole, and we are trying to pull it out. She comes to help us. Eleanor digs with a tusk, pushes with her leg. She helps us very much. When we meet a lion, right away Eleanor runs to us to be sure we are with the babies. Then she runs back at the lions to chase them away. If a baby dies, she stays with it a long time until she is sure it is dead. The next day, she is running a lot, pulling down things, breaking things, even long after we take the baby away."

Eventually, the young animals reared with Eleanor mature and go off into the wilds of Tsavo and an uncertain fate. At least they have been given a chance. On two or three different occasions, Eleanor herself went off, following wild elephants. But she always returned and resumed her duties as stand-in mother, Job explained as I stood at Eleanor's side. She had extralong lashes and very mild eyes, and I felt instantly secure in her presence. I would have liked her for an adopted mother. "She thinks the way people do," he said. "She is happy to be around people. If she sees or she hears someone she has not seen in a long time and it is someone she knows very well, she lifts her front leg in greeting and makes a lot of water from the places on the side of her head." Tourists regularly come up to spend time near her. Although she treats most with equanimity, she has been known to grab the wrist of people wearing an ivory bracelet and hold it fast in her grip for a while before finally letting go.

The work of Daphne Sheldrick could be interpreted as an extravagance. It was not cheap to have ten men bottle-feeding baby elephants in Nairobi and three more walking around all day with Eleanor and her orphan gang. What was the point of spending so much effort and money to salvage a handful of orphans with poaching so rampant? With human beings in this country going hungry and in need of care for their babies?

Daphne had heard such comments more than a few times. She

would answer by pointing out that the work is supported in good part by donations from some 30,000 visitors who troop through the orphanage every year. "Quite a lot are Kenyan schoolchildren and city people from here in Nairobi," she told me. "As you might expect, they may believe all kinds of nonsense about ferocious wild animals. These are the first elephants or rhinos many of them have ever seen. My babies are ambassadors for their kind. People go away thinking differently about elephants and their problems. Anyway, there are five young elephants now with Eleanor, and that is five more elephants than would otherwise be alive in Tsavo today."

Perhaps this project didn't make much sense when weighed against the problems of corruption, habitat loss, poaching, and overpopulation. Yet I found it all the more worthwhile because it was not particularly logical. It was a direct expression of someone caring for a creature, and caring unabashedly in the face of gloomy realities. I was very glad to have met Eleanor. Her presence said: Look, this too—this good and kind thing—is something humans can do to elephants. Just now, Tsavo needed a gesture like that. So did I.

FIVE

CENTRAL AFRICA: BANGUI

🔲🔲🔲🔲 IN THE VERY heart of Africa, where the southern tip of the Central African Republic (C.A.R.) projects like a spearhead between Cameroon, Zaire, and the Republic of Congo, an ecologist named Mike Fay from the Missouri Botanical Gardens was making his way up tributaries of the Congo River toward his remote jungle camp. Photographer Bill Thompson and I were going to look for him there.

I had done this sort of thing once before in the jungles of the Amazon Basin, searching for an ethnobiologist who was studying the cultural uses of insects among Kayapo Indians somewhere up a tributary of the Xingu River. "Find the house of the chief and talk to him first," the Brazilian pilot had shouted over the noise of his engine after depositing me on a raw landing strip cut from the forest canopy.

"Okay. Why?"

The pilot yelled something in a mixture of Portuguese and English. Something about the Kayapo being at war with nearby white gold miners and diamond hunters. Something like "The chief is the one who must decide whether to let you live or not."

"But I don't speak Kayapo. You know I don't even speak Portuguese. How am I . . . You're joking, right?"

The pilot waved as he roared off into the steam clouds forming over the rainforest canopy.

Now I was trying—in French—to arrange transportation in Bangui, the steaming capital of the C.A.R., where the locals call white people *moonjus*, a corruption of *monsieur* plus *bonjour*. The nation is roughly the size of Texas, with a population of less than 3 million. Infant mortality runs between 16 and 25 percent. AIDS is ubiquitous, as in Kenya, where I had just been. And, as in Kenya, elephants are prominent symbols on the country's currency, and the logo of the most popular brand of beer is a big bull tusker.

For centuries, the most valued commodities were gold, diamonds, slaves, and ivory. They were not so much exported by the region as looted from it, by Arabs and then by European colonialists. The C.A.R. now exports cotton and coffee, though coffee prices have fallen so low that many plantations have been abandoned. At the time of my visit, the true staple commodities remained gold, diamonds, and ivory, still traveling largely through channels older than the law. Elephant hunting was illegal and had been for a number of years. Technically, the only ivory that could be bought and sold in the C.A.R. was tusks taken as a result of official control actions such as killing crop-raiding animals.

As in neighboring Zaire, where elephant hunting for ivory was banned in 1977, there seemed to be a terrible crop-raiding problem, even in places where no crops grew. A recent inventory in Zaire had turned up 1500 tons of ivory, which meant a minimum of 65,000 dead elephants. In the C.A.R., a 1986 inventory of thousands of tusks turned up not one from an animal more than 35 years of age. Odd. Older, experienced elephants generally tend to be the worst crop-raiders; they should have been well represented in the inventory. Clearly, there were precious few elephants beyond middle age left in the entire country. They had been taken for their long ivory, and the ever-younger ones being shot since had little or nothing to do with filching crops either.

Much of the eastern C.A.R. is still depopulated from slaving, which sent captives along routes north to Chad and Sudan. You can still see the rock shelters and water catchments in the mountains of the east where people being stalked took refuge. Slavery officially ended in 1913, when the French killed the last major

Arab trader at his fortress, but it continued for a while after that on a smaller scale. Today, a number of residents toil as virtual indentured servants for Chadian Muslims, who form a powerful business network in the C.A.R. The workers are paid a monthly pittance and prevented from leaving by threat of physical harm. During my visit, I also noticed that in neighboring Cameroon, you could still buy young girls from a ring of military thugs— and not just for the night but as chattel for life.

🔲🔲🔲🔲🔲🔲🔲🔲🔲🔲🔲🔲

Day and night, the atmosphere lay over Bangui like a hot compress. Fishermen in long dugout canoes eased through the broad, brown waters of the Ubangui River flowing between the capital and the shores of Zaire. I suddenly realized that I had heard the name before: Ubangui. Ubangee. When I was a child, my friends and I used to talk about the Ubangees. To us, they were Negroes in grass skirts whose hair was tied up in a topknot with a bone stuck through it. They pranced around a big, boiling kettle, looking hungrily at the missionaries and explorers bound to a stake nearby. I couldn't remember whether we got this classic bit of cultural prejudice from television cartoons or comic books. I was embarrassed to be carrying around that kind of mental luggage on my first trip into the core of Africa.

On the other hand, Jean-Bedel Bokassa, a recent leader of the C.A.R., was an enthusiastic cannibal. He was so fond of human flesh that he served it at his mansion's table to unsuspecting dignitaries. At least, that was the local rumor.

"Did he really do that—*mange beaucoup de gens*?" I asked one of the locals.

"*Oui*, but Mr. Bokassa ate mostly people from the [some name I could not make out] tribe, and Mr. Bokassa's tribe has always eaten them," he shrugged. "They are said to be good to eat."

Africa and Its Exploration, published a century ago, contains a chapter by Sir Richard Burton entitled "Among the Fan Cannibals and the Gorillas," describing his travels north of the Congo

River in Gabon. "Anthropophagy," he wrote, "either as a necessity, a sentiment, or a superstition, is known to sundry, though by no means to all, the tribes dwelling between the Nun [Niger] and the Congo rivers . . . " For the Fan, cannibalism was engaged in only by warriors as "a quasireligious rite, practised upon foes slain in battle, evidently an equivalent of human sacrifice."

Having come to power in a military coup in 1966, Bokassa, a great fan of Napoleon I, proclaimed himself emperor in 1977. He somehow managed to spend $25 million on his coronation, a remarkable achievement in a country with rudimentary government services and a load of foreign debt. Not surprisingly, one of the major sources of foreign revenue under the Bokassa regime was poached ivory. Emperor Bokassa went on to involve himself directly in the torture and massacre of some hundred schoolchildren.

This was too much for the French, who had officially granted the C.A.R. independence in 1960 but have maintained considerable behind-the-scenes influence in the military and business spheres ever since. They quickly whipped up a coup to depose the man, even though he had thoughtfully been sending secret gifts of diamonds to the president of France for some time. Bokassa was exiled to the Ivory Coast. Several years later, he returned to the C.A.R. in the belief that his countrypeople would embrace him as their rightful leader. He was placed under house arrest and was still there, up on a hill overlooking Bangui, during my visit.

🙾🙾🙾🙾🙾🙾🙾🙾🙾🙾🙾

Bill Thompson, who arrived after I did, was nearly arrested for entering the country without a visa. When he exited Paris after a stopover, a customs official had mistaken his C.A.R. visa sticker for the identical-looking French sticker and stamped it canceled. Thompson emerged from customs at the Bangui airport after a couple of hours and several hundred dollars in "fines" that would never be recorded, only to be swamped by the inevitable gang of porters who grabbed his bags from his hands, threw them in a taxi, and then circled him screaming threats about not getting paid enough, hoping that he was not yet familiar with the C.A.R. wage scale or the exchange rate from U.S. dollars to C.A.R. francs. That scene over, he began making the rounds to get his visa restored, which meant hours and days in the particular level of hell that awaits wayfarers in any number of equatorial countries. . . .

It is a dark, stifling, hot little room in a building of moldy concrete and peeling paint, where an official sits hunched over an antique typewriter squinting at forms that neither he nor the foreigners required to fill them out fully understand. Around him, watching geckoes run down spiders on the walls or simply staring with an expression beyond despair, sit the would-be travelers. Many have already been here several times. They had not known the first time they came and waited that they needed an extra photo or an additional document or copy of a document. They did not know that the place where they could get such a photo or document or copy was closed until the end of a holiday or the next week or until further notice. They did not fully appreciate that the most important thing to the sweaty functionary hunched over the typewriter was the power he held over his supplicants, and the surest way to let them feel that power and respect that power was *not* to let them get what they wanted and needed. That was his purpose, as he saw it—*not* to make things work. Only a fool or a weakling would let these arrogant foreigners waltz in and do what they wished. Look at them. Hah! You can see in their faces how spoiled they are—how used to having things go their way. . . .

In the capital's main streets, people used long poles to pluck ripe mangoes off overhanging trees, and pigs rooted through piles of garbage. Mechanics repaired motorcycles on canvas tarps spread across dirt sidewalks. Several restaurants offered superb French cuisine, including duckling in bechamel sauce followed by raspberry torte. At intervals lay beggars afflicted with river blindness, deformed limbs, and leprosy. Elsewhere, those sidewalks suddenly gave way to deep pits where open sewer channels ran along the bottom. Since there was no illumination of the streets at night, and since nights here truly seem darker than in other parts of the world—a light-absorbing, palpable, moist, velvet dark that, in Bangui, smells of blossoms and excrement—it became important to walk with care. A *moonju* Peace Corps volunteer had recently tumbled down a sewer hole one evening and was shipped home soon thereafter with a useless leg and a variety of infections.

In the surrounding countryside, *les chasseurs des papillons*, butterfly hunters, stalked specimens with wings like white brush streaks on blue stained glass, vermilion wings that brought to mind the sacred powder I saw used for temple offerings in Nepal, and green wings that turn purple when rotated in the light. A great deal of this spangled, air-dancing beauty was netted over bait concocted of dog manure and human urine, taking advantage of the butterflies' attraction to salty minerals. A few *chasseurs* stalked prized specimens that kept to the sunlit top of the forest canopy. After climbing into the treetops, the men shot forked arrows carefully aimed to pin the butterfly against the bark by its abdomen. The more common species were brought by the sackful to Bangui. There the wings were sliced into fragments and then worked into mosaic art that was hawked in the streets to passing foreigners—mainly French businesspeople, technicians, foreign-aid *moonjus*, and their families. Recreational tourists were scarce.

I quickly grew fond of Bangui, which I don't think yet had a traffic light. In pace and scale, it was more like a village than the capital of a nation, and I could reach nearly every part of it by foot. But as the days passed, it seemed that we were farther than ever from reaching Mike Fay. There are only a handful of roads in all the C.A.R., and they were currently plagued by an outbreak of brigandage—ivory poachers again, AK-47–toting bands from neighboring Chad and Sudan who had run out of elephants. It looked as though the best bet would be to charter a ride on the private plane of a foreign timber company with a concession in the area near Mike Fay's camp. We wouldn't be able to lift off, though, until Thompson got out of visa hell. The signs were not encouraging. We had a U.S. embassy official working on the case, but the puffed-up tyrant who ruled the chamber of the government-form-damned was telling the embassy man that he, too, could come back later.

Of course, there was no guarantee that we could track down Fay in the jungle even if we ever got there, but that seemed to me the easy part. We would find him somehow. We had to find him—because Fay, who had been studying the relationship between vegetation and lowland gorillas, knew where we could find and watch a lot of forest elephants.

🮖🮖🮖🮖🮖🮖🮖🮖🮖🮖🮖🮖🮖

I once spoke with a man who had spent two years gathering information about forest elephants in Gabon, part of the same great tangled mass of lowland tropical rainforest. He was in the field nearly every day, and there were forest elephants everywhere, judging from the sign. During those two years, he actually saw the animals twice. Even then, he barely glimpsed them. That is how thick the jungle is, and that is why the habits and society of forest elephants remain virtually unknown.

If forest elephants were no more than typical African elephants that happen to live in dense forest, our lack of knowledge about them might not seem like such a shortcoming. But forest elephants are sufficiently different to be classified as a separate subspecies, *Loxodonta africana cyclotis*. With the biggest bulls standing less than nine feet at the shoulder, they are strikingly smaller than *Loxodonta africana africana*, the savanna, or bush, elephants found throughout most of the continent. *Cyclotis* also have smallish, rounded ears. Their backs are slightly arched or domed in the manner of Asian elephants, and their tusks tend to grow straight or even curve slightly downward. Savanna elephants have enormous ears, a more or less level back, and upward-curving tusks.

Any ivory dealer could tell you a further difference: the ivory of *cyclotis* tusks is much denser than that of savanna elephants and more highly valued for certain types of detailed carving work. Traders instantly recognize "hard" ivory, as they call it, for it has little of the porous grain or striations of the "soft" ivory taken from savanna elephants. Forest elephant tusks often appear more brown or orange-red than white. This is the result of surface staining from chemicals in the soil and vegetation. It can be washed or scraped off. In some regions, however, the inside of the tusks may have a darker cast as well, presumably from the inclusion of minerals in the dentine. Dealers may pay a premium for the pinkish variety of hard ivory, known as rose ivory.

As Western naturalists began probing through Africa's rainforests, many became convinced that a still smaller species or subspecies of elephant dwelled there. They called it the pygmy elephant. Some authorities still recognize a diminutive type of elephant labeled *Loxodonta pumilio* or *Loxodonta africana pumilio*. Safari operators in the region tend to confirm its existence, if only because they can then sell pygmy elephant hunts to trophy-seekers who have not yet shot such a creature. The same rainforest environment harbors pygmy human tribes, pygmy chimpanzees, and pygmy hippopotamuses. That it could have produced a scaled-down elephant does not seem unreasonable. We know that several different parts of the world produced pygmy elephants and mammoths during the Ice Ages.

Not long ago, what was thought to be a pygmy elephant was captured and shipped to a zoo in the West. A few years later, the animal had grown up and revealed itself to be an ordinary forest elephant, which is what most scientists now consider the so-called pygmy elephants of modern Africa to be. The confusion arises mainly from another quality of the forest elephant's hard ivory tusks—namely, that they grow very quickly. Whereas a juvenile savanna elephant will have relatively short tusks, a partially grown forest elephant only a few feet high at the shoulder may carry nearly full-length tusks. It can therefore easily be mistaken for an adult specimen of a very short elephant. (For that matter, the pygmy chimp, or bonobo, isn't a true pygmy form either. It weighs the same as the common chimp and is merely more slender, with a smaller head and shoulders and longer legs.

Less aggressive in its social groups than its more familiar relative, the bonobo is also more endangered, having been shot out of existence in all but one part of Zaire.)

Biologists haven't altogether written off the possibility of discovering true pygmy elephants. In 1991, two German zoologists published a paper asserting that *pumilio* is a genuine species, based on skull characteristics they measured and second-hand reports from the Congo region of social groupings consisting entirely of undersize elephants and their offspring. Who can be sure that races or populations of unusually small forest elephants haven't developed in, for instance, certain marshlands with highly acid soils and a poor supply of nutrients?

The Congo Basin still counts as anything-is-possible country. It is where the giraffe's closest relative, the okapi, went undetected by science until around 1900. And it is where expeditions periodically go today to follow up the latest reported sighting of *mokili-mbimbi*, the swamp-dwelling brontosaur—or something very like one. The tracks are said to be far bigger than those of the biggest elephant. Curiously, sightings by local people tend to increase in direct proportion to the number of *moonjus* with money in their pockets coming to look for the creature. But that is the nature of the monster-chasing business and always has been, and it still doesn't take the fun out of it.

The fellow who spent two years among forest elephants and only caught sight of them twice was Richard Barnes, head of the Forest Elephant Research Group based at Cambridge University in England. When I visited him there briefly, he pointed out that since savanna elephants had been so widely decimated, forest elephants probably made up one-third to one-half the elephant population remaining in Africa. Gabon alone held an estimated 85,000, more than all of East Africa put together. Not that people weren't trying every bit as hard to kill forest elephants as savanna elephants, but the rainforest remained infinitely harder to get to and get through, with dark, sluggish rivers forming the only available routes of transport to many realms. Once the poachers did reach the elephants, they still had to track them through the jungle a group at a time. For efficient commercial killing, this cannot match racing over open plains in radio-equipped vehicles after big herds with no place to hide.

So nearly one out of every two or three elephants left in Africa dwells in the equatorial jungles, protected for the time being to some extent by the impenetrability of their habitat. And, for the same basic reason, one out of every two or three elephants left in Africa remains an enigma to science. Richard Barnes shook his head and said, "They won't be safe for long. Oil exploration and development, hardwood logging, and schemes to clear the forest for agriculture are already creating road access far into the interior and transforming the rainforest. Now, suppose someone were to come to me and say, 'We want to set aside a reserve to protect our forest elephants, and we're going to really do it properly. Will you please tell us how big it should be?' Sorry, haven't a clue. We don't know what the usual home range is for these animals or how much their movements vary seasonally. 'Well, how many animals should our reserve enclose to maintain a healthy population?' We don't know. 'What is the typical family structure?' We're not exactly sure. 'What sort of herds form in the forest?' Terribly sorry, but we don't know that either."

🔲🔲🔲🔲🔲🔲🔲🔲🔲🔲🔲

I had all but given up on Thompson getting out of visa hell in time to catch Mike Fay when none other than Mike Fay showed up in Bangui. Shortly afterward, a direct appeal from the American ambassador shook Thompson loose from the bureaucrat's chamber of eternal irritation. To top it all off, Mike was sporting a brand new Toyota Land Cruiser pickup truck he had finagled through customs after months of paperwork. The three of us threw our gear in the back and tore away down the road. Periodically, we had to pull over to have our papers inspected by police stationed at barricades along the route. They checked and double-checked to make sure that this was indeed Mike's truck and that Mike was indeed Mike and so on, ad nauseum, because there was always a chance that something was not in order and they could throw us into a new level of hell in another concrete building complete with self-important bureaucrat, typewriter, and stack of official nuisance forms, overseen by a faded picture of the president, His Excellency, General of the Army Andre Kolingba.

In between, Mike drove at full tilt, reasoning that he could be past a bandit ambush by the time anyone started shooting. After midnight, we pulled off the road for a few minutes to eat in a roadside village of square mud huts with tin roofs. A fire burned in the center of a dirt plaza. Next to it were three itinerant drummers from Zaire. While they drummed, people danced in the firelight, and young men drank and fought in the shadows. One came by dragging a little boy by his shirt and kicking him in the face. We took turns guarding the gear piled in the pickup bed and waiting for the eggs and spicy vegetables being scrambled by a man at a table next to the fire. The drumming was incredibly complex and infectious, and I shuffle-danced through my tour of duty at the pickup. Then we hit the road again, and I tried to nap in the back between the bumpier stretches.

Before dawn, we came to a village called Bayanga. Mike led us to a house on stilts that had been built by Slovenia-Bois, the logging company with a concession in this area, which is known as Dzanga-Sangha. It was noticeably hotter and muggier than in the capital, which I had not thought possible. The house was big. Bats flew through it chasing bugs. Moving lines of ants patterned the walls. I crawled beneath a mosquito net and, too tired to sleep, lay listening to my pores drip.

Finally, I did doze. When I was awakened by noises nearby, I had to fight my way out of a snakelike torpor. Hunkered outside the door was a tall, nut-brown, very thin and thin-haired *moonju* wearing only ragged shorts and a hopeful grin.

"Ah. You're finally up," he noted. "Say, is that cereal in that box? Far out. When did you get in? Last night? I haven't had cereal for months. Actually, I haven't had any kind of food lately. Kept puking it up at first, and then I didn't want to eat anything. Malaria again. I still have it. You got any malaria tabs?" I rummaged for my bottle and shook out a handful, which he took without thanks. "I was staying in the forest with the pygmies.

Lots of malaria out there. Before I got this malaria, I got stung by bees and ended up with an allergic reaction. Man, it almost killed me, and now I have to be careful I don't get stung again. But there are bees everywhere in the forest. Especially around pygmy camps. They cover your whole body all day long sometimes. I have to do everything slowly so I don't accidentally trap one, like in the bend of my arm. I mean, one more sting, and I'm gone. It's weird. You got any bee-sting injections you could let me have? Powdered milk! You've got powdered ¢★@!$ milk! All right! Wait. We'll need to mix that with water. I'll get it. Be right back."

"Anybody we know?" I asked Mike as he padded into the main room and began to paw through our food boxes for coffee.

"Louie," he answered. "Screwy Louie. I think he's from New Jersey."

"I think he's hungry."

"He's always mooching food, but he does look a little skinnier than usual," Mike agreed. "I don't think he's had anybody to talk English to for a while either."

"I remember getting that way a few times," I said.

"He came here to record the pygmies' music," Mike explained, "and now he's more or less living with them. If we're not feeding him, they are. He's not really way out in the jungle with them the whole time. He lives in their camp at the edge of the village."

"They're camped close to here?"

Mike heaved a sigh of resignation and said, "Everybody seems to think pygmies live deep in the forest by themselves. But they've had a trading relationship with villagers for hundreds of years, maybe longer. They bring in smoked meat, medicinal herbs and their own special concoctions, honey, and other forest products they gather. They trade for machetes, fabrics, different kinds of food. They used to stay in the forest for most of the year and come in to hang around the villages for maybe a couple of months. Now it's almost the reverse in a lot of places. Other tribes have taken over a lot of pygmy territory, and the pygs are addicted to the villagers' tobacco and whiskey.

And starch. A lot of villagers treat them like crap, but they're still here. And their songs and dances—those are amazing," Mike continued. "I don't know how much longer traditions like that will last. I think Louie's on to something, trying to document them."

The door banged open, and Louie flew in along with a contingent of daytime insects. "Any of you guys have some extra batteries? I've used up all mine on my tape recorder. I was supposed to get some more, but they never came. The check I was supposed to get hasn't come either, or I could probably buy some off you. Man, I wish I knew where that check was. Could be anywhere. You making coffee? The head man wants me to marry his daughter. I like her. I guess I wouldn't mind marrying her. But he wants me to pay him 4500 C.A.R. francs. Whoa. That's, what, about fifteen U.S. dollars! That's a lot of money. What's this? Oh, tinned beef. Too rich for my stomach the way I feel now. You brought all *kinds* of supplies, didn't you. Wow! Spaghetti! I'd love to eat some spaghetti. We're going to need more water. What are you guys having? I'll go get the stove going."

When Louie ducked out, Mike said, "You know that pygmy girl he talked about marrying? She's beautiful. Fifteen dollars for a dowry, though. That *is* a fair amount of money out here. Big dilemma for Screwy Louie."

I was listening to a favorite tape of *Zairois choq*—good-time bar music from Zaire—on my pocket cassette player as Louie returned to the room. "Tell me about pygmy music," I asked.

Louie reflected a moment. "Pygmy music is very, very rich. Tremendously sophisticated. I consider it superior to Beethoven," he said, grabbing for a cracker. He did not make such comparisons casually, I learned later on. A candidate for a master's degree in mathematics before he lit out for the jungle, Louie maintained a lifelong and serious appreciation of classical music. Beethoven in particular.

"You have to hear it yourself," Louie went on. "You might get a chance to hear it in the right setting. Sometimes the pygmies sing around a fire, calling in the forest spirits while the fire dies down. When all that's left is a kind of red glow from the embers, the dancers come out of the shadows, where they've been hiding. They've covered their bodies with phosphorescent mold, like you see coating parts of the forest floor at night. You know? So, here they come, glowing and dancing and singing. It's pretty far out. Could you pass me another one of those crackers? Muummph. Pretty dramatic. There was a French film crew here not long ago to make a television special about the pygmies. The French heard about this phosphorescent dance and decided they just had to have that on film. Just had to. The pygmies didn't want to do it, though. There wasn't any traditional occasion for performing the ceremony, and they didn't want to do it for show. Well, the French crew kept on throwing francs at them until they finally decided to do it. So the pygmies rub on the mold and go through the motions, and this guy shoves a microphone into one pygmy's face and says, 'Tell us what the meaning of this dance is.' The pygmy just smiles and shakes his head. The film guy is going, 'But it is very important. Please tell us what this dance is all about.' Finally, the pygmy looks into the camera and says, 'This is a dance we are doing for money.' "

Mike told of another film crew working in neighboring Chad. They wanted to film a tribe known to hunt big game by walking among the animals while wearing a black cloak and a hornbill headpiece to disguise their human form. We don't do that anymore, the Chadian villagers told the filmmakers; we still know how, but the military has shot all the animals. So the crew arranged to bring the Chadians down to the C.A.R. and bought them all licenses so they could go on a hunt in their cloaks.

While lowland tropical rainforest robes the southern rim of the C.A.R., a broad belt of relatively moist, wooded, Ghanane (Ghana-like) savanna runs across the center, and the northern third is semiarid savanna. That is a good mixture of biomes, combined with one of the lowest human densities south of the Sahara—less than thirteen people per square mile. You would think the C.A.R. offered wildlife in abundance. But those Chadians in hornbill headgear didn't find the hunting all that much better on the C.A.R. side of the border. Poaching caravans from

Chad and Sudan had cleaned out most of the savanna game herds, particularly in the north. Highly organized, they came with camels, donkeys, and horses; cooks, scouts, and skinners. In many respects, they were merely continuing patterns of raids to the south many centuries old. But the weapons were deadlier.

The poaching gangs included soldiers of a rebel people's liberation army in southern Sudan, who used ivory poached from the C.A.R. and Uganda to finance their independence movement. Though well armed with military firepower, the Sudanese occasionally ran down elephants on horseback and severed the animals' foot tendons, slashing them with finely honed spear blades while galloping alongside. The Sudanese warriors did it this way for the glory and adrenaline, and to uphold a long-standing reputation for this method of slaying elephants.

What foreign poachers missed, the C.A.R. military and game rangers poached. Together, they had transformed some of the richest wildlife range in Africa into empty plains. Cattle were finishing the job, driven south by Chadian and Sudanese herders who had already overgrazed and desertified the arid range on their own side of the border. I met a *moonju* safari operator from the northern C.A.R. who had killed some 5000 trespassing cattle in his hunting allotment over the past few years. He asked the Mbororo herders from Chad why they persisted in coming when he shot their stock. They answered that the beasts would be even more sure to die if they stayed and starved back home.

Studying a C.A.R. map, I saw what appeared to be an impressive array of parklands. In reality, most of them had more illegal cattle than hooved wildlife within their borders and no park staff or facilities to speak of. One, Parc de Andre Felix, hadn't had a real tourist since the 1950s. Others were leased to Conoco for oil exploration and development. Still others became safari hunting concessions operated almost exclusively by and for *moonjus*, mostly Frenchmen. And a few parks had simply been degazetted in recent years.

A massive European Economic Community effort called Projet Nord was under way in the semiarid savannas. The intent was to develop agriculture and herding in tandem with a system of wildlife cropping that would produce a sustained yield of meat, hides—and francs from the sale of such wildlife products. This, it was believed, would demonstrate to local people the economic value of preserving wild creatures. In theory, the concept was sound. It was a very large project, though, involving water storage schemes, lots of road-building, and construction boomtowns. And a very expensive project. Some of the money actually reached the work sites. The rest, as ever, found its way into the pockets of officials, beginning at the ministerial level in Bangui and continuing down to local rural-development officers. Another megaproject, another round of direct foreign aid for corruption.

Meanwhile, it seemed that every laborer brought in to these previously remote rural areas was soon joined by a collection of his *bon freres* (the local phrase for good buddies and shirt-tail relatives), who came to hang out and poach. Enforcement of game laws was less than rigorous. Unable to countenance shooting poachers, Projet Nord had issued the local wardens whistles rather than guns. Whistles against AK-47s and submachine guns. This was a source of endless amusement to the foreign safari operators in the region, who had formed brigades that patrolled by motorcycle and dealt with poachers the same way they dealt with trespassing cattle. But the poachers were still thick, and poachers-turned-highwaymen had waylaid a couple of Projet Nord vehicles shortly before I arrived.

Mike used to work in the northern region. He once found eight hippos slaughtered at one waterhole. From each huge animal, the only thing taken was a strip of skin from the belly. It was to make a strap for a poacher's rifle. Of the hundreds of thousands of elephants found in the C.A.R. just two decades earlier, at least 90 percent were gone. As in Kenya, the survivors had banded together into frightened, often leaderless, and endlessly harassed refugee groups wandering from one region to the next in search of asylum.

The most intact wildlife habitat was in the rainforests of the Congo Basin region, which makes up no more than 15 percent of the nation. And the best habitat of all was probably right around us in Dzanga-Sangha.

Once we got ourselves and Louie fed, we went down to the riverbank to have a look around. The first thing that caught my attention was a tall, pale man with white hair, a white beard, a long, tattered, white robe, and sandals, walking toward the riverbank. His tread was slow and solemn, his hands clasped behind his back and eyes uplifted to the sky. He looked other-worldly, and he was. A French missionary, he was as indifferent to us as to the fact that the motor on the dugout that was to convey him and his satchel downstream into the Republic of Congo refused to start. He merely waited and prayed while some villagers repaired the motor. In time, he departed, eyes still on the heavens, which remained hidden by a haze of hot mist.

Then we started to do all over again what we had done in Bangui—make a series of visits to various authorities, fill out more forms, and then make courtesy calls to whichever other officials needed to be informed of our visit. This meant, first, a trip to the local gendarme—a uniformed cop in a little concrete building with a typewriter overseen not only by the president's photo but by handcuffs, bloodstained truncheons, and a poster-calendar of chimpanzees dressed in human clothes and posed in ludicrous situations. The gendarme informed us that he was very busy and would have to keep our passports for a while. Then we trundled over to the district official, who had us explain over and over again why we had no passports. Next we visited the guards of the Department of Water and Forests. In theory, they looked after the region's natural resources. In practice, they, along with the cops, were among the privileged few to have guns and used them to poach big game. Or else they loaned out their guns to the locals in return for the largest share of the poaching profits.

That evening, Mike raced down in his truck toward a little outpost called Lindjombo to retrieve some gear he had stashed, for his research camp was not far from there. He returned with a thief arrested by the Lindjombo gendarmes handcuffed to his tailgate for delivery to the Bayanga station. As the prisoner was being led away in Bayanga, he broke loose and ran for the jungle. The gendarme and his assistants quickly caught up with him. They took him to their little concrete house. The last sounds Mike heard upon driving away were the steady thwack of the truncheon upon the thief's feet combined with the wails of a grown man calling out for his mother.

Meanwhile, I had learned a bit more about pygmies. Not so long ago, their relationship with villagers in the Bayanga area apparently involved more mutual respect. The villagers put great stock in the pygmies' forest medicines and called on them to dance when someone in the village died. Then Bayanga was flooded by workers from outside, first for a coffee plantation and then for the timber company, and the newcomers had no special rapport with pygmies. The new people called the pygmies ignorant. Poor. People who have no houses and sit on the dirt. Apes. Chimps. Animals.

These days, the pygmies were often treated like indentured servants. Villagers conscripted pygmies to fetch and carry and work in their fields, paying them off with trifling amounts of manioc or liquor or sometimes nothing. Some treated the pygmies cordially, more in the manner of a member of a privileged class relating to a commoner. Others would beat a pygmy who ran away from work to the forest, or else take it out on the pygmy's family. A village man felt entitled to stroll into a pygmy's hut and take whatever he desired, including, sometimes, women. (A few days later in our sojourn, Bill Thompson gave a new T-shirt to a pygmy who had guided us, and a villager was wearing it the next day.) If you killed a villager in an auto accident, you could expect to have to pay the family U.S. $330 in compensation. Run over a pygmy, and the cost dropped to U.S. $66. The number of pygmies in the world is estimated at between 30,000 and 50,000, about the same as Asian elephants, which are considered endangered. How many of them in this particular part of the Congo Basin were true pygmies, as opposed to pygmy-Bantu mixes, was impossible for me to tell, but there were plainly a number of mixed-blood people in the pygmy villages.

The next morning, we were to continue calling on local officials, but Mike was slow in getting rolling. "Malaria," he grumbled and took a handful of pills from Thompson and me. He had spent the previous night telling us what he had been doing for the two-and-a-half months before he met us: surveying elephants through a largely unmapped section of the Republic of Congo. To get there, he first had to travel to the capital, Brazzaville, and make contacts with various authorities.

"It was ivory fever everywhere in that country," he commented. "You go to a restaurant, everyone's talking about ivory. Hop on a boat or a plane, they're still talking ivory. Shop at a store, walk through a village—ivory." Once upriver and nearing his intended survey area—ivory. He passed a Frenchman deep in the jungle who had a pygmy wife and 200 grass-skirted pygmies working for him—all hunting ivory.

A century earlier, Joseph Conrad's journey through the Congo Basin would leave him with fevers that recurred throughout the remainder of his life and with memories that went into his bitter vision of humanity, *Heart of Darkness*: "The word ivory rang in the air, was whispered, was sighed. A taint of imbecile rapacity blew through it all, like a whiff from some corpse . . . and outside, the silent wilderness surrounding this cleared speck of the earth struck me as something great and invincible, like evil or truth, waiting patiently for the passing away of this fantastic invasion . . . "

In the weeks that followed, Mike traversed several thousand square miles of the Congo Basin with a dugout canoe and pygmy guides, trying to get an idea of what the current elephant population might be. Like Richard Barnes in Gabon, he didn't try to count elephants directly. Rather, he relied upon a system through which elephant droppings, trails, tracks, feeding areas, and other sign are counted along a six-mile transect and fed into a formula that converts density of sign to density of animals.

Part of his route was through forest, part through marsh, and part through what Mike described as thorn swamp. "That was the worst," he said. "Day after day of nothing but sinking into mud with thorny plants growing out of it, and they weren't even tall enough to give you at least a little shade from the sun. You know what, though? There were elephants all over the place in that part of the Congo. It's got to be one of the best populations left anywhere. The poaching isn't that intense yet. It's mostly still undeveloped wilderness—one of the biggest, wildest places you could still hope to find in the world. Lowland gorillas all over the place. Chimpanzees everywhere. It's the same in the area where I've been doing research just downriver from here. Not many people work in this ecosystem or want to. They'll talk about how wonderful and diverse this rainforest is, but they'd rather do yet another study in someplace more comfortable, more convenient. They don't appreciate how many opportunities there are here to study species and relationships that are virtually unknown—begging to be understood. It's fantastic country. Unbelievable. You're going to love it!"

I studied this man closely. He was of average height and slightly built, with fair skin, dark hair, a moustache, and thick glasses. In sum, I thought he closely resembled photographs I had seen of James Joyce. Before coffee, before Mike had first admitted to diarrhea and a touch of malarial fever, he had dug a tiny tick out of the corner of his eye. This was his fourth case of malaria. Once, when the disease had been the virulent strain called falciparum, or cerebral, malaria, he had stopped breathing. Fortunately, that case had struck when he was on the road rather than in the jungle, and he had been able to get close to a hospital before he passed out. Now, as he struggled to put on his socks, I stopped him.

"What the hell happened to your feet?" They were a horror fest of red, seeping blotches and were missing half their toenails.

"Footworms," he said evenly. "They come from walking through the water. You'll probably get them. They never burrow very deep. It's just that you have to let them do their thing. If you dig in after them, the wound will go septic. I call them footworms; I don't actually know what kind of worm they are. You can get them anywhere." Mike showed me fresh festers on his bare shoulder. "I've got one on my ass, too. These other things on my feet are just thorn cuts and scratches. My toenails finally rotted off from all the wading. I must have waded more than I walked for a couple of hundred kilometers."

Thompson and I looked at each other and rolled our eyes, both of us clearly wondering whether we were going to be able to keep up with this guy. He hadn't paused to rest since leaving the Congo, and it didn't look as though malaria was going to stop him today any more than the hamburger feet that we could look forward to had.

SIX

CENTRAL AFRICA: BAYANGA

🌀🌀🌀🌀 BY AFTERNOON, WE had picked up a forest guard and two pygmies and were bumping along a partially overgrown Slovenia-Bois logging road in the Toyota, stopping now and then to hack away trees fallen—or pushed by elephants—across the track. The guard was noisily bossing the pygmies around until he realized that we were not the sort of *moonjus* who expected heavy-handed bossing, and he soon gave it up. He turned out to have a good rapport with the pygmies, as he had grown up in Bayanga and known them all his life. As for the pygmies themselves, the farther we went into the jungle, the more the zombielike mask they sometimes wore in the village lifted and was replaced by animated delight.

Some distance into the forest, we left the truck and slithered down a muddy trail potholed with elephant tracks and ripe with fresh dung. Where we encountered a shallow, sandy stream, we also met small crocodiles and a solitary bull elephant that had come to drink and to graze the shoreline grasses. He thundered upstream. We forded the water and on the opposite shore found the open, sunlit stretch of trail practically paved with butterflies of every size and hue. Uncoiling their proboscises—their thin butterfly trunks—they were busy probing mud enriched with fresh elephant urine.

"Twiners entwining twiners—tresses like hair—beautiful lepidopters—silence—hosannah." I had time to recall those lines scribbled into a notebook by Charles Darwin during one of his first excursions to the Brazilian interior. I thought of his successor Henry Bates describing butterflies like bright flakes of color racing each other down jungle paths. And then the forest closed around the trail, deep, twilit, and immanent, a three-dimensional maze that all but sealed out the sky. It was like walking into the earth without going underground. There was nothing to do but plunge in, for the others were already racing far ahead. Suddenly, I had no use for the sophisticated purposes I had carried with me to this place. I felt as though I were embarking on a journey into an ancient, sacred realm; that I should somehow have prepared my soul for it better, purified myself. The air smelled like steamed leaves. Doves hidden somewhere in the gloom overhead cried incantations.

With only slight variations in temperature and humidity from day to night and season to season, tropical rainforests are among the most constant of land environments. They have been for millions of years. Plants and animals face fewer demands from the physical conditions than from biological forces of competition, predation, and parasitism. In short, they are adapting mainly to one another. The struggle of each species to carve out a niche within an already crowded living space results in a proliferation of intricate, specialized lifestyles. Ultimately, this creates the stunning biological diversity characteristic of tropical forests.

For example, insects that eat a certain plant will tend to continually evolve better ways to attack it. These are countered by more effective defenses on the part of the plant. Often, it "invents" new chemical compounds that are toxic to the insect, inhibit its growth and maturation, or perhaps attract enemies of that particular bug. Other compounds are produced through natural genetic engineering to deal with larger, leaf-munching animals or with microscopic fungi and bacteria. Tropical rainforests, which hold more than half of all Earth's species on less than 5 percent of its total surface, amount to the most creative chemical laboratories on earth. Less than 10 percent of these plant species have been systematically screened for active compounds, yet half the pharmaceutical products used by humankind at the moment come from tropical vegetation.

A plant can also make itself more difficult to attack by becoming harder to find. Jungle species that grow in clusters or stands are vulnerable to infestation by insects and various diseases. Once such enemies have found the first plant, they can easily move on to the next, building up their own populations in the process until they begin to cause serious damage. The ecological solution for the plant species is to develop a more random distribution. As individual plants become better separated from one another, the creatures that eat them have to make their way past more nonfood plants and more of their own enemies to obtain a meal. At some point, starvation and predation begin to claim enough of them that they cease to be a threat. That point represents the plant's optimum density—the best balance between being abundant and being safely dispersed.

In the tropics, then, you rarely find a lot of individuals from one plant species in any one place. Instead, you find a few individuals from all kinds of species in almost every place. A single hectare (about two-and-a-half acres) selected at random from the rainforest of Borneo contains about seven hundred different species of trees, compared to four hundred for all of temperate North America.

In other words, as I made my way through the jungle, I had absolutely no idea what most of the plants I was looking at might be. The exceptions were a few palms and pineapplelike bromeliads—and one squashed-looking mess of pulp on the ground. Mike picked it up and pronounced it to be elephant chewing gum. "It comes from a plant called *Desplatsia dewevrei*," he told me. "The fruit is the size of a coconut, very fibrous and mucilaginous. It's also high in protein. The elephants chew on it a long time to extract all the value from the thing before they finally spit it out."

An hour later, the trail led to an opening. I could make out rain clouds thickening above what Mike termed *Gilbertiodendron* trees, whose branches mushroomed two hundred feet in the air, wreathed with flowering vines. Next to them grew ironwood trees with leaves that turned progressively more red toward the top, giving the whole plant the appearance of an immense, ripening blossom. Grey parrots with scarlet tails swept between the trees in raucous swarms. Mike held up his hand and cocked his head. From beyond the bushes ahead of us came other sounds—giant sounds of trumpeting and splashing. "The salines," he whispered. "Elephant time."

A series of salty springs—*salines* in French—issued from the ground to form marshes of low-growing sedge. In the course of seeking minerals here, generations of animals had enlarged the clearing, stripping and trampling nearby vegetation. We crept step by quiet step toward a position with a clear field of view. As I raised my head slowly from behind a fallen log, what struck me was not the sight of muddy elephants, which I had seen before, but the sight of muddy elephants, giant forest hogs, and sturdy, mahogany-red antelope striped with thin, vertical, white lines like sunlight slanting through palm fronds. These were bongos, perhaps the most rarely observed of Africa's nearly sixty species of antelope. A half-dozen of them stood together at one end of the clearing, shaking their heads to clear away clouds of insects. Several more bongos moved alone or in pairs between clusters of the round-eared, straight-tusked elephants.

The elephants numbered about twenty. As sunlight seeped in between the rain clouds, I could make out the swollen, white bodies of engorged ticks fastened here and there to their bellies and sides. Forest elephants *did* look small, now that I had settled down enough to focus on them. It was as if the fully grown adults in these families were off somewhere else for the moment. They weren't; I was looking at the adults. The tremendous size of the trees at the edge of the rainforest made the animals seem smaller yet. I was used to elephants standing out as one of the most conspicuous features in the landscape. My impression was that the irises of their eyes were generally lighter colored than those of savanna elephants, which would make sense, in that a jungle dweller needs less pigment to filter out strong sunlight than an open-country dweller does.

More elephants appeared. Like those present, they were generally in small groups of between two and five animals. That much is known about *cyclotis* society—that the average size of family units is considerably smaller than among savanna elephants. Animals associated with thick vegetation typically have smaller group sizes than those that dwell in more open terrain. This has to do with the patchy, scattered nature of the food supply in tropical forests. Shrublands and savannas have more homogenous vegetation, and larger groups are able to forage together within a given area.

Small group size also simply reflects the greater difficulty animals have traveling together in dense, tangled habitats. Another influence in the case of the elephant may be the virtual absence in this ecosystem of large predators that hunt in formidable social groups, namely lions and hunting dogs. Once a forest elephant grows large enough to cope with leopards, which usually hunt alone, it has little need for the security of a large family band. (Male forest elephants may go off on their own at a relatively early age. Seeing one of these juveniles, complete with large tusks and the sort of solitary habits that only fairly mature bulls exhibit among savanna elephants, an observer could be forgiven for thinking: Aha! No doubt about it—a fully grown pygmy elephant.)

What sorts of relationships exist between the small families of forest elephants? Are there bond groups that at least tend to occupy the same general vicinity and associate from time to time? Do related bond groups form clans, as among savanna elephants? Although you or I might not be able to see from one elephant to the next through the foliage, it is quite possible that the elephants themselves remain well aware of one another's whereabouts as they traverse the jungle. For in addition to their superb sense of smell, they have the ability to communicate through infrasound.

Infrasound is the trembling voice of distant volcanoes and earthquakes, the deep music of tides and rivers. Who knows what tales of the earth elephants hear? These frequencies are pitched so low that the wavelengths travel in slow swells, like a rolling sea or a long streamer gently undulating in the breeze. They are not easily blocked by objects in the way. They bend over and around. You can picture them slipping and snaking past tree trunks and branches. In a sense, elephant-generated infrasound may have been designed to do just that—penetrate the thick baffles of rainforest vegetation. The rainforest, after all, is where elephants probably evolved. They possess an ideal means of keeping in contact within such a setting. How often they use it and to what social purposes is still anyone's guess.

To discover the details about *cyclotis* social groupings and how they divide up available habitat, researchers will probably have to rely upon radio collars—ones that transmit at low enough frequencies to be effective in the jungle. For now, I would settle for the rare opportunity afforded by the salines at Dzanga-Sangha of being able to watch families interact for several days in a row.

Casually observed, forest elephant behavior appeared much the same as among savanna elephants. There were the usual sparring contests between young males. A four-year-old with strikingly well developed tusks raised his trunk in the air and repeatedly charged a big male bongo to drive it from a mud wallow. Subordinate families were displaced by dominant ones at favored seeps, where the animals plunged their trunks down to the hilt, presumably to find the saltiest solutions. And, as ever, the contact between mothers and their younger offspring was continual and affectionate. I did not notice many greeting ceremonies as various families joined at the salines, and those I did see seldom had the intensity I had come to expect from Amboseli. However, this could well have been a matter of chance and limited observation time rather than a genuine difference.

One morning, we arrived early at the salines and did not see the first elephant until nearly two o'clock in the afternoon, when a cow with twin six-year-olds and an approximately ten-year-old subadult appeared. They lingered at the jungle's edge, watching the same Hartlaub's ducks and cattle egrets that we had been watching all morning wade through the pools. The cow was tense and wary, apparently uncomfortable that her group was alone. When she finally did approach an open seep, a chase between the pair of cattle egrets there caused her to shy away. You would have thought the birds were lions. She cautiously returned and began to circle around them. Then she broke into an elephant dance, head-waggling and bouncing. The birds ignored her until she walked up and used her trunk to slap water at them. While the egrets circled through the clearing to alight at a different pool, she and her family drank briefly but suddenly broke off and shuffled away down the closest forest path through a storm of butterflies. Perhaps they had caught our scent. Maybe it was people that they had been nervous about all along.

The salines were empty of mammals once more until a solitary sitatunga, white spots dappling its orange fur, came into view among the taller sedges. The hooves of this marsh-dwelling antelope are elongated, with the two toes spread widely apart. Like the long-toed feet of egrets and other wading birds, they distribute the animal's weight so that it doesn't sink deep into the boggy ground with each step. The sitatunga therefore has an advantage over a heavy predator in a race through the reeds. And if it can't outrun the predator, it may escape by plunging into deeper water and staying completely submerged like a hippo.

Afternoon rain clouds once again formed above the treetops. The trees themselves were helping to build the clouds with moist exhalations—the tons of water drawn up by their roots and transpired through the pores of their leaves. I haven't seen a figure for the Congo Basin, but scientists calculate that the Amazon Basin's rainforests create 75 percent of their own rain.

By midafternoon, the sky had grown fairly dark, though not a degree cooler. I alternated my position between ground level and a platform some distance up in a tree. In the absence of larger beasts, I watched ants carve up a large fly and spiders stalking butterflies. I also noticed that each slight change in the atmosphere and each change in my altitude brought about a meeting with a new community of insects. For a while, it was mosquitoes, then filaria flies, which drill holes that erupt in tiny geysers of blood when the flies have finished feeding. Next came tiny, orange, biting gnats. Rather than endure long pants in the heat, Thompson had opted for shorts and insect repellent. But he kept sweating the repellent off and was often too absorbed with picture-making to remember to apply another dose. Looking down from the tree, I saw that his legs had become a mass of welts red as the poinsettialike leaf whorls of a liana growing at the clearing's border.

After the gnats came equally small bees that didn't sting but crawled all over my exposed skin, feeling no different from the dozens of gnats still there. Transpiring from every pore, I had become a salt lick—a saline—for bees large and small. Also for butterflies. At one stage, when I felt close to bursting blood vessels in this exasperating and eternal sauna, I realized that I was going to have to adapt mentally to my environment in fairly short order. I was all clenched up, as if called upon to defend against the thousand little insults to my flesh and endure until things got better. Things weren't going to get better. This was how they were. Always. If I didn't change my outsider's standards of comfort, I would become so worn down in a hopeless struggle to achieve them that I would be useless as a reporter within days.

I wondered how long I would have to live here before I could be like the pygmies lying on their side beneath the tree, talking in whispers, oblivious to the insects. I lay down and wiped the layer of sweat and bugs off my face and arms a final time, then fought to close off my awareness of everything external. I think I slept. Eventually, I felt a hint of coolness on my face. It was being fanned by dozens of butterfly wings. I sat up. The butterflies scattered, then reassembled, sipping, fanning, fanning. I stared at the sky without seeing, cooled wing by fragile wing, and was overcome by a feeling of absolution. Somewhere, drifting down the river that fed into the Congo, a white-bearded missionary in a tattered white robe was perhaps staring at the same sky with much the same expression on his face.

When it seemed that the air couldn't possibly become more saturated, the sky burst. Fat raindrops began to drum on the forest. The pygmies raced into the forest edge and returned holding umbrellas of palm fronds. I wedged myself into the crotch of a tree beneath a broad limb, hugging the main trunk like a damp monkey. After about half an hour, the downpour let up. Soon after that, nearly eighty elephants issued from the jungle at one end of the salines along with a herd of forest buffalo. Like forest elephants, forest buffalo live in smaller social groups than their savanna counterparts and are physically smaller as well. In fact, they, too, are sometimes confusingly described as pygmy buffalo. Another thing they have in common with forest elephants is that very little else is known about their home range and habits.

While Thompson crept forward to make impressionist photographs of elephants in the mist, I tried to sort out elephant groupings and keep track of interactions. But the afternoon was nearly gone, and the sky was growing darker by the moment. Thunder cracked straight over the clearing, rumbled, exploded again. An elephant screamed, and this time the sky opened up all the way. Even in a monsoon, I had never seen rain this thick. It descended in heavy sheets, dark and pounding, soaking us instantly. The whole sky had become a cascade.

A pygmy shouted something in pygmy language to his companion, who shouted in Sango, the national tongue, to the villager. He yelled in French about *la deluge* to Mike, who hollered to Thompson in English. I couldn't make out what he said for the sound of rain and thunder, but I heard enough to guess that it had to do with crossing the stream between us and the camp, where we had left a tent and supplies. We had to get back before the water rose too high. I shouldered my gear and looked back once through the rain curtains into the clearing. A series of lightning strokes etched into my memory a tableau of milling elephants and buffalo. It seemed that there were more than before, as if new ones were arising from the mixture of water and mud and taking life from the electrical discharges.

We began to run downhill along the elephant paths toward camp. Within minutes, we slowed to a stagger. The trails, worn deep into the poor clay soil, had become torrents of red mud and water. Our march ended with a flashlight crossing of the stream, which had grown wider but, fortunately, not too much deeper. Once again, we encountered an elephant bull wading there. His eyes reflected our light. But he stayed where he was a few strides upstream, watching our procession. We slogged into camp, listening to a gorilla drum on its chest in the distance, and began drying our clothes. Between sweat and rain, I would be drying them for the next month while worms and fungus helped themselves to my sodden feet.

꧁꧁꧁꧁꧁꧁꧁꧁꧁꧁꧁

Not many miles from the salines was another site where elephants came in search of minerals. There, they had dug into the side of a hill, creating a small cave. Crawling into the opening on their knees, they would tusk away the clay to get at fresh soil on the sides and stretch out their trunks to dig at the very end of the narrow passage. This is probably how the famed elephant caves of Mount Elgon in Kenya began. But those caverns of hardened volcanic ash and pumice could stand up to tunneling, whereas this little hole in the jungle hillside was destined to collapse on itself in a heap of clay, possibly trapping an elephant in the process. Or us, Thompson and I agreed as he arranged a trip wire and camera at the tunnel's farthest reach to record the giants' nightly visits.

On hikes around Dzanga-Sangha, we sometimes found where elephants had torn apart portions of fallen, rotted trees, again for pockets of minerals. We also occasionally came upon what appeared to be a round boulder resting on the dim jungle floor. Odd—there were no exposed rocks in this sediment-filled basin for hundreds of miles. Odder still, the sides of the boulder were rubbed smooth, and the ground for a short distance all around it was cleared of vegetation. The setting resembled that of a shrine, but Mike explained that these objects were old termite mounds used as salt licks by elephants. The mounds contained minerals concentrated by generations of termites harvesting plant material and packing it home to their cities of clay. One of the main food sources gathered by many termite colonies is the mineral-rich, haylike elephant manure that paves jungle paths and lies scattered throughout the forest. When elephants sought minerals from the mounds, they were once more recycling some of the same nutrients, closing the circuit.

Relationships of this type emphasize how precious minerals

are in many lowland equatorial forests. They are precious because they get leached out of the upper layers of the soil by pummeling rains such as we had endured almost daily. Silica-based compounds generally weather away the fastest, leaving mainly aluminum and iron hydroxides—the acidic, rust-red clay known as laterite, characteristic of many parts of the tropics. There is almost no organic layer, no humus, in this soil. A large percentage of the available nutrients remain locked up within the forest itself, cycling directly between one life form and the next. Competition for them is extremely intense.

Rather than feed upon the poor soils, many plants feed directly from other plants and from the decaying debris that accumulates high up in the canopy. This—plus the lack of sunlight on the forest floor—helps explain the prevalence of parasitic fungi and plants such as vines or lianas, with aerial roots; and epiphytes, including ferns and orchids, that root on the trunks and branches of other plants. A solitary fruit fallen onto the ground may soon be scavenged by surface roots from nearby trees. In the hothouse climate, those tendrils grow almost while you're watching, like science-fiction plants, rather quickly surrounding their vegetable prey to devour its nutrients before they are carried off by animals. Other roots snake along the ground capturing nutrients directly from leaf litter before they can dissolve into the ground.

Since the fertility of this ecosystem lies to such a large degree in its living cover, it follows that once you remove the rainforest, you remove the real wealth of the land. Yet that is precisely what developing nations around the globe are doing—practicing massive destruction of their tropical woodlands and replacing them with agriculture and livestock ranching. This is a case of wholly inappropriate technology in the service of a doomed idea.

The Kayapo Indians I met in the Amazon grow vegetable gardens on small plots within the still-intact structure of the jungle. They manage to do this by selectively burning certain forest plants to release their nutrients. For example, to plant maize, the Kayapo first soak the seeds in a growth-promoting extract taken from a wild forest plant, fell a palm and burn it on the ground, then sow the seeds along the strip of potassium-rich ash. These people have as many names for different kinds of ash residues as Eskimos have for snow and ice. They use old termite mounds to help mulch the soil. They also transplant mounds still occupied by certain species with strong-jawed soldiers to the borders of their garden, knowing that those termites will defend the area against species of leaf-cutting ants. That kind of integrated, finely tuned approach works splendidly.

But slash-and-burn clearing on a larger scale as practiced by colonists from the outside only yields two or, at most, three years' worth of crops before the minerals are exhausted and the cultivators are forced to move on to topple more forest. Because laterite lacks an organic layer, the increasingly barren, eroding ground is easily compacted into sun-baked hardpan. When trampled by livestock, it becomes bricklike all the sooner. Plowing is sometimes encouraged by agricultural advisors as a solution, but it only increases the rate of erosion and mineral-leaching from heavy rains. Large herds of livestock, like large fields and plantations of single crops, are monocultures. They violate the basic principle of diversity in this environment, which is that success lies in being abundant yet scattered.

Only now, late in the game, are scientists beginning to appreciate how rainforests work, how they may influence patterns of rainfall over a much larger area, and how they contribute to the global balance of oxygen and carbon dioxide. Only now are researchers such as Mike Fay beginning to reveal how much of the African jungle's natural richness and complexity reflects the presence of elephants. Here, even more than in the savanna, the giants' physical impact on their environment creates or maintains niches for countless smaller, less powerful creatures. *Cyclotis* also play a leading role in dispersing the seeds of scores, possibly hundreds, of tree species, taking all the continent's jungles as a whole. In sum, forest elephants are the very essence of a keystone species. Some biologists describe them as architects of the rainforest's diversity.

The basic elements of this architectural work are impossible to miss. As we made six-mile line transects through Dzanga-

Sangha to record elephant and lowland gorilla sign, hacking our way straight ahead with machetes, we were continually crossing and recrossing a dense network of elephant paths. And we sighed with relief each time one of the trails paralleled our course and we could stroll on it a while. It was like a broad, bare avenue scuffed free of all but the thickest roots. A better comparison might be to a high, wide tunnel through the encompassing walls of plant tissue. An assortment of tracks on these routes left clear evidence that they were major travel corridors for many of the jungle's other large creatures. Gorillas made frequent use of them. So did bush pigs, giant forest hogs, buffalo, bongos, and the various duikers in the region—black-fronted, yellow-backed, blue, and Peter's. Which was why leopards often liked to bide their time in branches overhanging the trails.

In the course of foraging, elephants are able to push over some of the skinnier trees, creating minor openings in the canopy. But the typical mature rainforest tree begins from a massive, buttressed base and soars upward like a cathedral pillar until it vanishes in the green firmament high above. The biggest *cyclotis* is no match for it. Not unless the elephant begins to yank on one of the lianas reaching like twisted climbing ropes from the ground to the very top of the canopy. As it happens, forest elephants do that a lot. Lianas are one of their favorite foods. Quite a few of the vines and creepers are packed with tasty starch. Others belong to the legume family, highly sought after for their protein content. Nitrogen compounds are as scarce as most nutrients in the rainforest's soils, yet they are essential building blocks of protein. Leguminous plants have root nodules that contain nitrogen-fixing bacteria. The microorganisms bind free nitrogen from the atmosphere and convert it to nitrates, which the plant in turn can convert to protein.

Trees with a fully developed crown are quite top-heavy with the combined weight of their own foliage plus that of epiphytes and lianas. Since strong winds seldom develop within such dense forests, top-heaviness is not ordinarily a drawback—no more than is the tendency of many trees here to have fairly shallow roots. However, when an elephant is pulling on one end of a liana, whole sections of the crown or, at times, the entire tree-top may snap off and fall. Or the tree itself may topple, perhaps carrying along one or two others trussed together by the same vines. If the elephant merely pulls down a liana alone, that still allows a good deal more light energy to filter through the canopy than before.

Mike estimates that about 10 percent of the forest elephant diet consists of bark. Just as in the savanna, giants seeking bark can strip away enough of the cambium layer to effectively girdle the tree, guaranteeing its demise. Lesser damage can still open the plant to invasion by insects, parasites, and diseases, which present more of a threat here than in drier climates. The point is that forest elephants remove trees in a number of ways, some faster than others, but in each case the result is the same: sunlight comes crashing down onto the damp jungle floor.

The seedling of a rainforest tree faces a daunting challenge. It must somehow establish itself in the light-deprived depths of the forest floor, avoid being turned into a meal by passing animals glad to find anything that hasn't already grown out of reach, and then rise up for a hundred feet or more to where its leaves can compete for sunlight in the crowded canopy. The majority of the woody species here belong to the division of flowering plants known as dicots. As a rule, they are extremely shade-tolerant in their early growth stages, adapted to extract the most energy from low levels of light. At the same time, they produce high concentrations of compounds called secondary chemicals (primary chemicals being those needed for growth) to defend themselves against being eaten.

The other main division of flowering plants is the monocots. These include grasses in all their various forms—bamboo being one of them—plus sedges, palms, lilies, and similar groups distinguished by parallel leaf veins. Since monocots tend to be herbaceous plants rather than woody shrubs and trees, they are much easier for most animals to chew and digest. They generally offer more starch than dicots, as well. Equally important, monocots have lower concentrations of secondary chemicals such as toxic alkaloids. Overall, monocots are the preferred food of grazers, such as the various forest antelopes, and of gorillas. And of elephants; herbaceous plants make up only a small percentage of forest vegetation but half the forest elephant's diet.

A key ecological difference between monocots and dicots is that monocots need more open, sunny habitats in order to flourish. In the rainforest, they are almost exclusively light-gap species. Like grasses and other herbaceous plants within northern woodlands, they are adapted to invade openings and prosper until the forest begins growing back high enough to shade them out.

Some trees within the forest are always dying, if only of old age, leaving gaps here and there in the overstory. Floods, fires, disease epidemics, and insect infestations create other opportunities for the monocots. And because tropical Africa has a pronounced dry season, lasting up to four months, its rainforest has a more open canopy to begin with than, for example, the Amazonian rainforest. So it would be stretching things to say that monocots in this ecosystem depend upon elephants. On the other hand, if elephants were not in the equation, the monocots would not be nearly as successful, and the survival of a tremendous spectrum of animals, from minute insects to lowland gorillas, depends in good part upon the success of these plants.

Elephants not only create openings but enlarge existing ones. Initially attracted by a clump of succulent bamboo or palms, for instance, they may go on to pull down nearby lianas and strip bark from surrounding trees. They help maintain clearings through their grazing and trampling and also by tearing up roots, which account for another 10 percent of their diet. Such disturbances tend to keep the vegetation in a successional, or subclimax stage, staving off the trees' efforts to reclaim the ground.

Monocots are adapted to handle a fair amount of grazing pressure. Quite a few produce runners, or rhizomes, that allow a plant to spread vegetatively instead of relying solely upon seeds as many dicots do. Rhizomes are not roots but horizontal stems. They hold the growth nodes that produce new shoots. Thus, if an animal grazes down the vertical growth of a monocot, it does not seriously harm the plant's ability to produce more. The animal can even tear up lengths of the rhizome, and other parts will survive, having put down roots of their own. This is why monocots have less need to rely upon chemical defenses than dicots do. Rhizomes allow grasses to coexist with great herds of hooved animals on the African savanna. Not so very long ago, rhizomatous grasses enabled tens of millions of buffalo, elk, mule deer, and antelope to graze the North American Great Plains year after year. For coping with foraging beasts of the jungle, the rhizome strategy works equally well.

"Okay, grazers eat grasses and herbs; browsers eat shrubs and trees. That's the traditional definition," Mike said. "We've always thought of forest elephants, gorillas, and most forest antelope as necessarily being browsers because they live in the jungle. But if you define a browser as an animal that focuses on woody dicots and a grazer as a monocot specialist, I think you could argue that a number of animals here are essentially grazers. In the case of elephants, we'd better call them generalists, because that's what they are. But they're doing more grazing than anything else. This is something of a new concept. It means that the difference in niches between forest elephants and savanna elephants, or between forest buffalo and savanna buffalo, may not be so great after all." It also means that in much the same way that elephants in a place such as East Africa transform woodlands to monocot-dominated grasslands, forest elephants help fashion the equivalent of savannas within the jungles they inhabit.

The most direct beneficiary, at least in the Congo Basin, appears to be the lowland gorilla. It prefers so many of the same monocot species elephants do that the two qualify as competitors. "Semicompetitors is a better way to describe them," Mike told me while we inspected a recent feeding area. He pointed out one of the most common gorilla foods, *Aframomum*, a member of the ginger family, Zingiberaceae. The base of each shoot consisted of new leaves still tightly rolled around a moist, starchy pith. The gorillas had stripped away the older leaves to get at this tender section, while the elephants had ripped up and munched the thicker rhizomes. It was the same with another plant, called *Megaphyrnium*, of the family Marantaceae. Gorillas ate the basal portions of the shoots, and elephants went for the bulkier rhizomes, which probably contained even more starch but also more of whatever defensive chemicals this monocot did produce. I tried the part the gorillas ate. It looked like an oversize version of a grass stem and tasted like a cross between that and celery.

Chimpanzees also seek out certain monocots in forest clearings. Mike told me he believes that in the days before they became more tied to villagers, the pygmies, too, used to get much of their starch from clearings left in the wake of elephants. Meat was comparatively easy for this race of people to gather; starch was always the category of food in limited supply. Today, the pygmies trade meat for manioc, imported to equatorial Africa from South America in slaving days to provide a fast-growing source of starch.

Later, Mike and I noticed where both gorillas and elephants had feasted on palm heart from a thicket of elephant-smashed raffia palms. The elephants had gone on to munch many of the leaves. They didn't eat just any leaves, though—only the newest, sweetest ones. Not far from the palms lay a modest-size tree that looked to have been snapped off by an elephant trying to drag down lianas. Although the tree was a dicot, the giant had eaten leaves from it as well. Yet it had once again chosen leaves from the younger sections. "Those have the least amount of coarse fiber and the fewest secondary chemicals," Mike noted. "You can see that forest elephants don't just rumble along through the jungle like bulldozers eating everything in their path that's green. Even though they can have the effect of a bulldozer on the forest structure, they are very selective about which species they actually eat and which parts of those species."

I wanted to know how Mike was able to identify so many types of jungle foliage in the first place. "Pygmies, my man. Pygmies," he answered. "Without them, my wife and I would still be doing vegetation plots and going crazy with plant taxonomy manuals. Besides, those manuals don't even list all the plants in a place like this. I hadn't been on this project long before I interviewed a pygmy named Bakembe. This one guy gave me at least ten times the data I'd gathered by myself up to that point. The pygmies know about 40 percent of the plants around Dzanga-Sangha, and I'd guess there are maybe 1500 species here. Minimum. They can pick out 400 different trees just by looking at the bark. That's fantastic, and it's really important." He pointed overhead. "Check out where the leaves are; you'd need a rocket ship to get high enough to pull off a couple for identification. The timber company used to hire pygmies to pick out the commercial tree species for them by the bark. They'd go out in teams of two villagers and five pygs and the pygs would do all the work. As usual. They got paid 200 C.A.R. francs a day [about two-thirds of a U.S. dollar] and the villagers got 600."

Mike rolled his eyes and wiped away the blood from a thorn scratch. "Now," he continued, "let's take this monocot feeding site. I'd guess we've got about six species of Marantaceae. They're reproducing vegetatively, so there are no flowering parts—none of the usual stuff identification manuals work with. But I can hand a pygmy a piece of a leaf, and he'll know the plant instantly. Same when we're on these transects looking for sign. I wouldn't get a tenth of what the pygmy sees. I never do a transect by myself. It would be an exercise in futility."

🙾🙾🙾🙾🙾🙾🙾🙾🙾🙾🙾🙾

On this transect, we were guided by a pygmy named Mbutu. Mbutu was not at all wiry like most pygmies here but, rather, barrel-chested with thick, solid thighs. Mike often referred to him as the Truck. Two heads shorter than I, Mbutu could carry three times as much three times as far through the tangles, while doing most of the machete work—all the while telling me how pygmies in Cameroon can turn into elephants at night and swim across the river to steal babies from villages on the other side— and still pick out dozens of elephant droppings for every one I noticed. He could also age the recent ones with precision, know-ing the sequence in which mold and insects in this sauna world reduce a heap of droppings to a thin, porous pancake, usually within little more than three days.

He never missed a beehive. Or a chance to shimmy up into the tree after the hive, which was usually hidden within a cavity. If he was unable to reach the honeycomb with his hand, he would poke in a stick to withdraw the golden syrup and lick it off. Gorillas here obtain honey with precisely the same technique. Mbutu was the first to notice cubiform termite mounds ransacked by apes. Gorillas break them up to expose the protein-rich insects; chimpanzees are the ones that use sticks as tools to poke into entrance holes and withdraw termites a few at a time to lick them off. When Mbutu came upon the white feathers of a bird at the edge of a stream, he stuck them in his hair and primped and promenaded, laughing at himself. He laughed all the time with high, soft, musical notes. He talked about how gorillas pointed to things with their chins, and he thought that was very funny. I would ask Mbutu where something was, and he would unconsciously point to it with his chin.

Oops. Is this beginning to sound patronizing? Does describing a pygmy acting like a gorilla set off all kinds of alarms about racial and cultural stereotypes? Good. I want to mention again that two kinds of prejudice are involved here. The first has to do with demeaning a fellow human by comparing him or her to our primate next of kin. Of course, it doesn't work unless everyone involved assumes that gorillas, chimpanzees, orangutans, and monkeys are inherently inferior to humans, and that is the second kind of prejudice.

I point out that Mbutu got honey the same way gorillas get honey and chimpanzees get termites because that is what he and gorillas and chimpanzees did. I say he made a gesture like a gorilla because he made a gesture like a gorilla. Mbutu would have been embarrassed to hear me tell it. Just as the villagers often speak of pygmies as chimps, the pygmies often describe villagers as gorillas. Some are sure that when villagers die, they in fact come back to life as gorillas. I do not consider myself prejudiced against any primate. As for Mbutu in particular, I often wished I were he. This man was the most inspiring mix of muscle and intellect I had met for a long time. Mike Fay was equally inspiring, but he was more a mix of intellect and sheer will-power. Together, they were turning this into an extraordinary trip.

Typically, Mbutu was the first to hear and then see elephants. He led me silently through a thigh-deep bog to within perhaps forty feet of a feeding mother and her half-grown offspring, and I still couldn't make out more than a tatter of grey here and there through the foliage. That encounter summed up a great deal about both the difficulties of research on *cyclotis* and the visual perspective of pygmies. Writing about the pygmies of the Ituri Forest in Zaire, anthropologist Colin Turnbull told of taking a group of them out onto the savanna. When they saw elephants thousands of yards distant, the pygmies thought they were looking at very tiny elephants only a short way off, because in their world, the farthest anyone could see most of the time was about thirty feet.

Yet inside that universe with a thirty-foot radius, a pygmy missed nothing. The quintessential newcomer, I was usually far too busy stumblebumming over roots and past webs of vines to spot an old rain-beaten elephant print, much less the duiker pel-lets and gorilla-bent plant stems Mbutu read in passing. A day-old trail of a porcupine would bring him screeching to a halt as if someone had laid a neon marker across the jungle floor. As we were walking along one grade, Mbutu pointed with his chin at an old elephant manure pile, lifted a hand toward a gorilla-opened termite mound in the fold between two buttresses of a tree, looked back at me to be sure I saw and learned, looked ahead again, and stopped cold. He began speaking in rapid pygmy, staring at the forest floor in total concentration.

"Mike! Translation, please!"

"Something . . . ," answered Mike, "He's saying something is not right. Something happened here. Something . . . there was a fight."

I stepped closer and saw the same chaotic carpet of moldering brown and purplish leaves and wandering roots I had seen for miles.

"The leaves are pushed around. Yes, a fight."

Now I could see that the leaves had been moved. A bit of bare ground showed between several. Mbutu hunched over it warily.

"Marks. Scuff marks. No, scratch . . . claw marks! Little claws. A squirrel. A squirrel was fighting. Something . . ."

With his eyes, Mbutu was following a path only he saw among the leaves, and he was tensed like a cat ready to leap. He took a step, another, and again stopped cold. He pointed with one hand and held the other up for caution. Again I found myself staring at leaf clutter and twisted roots. Then, as Mbutu pointed with a stick, I saw a pattern of diamonds exactly the same color as the leaves and a round eye edged with scales. It was the head of a rhinoceros viper. The body, thick as my upper arm and about five feet long, lay partly coiled like a root among the leaves.

"Mbutu says this snake is slow because the squirrel is inside it now." A few minutes farther along on our transect, Mike added, "Pygmies, my man. I'm telling you. Pygmies. The secret to science in this part of the world."

The next thing Mbutu picked out was a pomegranate-shaped fruit on the ground, which he handed me and indicated that I could eat. Elephants, along with gorillas, chimpanzees, pygmies, and assorted smaller primates all seek out the fruit of various trees in this area. At times, they proceed from one fruiting tree to the next as if working a trapline, checking to see what has fallen to the ground since they were there last. Often, the canopy is too far above and the tree trunk too straight and unbranched to make it worthwhile for any of the great ape family members to climb up and try to pluck the fruits. But an elephant can speed up the rate at which fruits drop off by shaking the tree or butting it with its head.

Seeds that germinate directly beneath the mature parent tree are fated to sprout in its shade and compete for precisely the same mixture of nutrients, a disadvantage for both parent and offspring. If new plants somehow succeed against the odds and join their parent to form a cluster, then they all become vulnerable to aggregations of their enemies for reasons previously discussed. The ideal strategy for typical rainforest species is, to repeat the theme, being abundant yet scattered. How to solve the problem of dispersal in the relatively windless environment? The solution is to attach the seed to a mobile life form.

Having coevolved with birds and mammals in the forest environment for millions of years, the plants have developed ways of enlisting them to move seeds around. Just as the bright colors, perfumes, and nectars of flowers lure animal pollinators, seeds coated with fleshy, sweet-tasting tissues attract potential dispersers. The seed and its supply of stored nutrients for germination are termed the endocarp, commonly described as the pit, nut, or seed. This is enclosed within the mesocarp, which is the pulpy edible portion, while any skin or rind is the exocarp. A common strategy is to produce an endocarp hard enough to pass through the digestive tract of the fruit-eater. It will then emerge to germinate in a fertile pile of dung wherever the animal happens to be when the urge strikes—preferably some distance from the parent tree by then. For that matter, a number of species have seeds that need to pass through some creature's intestine and have the tough outer seed coat partly dissolved by gastric juices in order to germinate well. This is probably a means of ensuring that new plants do not grow up directly beneath the parent tree and compete with it.

Insects disperse a great many seeds by carrying them in their mouth parts. Beetles and ants probably pack the greatest number around. Quite a few tropical plants are aerial germinators. Their seeds sprout up where the light and nutrients are, in the higher reaches of the forest, then send down rootlets to anchor themselves to the soil and tap its resources. Predominant among these are various figs, Ficus, the largest plant genus on the continent. Ants give many of these their start. As a measure of the complexity of tropical ecosystems, the ants are often secondary dispersers. After a larger animal eats fig fruits that have fallen on the ground and deposits the seeds elsewhere in its droppings, the ants take the tiny seeds from the dung pile and haul them up into the treetops. The endocarp still retains a thin but very sweet coating called the aril, and this is what the ants are interested in toting back to their colony. Bats and primates are also major dispersers of aerial germinators.

Different seeds are, in effect, designed with different animals in mind. For instance, the baseball-size fruit of a tree called gambeya (*Chrysophyllum*) has a lozenge-shaped seed coated with a mucilaginous aril just made for slipping easily down the gullets of mammals from duikers on up through large primates and elephants. Generalists and opportunists, duikers not only search out fallen fruits but follow along below monkey troops, scavenging half-eaten leaves, pods, fruits, and whatever other food is dropped or jarred loose from tree branches. Studies suggest that monkeys drop anywhere from a quarter to half of the food they handle. Mike said the forest duikers' role as vacuum cleaners was a little-known factor in the success of this ubiquitous group of small antelope. He also showed me where they had pawed apart elephant and gorilla dung to scavenge partially digested fruits of several varieties, notably those in the family Irvingiaceae. Knuckle prints near another elephant manure pile revealed where chimps had done the same. Mangabey monkeys and porcupines do this too, serving as additional secondary dispersers. Bush pigs are perhaps even more effective scavengers of seeds in dung piles, but they crack the endocarp and eat it.

At another site, we came upon fruits of a tree Mike identified as *Balanites*, in the creosote family. Its pit was the size of an avocado. Even gorillas couldn't have choked it down. It seemed to have been particularly designed with elephants in mind. Farther on lay a fruit as large as a basketball and considerably heavier, perhaps thirty pounds. Falling from a height of a hundred feet or more, it could take you out with a direct hit as surely as a viper could. "This baby is *Treculia africana*, in the fig family," Mike announced. "No hope of moving beyond the shade of the parent tree unless it gets broken up and transported by some big animal. Elephants and gorillas again." Before that day was through, he led me past a few tree species whose flowers and fruits grew directly from the trunk or lower branches, a condition known as cauliflory. One of the better-known species with this trait is the South American cacao tree, which produces the beans used to make chocolate. "I can't be completely sure, but cauliflory certainly looks like another adaptation to dispersal by big mammals," Mike observed. "Once you take gorillas and elephants out of a community like this, the whole ecosystem begins to make less and less sense."

Because the African rainforest possesses a more open canopy to begin with than other rainforests, it has long supported a greater biomass of large animals, which in turn exerted a greater influence upon the variety and distribution of plant life. While the animals evolved more means of exploiting the food energy available from plants, the plants were evolving more efficient means of taking advantage of zootic, or animal, forces in the environment. Over time, the two great divisions of the living kingdom became more and more closely bound to one another until they were resolved into an almost seamless whole.

In the throes of a jungle fever, you might even be able to look at a gorilla and see a mobile, hooting, chest-beating package of plant material—minerals, starch, protein, partly digested leaves, and expectant seeds—looking back through bright brown eyes. Or turn your blurred sight upon a bright little clearing of soft-leaved herbs surrounded by towering trees and sense millions of chloroplasts machining raw sunlight into starch molecules and flowers full of nectar and bees, and the bees churning out honey and the flowers metamorphosing into big, lozenge-shaped seeds enclosed by packages of fruit sugar . . . until you perceive a gorilla in the making. Or maybe the fever has you so fast in its grip that you imagine some great pod arising from the green center of it all and unfurling to release a pygmy, glowing as if covered with phosphor. You might be closer to the essence of things than if you were forever cool-headedly mouthing phrases such as "complex interrelationships favoring zootic dispersal mechanisms." After all, the rainforest is no less magical for being so overwhelmingly complicated.

Chief among the architects of that complexity, *Loxodonta africana cyclotis* could alternately be known as one of the foremost perpetrators of jungle magic. I rummaged through an elephant dung pile at random and came up with the seeds of at least eight

different tree species. Mike said he doesn't yet know what the total number of species dispersed by elephants might be. He could
list twenty from a single family, the Sapotaceae. He thought for
a moment and decided he could list nearly as many from the Irvingiaceae. The pygmies are known to take fruits from seven
elephant-dispersed tree species in that family, one for the mesocarp and six for the seeds themselves, which are laden with
oil. The oil-rich nut of *Panda oleosa* is also dispersed by elephants and used by the pygmies, who grind it into a buttery
paste. All this is in and around Dzanga-Sangha. Continent-
wide, elephants may be involved in disseminating the seeds of
as many as one-third of the trees in lowland tropical forests.

What happens to Africa's Irvingiaceae if elephants disappear?
What happens to *Balanites* with its avocado-size pit made for
elephant gullets? What happens to the scavenging duikers,
the monocot-dependent gorillas, the pygmies that still tap the
forest for provisions? The relationship of elephants with gorillas, chimps, and pygmies leads to another question. Considering
the elephant's key role in creating biological diversity within the
tropical forest, plus its equally major role in the dynamic
savanna-woodland balance, what influence might its kind have
had on the long sequence of primate evolution that led to *Homo
sapiens*? Who planted the tree where our ancestors were born?

🮚🮚🮚🮚🮚🮚🮚🮚🮚🮚🮚🮚

The recent history of Dzanga-Sangha covers a broad spectrum
of the relationships between elephants and humans in Africa's
tropical forests today. Early in the 1970s, poaching here was
minimal. People shot animals protected by game laws, but
everybody did that. The pertinent fact is that the killing remained more or less within the sphere of ordinary subsistence
hunting by the local villagers and pygmies. Then the timber
company came. The new logging operations didn't harm elephants directly, as the cutting was very selective. It had to be;
only a few tree species, such as African mahogany (*Entandro-
phragma*), were valuable enough to cover the cost of transporting

lumber made from them to foreign markets. The limited cutting may have increased elephant habitat by doing the same thing elephants themselves were: opening up patches of the canopy and encouraging the growth of successional plant communities dominated by monocots. Far fewer trees were felled for merchantable timber than in building roads to get at the prize trees.

Yet that was precisely the problem: the new road access. The main route to the mill made Bayanga suddenly accessible to poachers from elsewhere in the nation. The countless smaller timber roads radiating outward from the mill served as an easy way into the jungle. At the same time, the timber operation was markedly boosting the number of villagers. Most of those who came from other regions to work at Bayanga promptly spread snare lines of their own to go with those of the original villagers. These outsiders were not very comfortable prowling through the dank gloom of real jungle, so they found the road grid particularly helpful. To get meat from beyond the road network, they hired pygmies to hunt and trap for them.

Even then, elephants were not being heavily hunted. Systematic commercial killing did not get under way until enough timber workers were living in Bayanga that the government saw fit to establish outposts for the police and Department of Water and Forests. Other than the overseer of a coffee plantation in nearby Lindjombo, these functionaries had the first guns in the area capable of bringing down elephants, and they began doling them out along with orders to bring back tusks. In other words, elephant poaching got serious only after the law arrived.

"Here in Bayanga, we were always hearing the sound of guns from the forest," a pygmy I'll call Njoko (Elephant, in his language) told me through a translator. Njoko hunted elephants for an influential Arab trader, who provided a large-bore rifle. "He gave me five or ten bullets at a time. I could get maybe ten elephants in one week," Njoko said. "He always promised to pay me, and then, when I brought the ivory, he would give me maybe some drink." Moonshine, usually, the local, home-brewed white lightning. "Then the mayor of a big town came and shot an elephant and left it. The trader told me to go collect the tusks for him and his *bon frere* the mayor. When I found the elephant, the ivory was gone. The Arab said I took it and told his *bon frere* the gendarme to arrest me. They beat me with the *abanda* [a flat piece of pipe with a wooden handle]. They beat my feet so badly I couldn't walk right for six months. For the first three weeks, I had to crawl to go to the bathroom. They sent me to jail for a while in another town, but they let me go after not very long."

That mayor came down the new road to Bayanga to nail elephants whenever he could. A police chief came from the capital to hunt the giants. A minister of natural resources was caught with elephant guns at Bayanga; he was still minister when I visited. Three different poachers had been caught using the local Bayanga prefect's gun; he was still prefect. For years, the only real check on the slaughter was the fact that big guns were expensive and restricted to ordinary civilians. Word of the good poaching conditions at Bayanga even drew shooters from the Republic of Congo.

Mike and his colleague Richard Carroll, who was also studying lowland gorillas in the area, saw fewer and fewer elephants over the years. Only a handful of buffalo still appeared at the salines where large groups used to come. Bongos were on the way out. Then Carroll conceived the idea of a joint project of the C.A.R. government and the World Wildlife Fund to protect the area. He, Mike, and various officials went on to outline a plan for a reserve that incorporated a number of existing economic activities. Rather than fashion an off-limits estate in the old semicolonial park tradition, they wanted the reserve to function as an integral part of the resource base for local people. The result was the 1740-square-mile Dzanga-Sangha Dense Forest Reserve. Details of its final shape were still being worked out during my visit, but its guidelines were already in effect.

"Just in time," Gustave Doungoube, codirector of the reserve, had told me during an earlier conversation in Bangui. "Before, it was a no-man's land. Our goal is to protect not only important animals and plants but the pygmy people who depend on the forest ecosystem."

I had met Richard Carroll in Bangui as well, and he told me, "The government was interested right from the start. I think they see that the future of wildlife in the C.A.R. is now in the south, in the forest. And the pygmies needed a secure area. Their hunter-gatherer culture is changing awfully fast now that so many are living in permanent camps by the villages. The missionaries round them up and put them to clearing the forest, growing crops, learning French—acting like villagers themselves. We wanted to give the pygmies enough secure forest and wildlife so they could have at least a while longer to choose their way into another life, another economy."

As Carroll, Doungoube, and others have arranged this multi-use reserve, selective logging on a sustained yield basis will be permitted in certain areas. In other portions, safari operators can continue to offer hunts for select game, so long as they funnel 10 percent of the safari fee to the reserve and half the trophy fee to the local community; the going rate for a bongo safari while I was there was up to U.S. $30,000. Villagers can hunt and grow crops within a designated area. And the pygmies can hunt nearly everywhere, but only with traditional methods: spears, crossbows, concealed pits, and the driving of game into nets. Two small core areas are to be left strictly undisturbed by human activities. No elephant hunting is permitted anywhere in the reserve, not even by pygmies, who have always taken elephant meat as opportunity permitted. A buffer zone along lengths of the reserve's borders is designed to avoid bumping directly up against areas with no restrictions on exploiting the forest.

The elephants had quickly returned—in fact, so quickly and in such numbers that it seemed many of the giants had escaped shooting and merely abandoned the area temporarily to seek safer stretches of forest. On the other hand, Mike thought the increase might have been the result of elephants fleeing to Dzanga-Sangha from a newly logged portion of the Congo not far to the east. In any case, the challenge now was to keep them.

An Arab businessman went elephant hunting near Bayanga with a pygmy guide. A gorilla charged the pygmy, who was leading. It might have been a bluff charge; these things usually are. But the Arab tried to shoot the gorilla, and he hit the pygmy in the stomach. The pygmy died shortly afterward. That was only a couple of weeks before I arrived. And soon after I settled in, a safari operator discovered a fresh elephant carcass near Bayanga. Other reports of elephant hunting continued to surface, but most of it seemed to be on the reserve's periphery. The real ivory fever had broken for the time being.

Around noon one day along the road toward the salines, I encountered two seedy-looking *moonjus* and a huge African sitting by their vehicle sweating and sucking on beer. Not to jump to conclusions, but this trio somehow did not look as though they were here out of dedication to nurturing biological diversity. They gave me a cold beer, and we chatted a while. The Frenchmen were safari operators from the north; the African, a high official from Bangui. The Frenchmen were trying to convince the official that he should create an extra safari concession at Dzanga-Sangha and give it to them. They wanted permits to hunt a few gorillas and elephants and perhaps build a tourist lodge overlooking the salines. I took it as an ominous sign of possible things to come that would have less to do with promoting genuine eco-tourism than promoting disturbance to pocket more francs.

Most of the families in Bayanga still poached with snare lines. Many still employed pygmies to bring in meat as well. The village was doing more than feeding itself. It was looting the jungle to supply smoked monkey and duiker to several villages farther north. The situation would have been worse had not Slovenia-Bois gone broke and a lot of workers left for the diamond fields or other timber jobs. Mike worried about what would happen when logging got rolling again under a different multinational company, which had bought out Slovenia-Bois's timber concession.

"The problem is that we have a budget for ten rangers and six trackers," Gustave Doungoube had explained. "To cover the area set aside, we should have forty-two rangers and sixteen trackers. We will manage somehow. It is important to make this work. The Peace Corps is contributing through a program to educate the pygmies about the reserve. The pygmies need to understand which areas they can hunt in and why they are asked to leave the animals alone in certain zones."

When I was with pygmies in one core area, they showed me how to call in a duiker with a series of nasal, catlike yowls. This was the call made by a female duiker giving birth, they said, and other duikers in the area were attracted by it. The pygmy imitation worked. Duikers sometimes came to within a few feet of us. The pygmies understood that they were not to take such animals as prey, at least not when Mike was around. But when they grabbed a tortoise wandering along the forest floor and Mike tried to tell them why they weren't to kill creatures of that kind either, they looked at him in such amazement that Mike just laughed and turned to me, saying, "You explain it to them, okay?"

Peace Corps volunteer Anna Kretsinger had been taking pygmy children from Bayanga on nature outings, if you can call taking pygmy children into the forest that. To teach them the vital roles even animals as small as insects can play in the sustenance of a rainforest, she had them collect a variety of butterflies and termites. Unfortunately, before she got the specimens back to Bayanga for study, the kids had eaten quite a few of them, she told me. Her tale brought to mind the efforts of New Guinea explorer William MacGregor. High up among the mountain meadows of the interior, he collected three species of birds unknown to science. Two of them were to remain unknown for a while longer, since MacGregor's assistant, one Joe Fiji, had them for dinner. I don't imagine things would turn out much differently if someone speaking a strange tongue came through Montana and enlisted me and my friends to help collect specimens of local trout and morels.

༺༻༺༻༺༻༺༻༺༻༺༻

Mike wanted to survey elephants and gorillas in another expanse of rainforest some distance to the east of Dzanga-Sangha. Before leaving, he needed to gather some gear from a camp near

Lindjombo, the little riverbank town by the defunct coffee plantation. Thompson went with him. Upon arrival, they were obliged to check in with the local gendarmes. Two of them waited at the local guard post, and both were drunk. Imagine a couple of tie-dye hippies arriving in Cowboy Boot, Wyoming, on Saturday night, or a pair of urban African Americans running into the archetypical southern sheriff of Redneck, Alabama, while he is juiced. Now here come the *moonju* elephant boys to meet two drunken goons who had not had anybody to mess with for many a hot day at the end of the world. Thompson had forgotten his passport and soon found a more malevolent level of hell than any Bangui visa office. Happily, after much dispute and a short stay in jail, Mike's experience—and connections to higher levels of government—got the crew out and back to Bayanga.

To reach the other forest area, we had to retrace part of our route to Bayanga in the Toyota. We were scarcely under way when we passed a car full of Water and Forest guards returning to Dzanga-Sangha. They told us that bandits had been shooting up vehicles on the roads again, worse than before. A young American woman who worked with Anna Kretsinger, the Peace Corps volunteer with the pygmy nature club, had been shot in the arm during the robbery. Others had been killed. Farther down the road, in Nola, we asked how the bandit situation looked. A man pointed toward the highway and said, *"C'est le feu la-bas"*—it's a fire there. People said at least six or seven cars and trucks had been shot up in the last couple of days. Given the sparse traffic on C.A.R. roads, that was probably most of the vehicles that appeared to be carrying anything valuable.

We bought supplies from the market, where a pretty young bare-breasted woman watched us with an unshakable smile. She was shackled to the platform where she sat. An insane woman, we were told; the shackles kept her from wandering off into trouble. Then some kind of official, whose title I never got clear, came out of a fruit stall and began shouting at Mike, demanding to see Mike's permit for "his" pygmy, meaning Mbutu. Mbutu was lying in the back of the Toyota with me, eating mangoes from the market. The Big Man yelled again; but people here had few inhibitions about shouting at each other in public, and I no longer paid much attention to it. I was thinking that this was the best mango I had tasted lately.

While Big Man hollered, I contemplated the Irvingiaceae. This family includes *Irvingia gabonensis*, called the bush mango. Elephants eat the fruit and disperse the lozenge-shaped seed. People eat the fruit as well but prefer the common mango, such as I was slurping up now. The common mango belongs to an entirely different family. It originated in Asia and was brought to Africa only recently as an exotic. Yet it has an almost identical structure: a sweet, pulpy, fibrous mesocarp surrounding a large, lozenge-shaped seed. The fruit represents a striking case of convergent evolution, and one perhaps simpler to explain than most, for the common mango, the fruit half the people walking the streets and paths of the C.A.R. appeared to be munching on at any one time, had also evolved with primates and elephants in mind, but Asian primates and Asian elephants.

Mike finally told Big Man to stuff it. Big Man smoldered away down the street, and we stormed off in our Toyota, with Mike muttering about the absurdity of the affair: "*My* pygmy, he says, like people *own* pygmies. Mbutu's one of the best friends I have in this country. Besides, Mbutu wanted to come. His wife was giving him hell around home. Why should pygmies need permits to move around and do what other citizens do? I know, it's partly to keep someone from packing off half a pygmy tribe and forcing them to work for him somewhere. But it's nuts, because pygmies were here long before the Bantus. Pygmies are the original inhabitants."

After checking in with a district official and the Department of Water and Forests office to tell them of our survey plans, we saw the day giving out on us and decided to spend the night at Nola. A couple of women came by, insisting that we party with them, but we crawled into my tent, pitched beside the local Water and Forests chief's house, and listened to distant music and barking dogs until we fell asleep.

Another morning, another official. Then, at last, we were on the road again. Hours later, we turned off a narrow dirt route and beheld a strange sight: a superhighway of dirt, wide as a Los Angeles arterial and straight as a grand canal. It was an African Development Bank road, bulldozed through one of the last stretches of undisturbed jungle like the trans-Amazonian highway. Intended to link the capital more directly to the western part of .the country in order to encourage development, it was about two-thirds finished. Already, pygmy camps had sprung up along the strip between the roadside and the jungle, dusted with the passing of each giant dumptruck and log hauler. The pygmies were hunting meat for villages that used to be days away but were now just hours distant on the completed portion of the highway.

The road ended in a pack of bulldozers and earth-moving machines, any one of which would have dwarfed an elephant. A river lay ahead, awaiting construction of a ferry. For now, the little village of Bambio was the end of the line. We introduced ourselves to the mayor, Albert Essengamobe, who oversaw three village chiefs. He welcomed us and invited us to his house for dinner, honoring us with a chicken. Long remote, Bambio still had the quiet feel of a real community once night fell and the bulldozers' roar faded. There was none of the litter, hustle, and shouting racket of a large roadside town like Nola. But it was headed that way. Mayor Essengamobe told us that his village was unraveling. The young men were leaving for bigger places and bigger money. Road-builders were chasing Bambio's women. And they had guns, some of these builders, which was worrisome.

Mayor Essengamobe wasn't seeing the kind of wild game he used to see. No one was. And yet elephants had been raiding some fields 1.8 miles from Bambio, making off with pineapples, mangoes, papayas, and corn. It was just one group of six to eight animals, the mayor said, but no one had seen elephants here for a long time. He and Mike agreed that they were probably refugees from new logging and hunting in the portion of the Republic of Congo close by to the south.

Mike requested the mayor's help in obtaining a group of

pygmy porters, as we were going to hike through the forest to do transects for a number of days. The mayor sent the word out. All the pygmies ran away into the jungle. Mike explained to the mayor that he intended to pay the pygmies for their labor. The next morning, we found a crowd of them outside our hut along with a big villager named Alfred. Alfred informed us that these were his pygmies and that he would accept the money and dole it out to them, keeping a portion for himself, naturally. Mike hired seven pygmies and Alfred as a sort of foreman and made it clear that they would be paid at the end of our journey. Our designated gang ran off to pick up a few items from their homes, and a couple managed to get a little drunk before they returned and we marched off into the forest.

To be certain that each transect was exactly six miles, Mike wore a spool of fine thread of known length attached to his waist and let it play out behind him while he charged ahead along a straight compass line, pausing only to change spools. I nearly collapsed of heat prostration trying to keep up that first day. I wasn't in bad physical condition, but I wasn't in really great shape either, and I definitely wasn't getting nearly enough water to keep up with the rate at which I was losing it. My main fear was getting separated from the rest of the party. It wasn't even a very rational fear, since the pygmies could probably have circled back and found me handily. Still, every time I stopped to rest or wandered off a bit to investigate something and then looked up to find the others out of sight and no trace of Mike's string to guide me out of the labyrinth, an awful feeling of vulnerability welled up within me. In other kinds of wilderness, I go out of my way to trek alone. Here, I felt wholly out of my element and easily disoriented by the dark, immanent green and the absence of sky. Also by the stings, bites, and scratches that struck and struck again. Worse, I knew that my sense of helplessness was partly justified, because I had no more clue as to what to avoid than I did as to what I could eat and use to survive if left on my own. Even Mbutu, the all-seeing jungle Truck, had come within inches of stepping on a banana viper earlier in the day.

I would brush an ordinary branch amid the green profusion and suddenly be covered with ants whose bites made my skin swell so violently that blood oozed out my pores. I would duck under a liana and find myself in a flood of army ants and have to trot on, stamping hard with each step to keep from being overwhelmed. At times, I could hear columns of ants or of termites feeding nearby, a dry, rustling sound that pervaded my thirty-foot-radius universe. I took it as a reminder that in this ecosystem, the biomass of all the megafauna combined was minuscule compared to that of these social insects. Elephants and our search for them seemed to diminish accordingly. Only the wood and leaves and countless rustling little bodies mattered; only the growing and the chewing, the decaying and growing again mattered. I was a soft, succulent mass of tissue, a trove of scarce nutrients invaded by everything that bit, drilled, wormed, sucked, and licked. I had found ways to cope with that feeling of being under constant attack, but sometimes my tolerance evaporated. Sometimes at Dzanga-Sangha I would crawl into my tent and kill every damned thing that crawled in with me and just sit there, not being eaten for a while. Sometimes in the jungle I felt as if I had already been swallowed and was slowly being digested and absorbed.

We saw precious little sign of big animals that first day. Evening met us at an old pygmy hunting camp on a steep hillside above a clear stream, where we bathed and drank quart after quart of water. Pygmy huts are domes roughly the size of a doghouse, made of woven branches with broad leaves laid over them. Although an entire pygmy family will squeeze into a single such hut, I could not find room to stretch out in any of them and so slept again in my dome tent with Thompson and Mike. The pygmies curled near the fire, keeping far enough back to avoid its heat, while the night animals called to each other.

The second day was easier. My body had decided to match the pace after all. Better yet, the pygmies began to encounter more jungle groceries. That meant more rest stops; because at the first hint of wild food, the pygmies threw off their improvised manioc-flour-sack packs and went racing off after it, and Mike knew better than to try and stop them. The flight of bee squadrons led to honey, which had to be chopped free of a tree cavity up in the branches with machetes. Faint trails would lead to the underground burrow system of a giant forest rat. One man was stationed at each exit hole with a club or machete while another probed into the burrows with a long stick until the rodent panicked and tried to flee. Wham. Back to the transect. Porcupine trails led to fallen logs that were also probed and pounded until the animal emerged. Wham. To the transect again. In between, there were mushrooms and *coco* leaves (*Gnetum africanus*, a gymnosperm unrelated to cacao or chocolate but laden with protein) to be gathered.

Sign of larger animals picked up as well. We saw several elephant dung piles and trails, though none were as fresh as the evidence of gorilla feeding we noted. Until midday, we shared the feeling that we were about to come into megafauna territory now that we were pushing deeper and deeper toward the core of this tract of forest. But by afternoon, we saw that the elephant sign was no fresher and no more abundant than before. Even duiker sign had peaked out at an impoverished level. More telling yet, bounties of fruit—gambeya, *Treculia*, *Balanites*, various Irvingiacea—lay in putrefying heaps beneath the trees, unhandled, undispersed, writhing with ants.

We came upon a large pygmy camp with poles for hanging and skinning game, racks for smoking the meat, storage huts, and scattered shotgun shell casings. "You've seen our guys in action. They don't miss a single rat. Pretty damn hard for them to miss elephant sign," Mike said. "Now imagine thirty of them camped here hunting steadily for two months with a villager directing them. They can clean the place out. French and Lebanese timber companies have built roads to the opposite side of the forest, where we're headed, and what used to be a four-day trip to Bangui is now a matter of hours. This place is already getting stripped to supply markets there, and they're planning to go ahead and extend the logging all through the area we've been surveying. I don't see much future for elephants here, do you?"

That night, we camped where dark overtook us. I was badly

dehydrated again, and everyone was thirsty, as we had failed to find the stream that the map indicated we should have crossed by now. Mike said something to Mbutu, and the pygmies disappeared into the night with water containers. They returned with all of them full, having extracted the water from a vine in the grape family whose enlarged transport vessels held quantities of it. "They also know a couple of different trees in the fig family to use for water," Mike informed me. "They cut the aerial roots and sharpen them to a point and let that drip into a container overnight." We dined on giant forest rat and manioc, our staple, drowned in a gravy of *coco* leaves and peanut butter. The pygmies also had grouselike francolin meat and hard-boiled eggs. One of them had clubbed the bird, gathering up her body and the eggs she was incubating, almost without breaking stride.

Though a stronger hiker than I, Thompson was suffering constantly from an accumulation of insect bites and footworms. His body reacted violently to the attacks, swelling into welts, rashes, and suppurating wounds, as if his overloaded immune system was gyrating out of control. It was hard to find a normal-looking patch of skin on his body. On his cheek was an especially angry blot of rash that Mike thought might have come from being brushed by the wing of a particular moth. "They're toxic," he told us. "A guy I know had one fly into his eye around the campfire. That eye of his turned into a real mess." Looking across the fire, I found myself staring into the milk-white eye of one of the porters. His problem was river blindness, a common affliction caused by worms. He was convinced the cause was witchcraft. He never ate the mushrooms his companions gathered. They looked too much like his pale, ruined eye, and he feared they would turn his good eye the same way.

My worst scare had come one night when I began rubbing my eyes and brow to mop off sweat and felt a stinging, burning sensation. The harder I rubbed them, the worse they stung, and it became difficult to see. Before long, half my face was on fire, and I was growing a little panicky, until my companions pointed out that I had been cutting up dried chili peppers for dinner. Hot ones. All I'd been doing was transferring capsicum, the active ingredient, from my hands to my face while wondering which virulent little jungle organism had gotten hold of me this time. I laughed and looked up to see a single star showing through the trees, wondered at it, and laughed some more, the perfect example of a happy idiot.

On day three, we awoke, as usual, to the hum of hundreds upon hundreds of bees. Drawn by scents of food and perspiration, they coated our campsite like a yellow film. These were African killer bees, whose aggressive behavior, sensationalized by the press, was something they exhibited mainly in defense of their hives. Around camp, they were merely a nuisance, unless, like Screwy Louie, the occasional sting was enough to send you into anaphylactic shock. How Louie survived was beyond me. Even after I learned to move very slowly; to dress only after shaking each shoe, pant leg, and sleeve; never to reach into a food bag without first giving the bees foraging there time to escape, I still couldn't avoid the occasional mistake. Just wiping a brow or taking a bite of food without forethought would lead to a sting.

All morning, we passed through the innermost sanctum of this forest. Still, we encountered no fresh elephant sign and only sporadic, weathered evidence of gorillas, and still the fruits lay rotting beneath the trees. This land was being emptied of all animal life that was large, dappled, striped, curious, thoughtful, and kindred. By afternoon, Mike snipped loose his last transect string for the day. We moved from our straight-line route onto footpaths through the forest. Originally kept open by elephants, they now looked maintained by human feet. Bright-red plastic casings from shotgun shells used to bring down monkeys showed up at shorter and shorter intervals along the trail. Many of them marked cable snares tied to bent saplings off to one side. Several trap sites held signs of recent struggles, with the leaves all scraped away and the bare earth scored by the small, pointed hooves of duikers. One of the pygmy porters got caught in a snare laid across the trail and disguised beneath tamped dirt. We encountered a pygmy woman with a nursing baby and a long-handled, spoon-shaped instrument for digging up starchy tubers. Her husband joined her. He wore only a loincloth, and he carried a well-worn crossbow and a charm on his wrist for good luck in his use of the weapon.

The family directed us to their camp, and we arrived in late afternoon. The camp was fairly large and wonderfully situated on the edge of a broad clearing that was a mixture of sandy meadow and marsh. Breezes blew through this piece of savanna. Breezes! I sat with my eyes shut, savoring the wind, while Mike and Alfred spoke with the pygmies. They were mostly women and children and old men. Some of the children's toes were badly deformed by chigoes, parasitic insects that lay eggs under the toenails and in cracks in the skin. Their populations seem to build up to problem levels wherever campsites remain occupied for a long period. All the younger men were off hunting, the camp-tenders said. What were they hunting? Elephants.

They explained that of all the elephants that once lived in the forest, only five or six remained, and they had been using this place, feeding in palm groves at the edge of the marsh. The pygmies had been taking palms from the same groves to make wine. A villager had come and given the pygmies a gun. They had wounded an animal, and now they were tracking it. No one knew when they would be back. The villager would be angry if the bullets for his big gun had been wasted, for they were very expensive.

The stream we had been seeking trickled past one end of the savanna into a pool. The direct afternoon sun felt overpowering after the jungle shade, and the short, burning hike to the pool made the plunge into its water all the more delicious. We and the pygmies and the villager whooped and washed ourselves, then our clothes, and then simply lay in the water, unwilling to do anything more.

"Well, boys," Mike said after a while, "we finally found where the elephants are."

"Yeah," I said. "We've been going through jungle most people would consider as wild as it gets. And it *looks* as wild as it gets. It's pure, uncut, unsettled rainforest, and it doesn't have an elephant left in it. Amazing."

"It is amazing," Mike agreed. We floated in silence for some time before he spoke again. "You know, I'm a fanatic fly fisherman. That got me into entomology, and entomology drew me into other fields of science. I already knew I was going to be a scientist. I knew back when I was seven or eight years old. In Pasadena, California. I remember breathing that California smog and my chest hurting like hell one day, and I decided then and there that I was going to be outdoors all my life. Way outdoors. Here I am." He shook his head and sank lower in the water. "And we're going to lose this, too. Yes, indeed, it's amazing. We've actually succeeded in destroying the earth in barely half a century without really trying."

"How am I ever going to write this story?" I said. "I don't even know what it's about anymore, except seeing things disappear. Maybe I'll turn in a story with one sentence: Forget it, the elephants are screwed. The title will be . . . what? 'Here at the End of the World'?"

"How about 'I Was a Pygmy Love Slave in Mike Fay's Jungle Hell Camp'?" Thompson offered.

" 'The True Tale of the Transect: Fay Can't Find Crap.' "

"How about 'Researcher Sought in Murder of Two Useless Journalists at Remote Jungle Campsite'?"

Through much of the night, the pygmies sang, played a lyre-like instrument and another with a small keyboard of metal prongs, and danced beneath the soft moonlight. The next morning, Fay did find crap—fairly fresh elephant dung and tracks along with it after an elderly pygmy led us to the palm groves through a light, hot mist. Later in the morning, the hunters returned, and a villager emerged from the forest. He went into a pygmy hut and returned carrying a large-caliber rifle, 9.3-millimeter. Anger clouded his face, and I thought the situation might get tense in a hurry. As it turned out, he was suspicious of us, but his wrath was directed toward the pygmies. They had shot all seven bullets he had left with them, wounded three different elephants, and failed to recover any despite tracking one for three days.

"A couple of things pygmies aren't very good at sometimes,"

Mike said quietly while we watched the scene unfold at the camp. "One is tracking gorillas when they're stoned on marijuana. They think they're great, but they're lousy. Number two is shooting big guns. A lot of them just can't handle the things." After wandering back and forth for some time, the villager strode away down the savanna and out of view. Alfred, the villager who had accompanied us, mentioned that he himself had been planning to come here and hunt these last elephants but had changed his mind when we arrived and decided to go with us. Now he was glad of his choice, for at least he was sure to earn some money from this trip. Usually, he said, he went to Bayanga to hunt elephants.

Mike had been cagey about explaining exactly what he was doing, emphasizing his role as a scientist while downplaying any connections with officialdom and game conservation. That was perhaps why we never tangled with the gun-toting villager, and it was part of why Alfred spoke so freely. A more telling reason is that poaching was so open in this part of the world that no one bothered to conceal it anyway.

Toward noon, we traipsed off toward a village quite a few miles distant, following a series of sandy savanna clearings. Buffalo tracks crossed the path at intervals, scores of them. Elsewhere, clumps of bushes related to the pawpaw grew from the sand, and we gorged on the ripening fruits. In the heat of the afternoon, we approached a solitary hut in the center of a long, shimmering savanna. Outside the hut was a rack for drying buffalo meat. The hut itself was aswarm with insects of every description, and lying against one wall in the shade was a man, as small and wizened a pygmy as I had yet seen. His legs were like strips of biltong, or jerked meat, and his eyes seemed to gaze past us into the vacant white sky. Covered with flies and bees, he remained silent while we poked briefly around the camp and continued on.

"I feel like we just arrived from the starship *Enterprise*," Mike said.

I had been feeling almost exactly the same thing, thinking that I could not remember a scene quite so terminal and forlorn. A mile or so afterward, we saw a square, bulky object ahead on the sand among the scattered grasses. It was Mike's backpack.

"Hmmmm, and what do you make of this, Spock?"

I shook my head, but Mike pieced together the mystery. One of the pygmies had learned that there was palm wine to be had somewhere nearby and passed the word. The pygmy carrying Mike's pack had dropped it at once and run off for his share.

"At least some of this planet's inhabitants seem to be highly active," I noted.

"He'll be back for the pack," Mike shrugged, and we trudged on. Evening found us and the pygmies soaking in water again. The stream was wide, stained with tannin to a color like black pearl, sandy-bottomed, with a solid current, and women gathered to wash manioc in the side pools. At nightfall, we were pitching my tent next to the headman's house in a village where people strode up and down through the central courtyard shouting their opinions about the shooting of someone across the river.

We were not far from the new logging area. Mike said he had seen a map in the Republic of Congo showing a grid of projected logging roads for timber concessions sold to foreign corporations. They covered the better part of the country's rain-forests. Similar plans were being laid in portions of Cameroon. And Gabon, where new roads for oil development were already pushing farther into the backcountry. Gabon, the stronghold of tens of thousands of forest elephants, was where the director of wildlife and forests was recently busted as part of an international ivory poaching ring that involved Senegalese and Vietnamese with French citizenship. The killing was becoming multinational, like other forms of economic exploitation. This was not sustained development. It was much the same old pattern of foreign powers plundering raw materials from Africa's interior. True, the governments stood to make something in the short term from auctioning off their resources wholesale. Yet the serious money, what economists would call the value-added profit, gained from processing the materials and selling the finished products, was being made, as ever, outside the continent.

Suppose Africa's *cyclotis* all but vanished in the process, I reflected. The rainforest wasn't going to fall apart. It wasn't even going to change dramatically right away, despite the many effects elephants have upon species structure and distribution. Hardly anyone knew what these were anyway. Who, then, but a score of experts like Mike—and the pygmies, of course— would ever notice the subtle declines in various trees or obscure monocots? A change in the density of gorillas and duikers? These and other life forms would gradually become a little less than they were before, unperceived and unmourned. Only after many generations would the forest itself begin to disintegrate enough to reveal gaps obvious to all.

But by then it will hardly matter, for chances are that the jungle in question will no longer exist. All the computer projections based upon current rates of removal indicate that the globe's last major tracts of rainforest will be entirely gone within the next century, the majority of them within the next half-century. At the moment, less than 3 percent of Africa's equatorial forest habitat is protected in reserves. Most of those are quite small and already have problems with illegal logging and poachers.

I turned onto my side in the tent and whispered, "Mike, you awake?"

"Mmmmm. What's up?"

"I sure hope the Dzanga-Sangha project holds up. I just figured out how important it is. Good work."

"I'll second that," Thompson muttered. "Now can we go to sleep?"

The next day brought a blow-out hike of some twenty-seven miles back through the forest to Bambio, running transects again. We found less animal sign and more shotgun shells and snares. For the last ten miles, I entertained myself by wondering what a gorilla did when it found itself alone without any other gorillas in the countryside. I wondered what it was like to eat chimpanzees and gorillas, as many people did in these parts, and if you ate something for breakfast that was 98 percent human in terms of DNA, did that make it any easier to contemplate having a human for dinner? The youngest pygmy's knee gave out toward the end. He limped behind my flashlight into the village late at night, and that was the end of our rumble through the jungle. To return to Bangui, we had to bash Mike's Toyota along a rarely used, overgrown cart trail in order to avoid the bandits on the main road. Once we finally struck a larger road, we hid Mbutu beneath a tarp to smuggle him past a drunken cop at a checkpoint. Mike didn't want to hear "You got a permit for that pygmy?" again, and he needed Mbutu's help surveying an area farther east.

In Bangui, people tended to treat Mbutu as, at best, a second-class citizen. We took him to dinner at the fanciest French hotel we could find. We considered having Mbutu call the snobbish African waiter over and send the wine back, saying that he found the bouquet of this vintage a bit presumptuous, but decided that would be carrying our little fit of spitefulness against pygmy discrimination too far. This being the tallest building in Bangui, we went up to the thirteenth floor for a view of the city. Mbutu had been fairly high up before in trees, but he was uncomfortable the whole time we were up on the top floor. Even when walking on solid concrete steps, he trod as though he suspected the whole affair might snap off and tumble away at any moment. His high, soft laugh grew higher and softer and finally stopped. So we retired to my room and drank beer while Mbutu told stories. I stepped with him out onto the balcony. He seemed more relaxed at this altitude, about halfway up the building, and was adjusting to his new environment quite quickly. He leaned out to look, with his arms resting on the railing. I leaned out next to him, and together we watched the Ubangui River flow by in the moonlight.

🝰🝰🝰🝰🝰🝰🝰🝰🝰🝰🝰🝰

On the outskirts of Bangui stood a series of low, mud-brick houses with tin roofs from which issued steady hammering sounds. In some, women were pounding manioc. In the others, artisans were carving ivory tusks. In an adjoining shed, workers polished the finished products with abrasive leaves from the umbrella tree. Others stained the carvings a rich nut brown by boiling them in an extract of chicory. They were small tusks and small carvings, of crocodiles and women's faces, one like the next, and none of them especially well done.

The tusks averaged ten to twelve kilos, the owner of the business, Jean Ngbodjourou, told me. Small size was a problem for making decent sculptures, he said. More than half the ivory might be lost from a ten-kilo tusk in the working of some pieces. The most one could do with the fragments was salvage a few to make little ivory blocks for resting knives upon at the dinner table. Many of the tusks I saw being chiseled and rasped were only between one and two kilos to begin with; they appeared to have come from elephants barely past the age of nursing.

"Big tusks are few, and they go directly to collectors. The ones we can get are smaller every year," Jean complained. "We will have to turn more and more to wood, but there is not as much market for that." He was right, although I knew that ebony, also poached throughout Africa, had become scarce enough that it was selling for up to U.S. $300 per kilo abroad, nearly as high as premium tusks. Jean obtained his ivory from . . . private people, he said. And from the Department of Water and Forests. All from elephants taken in control actions, of course. His brother happened to be the *chef de cantonnement*, or district head, at Bayanga—an important man, I knew, and the owner of an important gun. In any event, Jean's supply was clearly drying up. Several of his carvers were working with wart hog tusks and hippopotamus teeth instead of elephant tusks.

Elephant tusks of less than ten kilos were not supposed to be traded. However, any piece, no matter how small, was legal as long as it was worked ivory. In fact, if the finished product weighed under one kilo, so much the better, since it did not require a CITES permit for export. I could not prove that the tiny tusks I saw were not simply the tips of larger, legal ones. The similarity between the two made the restriction on trading tusks of less than ten kilos all but impossible to enforce—even if someone were to bother trying. The majority of Jean's output went to a French colonel. I don't know how the colonel transported it, but impressive quantities of ivory passed from the C.A.R. to France on military transport planes, thereby avoiding such nuisances as duty and customs. Almost every returning soldier, advisor, businessman, and casual visitor went home with at least a statuette and a few additional ivory baubles and charms. In the ivory shops were bracelets, earrings, chess sets, crucifixes, and large and small carvings of women, pygmy hunters, madonnas, hippos, crocodiles, rhinos, elephants, and fruits.

Jean worked a ton of ivory annually. If his tusks really averaged ten kilos, that represented only 100 tusks, or 56 elephants (using the formula of 1.8 tusks per animal). But if his tusks averaged two kilos, as I thought they did, that represented nearly 500 tusks, or 278 elephants. And there were at least a dozen such shops still operating in the capital and more in outlying towns. Never mind the lucrative export of prime uncarved tusks. I could easily account for several thousand elephants each year felled for nothing more than hastily crafted figurines and baubles. Put another way, soft sales of ivory—the casual market for gee-gaws—alone was enough to keep driving the residual elephant population of the C.A.R. toward oblivion. Architects of the emerald realm, dispersers of bounty, the giants would be dribbled away in trinkets.

Another day in Bangui, I paid a call upon Alassan Garba, a Muslim ivory merchant. A huge man, he suffered painfully from gout. He received us while lying upon a couch in his parlor, surrounded by sculptures and ivory veneer mosaics representing a choice selection from his twenty years in the ivory trade, which began in the Republic of Congo. Several sculptures were so massive that I found it difficult to believe tusks of such thickness ever existed. He also sold ivory carved and highly polished to yield gleaming penises, a favorite among the French military.

But Alassan also complained of the difficulty of obtaining ivory of decent size these days. For what he did get, Alassan paid around U.S. $33 per kilo. Money could still be made in this business, but the big money, he said, was being cornered by the agents who shipped raw tusks straight to collectors and major international players.

Before departing the C.A.R., Thompson and I made careful arrangements through various officials to be certain we would have no trouble hand-carrying Thompson's film through customs. In keeping with the character of the trip, the man engaged to assist us took us almost as far as he could through the departure process, but then completely disappeared, and everything went spinning rapidly down toward an abysmal level of customs hell. We were soon locked in a screaming match with a security guard. He won. I am at a disadvantage when I try to think fast in French. Besides, he had the machine gun. The French overseer of the customs gate was worse than unsympathetic as I told him why Thompson's hard-won film should not be subjected to X-rays from antiquated equipment. He waved us off.

I rounded up someone from the crowd milling behind the customs barrier who could plead our case in better French. But that didn't help either. The machine gun–slinger pointed his muzzle at the film and then the X-ray machine and said, "It goes in there or you stay here. I will not tell you again." To stay in Bangui and try to arrange clearance again meant days or possibly weeks. Finally, Thompson, who was thinking more clearly than I, decided upon an end run around the devils of customs hell. After stuffing as many of his precious cameras as possible in my bags for me to haul through, he sprinted off to ship his film with the regular luggage at the last minute. It was risky, for luggage disappears forever on the best of airlines; a photographer friend lost six months' worth of work in Antarctica shipping his film that way. Thompson had to disperse liberal bribes to get someone to run out and load his package with the rest of the luggage. But at least he knew it was getting on the right plane at the outset.

A blur of hours and time zones later, we were in England, utterly astounded that the people with whom we dealt were actually trying to be polite and helpful. Several weeks after that, at his home in Seattle, Thompson went down with cerebral malaria. At the hospital, the doctors told him that he might not have survived if he had arrived a few hours later. Considering all the other places we had been, I thought he timed the whole thing extremely well.

SEVEN

JAPAN

ON MY WAY HOME from the Central African Republic in early June of 1989, I stopped in Washington, D.C., to meet with my editor at the National Geographic Society. I was asked to attend a meeting of the upper-level staff and brief them on the status of the elephant, which I did. Fresh from several months in the field, I offered what I thought was the very latest information. As soon as I finished, one editor said, "I guess you haven't heard," and handed me a newspaper clipping from the previous day. It was an announcement that the United States was banning further ivory imports and that the European Economic Community was expected to follow suit shortly. For the first time, I began to hope that the story of elephants might become more than a chronicle of ruin.

Apparently, the continuous stream of news reports about elephant poaching had finally begun to affect the political sphere. Demonstrations had helped as well. In both the United States and Europe, protesters had disrupted ivory sales at department stores. In Paris, a band called Robin des Bois (Robin Hood) dressed in papier-mâché elephant masks and trumpeted through the boulevards tusking shoppers at bijouteries selling ivory. "Robin Hood did not always act legally, but he always acted legitimately," noted cofounder Marlene Kanas, as the group repeatedly padlocked the door of one ivory dealer. Another French group, Amnestie Pour Les Elephants, pursued a strong anti-ivory campaign.

If one particular piece of publicity could be credited with helping to overturn the status quo, it would be the advertisement placed in major newspapers and national magazines by the

African Wildlife Foundation. The ad featured a photograph of an elephant kneeling as if resting on the ground with its head slightly turned so that one eye met the viewer. It was more or less a face-on portrait. The catch was that this elephant had no face. That had been ripped off, leaving white lumps of gristle amid tattered membranes. The animal was not resting but dead. The image was plainly in poor taste. Its message was that to wear part of such a creature's face as an ornament was not very classy either.

Not many consumers had given much thought to where the ivory they purchased came from. Hardly any realized that 80 to 90 percent of all the ivory sold in recent years, even in the most strenuously "tasteful" fashion stores, came from poached elephants. Some people assumed African villagers picked up old tusks they found lying around. A surprising percentage of the public wasn't exactly sure what ivory was in the first place. Many imagined the substance to be some sort of mineral mined from the earth, like jade. Others thought of it as something that literally grew on trees, confusing elephant teeth with material such as the extremely hard, white product made from the nut of the South American plant *Phytelephas macrocarpa*, sometimes marketed as "vegetable ivory." Still others simply thought ivory was a type of tree, like ebony. After the African Wildlife Foundation ad, however, it was not so easy to avoid the association between buying, selling, or wearing ivory and stealing elephants' faces.

As forecast, Europe's Economic Community did follow the United States in banning most further ivory imports. Now the critical question became what Japan would do.

In August of 1989, having discovered that a taxi from Narita Airport to downtown Tokyo could cost upward of U.S. $250, I was rolling along the freeway on a bus, peering out the window at mile upon mile of unliving scenery. There were individual structures—factories and apartment complexes topped by billboards, antennas, and mesh-enclosed golf driving ranges—but it was basically continuous concrete strata out there in equally grey air. Suddenly, amid the dullness, a swale of bright green: a rice paddy, also shaped by people, but nonetheless soft and vibrant. Farmers trying to preserve such plots had been fighting for years against expansion of Narita Airport, I recalled. And I wondered whether any would sympathize with the last elephants in patches of green forest falling before the chain saw, Japan being the major consumer of the world's tropical hardwoods.

The few scattered rice fields were quickly replaced by paved, inanimate landscapes again. Gradually, the buildings became more massive, taller, capped by larger and flashier billboards—more adamant. The smog and traffic congealed. Crowds thickened on the sidewalks. I was nearing the center of Tokyo, an inconceivably dense creation of steel and glass embedded in still more concrete. Part mall, part hive, it also struck me at moments as a vast mausoleum despite all the commotion and neon trappings. It wasn't just that the pervasive acrid, grey air seemed to wash the life from everything. It was my knowledge that this was the core of the island where seven out of every ten elephant tusks in the world had lately arrived. I had reached the elephants' graveyard. Marking the mood off as another mixture of jet lag and farewell-to-Montana culture shock, I shuffled into a hotel in search of a good bed. Even as I did, some forty tons of ivory from Hong Kong were being held up at customs, suspected of having illegal origins.

Unlike Hong Kong, Japan was at least making an effort to comply with international ivory-trading regulations these days. It had also agreed to limit its total ivory import to no more than 100 tons that year, down from 132 tons the previous year, the bulk of it coming from Hong Kong and the rest mainly from Belgium and Singapore. On June 19, 1989, Japan had followed the lead of the United States and Europe in banning the import of all processed ivory and ivory scraps, along with ivory from any country that had not joined the 103 member nations of CITES (Convention on International Trade in Endangered Species). Now the Japanese government was even talking of going beyond this to a total ban on all ivory imports. Europe had been contemplating the same move, and on August 18, the twelve-member European Economic Community announced that it was doing so. I was still just beginning to explore Tokyo that day, but I had learned something important: retail sales of ivory jewelry and statuary in Japan were already beginning to slow. Granted, this was partly because the price had become so exorbitant. But it was partly due to a growing awareness that the market for elephant tusks might be coming to an end.

Might be. On the other hand, I wouldn't have wanted to bet money on the possibility. Not given Japan's notorious defiance of world opinion by continuing to slaughter the only intelligent mammals greater than elephants—the whales—in order to subsidize an obsolete industry. The nation's various ivory manufacturers had joined together in trying to convince the government to simply cut back on the import of elephant incisors rather than cut off the flow completely. After all, their lobbyists were saying, some 30,000 Japanese depended upon the ivory industry for employment. A more thorough look quickly revealed that Japan had eighty companies with 600 employees directly involved in the business of carving or otherwise processing ivory. The other 29,400 "ivory workers" were clerks and salespeople in retail stores and import-export companies, nearly all of whom dealt with other materials as well. For example, a sales clerk in the jewelry section at a department store was included in the total if she handled an ivory bracelet or a pair of ivory earrings once in a while.

After time-consuming and rather delicate negotiations, the government-sponsored foreign press agency introduced me to officials in the ivory industry. Those gentlemen immediately presented me with a handsome color brochure entitled "Keep Ivory Legal" and a video, both showing the traditional use of ivory for carving and in association with musical instruments. The information implied that the venerable Japanese culture would all but disintegrate should ivory be banned.

On the video, nearly 100 musicians in black kimonos settled

themselves with dignity upon a stage and coaxed rich sounds from the bowl-bottomed stringed instrument known as the *shamisen*, a fretless lute. Strumming is done with a large plectrum, or pick—a very large one, called a *baachi*. Different *baachis* generate different qualities of sound. The best results come from those made of ivory, carved from a single large tusk. No ivory *baachi*, no pure, clear *shamisen* sound. No such *shamisen* sound, no traditional puppet theater. No Kabuki dramas. No living link to the past. Well, none of these things would be quite the same, insisted the narrator.

The video continued with someone playing the *biwa*, another stringed instrument, this one with frets. The frets are made of ivory, again supposedly because no other material produces such a beautiful tonal quality. Then came shots of *ganio*, a pigment containing ivory mixed with other minerals that is used to create the lucid white in certain Japanese wood-block prints. "Art can only be made by understanding the spirit of nature—becoming one with nature," the narrator was saying. He went on to conclude that we must save the legacies of culture and nature together.

It was pretty good stuff. Naturally, not a single scuff mark from one fallen elephant had made it onto the screen or into the brochure. I asked what the ivory dealers were doing to save the legacies of nature. Specifically, what were they doing to help preserve the great beasts that provide ivory, the apparent mainstay of so much Japanese culture? They replied that they had agreed to a self-imposed tax upon ivory imports. From funds raised by that tax, they had contributed $130,000 to CITES over the past three years. Moreover, they planned to donate another $10,000 to some conservation group that year.

Never mind that CITES was widely viewed as more representative of wildlife traders' interests than of wildlife to begin with. Never mind that $10,000—for Japan's eighty ivory companies, that works out to $125 each—was less than a pittance compared to the windfall profits they had made as the price of ivory went ballistic. Never mind that these same dealers were going to spend $142,000 in 1989 on pro-ivory "propaganda," as

Tamotsu Ishibashi, senior managing director of the Tokyo Ivory Arts and Crafts Cooperative, openly described it to me. Never mind that for years, while the average tusk brought in was becoming too small even to produce proper sizes of the *baachi* said to be vital to *shamisen* playing and related traditional art forms, the contribution toward elephant conservation from this end was zero. And never mind that when I asked what *baachis* were made of before ivory came into more widespread use, Ishibashi-san shrugged and replied, "Wood," and then shrugged again, knowing he had as much as admitted that wood had a longer tradition behind it than ivory did. Prior to the Edo Period (1603–1867), ivory actually had little place in Japanese society. Still, I found the arguments in favor of carrying on ivory carving compelling, for there is no question but that Japan has produced some of the finest pieces of sculpture in the world using the unique medium of elephant incisors.

Carvers from China, Southeast Asia, and India would surely contest the point, but their most elaborate creations can seldom match the achievements of Japan's ivory sculptors. At least, this is the opinion of many collectors. From what I have seen—and that includes a block of ivory carved by Chinese workers into twenty-seven lacelike balls, each imprisoned within the next larger one; and a screen, or jali, of wood and inlaid ivory that took an Indian father-son team more than a decade to complete—I would agree. Japanese ivory carving is in a class by itself. Their more refined and expressive, individual approach transcends artisanry to yield true, moving works of art.

After viewing the statuary made from ivory in the National Museum, I stood for hours in commercial establishments such as the Murasaki Gallery, Tokyo's oldest ivory carving gallery, savoring modern carvers' perfectly rendered ivory figurines of such subjects as courtesans, samurai, and the seven Oriental gods of luck. My favorite among those deities is Fukurokuju, whose huge, domed head reminds me of an Indian elephant. Originally a star god in China, he evolved into the Japanese god of riches, happiness, and longevity, with the power to raise the dead. In any good display, he and his companions stand near open jars of water on the shelves. In this gallery, the owner ran a humidifier that kept the whole room moist as well. Otherwise the ivory might dry and crack over time. For now, it remained flawlessly smooth and white as a geisha's powdered face, its inner glow almost like that of living flesh.

For many connoisseurs, the very finest and most sophisticated carved pieces are not the realistic statues but small, round ornaments with a hole in the center known as *netsuke*. Kimonos lack pockets; folks wearing them therefore had to stuff personal effects in the voluminous sleeves, the breast folds, or else the sash around the waist. Small, heavy, or easily spilled things presented a problem. The solution was to place them in a pouch, or *inro*, and hang that from the sash. In the old days, the pouch would have been leather and held flint and tinder. Later *inro* were silken purses containing a pipe and tobacco, along with perhaps a few medicines and other essential items. To keep the string holding the pouch from slipping off the sash, a toggle—the *netsuke*—was put on the end. Over the centuries, the preferred type changed from metal rings to thicker, more ornamented hoops. Finally, the toggle became a solid piece, often richly worked, yet still always smooth and rounded to keep from fraying the kimono's outer lining or tangling in its folds.

The practice of carrying *inro* developed during the fifteenth century and became widely popular among privileged classes around the end of the sixteenth century. By the Edo Period, both *netsuke* and *inro* had become fashion statements in themselves and the making of them a distinct art form. The *netsuke* in particular had to be not just splendidly carved but clever—smart, declaring a certain style and wit. Or embody the classical virtues of *wabi* (serenity) and *sabi* (elegant simplicity). Or be somehow clever and Zen-calm at once. Whatever the case, the old kimono sash toggles were obviously taking on levels of meaning infinitely beyond holding a pouch in place. They were prized possessions, speaking volumes about the owner's status and sensibilities. In the end, they might not be worn at all, only displayed. Yet they always retained the round or oval form plus the hole in the center for the string. It became a challenge for artists to incorporate these elements effortlessly into their design.

Throughout the Edo Period, Japan remained largely closed to

the West. Only the Dutch were permitted to trade in the country. They acquired a fair amount of ivory artwork and were really starting to load up on *netsuke* as the period came to an end. Once Japan opened its ports to all during the latter half of the nineteenth century, Western fashions supplanted kimonos, with the result that *inro* and *netsuke* became obsolete. At the same time, however, the popularity of *netsuke* was spreading rapidly among Western collectors. This proved most fortunate for Japan, which found itself with relatively few goods for export to gain foreign currency. Along with lacquerware and ceramics, *netsuke* helped put the island nation on a better trade footing. Pound for pound, these ivory pouch-holders fetched far higher prices than any other product. Japan exported huge quantities of them to the United States and Europe, which is where the majority of antique *netsuke* can be found today.

Tom Milliken, director of the Japan office of TRAFFIC (Trade Records Analysis of Flora and Fauna in Commerce), a division of the World Wildlife Fund, helped me immeasurably in following the various channels of the ivory trade in his adopted country. After providing introductions to key people, he freed assistant director Hideomi Tokunaga from his regular tasks to direct me to factories, shops, and offices. Once at a destination, Tokunaga-san continued to show the way, guiding me through discussions of sensitive subjects while translating, according respect where it was due, saving face when I overstepped invisible lines of protocol, and generally doing everything he could to make things scrutable. Without his self-effacing, mannerly presence, I doubt some of the older people with whom we spoke would have proved half so forthcoming around a foreigner.

An hour's trip by subway and train one afternoon brought us to a tile-roofed house in the suburbs with a garden to one side. Wasps were hunting insects trapped in spiders' webs among the petals, and goldfish swam among lilies in small, aerated pots. Shelf upon shelf of bonsai trees ringed the patio by the back door. Nature. Compressed and sculpted until it had become mostly symbolic, like the *netsuke*, but still nature. And still a refreshment for the spirit, parched for a bit of green after traipsing around central Tokyo. Projecting from another side of the house was a room with many windows, and inside, bathed in the day's light, were a workbench, tools, and blocks of ivory. This was the home of sculptor Maranosuke Okazaki, whose rather large, kindly face met us at the door. He had moved here ten years earlier, he said, to escape the rising costs of living at his old place in Tokyo proper, where the tall buildings that had risen on all sides obliged him to work in the shade even at midday.

Okazaki-san—or, more properly, Okazaki-sensei, denoting master—goes by the professional, or artist's, name of Koetsu. *Ko* is from a Chinese character meaning courtesy to parents; all this man's ancestors and carvers of the same school used the *ko* prefix. *Etsu*, he chose himself, for it comes from a character representing joy or pleasure, and he "works to create pleasure for people who appreciate ivory," he told me. He hastened to add, "I would like to continue ivory carving. As this is my life's work, I am most concerned for the future of the elephants." We were in his living room sipping tea while snacking on an assortment of sushi. The face of the clock on the wall consisted of numerals on a plasticized photograph of a family of elephants. Koetsu showed me the elephant-hide belt he wore around his ample girth and produced a business card from a wallet of snakeskin. I believe he considered these signs of his interest in the natural world.

Koetsu was born in 1935. His father was a famed ivory carver. Koetsu's elder brother followed in the father's footsteps. At the age of about twelve, Koetsu, too, began to learn carving, attracted to ivory by its smell and, still more, by its touch. "Ivory feels smooth and has a warmness that makes it become one temperature with your hand when you hold it," he informed me. "That is why the heads of stethoscopes used to be made of ivory. Ivory also gives a balanced heaviness. Not too light, like wood; not too heavy, like metal. A good heaviness. This quality is especially important with *netsuke*."

Since childhood, Koetsu had nurtured bonsai trees, a hobby usually favored by older people. He also became interested in painting. By the age of fifteen, he was apprenticed to a master carver while continuing to absorb his father's experience and techniques. "The most important thing an apprentice learns is how to cut the ivory into a basic form—and with as little waste as possible. Later, he learns how to employ progressively smaller chisels to bring out the details," Koetsu said as he shepherded us toward his studio. He had more than a hundred chisels that he had made himself arranged in drawers there. Swinging on an arm above those hand-crafted, palm-worn tools was a shining dentist's drill, a concession to changing times made by almost every sculptor nowadays.

Earlier, Koetsu had shown me a statuette that he described as a mixture of a god and a dragon. Its blend of the sinuous and ornate was spellbinding. Modestly insisting that the piece wasn't very good, Koetsu said he only kept it as a memento of the time during his mid-thirties when he was becoming independent of the influence of his father—"a great favorer of dragons." Now, from the workbench, Koetsu picked up a nearly completed *netsuke* and held it out for inspection. Its subject was another type of traditional Japanese figure—the *kappa*, or water imp. He had carved a gang of them playing golf, the current Japanese craze.

To finalize his ideas, Koetsu often carved a figure in wood first, but wood is too porous and soft to hold the detail that ivory can. Ceramic, jade, onyx, and other hard materials are too brittle; they might snap or shear under the strain when it comes down to the final intricate slices. "The basic advantage of ivory is its hardness-yet-softness. Its elasticity. This is what enables the carver to make such delicate parts," he explained. Like most ivory sculptors, he favored hard ivory—forest elephant tusks. They hold even greater detail than soft ivory while still retaining enough elasticity to be forgiving.

Koetsu's first love was *netsuke*, followed by conventional sculpture. For a bit of extra income, he occasionally carved accessories, the generic term that includes jewelry—bangles, baubles, and gee-gaws—and miscellaneous items from ear picks to chopstick holders. "My greatest reward is to make original works. To forget about money and just make happiness," he told me. "My greatest sorrow lies in not passing on what I have learned."

Having cut and shaped ivory for more than forty years, Koetsu had gained artistic recognition, financial success, and the current presidency of the Japan Ivory Carvers Association. Yet he had no apprentice, a catastrophic situation for any practitioner of traditional arts and crafts in Japan. "The old way is of teacher to student, then the student becoming a teacher, so that each man has his own stream," he observed, and in his face was an expression like that of someone just informed by a physician that he could never have children.

It takes at least ten years to learn carving. During that time, the apprentice is not paid, his reward being the master's unique knowledge. Along the way, though, the apprentice should be able to begin selling enough of his own simple sculptures and accessories to earn a modest income on the side. As Japan's post–World War II economy recovered and then began to build toward a boom, young people were lured away from traditional callings toward more lucrative jobs. Ironically, there was a greater demand for ivory than ever before as a result of the same economic boom, but it became so insatiable that it spurred a shift to mass production methods.

Some of the principal ivory dealers began to duplicate figurines with mechanical copying devices. (These days, many are driven by computers, and the reproductions are virtually indistinguishable in every detail from the original.) When even that failed to keep up with Japan's craving for ivory, the dealers turned to Hong Kong. Mass-produced accessories and sculptures were soon flooding in from expanded facilities there, and they undercut the salability of works by Japanese apprentices. As a result, fewer young men than ever were seeking to study under the ivory-carving masters. Almost none had come forward for the past several years. Even those who could somehow arrange to finance their apprenticeship foresaw a potential collapse of the ivory art tradition and turned toward vocations with a more promising future. The youngest apprentice ivory sculptor in the nation was in his mid-thirties. The average age of the sixty-one current members of the carvers' association presided over by Koetsu was now more than fifty years, and rising.

Looking at my open notebook, Koetsu spoke for his organization: "Art is important, but nature is more important than art. The elephants must not disappear. If they do, our tradition will also and never come back. I pray there will be total protection of the elephant until poaching is stopped. An effective way to do this is to stop international trade for a while—perhaps even five to ten years—while the herds build back up."

Patiently, Tokunaga-san described the basics of elephant population dynamics to Koetsu. He told the sculptor how females rarely reach maturity before their teens and how they then produce young only at intervals of several years. Elephants have a potential life span of seventy-plus years, yet the average female tusk now came from an animal about twenty-four years old—just hitting her prime, not even middle-aged, Tokunaga-san said. Meanwhile, the average male tusk came from an immature animal no more than eleven years of age. Elephant populations had not only been decimated, explained Tokunaga-san, they had been purged of older, experienced breeding animals.

Koetsu quickly grasped the point. "Ah so. Even ten years will not be enough," he said. He shook his head, then recovered. "We could accept that. We can use existing stocks of tusks and then continue traditional techniques in wood, returning to ivory later, whenever the elephants are safe. Collectors will grow bored with wood carvings. They will buy less. But I will even suffer a loss of business, if only we can have enough interest from collectors to survive and pass on our art to another generation." He stopped and shook his head once more. "The trouble is that many of my colleagues would lose their particular skills for working with ivory after ten years of other materials."

Closer to the heart of the city, Katsutoshi Saito sat cross-legged before the traditional low carver's bench. He was in the final stages of completing a *netsuke*. Having polished it with sandpaper of increasingly fine grade, he switched to a brush of stiff hairs from a horse's tail, then to a cotton cloth impregnated with powdery-fine sand, using a pointed bamboo stick to reach into crevices. As I watched, he spoke of ivory's unique "aero-dynamical form, a smoothness that cannot be brought forth as well in any other material." Finally, he started to rub the ivory by hand, using a powder made from burnt deer antlers. In his opinion, the best powder came from live antlers. He could get them from a temple where the priests cut off a limited quantity from the resident deer each year. Thus, the specialized bone of one species gave the finishing touch to the specialized tooth taken from another species. The result . . . if you can ignore the cost in animals, the result was luminous and sublime.

This *netsuke* contained a beast in metamorphosis—part tiger, part snake, and part monkey, each a creature of power and ca-lamity. Shifting from Japanese to English, Saito-sensei said, "It represents something very bad fortune." Though similar to tra-ditional *netsuke*, all of his subjects are at the same time wholly original outgrowths of his imagination, whose force I could feel. Some of his works writhed within the ivory as if straining to break loose. Others seemed still to be congealing from a dream. Many were marked by a sleek, voluptuous quality, their ivory warmth at once visual and tactile. In another *netsuke*, he had transmuted an ordinary rabbit into something mythic and erotic, a talisman almost too powerful to hold. Then he brought out the sleekest beast yet. "Otter. He always enjoys his life," ob-served Saito-sensei. "He seeks what I call applause for liberty. Adorement of liberty? Hmmm, celebration maybe? I seek the same thing—to take a beautiful abstract form from my brain and give it free expression." He had succeeded. Overall, his carvings were the most dynamic, limit-pushing artworks that I encoun-tered in my travels.

The professional name chosen by Saito-sensei is Bishu. It means beautiful country. Above his carving bench, Bishu had scrawled an exhortation to himself: Make the Line of Beauty. Next to that was a copy of Baudelaire's poem "Chanson de l'Au-tomne." Books on philosophy, art, and culture in several lan-guages hid three of the studio's four walls from floor to ceiling. Bishu cited Brancusi and Cézanne as major influences upon his work. "I have a theory that all nature takes these forms: egg, circle, cylinder," he proclaimed. "When I learned that Cézanne said nature should be treated as round shapes—round cylinder, round ball, and round cone that becomes the oval when you slice across it at an angle—I was so happy, because this is what I had been believing."

Bishu leaped from his tatami mat to snatch a publication from his bookshelf and began to read me passages from a manifesto he had written about *netsuke* for an exhibition: "And the imagination of the viewer must be carried to the sky and to outer space, where the stars are—or, to say it poetically, to create orbit in the palm of your hand." Before long, he was in *netsuke* hyperdrive, pulling out one book after another, telling me how we can use these sculptures in a world of international ideas and communication, modeling not just Japanese culture but the emerging global one. If you assumed, as Bishu did, that the oval *netsuke* represents one of the universe's ideal forms, then you might go on to perceive, as he did, that a *netsuke* is in fact a scaled-down version of the universe itself, a cosmos you can rub with your thumb. After that, it wasn't too hard to follow his train of thought at all.

Bishu chain-smoked menthol cigarettes while alternately carving and expounding ideas. He had a slender body, casually clothed in loose, black pants and a white polo shirt, and an equally youthful face. In a different setting, I might have taken him for a graduate student. He was forty-seven years old. In Japan, that is considered young to serve as leader of an official group of traditional artists; yet Bishu was the current president of the Netsuke Carvers Association. It was a measure of the esteem in which others held this man's talent.

The great-grandfather, grandfather, and father of Bishu were all carvers. He was apprenticed to his father at age fifteen. Three years later, his father fell ill, and Bishu had to assume most of the family carving duties. He believes that being forced to learn quickly for himself accelerated his artistic development. Now he had an apprentice of his own. A rare thing, these days, an apprentice Japanese ivory carver. But then the man was exactly the same age as Bishu.

"While the purpose of my life is to create good *netsuke*, I wish to strengthen my character so that I can carve with joy and tranquility," Bishu told me. "My course is only searching for beauty. In search of beauty is my final direction." Like Koetsu, he knew of no material that could compare with ivory's combination of warmth, strength, and elasticity. But instead of worrying about how ivory skills might be lost if tusks became unavailable, he put the situation this way: "I would need twelve years to make the transition from ivory to wood or some other material. Then I would need two or three years to learn the character of each type of wood. But I would continue without fail." To Make the Line of Beauty. In whatever was at hand.

I had arrived at a sort of moral crossroads, for I was beginning to view Japan's ivory sculptors in the same terms as the elephants themselves: incomparable and in danger of vanishing. At the same time, I was keenly aware that the "we're the real endangered species here" argument was so often invoked by the likes of polluters lobbying against regulation and logging companies trying to get at the last old-growth forest somewhere that it had been rendered almost completely bogus. Nevertheless, I saw a lot of similarity between the need to conserve biological diversity, as epitomized by elephants and their ecological role, and the need to conserve cultural diversity, as represented by traditional Japanese sculptors. Had the video and written propaganda I'd been given influenced my thinking? Not really. But sheer covetousness certainly had. The more I held and contemplated the work of artists such as Bishu, the harder it was to let go. For the first time, I wanted to possess ivory. I wanted those powerful figures and their glow-from-within beauty in my own room, wanted that orbit in the palm of my hand.

In African markets, I had passed thousands of ivory carvings and felt not a flicker of admiration, much less desire. Careless, graceless stuff for the most part, often still bearing the tooth marks of files, those rough curios only made the modern resurgence of ivory fever seem all the more foolish and a pitiful waste. But here in Tokyo, I finally felt for myself what had driven humankind's lust for ivory all those centuries. That alone made the trip worthwhile.

Or so I believed for a few days after visiting the sculptors.

Then confusion took over again. I was missing something—
something fundamental. All of Japan held only about 130 master carvers, so few that most of the 45-odd members of the *netsuke* carvers' group headed by Bishu also belonged to the ivory
carvers' organization of which Koetsu was president. A few
dozen large tusks taken from elephants that died naturally would
have kept the whole bunch supplied for a year, so any elephants-
versus-artists quandary was really beside the point—a nonissue.
Even if you added in journeyman artisans cranking out unin-
spired pieces, sculptures and *netsuke* still only consumed about 3
percent of the raw ivory coming into Japan. Where was the rest?

To find out, I crisscrossed Tokyo, looking through stores large
and small. Considering the hundreds of thousands of tusks that
had been sent to this island, I guess I expected to find evidence
of them stacked everywhere. But the trade in Japan proved surprisingly subtle once you were past the few galleries and expensive showrooms specializing in ivory. In the Shinjuku district of
Tokyo, I visited Isetan, a department store roughly the size of,
oh, Delaware, and found a handful of ivory accessories. The remarkable thing is that there were dozens more stores just like it
on all sides. Some of these places had a few ivory baubles in the
jewelry section as well, maybe a selection of ivory chopsticks in
another department, ivory buttons here, ivory chess sets there,
and so on. Yet the total seemed trivial, scarcely perceptible amid
the supernova of consumer goods and racing cash registers that
is late-twentieth-century Japan.

The mega–department stores graded directly into malls,
which in turn gave way to smaller stores, and, finally, shops
and curbside stands lining even the alleyways that led to the
next complex of colossal department stores. Time and again, I
heard myself say silently: So *this* is where most of the world's
money is circulating. I said it while staring open-mouthed at
$120 gift-wrapped pairs of melons, $1500 off-the-rack suits,
$100 breakfast menus, young people who smiled pleasantly

while requesting $500 per day to serve as interpreters; while fording endless streams of shoppers in the glittering stores, endless crowds of determined-looking businesspeople on the almost spotless and relatively crime-free sidewalks, endless parades of brand-new automobiles on the streets. This is what it must have been like for someone from the so-called Third World to visit a major city in the United States once upon a time, back when we had most of the money. (Not long ago, the value of the area encompassing Tokyo and nearby Yokohama surpassed the combined value of all the real estate in the United States plus the majority of western Europe.)

Eventually, I visited enough places in Tokyo to realize that if you added all the ivory jewelry and other minor accessories in all the stores that sold them, the sum would no longer be trivial. Adding all the stores from other parts of the nation as well, you could account for about 25 percent of Japan's ivory imports. The rest was still missing—until I looked in a quite different section of one department store. There, at a counter displaying pens and other writing materials, I happened upon my first array of *hanko*.

Hanko are personal signature seals, commonly called chops, as in "He agreed to the deal and put his chop on it." Like the word *chop*, *hanko* is something of a slang term. Signature seals also go by the name of *inkan*, *inbou*, or, more formally, *jitsuin*, the common root being *in*, which means seal. *Inro*, the pouch held by *netsuke*, means seal bag, since it was often used to carry one's personal chop. The days of the kimono may have faded, but one thing that has not changed is that written signatures have little meaning in respect to official documents. Bills of sale, other major business and legal contracts, certificates of birth, marriage, and death—none of these are considered valid unless stamped with a personal seal dipped in ink.

Accordingly, each person selects an individualized chop pattern that is then carved onto the head of a *hanko*. The resulting print is registered with a central office, making it the legal mark of that person. Corporations also have distinctive seals and go through the same basic process to obtain and register them.

Hanko may be made of boxwood, ebony, or cheap bamboo; jade, malachite, or common soapstone; buffalo horn, ceramic, or plastic; gold or pot metal; and all manner of other substances, including ivory—from hippopotamuses, walruses, wart hogs, or elephants.

Wood and horn predominated in old Japan, whereas China always favored stone. Sometimes the handle was made of something different than the head, which, ideally, should be hard enough to hold up to repeated use, yet absorbent enough to transfer a proper amount of ink onto paper. Ivory fits the prescription nicely. It was often glued onto a horn or wood shaft. More ivory was occasionally inlaid on the shaft for decoration. Yet *hanko* of solid ivory were not considered especially desirable.

Once elephant teeth became so expensive that they could serve as status symbols, though, seals made of them grew popular among the well-to-do, and Japan's unprecedented economic growth proceeded to make growing numbers of middle class people well-to-do. Beginning in the 1970s, ivory *hanko* became the rage. They were perfect—something you could pull out of a pocket and flash around on important occasions without seeming to call attention to your wealth *too* loudly. Once everybody and his brother were acquiring ivory *hanko*, you could still stand out by opting for one of the thicker, costlier versions. Preferably, it would be made of seamless hard ivory to distinguish it from those cut from less expensive soft ivory, whose crosshatched internal structure is more evident upon close inspection. Miniature etchings or inlays of gold or precious stones added a further touch of prestige value to any *hanko*.

The department store counter where I first noticed *hanko* had both plain and decorated styles on display. When I asked where I might find a still wider assortment, they directed me to a shop that dealt mainly in *hanko* a few streets away. It was called Nita (the family name of the owners) Inbou (seal). Mrs. Yochiko Nita showed me a selection of ivory chops ranging from about $100 to more than $6000. She informed me that the high price of ivory combined with reduced imports had resulted in a return to the style of *hanko* with a buffalo horn handle and an ivory head. Still, she had more solid ivory *hanko* than any other kind. And Japan had something like 11,000 *hanko* shops. Maybe 12,000, counting stationery stores that also carried an array of *hanko*. It didn't matter. The point was that every one of the people in the crowds eating, shopping, and hurrying all around me owned a *hanko*, and a high percentage of those were made of ivory. By 1981, the country was manufacturing personal seals from ivory at the rate of 2 million per year.

I rode the bullet train from Tokyo to Osaka to meet with Kageo Takaichi, chairman of the Ivory Division of the Japan General Merchandise Importers Association, chairman of the Osaka Ivory Arts and Crafts Association, director of the Japan Federation of Ivory Arts and Crafts Association, president of Takaichi Ivory Company, Ltd., Japan's biggest manufacturer of *hanko*, and surely one of the wealthiest men I had ever met.

The way to Takaichi-san's office took me through room after room stuffed with tusks and antique ivory pieces. The majority were part of his family's private collection. I had never seen the likes before and never would afterward. The collection leaned toward the strikingly large, either carved from enormous old tusks or built from joined pieces. He had child-size human figures from India, China, and Myanmar (Burma) as well as Japan; flocks of ivory birds and sprays of ivory flowers and nests of ivory dragons; elephants—a favorite theme of carvers everywhere; ivory streams flowing off ivory mountainsides; giant ships with sails of fine ivory plate; even composite pieces representing entire village scenes. We passed carvings inlaid with gold and silver, others coated with gold lacquer, and a single set of figurines he said were valued at up to a third of a million dollars. And tusks stacked upright in the corners. Then tusks too long to fit that way resting on the floor, curving across an entire section of a room. One of these was a 140-pound tusk from Zaire for which he paid $500 a kilogram—$31,500 total. And mammoth tusks with cracked grey rinds, smelling of dirt and powdery decay.

In his office stood still more impressive works and, behind a false panel, shelves of erotic ivory sculpture. The movable parts were, ah, intriguing. As for the carved ivory skull that opened along hidden lines to reveal female genitalia in full bloom, words completely, fortunately, fail me. I followed Takaichi-san to his house to see what he said was something else he liked to collect. After sex and death and the fatal beauty of ivory, here came. . . . "Harley-Davidson, my friend. Now this is a bike!" he exclaimed, leading the way past a line of big American motorcycles. Once or twice a year, he would jump on one of these hogs and roar off into the countryside. Just ride the mountain roads for a couple of days, he said; get back to nature.

In the basement of his home more tusks were stacked. This is where he kept the flawed specimens—the chipped, streaked, decayed, or deformed. Several had bullets embedded in them. Other contained lead that sellers had poured into hollowed-out portions on purpose to raise the weight and bring a better price. The practice of stuffing tusks with metal or heavy stones goes back to the earliest days of trading, as does soaking the fine-pored ivory in water prior to a sale.

"Ten years ago, the tusks we were getting averaged seventeen to eighteen kilograms," Takaichi-san observed. "Today, eight kilograms is the average." Most of the tusks were hard ivory from Zaire, Gabon, and the Congo. To turn them into *hanko*, workers began by cutting them across the grain into blocks about three inches long. Each was then carefully studied and marked so that the band-saw operator could slice the maximum number of *hanko* blanks from the block, much as a saw operator in a lumber mill tries to get as many boards as possible out of each log. As soon as the blanks were cut, another worker ground the rough edges on a wheel until they were perfectly cylindrical and ready for polishing.

White powder from tooth dentine thickened the air and coated every object and person in the factory, giving the whole place a haunted quality. I suddenly remembered the ivory craft shop with mammoth tusks that I had visited in Siberia and my later dream of wandering through a graveyard of long-dead giants by the sea. All around me now were stacked boxes of rough *hanko*, finished *hanko*, waste chips, and sweepings of ivory dust. The chips used to go to Hong Kong to be made into small jewelry such as earrings and beads. No more, said Takaichi-san, due to recent trade restrictions. But the powder was still used in Japan for fertilizer and in the preparation of a few folk medicines. Throughout the Far East, many people held that ivory purified the blood while serving as a general tonic. Boiled with meat in soup, it was also taken as a remedy for irritated eyes.

Other boxes contained sheep horn from China that had been melted down to a gluey consistency and reprocessed into amber-colored *hanko* cylinders. Takaichi-san was going to affix ivory heads to them. He planned to do the same with reprocessed cow horn, natural buffalo horn, and boxwood, thereby stretching out his supply of ivory as long as possible. I imagined he would find some way to keep going. After all, a few decades earlier, the main business of the Takaichi Ivory Company had been making ivory cigarette holders.

Lately, conservationists had put a lot of effort into trying to analyze the Japanese view of the living world. Why *was* this nation so willing to keep accumulating ivory when to do so was to visit disaster upon elephants? Why was it continuing to lead the way in knocking down the globe's tropical rainforests for hardwood, threatening the richest of all terrestrial ecosystems, whose residents include both elephants and native peoples? Why was Japan still attacking great whales, dolphins, and sea turtles? And, while it was at it, the rest of the open ocean community, first through its huge fishing fleets and factory ships and secondly through drift nets, mile-long curtains of death hung vertically from floats and loosed to sweep through the sea wherever currents carry them, tangling and killing everything in their path? Aren't these people who strive for the perfect expression of a dragonfly in a brush stroke? A moonrise through plum blossoms in haiku verse? Don't they teach courses to pass on venerable techniques of flower arranging? Isn't Japan where Zen monks might sit for hours by a stream contemplating the pattern of moss on stone?

Yes. In gardens and parks, as in poetry, painting, and the exquisite ceramics and sculpture of this island nation, nature is nurtured and praised. Japan is indeed synonymous with an extremely refined appreciation of nature. However, the operative term here is not nature but extremely refined, as epitomized by the stunted, root-starved, strapped, and carefully twisted little trees called bonsai, such as ringed Koetsu's patio. Wild things and places apart from the human sphere are something else again. Japanese culture has not traditionally accorded them much sympathy or respect. Then again, neither has the West.

Judgments about other societies are dangerous to make and rarely fair, so I would be glad to avoid going beyond what I've already said. Besides, I really don't think I need to. Japan is placing exceptional pressures on the biosphere just now not because of some rapacious streak in the national character, and not because its citizens are exceptionally greedy, but simply because the Japanese are humans and their country has an exceptional concentration of capital and technology at the moment. Japan is only doing what the United States did as it spearheaded the Industrial Age, what Europe did during its colonial Age of Empire, and what the Moghuls and China and Rome each did in their respective heydays, when they had the edge in money, organization, and know-how.

With a population of about 120 million on an archipelago whose total acreage is roughly the same as that of California, Japan had been importing 70 percent of the ivory in the world through much of the past decade and using 70 percent of that for *hanko*. Unless my calculations are off, this means that around half of the elephants taken through the height of the slaughter died to make finger-size chops so that the citizens of Japan could have one more way to display their affluence. I was wrong to think I had understood what had driven the ivory trade through history. It wasn't a compulsion to own and cherish something of transcendent beauty. To a far greater extent, it was the desire to gain in social status. Acquiring ivory as a symbol of wealth and rank was just one more form of the same old one-upmanship practiced by all but a few human groups—and other hierarchical primates. Unfortunately, this form encouraged the annihilation of the grandest land mammal still in existence.

An estimated 700,000 elephants had been destroyed during the 1980s. Traditions (that word brought up so often by the Japanese) passed on through generations by the matriarchs had been obliterated as well. The social structure of the survivors was a shambles. This is not to mention the toll of rangers and other law enforcement officials, the destabilization and corruption of governments, and the consequent degradation of national parks, preserves, and other biologically rich areas. And the toll of poachers' lives as well. *Hanko* . . . Yes, this transaction is now official. Uromara-san has put his chop on it. By the way, did you notice that chop? Ivory, and such a flawless piece. Very nice. Everyone seems to be getting one. I must look into it for myself. . . .

I had come a long way to rediscover the banality of evil.

🕮🕮🕮🕮🕮🕮🕮🕮🕮🕮🕮

A close parallel exists between the modern ivory crisis and the last great spasm of wholesale elephant killing. That one lasted from the middle of the nineteenth century until around 1930, at which time game laws and preserves began to be widely instituted. Actually, much of the hysteria went out of the market as early as 1914, as the price of ivory collapsed with the onset of World War I. Until then, between 25,000 and 100,000 elephants per year were being taken, the average probably being about 50,000 to 60,000. Missionary and explorer David Livingstone estimated that 44,000 elephants were taken to supply just the English markets in 1870. In terms of tusks, the worldwide take doubled from 500 tons in 1800 to roughly 1000 tons annually through the latter half of that century.

Why? What was the bulk of the ivory used for back then? In an excellent recent article for *Audubon* magazine, Richard Conniff provided the answer in the title: "When the Music in our Parlors Brought Death to Darkest Africa." Most of the elephants that died did so to supply the raw material for piano keys. The next most common use of ivory involved another entertainment that became popular in Victorian parlors—billiards. The balls were made of elephant teeth.

Conniff lists some of the other principal uses of ivory at the time: ". . . combs, of course, and cutlery handles . . . page markers, letter openers, erasable reminder sheets, business cards, domino pieces, fold-out toothpicks, cuff links, collar buttons, nit combs (small and fine-toothed for picking lice and their eggs out of the hair), 'Congress-folders' for creasing paper, and spatula-like 'flour-triers' used in checking flour for worms. Scraps were sold, or burned to make ivory black, which copperplate printers used in their ink. Ivory dust was . . . prized as fertilizer. . . . The workers in factories learned to shave a tusk into sheets, like paper, for painters of miniature portraits. (In 1851 one of these sheets, fourteen inches wide and fifty-two feet long, was sent to the World's Fair in London and hung from the dome of the Crystal Palace.)"

More ivory went into making barrettes, hairpins, hat pins, jewelry of all kinds and boxes to put it in, snuff boxes, tissue dispensers, and so forth. Accessories and more accessories— mainly nonessential personal and household items, nearly all of which could have been made of other materials. Before long, many would be replaced by mass-produced plastic versions.

But nothing can equal ivory for piano keys, said the salesmen. Nothing else combines such smoothness with a porosity that offers just enough friction to prevent slipping, especially when slightly perspiring fingers begin to fly up and down the octaves. There is truth to that, or was, before modern advances in synthetic materials. Yet the factors underlying the piano's surge of popularity had little to do with the qualities of ivory for concert-level playing. They had to do with the Industrial Revolution and the aspirations of the burgeoning middle class. Ivory was what keyboards happened to be made of at the time that a national mania for the piano, as Conniff describes it, swept the United States. Europe, notably England, experienced the same fad, though not quite as intensely.

The Industrial Revolution was creating a great deal of purchasing power while simultaneously making it possible to manufacture pianos quickly and relatively cheaply. The middle class could now partake of goods and leisure activities once restricted to the wealthier, more genteel social strata. A piano in the parlor was a sure sign of upward mobility. All at once, it seemed every well-brought-up woman in Victorian society was expected to learn to play one, and every woman wished to appear well-brought-up. Men, too, were encouraged to add piano playing to their social skills. Production of pianos in the United States grew from 9000 annually in 1852 to 22,000 annually by 1860 to 350,000 in 1910, at which time one American in every 260 was buying a piano every year. Piano purchases per household began to taper off after that, along with Victorian lifestyles.

Bringing death to darkest Africa refers to more than the deaths of elephants. Before pointing out that a pound and a half of ivory went into each keyboard, Conniff quotes explorer Henry Stanley's estimate that every pound of ivory "has cost the life of a man, woman, or child" in Africa. Although Arab countries and many of the African tribes themselves had long dealt in captive labor, the slave trade became a truly major industry only after colonial European powers began directly exploiting African resources during the fifteenth and sixteenth centuries. In many cases, tusks were what the traders wanted most; enslaving people was merely the most expedient way to transport the teeth great distances through trackless countrysides. Arab traders, who continued to control the main trading operations, sometimes captured slaves only to ransom them for ivory. Then they would snatch more slaves to haul the tusks out. Once at the coast, both tusk and transporter were sold, the tusk typically fetching at least twice as much as the person who had carried it.

The European colonial powers were also, of course, competing for territory and resources in the Americas. Some of the native Indians of Central and South America had kept slaves. Abruptly, they were made slaves themselves. But imported European diseases quickly decimated their numbers, and Catholic missionaries were having a hard time convincing brutalized Indians of the superiority of the white man's God. The priests and white overseers went to Charles I of Spain and got him to permit the import of black slaves from Africa to provide labor instead. Portugal followed suit. The era of plantation slavery was soon under way, fueled by Europe's growing consumption of sugar from newly established cane fields in Central America and the Caribbean. Before long, Europe's sweet tooth and the spread of plantations through the southern United States had combined with the ivory trade to drain Africa of elephants and humans alike.

David Livingstone reported that only about one in five slaves captured in the interior made it to the sea alive. On some routes, he figured, the ratio was more like one in nine. The hellish stories have been told many times of routine starvation, torture, and rape; of how the sick and weak were prodded and beaten forward until they collapsed. When they fell, the yokes sometimes broke their necks. If alive but unable to rise, captives were quickly slain as an incentive to the rest. In the early days of the slave trade, elephant incisors weighing 100-plus pounds were common. No one would have bothered with the little tusks poachers sometimes trade their own lives for today. As late as the nineteenth century, the average tusk weight was still more than sixty pounds. When a mother carrying a baby showed signs of having trouble carrying a heavy tusk as well, you can guess which weight was disposed of.

And all this was before the trials of a voyage across the sea with the slaves stacked like cordwood in filthy holds for weeks on end. Still chained, of course. The shackles were thick and heavy. Once England took a stand against slavery, British vessels often patrolled Africa's coasts to intercept slave ships. But an alert slaving crew could begin tossing iron-weighted slaves over the side, and they in turn would drag down the others. Thus, by the time the British sailors came aboard for an inspection, all the human evidence would be on its way to the bottom of the sea. A typical slaving ship might hold 300 to 400 captives.

Between the start of the sixteenth century and about 1870, the number of Africans shipped to the New World was on the order of 10 million, some experts believe. Five times as many black slaves as white immigrants came across the Atlantic before 1820. Their free labor not only developed the Americas but garnered tremendous wealth for the colonial European powers and, later, the United States. This capital accumulation helped set the stage for still more rapid economic development, including the Industrial Revolution.

One of the two leading industrial consumers of ivory in the United States was Pratt, Read & Co. The company's chief product was piano keys. According to Conniff, co-owners Julius Pratt and George Read were both staunch abolitionists. Pratt's church group sponsored antislavery speakers. Read even housed runaway slaves. Most Westerners did not really understand how ivory was brought out of Africa. Maybe these two men didn't either. Yet if that were the case, maybe they didn't try too hard to find out, for they did business with dealers who knew Africa intimately.

History can be a study in irony. England led the way in outlawing slavery in 1833, and the United States fought a civil war from 1861 through 1865 to expunge the practice. And yet the popularity of pianos and ivory continued to increase by leaps and bounds in both countries afterward. Slaves still carried most of the ivory to market. Only now, the captives were sold to Cuba or Brazil instead of England, France, or the U.S.A. And, of course, the elephants still died in huge numbers. As they grew more scarce, the price of ivory increased, which only made it more desirable and prestigious.

The Arab-dominated slave trading network finally collapsed in 1890. But by then, patterns of wanton ivory consumption in the West were so entrenched that the pace of elephant slaughter never faltered. In fact, it quickened. The main difference was that the Arab-led bands who had gained tusks from native peoples through theft, trade, and force were replaced by profes-

sional hunters. Great White Hunters. They began to systematically work over herds the way the buffalo hunters had done in
North America's now empty savannas.

To summarize, the average consumer of a *hanko* in Japan paid
little more attention to the consequences of his or her purchase
than the consumer of a piano had in the previous century. Well
before the turn of that century, travelers were already reporting
that they could cross long stretches of East Africa without
seeing a single elephant. Between 1608 and 1612, two centuries
before British explorers penetrated the upper Nile, Dutch Boers
were exporting more than 25 tons of ivory per year from South
Africa. Only a few hundred elephants remained there by the end
of the nineteenth century. Portuguese traders wiped out the
coastal populations of elephants in Angola early on. Other traders and slavers from all over Europe had depleted populations of
elephants and people along the coast farther north—the Slave
Coast, with what are now Nigeria, Togo, and Benin at the center. So the Great White Hunters had to move on toward the very
core of the continent, then generally referred to as the Congo,
now the Central African Republic, the Republic of Congo, and
Zaire, the former Belgian Congo. An estimated 585,000 elephants were taken from Zaire alone between 1889 and 1950.

꘡꘡꘡꘡꘡꘡꘡꘡꘡꘡꘡꘡

The latest bulletin from Kenya was that beefed-up antipoaching
troops with G-3 semiautomatic rifles and special training from
British commandos had killed thirty-two poachers during the
past ten weeks, while not one elephant had been lost. Such news
was getting well disseminated, in part because Kenya's new national parks director, Richard Leakey, hired a Washington,
D.C., public relations firm to help do it. Spreading the word
that Kenya's parks were being brought back under control was
essential to reassure potential tourists after the spate of shootings
by bandits there. Leakey was being called the Rambo of conservation. Some meant this as a compliment; others considered
it a sorry comment that Kenya's most imaginative solution to

poaching appeared to be more killing. Without a doubt, many in the poaching gangs were ruthless, mercenary thugs. But many more were simply poor, rural people who served as pawns for corrupt officials and wealthy international ivory dealers.

Then another bulletin from Kenya: George Adamson had been killed by *shifta*. A former Kenya park warden, George was the husband of Joy Adamson, author of *Born Free*, the internationally acclaimed account of how the Adamsons raised Elsa the lioness and other young lions whose families had died or been killed. Years after the appearance of the book—and subsequent movie—Joy Adamson was murdered by a local man, who tried to make the killing look like the work of a lion. Later, George moved with his remaining big cats to the north of Kenya, where he strove to return them to the wild. Over the years, Somali poaching gangs and herders swept the area almost clean of elephants and other wildlife, including, no doubt, most of Adamson's lions. Unable to enforce the law in this region, officials repeatedly warned Adamson to leave. He ignored their advice, convinced that his lions might still be out there somewhere in need of him, that the once teeming wild might yet be restored. Now he was dead as well.

With the huge shipment of suspect ivory from Hong Kong held up at customs in Japan, rumor had it that large quantities of mastodon and mammoth ivory from Siberia were being shipped in to make *hanko* and ornaments. Hong Kong's own stocks of ivory had finally been officially weighed and documented as part of an international effort to assess the scope of the ivory trade. Surely much was hidden away from the officials' eyes; it always was in Hong Kong. Even so, the total came to 500-some tons of raw ivory plus at least 170 tons of worked ivory. Hong Kong was whining loudly about being stuck with so much, now that its past trading partners had grown cautious about imports. The dealers wanted an exemption from the mounting bans and restrictions until they could liquidate this supply they had accumulated in anticipation of ever-rising prices. Holding the tusks from at least 60,000 to 70,000 elephants, the great majority surely killed illegally, Hong Kong was appealing to the international community's sense of fairness. And I was headed for Hong Kong.

EIGHT

HONG KONG

🅂🅂🅂🅂 IN 1989, QUITE a number of Vietnamese boat people made their way to Hong Kong, only to be incarcerated in an island holding camp pending a forced return to their country. They were rioting as I arrived late in August. With a population of 5.4 million, Hong Kong already averaged well over 13,000 people for each of its 410 square miles. That didn't leave much room for more. Still, you might have thought people in this British crown colony would be especially sympathetic to refugees. Under the terms of a ninety-nine-year lease drawn up in 1898, mainland China is due to take the port back from the British in 1997. Three out of every four residents of Hong Kong say they want out before then. But, like the Vietnamese, they are having problems finding a country that will accept them. The passport offices have been mobbed with men and women competing for the limited number of special openings made available elsewhere in the United Kingdom for immigrants from Hong Kong.

For a while, the People's Republic of China under Mao Tse-Tung's successors had shown signs of growing flexibility and openness, even of promoting private enterprise, and Hong Kong's citizenry had relaxed a little, thinking the transition might not be so rough after all. Then came the crackdown by hard-liners that included the shooting of prodemocracy student demonstrators in Tiannamen Square. Hong Kong, bastion of freewheeling capitalism, a consumer paradise with a skyline of grand glass towers in the latest architectural styles, was scared witless. Citizens and corporations wanted ways to get themselves and their capital out *now*. The United States had more than a passing interest in the drama. Having long been both a key supplier of raw materials to Hong Kong and a key consumer of its finished products, taking about a third of the total, the United States was also responsible for about 45 percent of the total foreign investment in Hong Kong itself.

The crackdown devastated what had been a rapidly growing tour business within China. As a major staging point for excursions to the mainland, Hong Kong had seen tourism suddenly drop off 25 percent. Between the decline in visitors on shopping sprees and tightening international restrictions on ivory, retail stores were beginning to post hastily made signs in their windows. They read: "Ivory Sale!" "Special Bargains on Ivory," "Low Discount Prices on Ivory," and even "50% Off on All Ivory."

Consisting of the Kowloon Peninsula, strips of the Chinese mainland, Hong Kong Island, and more than 230 smaller islands nearby, Hong Kong claims to be the third-largest port in the world. For a long time, the archipelago supported only scattered fishing villages. It was also the haunt of sea pirates known as *hoklos*, which may be why other ships seldom used the area even though it is the snuggest harbor for many a sailing day along the typhoon-ridden outer Chinese coast. At the head of a nearby bay, the British occupied a segregated trading depot at Guangzhou (Canton). This was the only place they were permitted on Chinese soil during the early nineteenth century, and they were busily acquiring silk, porcelain, and tea. Especially tea. Lots and lots of tea. The craving for this stimulant—not to mention the pomp and ritual of tea ceremonies—was at its zenith throughout the British Empire. Unhappily for the British, the insular Chinese wanted little from them in return in the way of goods. Instead, the trading monopoly, or *hong*, with whom the British dealt demanded payment in silver. Lots and lots of silver.

To overcome this bothersome trade imbalance, the British started pushing opium. "Foreign mud" the Chinese called it.

Portuguese traders had already made the drug fairly available in China during the seventeenth and eighteenth centuries, but it was used largely for medicinal purposes. The British East India Company now brought tremendous quantities from its colonial holdings in India and made this opium cheap enough that the Chinese were soon hooked by the thousands. In 1834, 16,000 chests of opium moved through Canton, and the flow of silver was already beginning to reverse in favor of Great Britain. By 1839, the number of opium chests had surged to 40,000.

Facing bankruptcy as well as massive addiction of its populace, China seized British facilities in Canton, along with 20,000 chests of opium. The foreigners beat a retreat to Macao, across the bay from Hong Kong. Once a fair port, Macao had suffered badly from siltation by the Pearl River due to deforestation and overly intensive farming upstream. The British demanded a better trading site. Skirmishes off the Hong Kong archipelago led to the First Opium War, from 1839 to 1842, with Hong Kong Island finally being ceded to the British. They later expanded their holdings and arranged the ninety-nine-year lease. Some authorities argue that although a variety of modern forces came into play about the same time, the widespread opium habit fostered by Britain played a substantial role in weakening and eventually bringing down the 4500-year-old Chinese Empire.

While expanding as a trading nucleus, Hong Kong continued to have its share of pirates. At first, most were simply well-armed raiders. But over time, many developed smuggling rings that dealt in opium, gold, guns, and anything else that was either illegal to transport or subject to stiff customs duties. I was told that for a while during the 1950s, women coming from Macao were required by Hong Kong customs officers to jump off a platform two feet high. The idea was to shake loose any substantial quantities of gold carried in the vagina. Dope was still a prime smuggling commodity at the time of my visit. In addition to hard drugs, ordinary cigarettes proved immensely profitable to sneak by customs, since tobacco was heavily taxed and most adult Chinese males were addicted, creating an enormous demand.

Together with Taiwan and North Korea, modern-day Hong Kong was also a hub of trade in illegal wildlife. Hong Kong in particular moved rare species and contraband wildlife products in and out of China, from rare reptiles and birds to bear gall bladders and musk deer glands. And Hong Kong was where the bulk of the world's raw ivory arrived and was reexported, coming and going via legal channels and otherwise. Japan may have been the largest single consumer among nations, but most of the ivory it obtained passed through Hong Kong first.

The ivory stockpiled in Hong Kong at the time of my visit was valued at around $11 billion Hong Kong, or roughly U.S. $1.5 billion, and a high-ranking official was touring Europe and the United States in an effort to persuade other governments to let Hong Kong unload its elephant teeth hoard. Several Hong Kong banks were rumored to be holding piles of tusks in their vaults as collateral for loans they had issued.

It wasn't often that Hong Kong traders—or bankers—got stuck in a big way with unwanted merchandise. But they had not bargained on an orchestrated effort by international conservation organizations to expose the full extent of the current elephant-killing orgy. Open a magazine or newspaper, and there were pictures of paramilitary poachers playing with models of AK-47 rifles carved from ivory, and those faceless elephants with strings of connective tissue all but falling onto the page, and advertisements by conservation groups with the admonishment *Don't buy ivory*. The chain reaction of the public in the West caught the dealers flat-footed.

Not only was it illegal nowadays to return to Europe or the United States with ivory from a Hong Kong trip, it was definitely getting to be uncool. Whereas just the other day, it seemed, ivory had been a mark of high fashion and disposable income, Westerners were starting to view it, as they did fur coats, as unfashionable and a sign of poor style. *Don't buy ivory*. Don't buy it. Don't sell it. Don't wear it.

Unlike the situation in Japan, ivory was highly conspicuous along the sweltering streets of Hong Kong. Camera and video shop, watch shop, gold watch band and necklace shop, imitation

Ralph Lauren polo shirt shop, ivory shop. You stopped, looked around a while, left, and passed another camera shop, imitation Rolex watch shop, purse and wallet shop, then another ivory shop stuffed with elephant tooth wares. First, and always prominently displayed in the window, was the tooth itself—maybe two or three big, perfectly shaped tusks—polished and often capped on one or both ends with gold- or silver-plated, ornately worked metal. Smaller whole tusks—teenage elephant teeth and baby elephant teeth—were mounted upright on a fancy base. And then, the worked ivory: Magic balls, the carved spheres within spheres from China. Miniature scenes with pagodas and maidens on arching bridges and romantic cloud worlds carved in minute detail from a single tusk. Japanese-style figurines and *netsuke* of a quality created with the budget-conscious shopper in mind. And the ubiquitous train of elephants on the march, with each animal holding the tail of the one in front with its trunk, the entire group also carved from a single tusk. Additional shelves were crowded with small, copulating human figures—action figures. They were another great favorite and easy on the pocketbook. After a while, it all began to look the same. Because it was the same. The same carvers had turned out the same little fornicating people day after day. The same duplicating machine had crafted those graceful goddesses in flowing robes by the score.

In all, Hong Kong was said to have about 3000 stores that sold ivory. It was not moving well there, but it was moving. Mexicans were buying fairly heavily, several shop owners said. Others mentioned Taiwanese, saying (with no small amount of envy) that they have all kinds of money these days. No, the prime buyers were still Arabs—Saudis and Iranians—others insisted. At still other shops, I was told the main ivory purchasers were Colombians; God knows they have plenty of dollars, the shop owners agreed. (I remembered reading that more money flowed out of the United States for cocaine than for any other single imported consumer item—a bit like China in the heyday of British opium.) A couple of storekeepers even mentioned Nepalese as important buyers. A shop owner's conclusion as to who were the big purchasers of ivory seemed based upon whichever nationality had last stopped in to spend an impressive sum.

Hong Kong citizens were also buying some ivory, I was informed. These were people who had won permission to emigrate to another part of the British Commonwealth—Canada in particular had agreed to accept a large share—and they were permitted to take ivory with them as a personal possession. For some families and businesses, this could be used as a way to spirit wealth out of the country without bumping up against laws designed to prevent massive flights of capital from Hong Kong.

I did notice a number of Taiwanese browsing while I was in different ivory shops. Beyond that, the most striking thing about the clientele was its absence. Store owners had plenty of time to talk between customers.

"We haven't slowed down all that much in business," insisted Edmund Ho, export manager of the Sovereign Company, which specialized in ivory and metal sculptures. "The Taiwanese come in and don't even look at the price. But things are changing. Almost 60 percent of our sales used to come from Americans and Europeans. Japanese still buy, but they must slip the ivory back into their country now. You, yourself, could probably bring back small to medium pieces and take your chances. But you *would* have to take your chances." Edmund Ho was one of perhaps three or four ivory dealers in all of Asia and India who let on that it might be illegal for me to take ivory back to the United States, and I talked with hundreds.

My standard approach was to poke around an ivory shop for a while, admiring the goods. Then I would chat up the person behind the counter, eventually stating that I was an American citizen and had heard that ivory was no longer legal to take home with me. Was that true, I would ask? Almost invariably, I would be assured that I could walk out with anything—except possibly the largest pieces. A common line was that it was fine to take whatever I happened to be looking at; I should just avoid the grand tusks and showy composite sculptures—the multithousand-dollar stuff the shopkeeper could tell I had no hope of affording anyway. Those were restricted. Are you sure about the others? I can take them home legally?

Yes, yes. Okay, no problem. Only big pieces are illegal.

While "Don't Buy Ivory" signs and stickers proliferated in the West, Nathan Ivory in Kowloon had a sign in the window that read "Buy Ivory—Help Save Elephants." Below this confusing request was a smaller-print summary of arguments purporting that elephants were overcrowded and in need of culling and that the ivory sold from culling operations supported conservation work. There was no mention of the fact that South Africa and Zimbabwe, the main proponents of the shoot-them-for-their-own-good school, were among a bare handful of nations whose elephant populations were not declining; they had already declined, and the remnants were mainly confined to reserves with scant room for the giants to grow again in numbers. Nor was there mention that little or none of the ivory inside most shops actually came from those countries anyway.

The sign on the window hinted at the intense propaganda battle being waged worldwide between the majority of conservationists, who were now requesting CITES to place the African elephant on Appendix I of the Endangered Species List, where its cousin the Asian elephant had been since 1977, and those who felt the African elephant should remain on Appendix II, permitting trade in legally obtained ivory to continue.

Since every dealer already claimed to be handling only legally obtained ivory, it was difficult to see how a continuation of Appendix II would be anything but a continuation of the ongoing holocaust. Not so, argued the pro-ivory faction. With better enforcement, regular culling of healthy populations could produce a sustained yield of tusks. These could in turn sustain a healthy ivory industry. It was not fair to penalize countries with good wildlife-management programs and viable elephant herds for the corruption and mismanagement that had led other countries to massacre their giants.

South Africa loudly voiced this opinion despite the fact that high-ranking members of the South African military had been caught red-handed more than once smuggling tusks into their country from Angola and were believed to be involved in bringing illicit tusks from both Botswana and Namibia as well. Once in South Africa, the tusks were documented as having been legally culled from elephants in the country's best-known national park, Kruger. They were then shipped to Asia through trade connections the military had established with Hong Kong.

More confusion: not far from Nathan Ivory, at the Shing On Ivory Factory showroom and shop, I spied a plaque on the wall in English telling prospective buyers that it was all right for American citizens to buy ivory. Just below the plaque was an official statement to that effect bearing the letterhead of the U.S. Fish & Wildlife Service. Or so it appeared. If you stepped close enough to read the small print, though, you discovered that the only ivory items approved for import were ivory from hunting trophies and personal items that were part of a household move to the United States.

Lee Chat, Shing On Factory director and chairman of the Hong Kong & Kowloon Ivory Manufacturers Association, spoke with me from behind the counter while his daughter Adeline translated. "Companies may try to keep up appearances and tell you they still have good ivory sales," said Lee Chat. "But I know that for the last three months, from June until now, our business has been only 30 percent of what it used to be. For some shops, business is off as much as 90 percent. Casual tourists take only a fraction now. We rely upon direct exports. South America is still a good buyer. Also the Middle East. But there are going to be many ivory people out of work before long, the way things are looking. We all await the ruling of CITES for our future."

The fateful CITES meeting would be held in Lausanne, Switzerland, in October, only a couple of months away. Appendix I or Appendix II? The decision would be made by a vote of all the 100-odd member countries. A preliminary meeting held in July in Gabarone, the capital of Botswana, had served mainly to emphasize how far apart the two camps were. Lee Chat had attended. He told me that he and other ivory dealers were sure the conservationists were seriously underestimating the number of elephants left in Africa when they claimed the total was no more than 650,000; there were officials who thought the true number was more than a million. "African countries are poor and undeveloped," he said. "Ivory is an important natural resource. We can help them develop." He also said the representatives from mainland China let him know that if the October vote favored Appendix I, their country would probably take an exception— that is, China would refuse to abide by the decision and would continue to deal in ivory. Zimbabwe and South Africa were threatening to do the same.

By Lee Chat's reckoning, China was importing an average of sixty tons of ivory a year. Roughly half of that came through Hong Kong. Rising prices had temporarily slowed China's purchases of raw ivory. Yet sources I consulted elsewhere were reasonably sure that China had been paid in tusks for a number of large-scale, quasi–foreign aid construction projects in various African countries. Some 20 percent of the ivory goods coming into Hong Kong these days were finished carvings from China. Nearby Guangzhou was probably the center of the modern Chinese ivory industry. Additional details were scarce, but Lee Chat thought the country might still have anywhere from 4000 to 5000 carvers. They worked with wood and stone as well as with ivory in enormous factory buildings.

Chinese carvers specialized in detailed, time-consuming work, notably the magic balls. Lee Chat had heard of up to thirty balls nested within one another. Three men typically took forty days to carve a typical piece with between ten and twenty magic balls. The first man turned an ivory block into a large sphere. The second man fashioned the elaborate dragon pattern that generally decorated the outermost ball. The third man carved out the internal balls with a specially designed, more-or-less L-shaped tool, cutting each new ball through holes made in all the ones above it as part of their overall design. Artisans have been working ivory in China for at least a thousand years, far longer than in Japan. Of course, China long had elephants of its own. Between twenty and perhaps 250 beleaguered survivors may still roam forests of the upper Mekong River Basin in the Yunnan Province, near China's border with Laos.

Lee Chat was born in China in 1933. He emigrated to Hong

Kong after the close of World War II in search of work and began carving ivory at age fourteen. He served as an apprentice for
the next five years, compensated at first with two Hong Kong
dollars per month and four days of vacation per year. He continued carving until 1970, at which point he was able to open his
own shop with money he had saved. Of the thousand or so ivory
carvers in Hong Kong who had been working full time, 70 percent were presently idled by the slowdown in trade, he guessed.

Estimates of the number of carvers in Hong Kong ran as high
as 4000 to 5000, on the order of China. But those figures included part-time and apprentice ivory carvers and artisans who
worked in other materials, mainly stone. Moreover, many
Hong Kong carvers worked at home, where they could keep
their own hours—usually longer than office hours, since most
got paid by the piece—and turn the polishing chores over to
wives and children.

In the Shamshuipo district of Kowloon, ivory carver Lee Chi
ushered me up several flights of stairs to his workplace, a small,
dimly lit room shared by a couple of other carvers. The view
was of a narrow street running between similar high-rise apart-
ment buildings and webs of electric lines. His specialty was the
elephant group walking trunk to tail. The tusk he was at work
on had fifteen elephants emerging from the dentine and would
represent five days' total labor by the time Lee Chi was finished.
Also originally from mainland China, Lee Chi had been carving
for forty-four years, beginning at age fifteen. Now he had no
idea what the future held.

"We have five or six orders left to fill," he said, looking up
from his workbench past the half-glasses he wore and wiping
ivory dust from his fingertips onto his T-shirt. "After that, nothing. Instead of six or seven shops giving us orders as usual, there
is just one now. It may close soon, any time. We had six people
working in this room just a month ago. Half of them have left
already. You can see how it is. People who want to save the elephants should punish the poachers, not us. Hong Kong had ten
carvers who could do Chinese-style magic balls, and eight have
quit. We had dozens of people carving elephant chains like this
once. I am the only one who is still making them. What will I do

after I fill the last order? Working in stone is not as good for money or for art, and it causes diseases of the lung. Finding another kind of job in Hong Kong is not so difficult, because people are leaving. The problem is that I am too old and other jobs don't pay as much."

I asked what the best part was about his job, his art, and what he would miss most if he had to abandon it. "Making money," replied Lee Chi. "It's a job to make money." An honest enough answer. A good ivory carver could make $10,000 Hong Kong (U.S. $1300) per month, three to four times the average wage. I turned to the thirty-seven-year-old man at the next workbench, So Kang Sang. A carver for twenty years, he specialized in small, inexpensive birds and flowers. He occasionally made them from hippo teeth, which were very hard ivory and subject to cracking but still adequate for minor pieces. I asked him what the future would be for his work. "No future," he said. "I came to Hong Kong to learn carving and studied five years under the man who used to sit at this table. It doesn't really take that long to learn what we do. It was a way to get apprentices to help the master for as long as possible for less money. People stopped entering the trade, so the time of apprenticeship was cut to three years. But all that is behind. I am leaving the industry before the mid-autumn festival."

Earlier, David Melville, the World Wildlife Fund's ivory trade specialist in Hong Kong, had told me that he couldn't get any carvers or their bosses at the factories to try samples of a new synthetic ivory made from a petroleum base, though it might help preserve their craft if accepted by buyers. Nor was there any interest in shifting to *Phytelephas macrocarpa*, the so-called vegetable ivory derived from a South American palm. (Later, in 1991, Sakai Research Laboratories of Japan announced the invention of an artificial ivory made from whole eggs and milk that it claimed was virtually indistinguishable from the real thing. But this substitute hasn't yet won a following either.)

Lee Chi thought there should at least be a grace period in which Hong Kong could sell its stocks of ivory. Better yet, he said, people at the upcoming CITES meeting should agree to buy up all the ivory in Hong Kong and distribute the money to dealers and carvers so they could retire on it. "I hear the World Wildlife Fund spends a hundred dollars a day on each elephant," Lee Chi told me. "Why don't they spend it on us?"

A hundred dollars a day per elephant for the remaining 600,000 elephants would be around $22 billion annually. What a concept! If conservation groups could claim wealth of that magnitude, the Endangered Species List would surely not be lengthening almost by the hour. Such misinformation about the World Wildlife Fund and the financial resources of environmental organizations was almost as ludicrous as the theory mentioned by one dealer that the whites were conspiring with the blacks through all these new restrictions in order to force the yellow people out of the ivory trade and take over.

Yet another ivory dealer outlined what I thought was a much more sensible attitude. If you're looking for someone to blame, he said, blame the Poons. Blame the Wangs. Blame the Lais. These Hong Kong–based trading families had developed and controlled the huge international ivory network. It was they who probably did more than anyone else to encourage the excesses that had brought down the elephant and were now in the process of bringing down the ivory industry.

The dealer who said this asked that I never use his name. Everyone knew about Lee Chat. In an *Asia Week* exposé of the ivory industry, the involvement of certain families was mentioned, and it appeared that the information came from Lee Chat, since he was the primary dealer interviewed. Soon afterward, Lee Chat received anonymous threats. Then a car was driven through the window of his shop—the one at which I had met him during my visit.

According to information gathered through undercover investigations by the conservation community, the paterfamilias of the Poon family was Poon Chow, owner of the Tat Hing Ivory Wares Factory. (I had passed the factory in Kowloon, but a sign on the door said that it was temporarily closed.) He helped found the Hong Kong & Kowloon Ivory Manufacturers Association in 1954. These days, Poon was not well. Apparently afflicted by a stroke, he was thought to be living in a flat atop a high-rise complex he owned. The active members of this ivory dynasty were son Poon Tat Hong (T. H. Poon), who oversaw the Hong Kong operations; son Tony Poon (K. Y. Poon, from the Chinese name Poon Kwok Yuen), who ran Poon's Ivory Carving Factory in Hong Kong; George Poon, either a brother or a cousin, based in Paris and connected to French-speaking central African countries; Poon Moon Lee, possibly a nephew (other sources said he was unrelated), manager of the M. K. Jewelry Company in Dubai, United Arab Emirates; and M. K. Poon, a partner of T. H. Poon, exact relationship unknown. Some said Tony Poon was M. K. Poon's son. Obviously, the trail the investigators followed was a convoluted one.

That trail led to the following holdings: in addition to Tat Hing Ivory and Poon's Ivory Carving Factory in Hong Kong, there was Tat & Company (an ivory retail shop), Tat Hing Investments, and Kin Ming Ivory Factory. Along with the M. K. Jewelry Factory in Dubai, there was the Dubai Ivory Factory. Paris had a boutique called Hong Kong-France and Tat Hing Ivoire, both managed by George Poon. Macao had Son Ian Chop Hau, where T. H. Poon stored tons of ivory in 1986, before authorities tightened regulations there. Singapore had Fung Ivory Manufacturing Ltd., managed by Mrs. Choy, wife of Choy Tat Hing of Dubai, and Kyomi Handicraft and Trading Ltd. GBL & Associates in Dar es Salaam, Tanzania, was also a Poon front, as was an ivory factory called Jewelry World, opened in Zaire.

The Hong Kong ivory syndicates were implicated in the following operations, to name only a few: The transfer of 130 tons of ivory from the Republic of Congo to Paris in 1984. Tampering with French diplomatic mail. Smuggling ivory in *dhows* from East Africa to Dubai, and then flying the ivory to Zaire, where it was given CITES certification and reexported as legal ivory. Establishing a route from Dubai to Malaysia and Singapore. Bringing 17.5 tons of poached ivory into Singapore under false papers. Taking illicit ivory out of Sudan. Transporting illegal ivory from Tanzania into China. Manipulating much of the illegal trade out of Burundi prior to 1987. Inventing the scam of having someone scratch a ring or other design on the base of a tusk so that it could be imported without registration to Hong

Kong as "worked" ivory—an expression of craft and artisanry—rather than raw ivory, thereby wriggling through a loophole in existing laws. Devising schemes for transferring CITES certification from old stocks of ivory to new, smuggled-in tonnage. And claiming a high (40 percent) rate of wastage in carving figurines (the average is more like 5 to 10 percent) and selling certificates covering the difference to traders with illegal ivory.

I am passing on allegations. Despite all the poachers shot and all the middlemen caught, no one has indisputably proved the Poons or other families guilty of any wrongdoing. At one point, prominent importer K. T. Wang claimed to control 50 percent of the legal ivory trade but steadfastly denied any ties to illegal activities, and he was never proved a liar.

As the unnamed ivory dealer told me, he and others in Hong Kong were reluctant to criticize the ivory syndicates for three reasons. First, respect for elder members of the families. Second, people feared having their ivory supplies cut off by these powerful importers. And, third, they grudgingly admired the dealers' ability to stay ahead of the game. They never overtly broke the rules; they kept redefining them. They followed the Eleventh Commandment: Don't get caught. They didn't. (An exception was George Poon, indicted for illegally importing ivory into Paris after more stringent regulations had gone into effect. Still, his getting caught was a mere inconvenience; how serious could the threat of a minor fine be to a man with an income reported by the London-based Environmental Investigation Agency to be close to U.S. $1 million per week?)

The Poons and their fellow traders simply took the old buccaneering tradition of Hong Kong and applied it on a grander scale. The British opium dealers of yesteryear would have winked and nodded at such goings on. Interestingly, modern Hong Kong's request to be allowed to dispose of its ivory stockpiles was eventually granted by Great Britain's prime minister at the time, Margaret Thatcher. She agreed to give Hong Kong six months to sell off what it could.

NINE

INDIA:
THEPPAKADU

🔲🔲🔲🔲 In 1901, INDIA held 236 million people. Even then the country was known for its combination of overcrowding and poverty in many regions. Half a century later, as of 1951, the population stood at 361 million, and by 1981, it was 685 million. It is already closing in on 900 million as I write. This is one-sixth of the entire human population on 2.2 percent of the earth's land surface, or an area approximately one-third the size of the United States. It is more humans than yet exist in all of Africa, which has closer to 700 million people on 20.2 percent of the planet's land surface.

The fact that India also holds between 35 percent and 50 percent of the elephants in Asia is at once discouraging and hopeful. Discouraging because it shows how few elephants are left. Counting those in India, Asian elephants total just 35,000 to 55,000 in the wild and another 16,000 in captivity. Once spread across the largest of continents in the millions, from the Tigris-Euphrates fertile crescent in Syria to fairly far north in China, the wild population now inhabits areas totaling just 168,000 square miles, scarcely larger than the state of California. Only about 30 percent of that remaining range lies within national parks, game sanctuaries, forest reserves, or other kinds of protected lands. All the rest is at risk, and so are the elephants inhabiting it. For that matter, many of the reserves themselves are at risk of being swamped by people. Equally troubling, neither the remaining elephant herds nor the ranges they currently inhabit are continuous. On the contrary, they are spread out in bits and pieces over India, Southeast Asia, and assorted islands in the Indian Ocean claimed by Indonesia and Malaysia. They could scarcely be more fragmented. Which makes prospects for the long-term survival of *Elephas maximus* even slimmer.

The hopeful part is this: it is something of a miracle that India, given its current human population, should have room to support a single elephant, much less 17,000 to 22,000 in the wild plus close to 3000 to 5000 domestic ones. India, therefore, might be able to tell us something important about how to coexist with giants in an overcrowded world.

After entering India at Madras in early September, I flew to Bangalore, a rapidly expanding city of millions in the southern state of Karnataka. I had arranged to meet a professor at the Indian Institute of Science in Bangalore who was a leading authority on the Asian elephant. His name is Dr. Raman Sukumar. Sukumar was in his thirties, tall, slender, and bespectacled. Although he had a casual, friendly style, he was also a very thoroughgoing scholar. He loved practicing science and teaching science and was eager to see that I absorbed his information. We started talking elephants from the start and never let up.

In short order, we were on our way out of the city in his jeep, dodging pedestrian hordes, holy cows, and wooden-wheeled carts pulled by oxen. The cart drivers conducted delicate little symphonies of pain to get on down the road, constantly poking, prodding, and lightly whipping the animals' flanks while Sukumar steered the jeep in a slalom course around them and told me that elephants were seen now and then right here, a few miles from the southern edge of Bangalore. Not long ago, they came right into the city's outskirts by a college campus not far from where he teaches.

From Bangalore, a series of rolling, forested hills lead along the Mysore Plateau to the heart of an elephant stronghold where the states of Karnataka, Tamil Nadu, and Kerala all meet in a swell of ridges and peaks. Throughout most of Asia, surviving elephants tend to be found in the sort of steep, rugged terrain that is the last to be converted for agriculture and human habitation. This area is a prime example. It includes the Eastern Ghats, the Western Ghats, and the Nilgiri Mountains, which run between the first two ranges and are basically a lateral extension of the Western Ghats. These highlands escaped heavy use by humans for centuries and were then set aside as forest reserves or wildlife refuges before the momentum of modern change could overrun the more accessible portions.

In the case of what is now Bandipur National Park and Tiger Reserve, the lands were first protected as the exclusive hunting estate of the maharajah of Mysore, just as many reserves in Europe began as grounds where high-ranking noblemen could indulge their love of the chase. Local stories tell of one particular heir to the Mysore palace who was very fond of alcohol and would go riding out on his elephant to hunt tigers in Bandipur while royally drunk. Every time he aimed and fired, two or three sharpshooters by his shoulder would aim and fire at the same time. No one could be sure this maharajah ever hit what he aimed at. But then only on the rarest of occasions could anyone ever say that he missed.

Not long ago, Bandipur, nearby Nagarahole National Park, Mudumalai Wildlife Sanctuary, and Kerala South Wynad Sanctuary (a *wynad* is a wetland area) were linked with adjoining forest reserves to create the 2150-square-mile Nilgiri Biosphere Reserve. As intact elephant habitats go these days, this represents a substantial chunk.

The first thing we had to do in the reserve was make a courtesy call at the headquarters for the Mudumalai Sanctuary, located in the village of Theppakadu. I did not much want to stop. A part of the wild world I had never seen was beckoning all around me—a green, southern Indian jungle filled with bright birds and strange calls—and I was desperate to touch it. I had just spent almost a month in artificial habitats dominated by increasingly identical consumer goods. This monolithic environment—the mall-osphere—now stretched along the Pacific Rim from Japan to Hong Kong all the way to burgeoning Bangkok, where I made a stopover.

I needed bush time to clear my head and recalibrate my senses. I had wasted almost a week fuming back and forth in Bangkok's near-gridlock traffic just to meet with officials at the Laotian embassy and fill out the stacks of forms they gave me. Visitors to Laos were generally confined to a zone around the capital, Vientiane. Since I wanted to look for elephants, I needed access to the countryside beyond, and I had been told that the embassy in Bangkok was a good place to pursue this. I had already been stonewalled by the Laotian embassy in Washington, D.C. Nobody said no; the functionaries just never said anything. Every so often, I would call and be told that my repeated petitions were surely being passed along by somebody somewhere.

If the Laotian bureaucrats gave my application any thought at all, it was most likely to wonder what it was I *really* wanted. I've run into this time and again with countries that lack experience with wildlife tourism. Having no serious interest in wild creatures, except perhaps as commodities, the officials cannot imagine that I do either. You want to spend all that time and money to go halfway around the globe so you can run through the jungle getting hot and filthy and leech-sucked just to watch elephants? Right. I had to be crazy, crooked, or a spy.

Spy was probably their choice of the moment. I had specifically requested permission to visit a part of southern Laos where people still used domestic elephants to plow fields and as the main means of transporting goods between villages. The next thing I heard about the area was that it was the focus of an active prodemocracy movement such as swept eastern Europe and briefly flourished in China. The communist government of Laos was in the process of bloodily suppressing it. I would take up my request to enter Laos on my next trip through Thailand.

So now, heading toward Theppakadu, I pleaded with Sukumar to just keep going straight into the heart of elephant country and bypass as many paperwork formalities as we could. I whined about my trials in central African government offices, the Laotian embassy, and a score of other Kafkaesque night-

mares along the elephant trail. I grumbled that my tolerance for
the tyranny of bureaucrats was worn down to the tearing point.
I even admitted that I was a spoiled American journalist who did
not think he should have to follow the same rules everybody else
did. At least not until he'd gotten in a good hike first. Sukumar
stopped in Theppakadu anyway.

Across the street from the Mudumalai Sanctuary headquarters, a man was beating a dog. A disheveled old madwoman
came wandering down the street and stopped to shriek at him.
Bonnet macaques in an overhanging fig tree took up the cry and
dropped down to the roof of a nearby building, where they
formed a row of hooting, arm-waving spectators. The woman
ran over and swept the dog up in her arms. Both she and the
beaten animal turned with bared teeth toward the man, and he
eased away, trying to appear as if he were still in charge. Only
after the small drama had wound down did I notice that his
stained khaki pants and sweaty shirt amounted to a uniform.
This was our park official.

I was more than prepared to loathe this fellow. I had a month's
worth of ivory trade madness and mall-dweller frustrations all
ready to heap on the first son-of-a-mutant-mongoose who tried
to keep me from getting my feet back on God's green earth. Yet
when the official did indeed set about demanding more paperwork and letters of approval than we had, threatening to delay
us interminably, living up to every foul expectation, I didn't do
a thing. I couldn't. This was Sukumar's study area. I was his
guest. It wouldn't have been fair for me to make the situation
any more difficult.

Sukumar placated the official well enough to keep us going in
the field for a few days. Later, the man did manage to create
trouble for us, but not an unmanageable dose of it. In the meantime, we were out in the thick of the Nilgiri animal kingdom.

Sukumar began by driving high into the Western Ghats to a
temple site from which we looked across rippling hills and hundreds of square miles of uninterrupted forest. A series of light,
premonsoon rains begin to sweep across the region in April or
May, and they come first to these uppermost elevations, which

wring the moisture from passing clouds. Where undisturbed, such sites give rise to true tropical rainforests of immense trees sprouting ferns and other epiphytes and draped with lianas. When the premonsoon starts in earnest, these areas are where the elephants will be, for the more open parts of the forests will have carpets of sprouting *Themeda* and *Imperata* grasses.

The southwest monsoon season doesn't really get under way until about the beginning of June. When it does, the well-watered grasses shoot up as high as an elephant's eye, becoming more coarse and fibrous and less nourishing. By then, the rains will also have begun falling downhill from the peaks and ridge-lines, and that's where the giants will be, seeking the more recently sprouted grasses and forbs there. Eventually, this pattern takes them down to the lowest elevations, where a dry deciduous forest prevails, mixed with a protein-rich thornscrub in its more arid sections. This is also where the animals come into contact with agricultural and grazing lands outside the reserve.

The rains taper off during August, but are soon replaced by the northeast monsoon, beginning in September. Once it finally ends and foliage begins to dry up, usually toward late November or December, the elephants migrate toward riverine and *wynad* habitats, still seeking plant species with a high level of moisture and flowing nutrients. Over the long, rainless months to follow, such wet areas as remain cannot provide enough forage. The elephants shift from grazing to browsing—stripping bark from trees and munching on select shrubs. At times, they dig and tear up roots to eat as well.

Overall, the downslope movement during the monsoons takes place from west to east. With the onset of premonsoon showers in April, the bands of elephants that are dispersed through the lower elevations of the forest gradually begin to gather into larger herds and migrate westward, returning to the uppermost elevations with new sprouting grasses to begin the cycle all over again.

The average group size Sukumar recorded throughout the year was fairly small—just over eight. Yet it was not uncommon to observe herds of between ten and twenty. Large temporary groups formed around waterholes during the dry season, and herds of up to a hundred animals were recorded during the time of migration from the lowlands back up toward the top of the Western Ghats.

Together with the still relatively lightly developed countryside surrounding it, the Nilgiri Reserve supports close to 4000 elephants, Sukumar figured. This amounts to one of the brightest prospects anywhere for the species's survival. Females here were first breeding between the ages of fourteen and eighteen, with a mean of seventeen-and-a-half. (The earliest age of pregnancy recorded among domestic elephants was sixteen in Burma and 13.6 in India.) Calves were born at intervals of four to six years. Reproduction was not high, but it was adequate for replacement and perhaps a fractional increase. In the portion of the countryside Sukumar chose for a study area, the population density averaged about 1.3 elephants per square mile.

An elephant population as robust as that found in the Nilgiri region should be an indication of an abundant and diverse fauna in general. It is. The Indian subcontinent contains wildlife communities nearly as rich as the better-known ones of Africa. India had cheetahs until the last century—Asiatic cheetahs. It still supports lions and rhinos—Asiatic lions, the kind seen engraved on ancient stones in Greece and Persia, and Indian rhinoceroses. Since both have become rare and restricted in their range, the Nilgiri Reserve holds neither, but it can claim its share of leopards, striped hyenas, jackals, and mongooses, plus a gazellelike antelope known as the blackbuck. I think comparisons with Africa also came to mind for me because we were finding these animals or their sign among tall termite mounds, thorny acacias, and terminalia and combretum trees, all common to both Africa and the Indian subcontinent.

As we drove and hiked through the countryside, we encountered some of India's members of the deer family as well. Sambar are related to Europe's red deer and North America's elk. Chital, also called spotted, or axis, deer, have a coat that always looks as though it were dappled with sunlight; it lets the animal blend easily with the understory of the dry deciduous forest with its relatively open canopy. Muntjac, or barking deer, are characterized by tusks, or tushes, formed from elongated canine teeth that are used in battles between members of this semisolitary species. And in the largely nocturnal chevrotain, or mouse deer, the males also carry tusks, though the entire body of the creature is barely a foot tall.

Chital, muntjac, and, in the north, the para, or hog deer, are all secondary feeders at times. Much like duikers in African woodlands, they follow below monkey troops, which are very messy eaters and drop all kinds of fruits and leaves. The deer also follow elephants to glean leftovers in their wake. Elephants break a lot of trees. In fact, they probably keep certain tree and bamboo species in young stages of growth—maintain them in subclimax condition, as an ecologist would say. Sukumar thinks that the prevalence in the region of trees that revegetate readily from roots or branches suggests an adaptation to elephants over the ages.

Along the crest of the Nilgiri Mountains lives the Nilgiri tahr, a shaggy mountaineer intermediate between wild sheep and wild goats. After circling downhill through an open teak forest to gain a closer view of a solitary bull elephant, we noticed a herd of another type of bovid half-hidden in the moist ravine bottom, where woody brush was interspersed with clumps of bamboo. These were gaur. They stand seven or even eight feet at the shoulder with a sleek, blue-black coat and short, incurving horns like bison. Although sometimes called Indian bison, gaur are more closely related to India's yaks and domestic cattle. The group we came upon was extremely wary, and it was a challenge to creep close enough to be able to observe these huge wild oxen through the underbrush without disturbing their behavior.

India also contains wolves. They have a history of carrying off children here, I discovered, and were at it again in a northern state during the time of my visit. Let me rephrase that. There is a history of *reports* of wolves killing children and the wolves were *reportedly* at it again. Good documentation is still lacking. After centuries of persecution and habitat loss, their numbers are low, and the animals are rarely seen. We crossed no spoor of any.

However, I saw my first dhole, or Indian wild dog, in the Nilgiri Reserve and was able to watch it for nearly a quarter of an hour.

A sloth bear watched us for a few moments before racing away. We followed to see where it had been foraging. Sloth bears are neither slothful nor related to sloths but were classified that way for a while on the basis of worthless field reports about their behavior from colonial big-game hunters. During a sojourn in southern Nepal, I had heard stories of how sloth bears use their long, curved claws to attack people. Villagers said they go for the face. As the feeding site we looked over showed, the formidable-looking claws are mainly used to tear open termite mounds. Aggression toward people by this animal is unusual.

Besides, when you are in tiger country—and we were in some of the best—a sloth bear seems almost innocuous. This bear weighs a couple of hundred pounds, three hundred maximum, and is so specialized for sucking up termites that it has no front teeth. An Indian, or Bengal, tiger can weigh five hundred pounds, sometimes more. And a cat that size can eat pretty much whatever it wants. You simply have to hope none takes up the habit of adding people to its diet, as occasionally happens, while you are around. Given good protection in India through Project Tiger, a program emphasizing conservation at the ecosystem level, tigers have increased from a low of less than 2000 to more than 4000. In the Ganges Delta area, fishermen have lately taken to fashioning straw men to ride in the back of their little skiffs to take the brunt of any tiger attack, of which there have been dozens. The tiger is probably the one predator that poses a serious threat to Asian elephant calves and to any small juveniles separated from their families.

Following a map sketched on a napkin, my wife, Karen Reeves, and I once trekked for days through prime tiger country in Nepal's Chitwan National Park near the Indian border. We were more or less lost. Happily so. One night, we camped along a sandy riverbank by a flood plain thick with elephant grass fifteen to twenty feet tall. We worried about the rhinos stomping about. We worried about mugger crocodiles, and we worried about snakes. But not about tigers. In the morning, we found fresh tiger prints within a foot or two of our joined sleeping bags. Huge prints. We had been sniffed and spared while dreaming. I am a coward about plenty of things, but I never worried about tigers before that, and I never have since.

⌸⌸⌸⌸⌸⌸⌸⌸⌸⌸⌸⌸

The animal I finally started to get nervous about was the one I had come to see. My impression had been that Asian elephants are not as aggressive as the African species. This view is widely shared and based on several premises, including the Asian elephant's smaller size and the fact that it is more of a forest-dwelling creature, forest dwellers being generally more secretive and retiring than their open-country counterparts. There is also the understanding that Asian elephants prove more tractable in captivity, whereas African elephants have seldom been tamed, at least in recent centuries.

Yet I noticed that Sukumar was very cautious around elephants in the Nilgiri Reserve—much more cautious than his counterparts were in African reserves. Not that Sukumar was wildly impulsive to start with. But even taking his systematic, let's-stick-to-the-data style into account, Sukumar still seemed exceedingly wary near these elephants. He told me that the head of wildlife at the Indian Forest Research Institute had visited here once and ignored warnings about approaching the elephants too closely. A bull ran him down and trampled him to death on the road. I was only mildly interested in this account until we stopped to watch a family feeding by the road and a five-year-old male suddenly whirled and charged our jeep.

Typical, and not just of males, Sukumar let me know as we left. One group of four related females he had observed for years was usually ready to give chase at the slightest provocation. He named them the Torone sisters, after a particularly testy sorority of African elephants that Iain and Oria Douglas-Hamilton had studied in Tanzania's Manyara National Park.

As it turns out, elephants poach 150 to 200 people a year in India. Sukumar had documented 160 deaths from elephants in the biosphere reserve area alone over the preceding fifteen years. A couple of people had been nailed quite recently. One was a man killed while rounding up his buffalo in the reserve a week earlier. Just the other day, a guide leading a man within the reserve had been cornered by a four- or five-year-old male and injured, and on the park's edge, a woman had been chased by an elephant and wound up with a broken arm. It wasn't clear yet whether she broke her arm when she fell or the elephant smashed it. No matter. I still wasn't paying close attention to the implications, not even when I went for a late-afternoon hike at the reserve's edge, close to where the woman's unlucky encounter had occurred.

I went with Varman and Arumugham, two students working as field assistants for Sukumar. We were in fairly dry habitat, where the forest tapers off into thornscrub, but it was flowering exuberantly in response to a spate of recent showers that heralded the onset of the real monsoons. The high country was already well soaked, and mists clung to the top of the Nilgiri peaks in the distance. Varman pointed out *Acacia pennata*, a shrubby legume whose long, pealike pods were favored by elephants. He called it Indian laburnum. I had little trouble recognizing another common shrub. When I brushed against some branches, double-hooked thorns stopped me in my tracks. Hello, *Zizyphus*. This genus had cost me pants, shirts, and blood in the African thornscrub. Varman said the elephants here ate both the new branches and the berries and probably played a role in distributing the seeds.

Walking fast and easy in the fragrant air, we intersected scores of chital with their fawnlike coats of soft chandelier light. In one band were two female blackbucks that had wandered into the area but found no mates, populations of the species having grown scarce and widely scattered. As evening approached, we began to concentrate our attention on birds: a brown fish owl hunting by a pool along a stream; plaintive cuckoos—the name describes the call—in a berry-laden *Zizyphus* bush; hoopoes, bee-eaters, and rollers, all common in Africa as well; mynas, munias, and magpie-robins; and then, finally, peacocks. We followed them until we realized that we had four miles to go to reach the road, where we were to be picked up by a driver, and darkness was nearly upon us. Soon, we could only make out vague silhouettes of things right next to us.

I carried my flashlight in my hand toward the end of our march and turned it on to signal the driver. As soon as I did, a trumpet blast shot forth from the darkness in front of us. Directly in front of us and awfully close. I snapped off the light. Footfalls sounded. We broke and ran in a short loop. As soon as we started to turn back toward the road, another trumpet cut us off. We veered at once and began running away. Footsteps fell close behind. I could feel them in the ground through my own feet, feel them inside my skull.

"Go back and forth . . . through the trees," shouted one of the researchers. Where were the trees? Here? Yes. I zigzagged for all I was worth. Giant footfalls still thudded behind. All I could do was race on, cutting sharply back and forth and hoping I didn't smack into a tree trunk, until I became aware that the only thunderous sound left was from my own heart.

We didn't dare return toward the car. I wondered if we were still being stalked. How to tell? It was pitch black. With those layers of fat and connective tissue on the soles of their feet to help cushion their weight, elephants can be amazingly quiet when moving, if they want to be. I remembered being told of an elephant researcher surveying a remote part of Southeast Asia a few months earlier who described an elephant trying to hunt him down. He would get some distance away, out of sight, and stop to rest, and there would come the giant again, using its trunk like a bloodhound to track his scent along the jungle floor. A couple of Great White Hunters in Africa had described similar incidents in their journals. I hadn't put much stock in them. But now, in the dark, I felt like elephant prey. My whole attitude toward elephants was zigzagging around through the flower-scented night.

We made it to another section of the road and eventually flagged down a passing bus. Safe. Now we had to get to the man who had been waiting for us in the car. He would still be there, locked in behind the park gate for the night while we had the key. He would be stewing over our fate and possibly in trouble himself. Elephants in a foul mood sometimes squash cars. We reached a village and located someone who had a vehicle he could spare for our mission. Unfortunately, this someone was merrily slugging down rice liquor—*rakshi*—in a tavern, and impressing the urgency of the situation upon him took a while. Finally, he consented to help us go find our friend.

Our friend was there, still waiting. Though unsquashed, he was badly shaken mentally. The elephant had come upon the car in the gathering darkness without a sound. The first the driver knew of its presence was when it trumpeted at us, right next to the car window. I will never know what the elephant had in mind that night, but upon reflection, I have to credit the animal with giving us fair warning. If it had really been out to smoosh us, it could have merely waited where it was and let us bump right into it.

I soon met two more young men studying elephants in Mudumalai. Sukumar introduced us, but they were working independently of him, affiliated with the Bombay Natural History Society. The first was Ajay Desai, who was gathering detailed information on the social relationships and behavior of individual elephants. The other was N. Sivaganesan, called Siva. He was collecting equally detailed data on the elephants' feeding habits through direct observation.

Both projects were breaking new ground with their intensive, close-up approach to studying wild Asian elephants. The behavior and ecology of this species had been little enough studied from a distance. Ajay was discovering that beyond the mother-young social unit, allegiances between elephants did not appear to be strongly fixed; that is, a six-year-old female seen following a particular cow one day might be recorded walking behind another adult female in a separate group the next day.

This was quite different from the more constant family

groupings found among savanna elephants by the Douglas-Hamiltons, Cynthia Moss, and Joyce Poole. On the other hand, there were hints that African forest elephants might have a social structure similar to what Ajay was observing. Ajay noticed that even the mother-young bond wasn't constant, as calves spent a fair amount of time in the company of sisters and aunts. But that seems in keeping with observations of African elephants, whose babies sometimes spend more time around an older female—a grandmother or auntie type—than their own mother for long periods. Unlike African cows, Asian females rarely secrete from their temporal glands when excited.

Ajay agreed with Sukumar's findings of small group size, averaging between six and eight—another characteristic the forest-dwelling Nilgiri elephants seemed to share with African forest elephants. The larger Nilgiri groups that formed appeared to involve related families—bond groups and even larger clans—but Ajay wanted more observations to be sure. He told me that the interactions he saw during get-togethers around waterholes or in the bush were essentially the same as those of African elephants. Matriarchs greeted one another with clasped trunks and generally avoided overt conflict, while young males couldn't wait to begin jousting and sparring.

Dr. A. J. T. Johnsingh, who advised Ajay and Siva, insisted that they spend every day for an entire year working with domestic elephants before undertaking field work in the Nilgiri Reserve. The idea was for them to become intimately familiar with the animals, with each nuance of expression and the meaning of each sound. The better they were able to interpret an elephant's intentions, the higher their chances of staying alive in the bush.

Siva admits that he was frightened half to death when he began working with elephants in the wild. He stayed that way for the better part of a year, terrified day in and day out by what he was doing. Now, more than four years later, he had still only met one elephant, a female, that tolerated him at close range. Only one—and he may owe her his life. Siva was watching her group when a ten-year-old male attacked him. He decided that his only possibility for escape was to run in among the females and hope the male would hesitate to charge among them. The ploy worked, or Siva wouldn't have been here now in mid-morning, directing me past *Kydia* and *Anogeissus* trees toward a group of elephants. The family consisted of two adult females, a five-year-old female, and a two-year-old whose sex wasn't yet obvious, and they had an adult musth male in attendance.

The bull's presence put both us and the female elephants on edge. They moved along quickly through an understory of tall, dense brush dominated by an orange-blossomed shrub called *Lantana*. We followed downwind. Siva had found that as temperatures grow warmer during the day, the elephants are more likely to use shadier, moister areas. He guessed this group was on its way downhill toward a ravine, or *vayal*. Thick, ropy fig vines coiled around some of the larger trees. The shrubs were strung with *Ipomoea*, a flowering vine I had seen brightening wide sections of Tsavo National Park in Kenya after the rains. Exactly how dense some of the thickets were was hard to appreciate until the whole mass of elephants would suddenly disappear from view while still close enough that the sound of their chewing filled the air.

So far, Siva had accumulated 720 hours of direct feeding observations. Between poor visibility and the animals' aggressiveness, it had taken him several years. He gathered a lot of his data the same way other primates do—by racing from tree to tree and climbing up into the branches to peer around. He needed to be high up in order to see over intervening vegetation and make out which plants the giants were actually selecting, and a stout tree was generally the safest place to be for someone trying to stay as close as possible to elephants without disturbing them. In all, his was one of the most unusual and adrenaline-rich research projects I had come across.

Siva took another precaution in his work that was every bit as valuable as the year he invested with captive elephants. He always brought along at least one extra pair of eyes and ears in the form of a local tracker and guide. Not only did he need help keeping tabs on various members of the group he was following, he had learned through harsh experience that he needed someone to look out for other elephants that might suddenly appear behind him.

On the day we followed the family being visited by the musth male, two trackers led the way: Chenna, a villager from Theppakadu, and Bomman, a member of the Kuruba tribe, an indigenous group still living within the reserve.

Like the Sholagas, another group native to the Nilgiri area, the Kurubas are thought to represent an aboriginal line present in southern India before even the Dravidians arrived. Bomman was dark-skinned but, unlike the Dravidians, had a short, stocky build with broad feet and broad features, especially the nose. I thought he bore a marked resemblance to Australian aborigines. Later, I learned that these early inhabitants of southern India are referred to by some authorities as proto-Australoid.

Before I met Bomman or any of the area's other indigenous people, I had been walking through a chital-grazed patch of forest trailing elephant sign when I came upon a low log hut with a roof of packed earth and sod. Inside were stones. Simple, smooth stones. They were offerings to Bummi, I learned, a goddess venerated by the Kurubas and represented only by uncarved naturalistic objects in a continuation of animistic practices that predate Hinduism.

The Kurubas subsist by hunting some game and fish and gathering other forest produce, from green shoots to fruits and nuts. If they need to get outside materials or raise a bit of cash, they can usually gather extra wild honey or medicinal herbs to trade or sell. In the past, Indian authorities sometimes tried to relocate such groups from reserves and encourage them to take up agriculture. Sometimes they were allowed to stay but forbidden to hunt or gather in the protected zone, which merely turned them into full-time poachers. Nowadays, the government is more inclined to let indigenous tribes remain in their homelands with only a few restrictions on what sort of animals they can hunt. The situation is still confusing, though, because the regulations imposed on indigenous peoples vary from one Indian state to another even within the reserve. Some of the Kurubas flee into the forest when they encounter any visitor from the outside.

Chenna kept an eye on the rear while Bomman kept vigil to one side. His vantage point was a high tree limb that he had climbed, as usual, with a machete in one hand. Siva and I were together in another tree. Birds chanted in the bush. Once, we heard crashing behind us, but it turned out to be a herd of gaur. Butterflies in great flocks danced between the thickets like wafting petals or dispersing seeds. Hot, thick air rich with perfumes and colors enwrapped us; high overhead a black eagle circled, its silhouette stroboscoping through the leaves of the canopy.

Our elephants were the grey splotches visible now and then behind screens of orange lantana blossoms. "Lantana is an exotic shrub, from South America, I think," Siva whispered as we rested on adjoining limbs, looking down toward the elephants. "It takes over on disturbed ground. People grazing cattle and buffalo have spread it through the reserve. Beautiful, the flowers. But this plant is poor forage for animals. The elephants may tear it, but they are not eating it. They are trying to get underneath to the grasses."

Bomman bounded down from his tree to take up a position in one closer yet to the elephants. He looked back toward us and waved his machete for us to join him. We did, and waited a while in utter silence. Then Siva and Bomman began whispering. I couldn't begin to follow, but some of the words Bomman used sounded very odd. Was this the Kuruba tongue, I asked? No. Bomman had memorized the Latin names for the vegetation, Siva said. "The grass there looks like *Setaria intermedia*," he continued. "That one. See it? Very tasty, because it is just sprouting now with the rains, so it has a good concentration of nutrients."

Biologists say elephants process their food at only about 50 percent efficiency. It is one of the things that makes them particularly good seed dispersers. They not only spread them around but enhance their chances of germination by passing them through with only minor processing and dropping them in fertilizer that makes a good, rich mulch without being too concentrated in nitrogenous chemicals. Siva found that 80 percent of seeds sprouting in elephant dung were viable, whereas only 40 percent of seeds sprouting apart from dung survived. Wild boars, mongooses, hornbills, and jungle fowl, the ancestors of

all domestic chickens, scavenge seeds from elephant manure, becoming secondary dispersers. Interesting to think that the
chicken on tables around the world was originally shaped in part
by the presence of elephants in Asia's forests.

"Since elephants eat several hundred pounds of forage daily,
people think these animals just bash along eating everything as
they go. But they don't, and it is because their system is unable
to digest rough forage that efficiently," Siva noted. He swept an
arm toward the west and said, "Look. There is the whole high
country full of grass taller than your head and not a single elephant in it. To keep in good condition, they must constantly seek
out the highest quality foods. For creatures so huge, they are actually fairly picky eaters. They have to be. This has important
implications for their range and movements. You can't stick
them into inferior habitat and say, well, they will just have to
spend more time looking for food and less time resting. They are
already eating sixteen to twenty hours a day in good habitat.
Now, . . . Uh-oh."

For some time, the sounds of contented foraging—blowing,
rumbling, branches snapping, molars grinding—had issued
from the elephant group in a steady flow, even when we couldn't
see what they were actually doing. They had slowed their pace
quite a bit. We were nearing the midday resting period during
which elephants often stand about in a shady spot and feed list-
lessly if at all. Abruptly, a louder rumble had cut off the other
sounds. A high-pitched squeaking followed. "Alarm call," Siva
whispered, and all at once, the elephants were coming our way.

The wind must have shifted. Chenna materialized on a lower
limb of the tree, gesturing frantically. Siva and Bomman started
discussing something in equally great haste. Once again, I was
in a strange place listening to people I didn't really know talking
in a tongue I couldn't fathom about what to do about something
that could kill us and was drawing ever closer. When I queried
Chenna and Bomman earlier, they had agreed that, yes, the elephants here would track people down through the bush by
scent, like a hunting dog.

We were too low in the tree, and I was not sure it was thick enough to withstand the bull if he decided to try and shake us out. Luckily, the elephants solved everything by stopping short, moving off at an angle, and half-vanishing again in a different thicket. The only problem was that Siva would now have to wait a quarter of an hour or so before the elephants were relaxed enough to provide normal, rather than disturbed, feeding data. All things considered, not a bad problem. I climbed slightly higher and caught a nap in the crotch of a limb. When I awakened, the elephants were just emerging from the shrubs into an open, parklike stand of teak and themeda grass, another favorite food. This was our best view of the elephants yet.

"Ho!" exclaimed Chenna under his breath. At the heels of one female was a calf barely a month old. This littlest elephant explained the extra caution of the group earlier after smelling us. The reason they didn't run away altogether was that the animals were somewhat used to human scent.

Many Indian reserves differ from Western exclusionary models. In addition to the tribal people permitted to live inside the Nilgiri Reserve, nearby villagers were allowed to gather firewood and graze livestock on a limited basis within the periphery of the protected area. Some selective commercial logging of teak was also allowed. To integrate the biosphere reserve with existing land-use practices and local economies was the strategy. To some extent, it was an effective one. However, the number of people using the periphery far exceeded the guidelines; villagers penetrated farther into more pristine core areas than they were supposed to; and quite a few people were simply squatting in the reserve. If the wild creatures were to flee every time they smelled people nearby, they would soon be exhausted.

The elephants we were observing continued across the open understory. We jumped down from the tree and followed at a distance. The group came to a spot where we had crouched earlier while first locating the animals. Trunks probed the grasses and inhaled our spoor, possibly testing it for freshness. Then those trunks reared upward and waved toward us like so many tentacles. I thought of Rudyard Kipling's "Just So" story about how the elephant got its trunk: A nose of the everyday short-snout kind was grabbed and stretched by a crocodile on the banks of the great, green, greasy Limpopo River. My thoughts swirled back to Tsavo, where an observer wrote of seeing a bull elephant having trouble withdrawing its trunk from Mzima Springs after drinking. A great heave finally got the trunk out— with a good-size crocodile attached to the end. The bull wound up and swung the reptile twenty-five feet through the air.

"Elephants can smell fear. You must not show fear," Chenna was whispering. "You must not think fear either." No fear. No fear.

Following the matriarch's lead, the giants all turned in our direction. No fear. My attention was riveted on a life form at my feet. It was one of the long, twiglike insects known as walking sticks. The fore and aft legs were green, the middle pair brown as dead branches. And the digestive system was spilling out of its split abdomen. Someone's heedless shoe had crushed the bug in the grasses, and it was dragging itself along toward oblivion, noticed only by me and the flies already feeding on its guts. Crashing noises brought my head up. The giants had turned again, this time in the direction they had come from, and they silently melted back into the jungle thickets.

Chenna said the lead female never would have rushed us for any distance. Why? Out of fear of becoming separated from her baby. But you never knew whether one of the lower-ranking females might try her luck. And a musth male—you never knew what he was going to do next because he didn't know either.

Chenna happened to be a genuine authority in the sphere of elephants, fear, and charges. "If an elephant comes running at you, you just stay and watch, and if it slows down its speed just a little, just very slightly as it charges, you can continue to stand still, and it will come to a stop," he told me. Siva vouched for the fact that Chenna was willing to stand his ground in the face of an onrushing giant. Elephants had come as close as twenty feet before putting on the brakes, and Chenna never faltered. He was even known to chase elephants. Chenna said he was twenty-two years old when he learned the trick of not showing or thinking fear. As he was twenty-nine when we met, I suppose there is something to it. Possibly, the secret has to do with becoming motionless, for Chenna insisted that it was as important to avoid moving as to avoid feeling or revealing fear.

Suppose the elephant is twenty feet away and still shows no sign of stopping? "If the elephant comes on at full speed, no slowing—that is the sign, no slowing—you had better fly. Throw stones. Yell and throw and run to a new place. And then stop moving. It really works very well," Chenna assured me. I believed that it worked. For Chenna. He was lithe and extremely quick, as well as confident enough to avoid making any panicky moves. If he had to, he could probably be zagging before the average giant was done zigging. I recalled Iain Douglas-Hamilton's tales of standing off some elephant charges by swinging a survey tripod over his head, and I had grown somewhat used to low-level bluff charges by African elephants. But I had no urge to test myself Chenna-style around these Asian ones.

The reason I am paying so much attention to rip-snorting elephant chase sagas is that I believe the surprisingly aggressive behavior of the giants here reveals a great deal about the forces currently affecting them and their ultimate chances for survival. The strongest force is the relentless expansion of the human population around the reserve. Acre by acre, the buffer zones of forest once lightly used by people are being converted into intensively used pasture and farmland to feed the exploding populace. More and more, the Nilgiri elephants' use of low elevations brings them into contact with agricultural areas, and it does so at exactly the wrong time for the local farmers.

Farmers usually plant some sorghum, maize, and other crops during the period of light, premonsoon rains that begins in April and May. More extensive plantings, mainly of *ragi*, or finger millet, are made from late summer onward in anticipation of the true monsoons. Elephants are down frequenting the thorn-scrub soon afterward, having abandoned the tall, rank grass of the highlands in search of more palatable fare. In keeping with their strategy of exploiting the most nutritious, high-energy food resource available in any given season, they could hardly do better than to move on into the nearest fields to get at the growing grains in monsoon time. And it is never that far a march from the mountains to the fields in any season for an elephant that remembers dining on the sort of plants that flourish year-round near villages: banana, jackfruit, mango, coconut, and sugar cane.

Elephant crop raids nearly always take place at night. Females and other family members tend to linger by the forest edge when they come into fields and are fairly easily spooked off by approaching people. Mothers with young babies almost never raid by themselves. Bulls are more likely than cows to stomp right out into the open and remain there despite disturbances, though the younger bulls often wait until they can join with other males before venturing into the fields. Sukumar saw one old, experienced male arrive at 6:00 P.M. and gorge itself steadily until 6:00 A.M., by which time it had removed between 440 and 660 pounds of millet.

Twice the weight of females when fully grown, Asian males consume twice as much during a typical raid. They also raid much more often and are much more dangerous to deal with. Of the 160 deaths from elephants that Sukumar recorded for the Nilgiri area, 45 percent were on cultivated land. All but one of them were caused by bulls. The other deaths occurred within the reserve but were in large part associated with settlements located within the reserve. About 80 percent of those were caused by males too.

A particularly notorious bull that Sukumar monitored was in crop fields at least 120 nights, a third of the year. In the Nilgiri area, the average adult male raided fields on 49 nights of the year and caused U.S. $600 worth of damage to crops, while the average family member raided on 8 nights and did more like $30 of damage—still a substantial amount in a land where the annual per-capita income is under $200. This is why farmers average something like 100 nights a year in the fields themselves. Some, especially owners of the newest plots to have been hacked out of the forest along the reserve's edge, spend more than 150 nights among their crops, trying to ward off raids.

Sambar, chital, and troops of langur monkeys all filch a share of human produce and must be guarded against. The two deer species usually arrive for the early sprouts. Elephants are more likely to wait until a grain field is tall and golden and almost ready to cut, then come in and break farmers' hearts. "One year, they took three-quarters of my crop just days before the harvest," I heard from Boran Gowda, the owner of several plots. "Last year, I spent six months in the fields at night. When there were maybe two days left until harvesting, elephants came. They didn't take everything from me, but they took too much. They took the whole field next to mine."

It was getting close to ripening time when I was there. Boran's fields of *ragi* were once again full of promise. They lay at the edge of a village called Masinagudi, meaning temple (*gudi*) of Masina, a local fertility goddess. Back in April, an elderly man from Masinagudi—too old to have reflexes like Chenna's—had been resting against a tree in the reserve to keep an eye on his grazing cattle when he was attacked and killed by a male elephant about ten years old. Now the scene of encounters had moved to the fields. There had been interactions between people and elephants almost every night.

Several took place the first night we visited, as a young bull rummaged through fields close to Boran's. Sukumar guessed the male's age at five to seven. He was not big, but big enough to smash through live fences of thornbush and a euphorbia with toxic sap planted along the boundaries of fields to keep cattle out. Big enough to mash a grass sleeping hut and intimidate those on guard, then go on to feast upon millet turning from green to gold.

We heard the commotion, but I never caught sight of the culprit. Operating alone, he was fast and furtive. When morning arrived, we inspected the damage, with Sukumar carefully measuring out the dimensions of trampling and grazing in the millet patch. We spent the day observing wild elephants within the reserve, briefly following a group of seventeen, then returned to Masinagudi by late afternoon. Evening came and gave way to lavender twilight, and we rejoined the farmers out in the fields. For some of them, the busiest part of the twenty-four-hour period was just beginning.

The scene was of preparation for battle, and it could have been from any century in the past several thousand years. Across the grain-patterned landscape, men squatted over small fires beside grass huts and piles of throwing stones they had gathered. Others moved between outposts carrying torches. Stout trees had been left standing here and there amid the plots. Almost every one had a ladder along its trunk leading up to a watch hut or platform in the branches. Boys as young as twelve joined the defense force, and they were usually stationed in the trees, straining to see through the gloaming. From the trees, from the ground huts, from campfires glowing in the distance, the farmers sent a growing chorus of hoots and clangs out against the night.

Boran had cobbled together a wind-driven mill of tin cans with pebbles inside. Each gust sent the contraption ratcheting and clattering with renewed strength. Other men carried rattles. A few had whistles. The night before, an unearthly hybrid of a moan and a squeal had put the hair on my neck on alert. While wandering through the moonlit fields in search of the marauding bull, we had come upon a man squatting next to an inverted tin can. The shaft of a peacock feather hung from its center like a bell clapper. He showed me how to moisten my fingers and pull them down the length of the feather vane, which had a rough feel. The friction generated the weird moan-squeal noise, and the can amplified it to a startling volume.

Whatever works. Sometimes, nothing does. I was told that experienced crop-raiding bulls would ignore thrown firecrackers and even gunshots aimed close to them. "I once put five rounds over an elephant's head from the verandah as he was raiding our area. This gentleman did not even have the courtesy to stop chewing," sniffed Siasp Kothavala, the owner of a small plantation in Masinagudi.

This night, the moon would rise late and be close to full. We waited by Boran's little fire. Periodically, an alarm arose in some quarter and surged across the fields, raising cries on all sides, then gradually ebbed as it was proved false. As the hours wore on and still no elephants came, I drifted off to sleep by the coals. It was a fitful sleep, roiled by the wind-powered rattle close at hand, twisted by sporadic cries and whistles from afar. Before

long, I slipped into truly evil dreams, one bloody phantasma-
goria soaking into another. At some point, I roused myself long
enough to think: God help me, I must have had other lives to put
details in my head like these; what bitter proof of reincarnation.
Then I drifted off again.

Sometime after midnight, I was shaken out of my horrific
drowse and led stumbling through pools of moonlight toward a
great roaming boulder of darkness. At first, we were expecting
the smaller bull that had come the night before. Then we were
expecting a teenage bull that had been reported while I was
sleeping. But this one was enormous and trumpeting like doom.
Once enough men had gathered with torches and flashlights,
screaming and hurling stones, he finally gave way. But he returned from the forest at a different point fifteen minutes later,
was driven off again, returned. . . .

Back at his hut Boran rubbed his eyes and said, "I believe the
elephant is a god. If I lose my crops, I never blame the elephant.
I blame myself. I wonder what I have done wrong. I pray to Ganesh not to destroy my food."

Ganesh, also revered as Ganesa and Ganapati, is Lord of the folk,
Remover of obstacles, God of wisdom and success. He is the son
of Siva, mightiest of all the Hindu deities, and his consort, Parvati. In one version of Ganesh's origin, Parvati formed him from
rubbings off her own body, then stationed him by the door to
her chambers to stand guard while she took a bath. Returning
from his cosmic errands, Siva flew into a rage when he found a
handsome stranger by his wife's door. (Some versions say Ganesh was conceived and grew up in the normal manner, but Siva
had been away so long that he failed to recognize his own son in
Parvati's room.) The upshot was that Ganesh got his head cut
off. Emerging to see what the ruckus was about, Parvati let Siva
know that he had just murdered her offspring. A chastised and
repentant Siva at once dispatched his minions to cut off the head
of the first living thing they came upon so they could replace Ga-

nesh's with it. That first living thing happened to be an elephant. Hence, another name for this god: Gajamukha, the elephant-faced.

Though a subsidiary deity in terms of rank and power, Ganesh the facilitator, the intermediary, chief among Siva's attendants, is generally the one first called upon whenever a supplicant arrives at a holy site to address other gods. He is also worshipped in his own right, and worshipped often, because as lord of the folk, Ganesh is the one who takes the time to sympathize with householders' everyday needs and worries. When bare feet first touch village streets in the predawn light, when hands move through the mist and dust bearing lighted candles and offerings, when the cupped flame and fruits and rice grains and vermilion powders are brought before images of the holy, the first word on the lips of millions as they begin their morning prayers is Ganesh.

I saw Ganesh temples old and new on the way to the Nilgiri Reserve, Ganesh shrines among the houses in villages, and Ganesh icons at the entryways to homes. He is carved with a realistic trunked elephant's head—a tusked male head, with one of the tusks usually depicted as broken. The heavy head rests upon a four-armed body, which typically has a smooth potbelly and short, bandy legs. Beneath the legs is the image of another creature. Each major Hindu deity is associated with one—a living vehicle, an animal that he or she rides through time and space. Siva's vehicle is a bull, Vishnu's a bird, and so on. Ganesh rides upon a rat, which is interesting in light of the Western myth that elephants are terrified of small rodents. This belief is an old one. Pliny records that "They hate the mouse worst of living things, and if they see one merely touch the fodder in their stall they refuse it with disgust." One trainer at an American zoo told me that captive elephants in earlier times may indeed have been terrified of small rodents, but because rats came to gnaw at their shackled legs. However, another trainer said he had seen elephants squash mice and roll their little bodies underfoot until the skin came off. And Dave Blasko, of Marine World–Africa, U.S.A. in Vallejo, California, knew of a captive elephant that regularly set aside a small portion of its ration of grain for a resident mouse, perhaps a case of a tame animal keeping a pet of its own.

The four hands of the elephant god variously hold a cattle goad, a noose or halter, a rice pot, a scepter, or boons for worshippers. More likely than not, one of the hands holds Ganesh's broken tusk. In another of his roles, that of the sacred scribe, Ganesh first put the epic *Mahabharata* into written form, furiously scribbling in Sanskrit on papyrus leaves as the sage Vyasa dictated. Partway through, Ganesh's writing stick broke. Without hesitation, he snapped off his own tusk to use in its place and carried on. He stands as the patron of letters and learning, and I left offerings to the Elephant-headed One many times, asking him to help me gain knowledge and pass it on to others. This was also a way for me to express the respect I felt for the power and intelligence of the elephants themselves.

Yes, some elephants were out there at the same time stomping around on fields, huts, and people. Sukumar described places where the giants went after the grain even after it was harvested, breaking into storage houses. They also had a knack for smashing illegal stills in the forest, where the grain was being fermented into liquor, wallowing and swallowing in piles of mash. In one village, a bull found a whole barrel of palm toddy, sucked it down, and proceeded to act about like you would expect a megaton drunk to act. He tore up and smashed and trampled the village and quite possibly enjoyed the hell out of himself. But, as Boran knew, that's the sort of things gods do. Whether they have elephant heads or some other form, they will test you, taking away the very things you most cherish to check on your soul. Who can say why?

The special reverence Hindus feel toward elephants is reinforced at a broader level by the Hindu reverence for all life, a concept known as *ahimsa*. You could also describe *ahimsa* as nonviolence, the avoidance of harm, or simply as compassion. It springs from a conviction that even the smallest and most common of creatures with no direct link to the Hindu pantheon are nonetheless manifestations of the divine.

Given that the object is not to destroy these animals, farmers quickly run short of ways to contend with crop-raiding giants, beyond attacking bravely with stones and torches. Trenches rather like those used to block tank movements have been tried out as barriers in a few places. With their columnar legs, elephants lack the flexibility to contend with abrupt drop-offs. But they make up for physical shortcomings with mental abilities. Local Nilgiri tales describe elephants using logs to make bridges. One farmer swore to me that he had seen an adult elephant climb down into a trench and let the smaller ones cross on its back. I can't vouch for the accounts of either technique being genuine, though zoo elephants are known to have made log bridges over lesser barriers, and the Roman author Aelian wrote of an elephant going down into a trench so that others could use its back as a bridge. In any case, many Nilgiri elephants quickly learned to simply kick down the earthen embankments with their feet to create crossings. An equally serious shortcoming of trenches is the sheer amount of labor required to dig them and then maintain the steep sides against monsoon thunderbursts and general erosion leading to slumping.

Asian elephants can learn to overcome electric fences as well, using the thickly padded, insulating soles of the feet to depress the wires. Bulls discover that their tusks are also poor conductors and use them the same way. And some elephants apparently learn to push trees down across the fences. Observers claim to have seen the animals drag in trees or branches from some distance away to throw them across fences—making bridges again. I had already heard about each of those techniques in Africa, along with stories of mothers lifting young babies completely over a fence with their trunks.

Not every elephant improvises ways around electric fences, though, and those that do may still receive shocks often enough through slips and miscalculations to result in negative conditioning. Consequently, this sort of barrier has proved effective in a variety of situations and holds real promise. The main drawback at the moment is that few individual farmers in developing nations can afford such fencing, much less the generators or solar panels necessary to power them in remote areas. Agricultural cooperatives can sometimes come up with the funds but seem to run into difficulties getting people to maintain long stretches of fencing. Without periodic wire-mending and clearing of vegetation that can grow up to short-circuit fencelines, the whole structure is little better than string. The most successful operators of electric fencing in elephant country have generally been well-to-do individual farmers and highly organized estates and plantations.

The subject of electric fences is a reminder that the elephant's aura of the divine is not enough to protect it from some Indians. There are farmers who will run a strand of wire along the border of their fields and hook it up directly to a 230-volt electric transmission line. An elephant touching this illegal barrier will be instantly stunned or killed (and the same holds for any unsuspecting person happening upon it). This is the most common way of dealing with giant marauders. One farmer fried an elephant by putting one end of a wire into a nice, ripe bunch of bananas and throwing the other end over a high-tension power line. A few wealthy farmers and plantation owners have been known to hire someone to surreptitiously shoot problem elephants.

The number of elephant deaths caused by people taking extreme measures to defend their fields has been relatively minor in the Nilgiri ecosystem. But one more factor remains to be accounted for in elephant-human relationships here, and that factor is ivory poaching. Rampant ivory poaching. It has not devastated the population for one simple reason: Asian elephant females lack tusks; therefore, the breeding segment of the population has been left more or less intact. Sukumar feels that the Nilgiri population has held its own numerically and possibly even increased by 1 percent to 2 percent a year. But the killing of males has been so pervasive that it threatens the genetic and behavioral make-up of the species over the long term, together with its very survival.

Beginning in the late 1970s, poachers in southern India killed a minimum of 90 to 150 bulls each year, Sukumar figures. That toll may not seem too dramatic, considering that the region holds 5000 to 7000 elephants, counting the Nilgiri animals. Over the years, however, it added up to the removal of nearly all the big tuskers in many areas. In 1987, when Sukumar recorded the age and sex of 1188 elephants in the Nilgiri area, he found only 46 males older than fifteen. And the pace of killing had picked up since then. Ajay and Siva thought that about 500 elephants, or 12.5 percent of the Nilgiri population, had been poached within recent years.

In preparing to publish a book based upon his studies (his excellent *The Asian Elephant: Ecology and Management* came out later in 1989), Sukumar had made it his business to collect updated census estimates from throughout the species's range. He could list seven elephant populations large enough to possibly avoid slipping away over the long run through increasing isolation combined with genetic drift and inbreeding. One inhabits the state of Sabah in Borneo. One is in the Irrawady-Chindwin valleys and northern hill ranges of Burma. Another dwells in southeastern Sri Lanka. Between political instability and massive deforestation, none of these three can be considered secure. The Sabah population was becoming thoroughly fragmented by the time the book came out, and Sri Lanka's model system of connected reserves was a casualty of war, with dead rangers, poisoned waterholes, and rebel groups using the wildlands as bases of operations.

The other four major elephant populations are in India. Three of them are in the north of the nation and also subject to political instability along with accelerating habitat transformation. The last population consists of the inhabitants of the Nilgiri area. They, too, are steadily growing more confined by conversion of wildlands. Traditional migration corridors between the Eastern and Western Ghats are being whittled down to a scattered sequence of microhabitats—swales and thickets, stringers and brushy bottoms—that are just barely usable anymore. Forests linking the ecosystem to the Lake Periyar area and other prime elephant range to the south are already in the next stage—transformed into a belt of farmland and villages wide enough that it now acts as an all but impermeable barrier.

Within the Nilgiri Reserve itself, heavy grazing and firewood gathering remove a certain amount of forage from the elephants. Of greater concern are the fires that repeatedly sweep through the forest during the dry season every year. They are set by herders to maintain grassy pasture, by gatherers of honey and herbs to make travel easier and dangerous animals more visible, and by poachers to drive game and make their prey more visible. In sum, almost everyone using the reserve except tourists is likely to be tossing out matches during the dry months. Lightning-set wildfires grow fine grasslands and are an important agent of natural habitat diversity within the monsoon forest. But fires set too frequently by people discourage regeneration of the very trees that build the forest.

Frequent fires also suppress the growth of bamboo. The Nilgiri area harbors two species of these huge, fast-growing (up to a foot per day) grasses. They serve as a favored and nutritious food source for elephants and other herbivores and also as a refuge when dense groves develop. Typically, all the individual plants of a bamboo species in a given area flower simultaneously. But they usually do this only at intervals of several years. When it happens, the flowering provides a tremendous bounty of seeds—natural grain—for a host of insects, birds, and rodents, as well as for larger animals up to elephant size.

Because of human activities, then, the Nilgiri elephants are becoming increasingly cut off from other herds and habitats, and the habitats within the reserve that they are supposed to be able to count on are subject to some degree of degradation. The combination of fire, overgrazing by livestock, excessive firewood cutting, and clearing of adjoining buffer zones for agriculture is most intensely felt in the dry forest and thornscrub habitats at the low elevation end of the spectrum.

Even so, this population ought to stay strong. Scientists believe that the smallest number of breeding individuals required to maintain a healthy gene pool is about 500 for most species, and the Nilgiri total of about 4000 elephants is eight times that. But there is a catch. Unless all the animals in a population are in fact breeding (which is never the case, due to the presence of immature, infertile, or very old animals), and unless a number of other idealized conditions hold as well (the sex ratio is exactly fifty-fifty, all mating pairs produce exactly the same number of offspring, etc.), the minimum number of individuals must be considerably larger than 500 in order to maintain viability.

I'm not trying to make this sound complicated. I'm trying to explain that because of the highly skewed sex ratio in the Nilgiri elephant population, only a small number of males are contributing genes. As a result, Sukumar points out, the *effective* population size for the whole Nilgiri area is already getting dangerously close to the minimum of 500 breeding individuals. Thus can poachers threaten the future of one of the last best hopes for the Asian elephant almost as certainly as poachers in Africa have laid waste to the great herds there.

෴෴෴෴෴෴෴෴෴෴෴෴

India developed an ivory-carving industry early in its history. It exported ivory goods to Greece, Rome, Persia, and other Mediterranean empires, and to the Orient as well. But from which elephant species the ivory was obtained is hard to determine, for India also began importing tusks from Africa early on. Elephant teeth were being shipped to the subcontinent from Ethiopia by the sixth century B.C. By then, elephant habitat in India had already been substantially reduced, and over the centuries that followed, the surviving herds were increasingly prized as sources of elephants for war and ceremonial display.

In his illuminating research on the ivory trade, Esmond Bradley Martin revealed that modern India probably had far and away more ivory carvers than any other nation. As late as 1978, some 7200 Indian men and boys made their living working with elephant teeth. They produced vast quantities of figurines and jewelry. But India's specialty was meticulously worked ivory *jalis*, or screens, and inlaid furniture. The carvers also made thin sheets of ivory, upon which painters daubed classical scenes and portraits, as well as ornate ivory picture frames.

And who were the consumers? Ivory bracelets had become standard gifts for brides in India, but more than 85 percent of the finished ivory went to foreign outlets in Europe and the United States. An unknown quantity left India in the luggage of tourists, again mostly Westerners. And a quantity both unknown and illegal went by *dhow* to Arab nations.

During the 1870s, the peak of the elephant slaughter by colonial powers in Africa, India was importing some 250 tons of ivory annually, more than Japan in the 1970s. Ivory imports remained high until about the middle of this century, when steep import duties dampened them. Further regulations and restrictions followed, but the value of ivory products kept rising apace with the world market. In other words, ivory became harder than ever to obtain legally, yet pricier than ever with each passing year. You could scarcely design a more ideal incentive for poaching.

India had always continued to supply some ivory from its own elephants. The country experienced an elephant massacre in the nineteenth century at about the same time as Africa, thanks to India's British colonists. Besides hunting elephants as trophy game, they were shooting up herds to prevent depredations on newly established plantations of tea, coffee, and other commodity crops. Until 1873, the British raj even offered a bounty on elephants. After game laws came into effect, tusks were still available from sportsmen's kills, legally shot crop-raiders, domestic elephants that had died, and remains of wild bulls found in the forest. The Indian carving industry quickly absorbed whatever was available.

Nearly half of all the carvers were concentrated in a fairly small part of the country—the southern state of Kerala. Whereas northern carvers, based mostly in Delhi, shifted to electric lathes and drills, the southern carvers continued to work with traditional hand tools and were known for the more artistic quality of their sculptures. Kerala happens to have a large Muslim population and close ties with Arab countries, and it is where heavy poaching first became noticeable during the 1970s.

Lake Periyar Tiger Reserve, a major elephant stronghold

south of the Nilgiri area along the Western Ghats, took the first big hit. By the end of the 1980s, biologists were counting just one mature male for every twenty mature females there. As a precaution all too familiar to an African traveler, visitors were no longer allowed to travel in the park's interior due to the danger of poaching gangs, some of which were up to two hundred strong. Smaller, loosely organized bands—the freelancers—made do with muzzle-loading guns, but the big gangs relied upon modern automatic rifles. Some used dogs to track elephants and help separate young bulls from family groups.

The most dangerous gang of brigands was led by a man named Veerappan, who by then had a bounty on his head of a million rupees (about U.S. $80,000 at the time). He and his outlaw bunch were responsible for the deaths of several policemen and rangers as well as many scores of elephants. Authorities caught him once, but he bribed his way free and went on to kill more rangers. He was said to be a great drinker and womanizer, cruel to underlings who failed to do his bidding, and lethal to villagers who informed on him. At the same time, some hailed him as a sort of Robin Hood, for his poaching operations spread wealth among squatters and indigenous forest people displaced or suppressed by officialdom.

Sukumar was put off by the quasilegend, for he had lost a good ranger friend to the bullets of Veerappan's desperados. (In 1992, I learned from Sukumar that Veerappan had just killed another ranger after luring the man to a rendezvous site at which the outlaw was supposed to turn himself in.) Siva had come upon bandit gangs on three different occasions while following elephants in the backcountry and was alive because no one recognized him as being associated with the reserve. Tensions were high. Under Indian law, a strong burden to prove guilt lay upon any enforcement official who killed a person in the course of duty. As a result, I was told, rangers found it simpler and cleaner to either ignore poachers or leave their bodies in the bush. Given the size of the gangs and their network of village informers, rangers often chose the path of willful ignorance.

"You will no doubt hear officials say we have the problem under control now," Sukumar told me. Officials had already said exactly that to me. "The truth is that the killing slowed only because the poachers at last began to run out of bulls to shoot." The gangs were still intact and had moved on to poaching sandalwood, which was now bringing 150 to 300 rupees (U.S. $12 to $14) a kilo and becoming as scarce as bulls with tusks. In fact, the bandits were being forced to turn from sandalwood to poaching rosewood in the reserves. You couldn't help but wonder what would be next.

Between 6 and 9 percent of the dead bulls Sukumar recorded had succumbed to wounds after eluding the hunters who shot them. He knew that because he found the bullet-punctured bodies with tusks still attached. How many wounded bulls stayed alive but full of infection and irritation? How did this influence their next encounters with people in the forests and fields? How much of the aggressiveness of the Nilgiri elephants toward people in general was due to the basic nature of *Elephas maximus*? How much was due to the fact that they had a lot of interactions with people and a high percentage of those interactions were painful and threatening? In the jungle, they were shot at; in the fields, they were continually stoned and harassed.

Poaching gangs took other game as well as ivory-bearing elephants. In Sukumar's opinion, chital and elephants hung out near fields and villages not only to get at crops but for the same reason many species had taken to lingering by ranger headquarters in certain African parks: because they were safer from poachers there than in the depths of the forest. In a vicious cycle, poaching probably increased crop-raiding and the likelihood of raiders killing villagers, which increased villagers' resentment of the animals and led them to believe that there were too many around, which meant the villagers would be more likely to look the other way around poaching networks, maybe even take part in them.

We may never know the answer to the question of how much of the Nilgiri elephants' aggressiveness is genetic and how much learned, because there are no nearby groups of undisturbed elephants for comparison. In all of Asia, it would be hard to find a group harassed neither by hunters nor by encroachment upon their habitat. Circumstantial evidence from earlier decades in different countries suggests that groups free from direct harm were more tolerant of humans. Common sense says they should be. The Kuruba and Soligal natives in Nilgiri said that the elephants didn't used to be so hard to scare away, nor were they so quick to give chase.

Extreme intolerance is learned, just as the sort of friendly tolerance seen in special situations such as Kenya's Amboseli Reserve is learned. Just as pet owners and trainers know from ordinary experience how different approaches can yield a gentle dog or a mean one. You can even produce a vicious pet rabbit if you punish it often enough. The wonder is that the Nilgiri elephants did *not* bother the overwhelming majority of local people and visitors passing through the reserve. A number of those who were harmed were drunk, crazy, or acting like typical tourists and photographers who insisted upon getting way too close and violating the elephants' sense of personal space.

With its huge, convoluted brain and prolonged period of dependency, the elephant is designed to learn from experience. It is prepared to absorb, process, and store information about the route to a dry-season waterhole, the status of members in a neighboring herd, where it must be wary, where it may relax a bit, and so on. This is part of what its much-discussed memory is all about, part of the reason those in captivity can be trained to respond to more than sixty different commands.

Bernhard Rensch trained a young Asian elephant female to discriminate between twenty pairs of symbols presented on cards. After a year went by during which the animal had no exposure to the symbols, she was tested again and remembered thirteen of the pairs. Recently, Charles Hyatt and his colleagues at the Georgia Institute of Technology's Psychology School repeated the experiment with African elephants. One subject was taught the same twenty pairs of symbols and, when retested after a break of eight months, remembered sixteen of them.

These were not simple dots and squares that the animals learned and later recalled, but complex symbols. Very complex.

"It is also interesting to note," Hyatt and his coworkers wrote in their report, "that in both elephant studies, even after thousands of trials, the human experimenters relied heavily on written notes to identify the correct stimuli." In other words, the humans couldn't always remember which cards went with which. A study conducted in the mid-1970s challenged three Asian elephants to operate panel keys in certain sequences to obtain a reward. Eight years later, having had no exposure to the testing device in the interim, one of the animals remembered most of the correct sequences.

Would experiences such as being hit with stones, wounded, or watching family members die alter behavior in an animal this bright? Surely it is only because science does not yet know how to speak about animals in nonmechanistic terms that it has so much trouble answering. Is there any doubt that these sorts of experiences affect attitudes in people? They shape ethnic and national psychologies, borders, wars, vengefulness carried across the centuries. Indeed, they drive history. In my opinion, each population of elephants, including those in the Nilgiri area, has developed unique psychological attitudes as well as unique day-to-day patterns of living. They merely wait for us to accord them some of the qualities of consciousness we so insistently reserve for ourselves.

All right. Granted, the Nilgiri elephants have an attitude. But what's the norm? This gets back to the question of where in Asia there is an undisturbed elephant population for comparison. But then, how long ago was "undisturbed" the norm? Elephants in India and much of the rest of Asia have been hunted by various tribes since long before the written word existed. And for at least the past 3000 to 4000 years, they have also been squeezed out of traditional ranges and captured to be pressed into the service of human society.

In the south, Indians captured elephants singly in pits dug in the forest floor. In the north, the capturers used the *keddah* method, driving entire herds of elephants into corrals built of massive logs. To help build the corrals and drive the wild elephants into them, tame elephants were used. They also plowed

fields and logged forests; how many species are forced to participate in the destruction of their own environment? Most importantly, as far as the rulers were concerned, the giants waged war,
serving as the precursor of tanks and heavy trucks.

Sultans and maharajahs boasted of armies of thousands of elephants. They were probably lying to impress their neighbors
and enemies; yet they certainly had armies of hundreds of elephants trained for fighting and hundreds more to transport supplies. For example, the Delhi sultanate of the thirteenth and
fourteenth centuries claimed to have 3000 war elephants. In
truth, only about a third of them were fit and trained for battle.
Yet think what it took to muster just 1000 grey giants upon a bat-
tlefield. Think what it was like to see rank upon rank of such
beasts shining in full armor, two-story wooden towers for arch-
ers swaying upon their backs, horns of hammered metal jutting
from the headdresses covering their foreheads so that, with their
tusks, the animals looked like triceratops. It got to be a measure
of wealth and prestige simply to have huge numbers of elephants under royal care and available for display in processions.
Vassal states sent elephants as tribute, and the capture of an enemy's elephants was considered one of the great spoils of war.
Symbolic of the old wars that pitted massive tuskers against one
another, *sath-maru*, or elephant wrestling, remained a spectator
sport in India up until World War II.

In the third century B.C., the great Indian emperor Ashok
converted to Buddhism. Soon afterward, he issued India's first
known conservation law, the Fifth Pillar Edict, forbidding the
slaughter of certain animals, including elephants, and the burning of forests. A work on statecraft called the *Arthasastra*, written sometime between 300 B.C. and A.D. 300, also addressed the
need to preserve elephants in the forests beyond settled land. To
that effect, rulers were advised to set about establishing elephant
sanctuaries complete with guard patrols. Elephant poachers
were to be killed.

Thinking about the battles between rangers and Veerappan's
outlaw brigade in the Nilgiri Reserve, it seems to me that things
have not changed much over the centuries. Of course, the pur-

pose of those ancient sanctuaries was to ensure a supply of giants for military purposes, not for wildlife appreciation. Sukumar told me that Ganesh worship was not common before the third or fourth century, and he wondered if it might not have been fostered by officials as a way of reinforcing elephant protection as the giants became scarcer.

The norm today, and for thousands of years past, is of Asian elephants contending with an array of human depredations. If one day we wanted to restore a population of *Elephas maximus* within a truly pristine setting, it would be hard to know what sort of ecological and behavioral patterns to promote as "natural." The biological data painstakingly gathered by Sukumar, Ajay, Siva, and others in the Nilgiri Reserve tell us about animals whose habitat use has been rearranged by disturbances and whose population structure lacks adult males. It can only go so far in telling us which things to save in an effort to save the species.

For example, Sukumar had never seen a band of bulls larger than three in the reserve, and 93 percent of the mature males he saw apart from female-led groups were solitary. Is this a characteristic trait of *Elephas maximus* that has helped it adapt to its environment, or a consequence of *Homo sapiens* looting herds for teeth? Some Nilgiri males seem to become independent of family groups at an earlier age than is typical for African savanna elephants. We also noticed wild Nilgiri males showing signs of heavy musth at age twenty or so, whereas Joyce Poole seldom saw full musth in African savanna elephants before their mid-thirties. Was the difference natural? Did it suggest the intriguing possibility that Asian elephants are more similar to African forest elephants, which also appear to become independent at a young age? Or was it another artifact of poaching and the resulting absence of mature bulls?

Consider the saga of the first of several small Nilgiri herds that made their way into the Chitoor district of the state of Andhra Pradesh. Wild elephants had not been seen there for generations, possibly for four hundred years. Did the elephants disperse as a result of normal population dynamics, or as refugees trying to escape attacks by poachers and the social instability that followed? Totally inexperienced with wild elephants, folks in Andhra Pradesh came bearing offerings of fruits and sweets as they would to elephants at temples. They hoped to touch the sacred beasts and be blessed. Instead of blessings, they received blows. Others, hearing a commotion in their fields at night, ran out with sticks to shoo off what they thought were buffalo. Smoosh. The first seven elephant colonists had so far killed something like twenty-eight people. A research student recorded one of the elephants dragging the body of a man it had killed into a pit and covering it with mud.

Was this degree of violence to be expected if wild elephants were lucky enough to increase in number and expand their range elsewhere? Or was it because this herd had particularly unpleasant memories of Nilgiri? Or some other reason: a biologist told me that early in their travels beyond the reserve, these elephants had been involved in a nasty encounter with villagers, who killed a baby elephant while trying to capture it. Was that what made the animals so quick to lash out?

From here, the questions could lead into moral territory, and maybe they should. The tale of the Andhra Pradesh elephants almost demands that we consider whether the attitudes of those animals were not in some part justified. What about the attitudes of the crop-raiders in Masinagudi? Is there or is there not any justification for putting the desires and reactions of elephants on an equal footing with the desires and reactions of people? Odd though it might seem by Western standards, hard-pressed farmers such as Boran Gowda would be among the first to answer: there is. Animal rights are built into his view of the world. If there were ever a place to pursue the subject of species sharing our moral realm, it would be India, where elephants, real and sacred, are inextricably linked to the efforts and aspirations of human culture, and where the potent concept of *ahimsa* is part of everyday life.

TEN

INDIA: MUDUMALAI SANCTUARY

🖸🖸🖸🖸 CLOSE BY THE village of Theppakadu in southern India's Nilgiri Biosphere Reserve is the Mudumalai Sanctuary Elephant Camp. Here, at the time I visited, in September of 1989, government-salaried mahouts, or elephant handlers, were training young elephants to perform a Hindu ceremony as part of a show for tourists. The prospective devotees, whose juvenile hair made them look to me like balding mammoths, learned to circle a shrine clockwise, the holy way. While circling, each held a bell with its trunk and rang it—the Hindu method of calling the gods to a site of worship. Then, facing the shrine, the elephants would put the bells down and swing their trunks repeatedly back over their heads the way a human worshipper would pass an arm over his or her head as a sign of reverence. Finally, the young elephants touched their ears, another sign of reverence, prostrated themselves together before the altar, and nodded their heads as if in prayer.

In the meantime, older elephants from the camp were taking visitors on rides through the forest and along a canyon rim to a scenic waterfall. "Please don't be telling any tourists," a mahout said to me, "but one of our riding elephants is blind. She is an old woman now and totally blind. We are putting her in the middle of the line, and she follows the others very well. You would never know this old woman is using her ears to find the way instead of her eyes. If it is necessary, she is using her trunk too, like the cane."

Trust. And all the while, wild elephants rambled by within

earshot of the camp and trails. Others waited near the forest edge for nightfall and a visit to the fields. Once in a while, tame bulls were ridden from the camp to agricultural areas and put to work driving off wild crop-raiders.

The camp elephants are primarily kept to be used for selective logging within the reserve; they haul heavy, green teak logs off the hillsides and out of ravines to trucks waiting at the end of the nearest road. Elephants are cheaper to purchase and cheaper to operate than bulldozers and skidders. And their working life span is around three decades, compared to eight to ten years for the average machine. Of equal importance, since this is a protected area, the elephants cause much less damage to the ground-cover than machines do, leading to less habitat change and erosion. More trees must be felled just to give heavy equipment sufficient room to maneuver, and even then the machines simply cannot get to a lot of places the elephants can in steep-sided country.

Muddy roads, slick slopes, and flourishing leeches shut down logging operations during monsoon time, which adds up to a third of the year. Providing rides and putting on demonstrations of log handling for tourists at that time gives the elephants exercise and the mahouts a chance to continue training. Once the demanding labor of logging resumes, some of the weaker, older, and pregnant animals remain behind at the camp and continue to provide visitors with a hands-on experience of giants.

The rains had pushed the last loggers out of the high forests shortly before I arrived, and the slow, easy months for working elephants had begun. Each morning, men and boys took them a short way downhill from camp to a river for a bath, scrubbing them with the cones of *pandanis*, a local tree, until pink skin showed here and there through the grey pigment and caked dirt.

I loved to wander along the riverbank among the beasts and their keepers in the early light. Morning is the time of ritual washing for Hindus everywhere. On the porches and by the windows of countless homes, men and women were performing ablutions and offering praise. Millions more waded into streams and rivers throughout the land to cleanse themselves for the new day. It seemed only right that the elephants would be doing the same.

After wading in to splash, suck up water into their trunks and squirt it into their mouths (one of the 121 Sanskrit names for elephant is "the one who drinks twice"), and shower themselves for a while, the beasts lay down on their sides in the river on command. Sometimes their heads went completely under, leaving only the trunk tip above the water as a snorkel. Legs sprawled to the side like half-submerged logs, and the mahouts paid careful attention to washing the feet and nails. They then crawled up the legs onto the round bellies, which bulged above the surface like boulders, smooth and sunstruck, glistening with droplets. Clambering about on elephant terrain, the mahouts chatted to each other and to their animals while scrubbing away at square yards of flesh.

Many mahouts washed their elephants twice daily in the slow season. One purpose of such regular care is hygienic—to keep the animals free of parasites such as ticks, mites, lice, and leeches and to cleanse any scrapes or wounds to ward off infection. But the mahouts feel that it is equally important merely to have a time each day for extended care and tending, a laying on of hands to reinforce over and over this most unusual and crucial bond between a titan and a human. And anyway, they told me, the elephants loved the water. They recalled stories of elephants brought from dry regions such as Bihar and introduced to standing water for the first time staying immersed for days, refusing to get out. At wits' end, some handlers tried to dislodge one such animal by sending burning tires down the river toward it. The beast supposedly snuffed them out one by one, having also discovered the delight of squirting unlimited amounts of water with its trunk.

Children and bonnet macaques scrambled along the banks beside me as I watched the morning elephant wash. Women came in pairs and small groups, dipped vessels in the elephant-churned water, set them on their heads, walked back uphill. Such a simple, practical sequence, and yet the grace that emanates from a woman sheathed in a bright, silken sari scooping water and walking while balancing a vessel upon her head is boundless. Moving through golden light reflected off the river, the women seemed themselves perfect vessels of the spirit. Arising from the water, the elephants shone as well—part god and part Pleistocene behemoth. With their hairs freed of the usual thick coating of mud and dust, even mature animals showed a touch of the old mammoth shag, and each hair sparkled with crystal droplets.

The mahouts led the younger elephants back to camp and rode the older ones, then cooked them breakfast: balls or cakes of rough wheat and *ragi*, the same stuff elephants and farmers were fighting over nightly not far away. The mush was mixed with *jaggery*, a kind of molasses distilled from sugar-cane juice, and, on occasion, salt and mineral supplements. Rice and coconut go into daily rations for the ill and pregnant.

Laden with cakes, I stuffed them one at a time into the mouth of an old, sunken-templed female towering above me. Her name was Godavri, age seventy-three, retired after a lifetime of work. The mahouts call such elephants pensioners. One named Tara lived on here until the age of seventy-eight. She had retired in her mid-sixties, and the first thing she did upon being pensioned off was to get pregnant, a decade beyond the age at which most females cease breeding.

Toward evening, most of the elephants would again be taken to the river to drink and bathe. Afterward, they would be led into the jungle uphill, where they would be turned loose to feed through the night. Not entirely loose. They would be hobbled by a short, thick rope or chain between the front legs. A very long, heavy chain would be placed around their neck with one end dragging free to help mark a path for mahouts coming to collect their animals in the morning.

Every so often, an elephant learned to haul the chain in with its trunk and to carry part of it coiled there and the rest slung over its back so that it left no trail. That way, the animal might get in a little more foraging time before the mahout found it. The mahouts would place bells on one or more of the elephants in a group to better mark their whereabouts, but some elephants learned to stuff the bells with mud so the clapper couldn't give them away either. On the other hand, I also met a big bull newly laid off from logging work by the rains who had come back to camp on his own in the morning. He was carrying a huge log he had found in the forest.

Not far from the Nilgiri Reserve once lived a mahout who, like many in the elephant-riding trade, worked mainly in logging, and, again like many in his trade, was fond of *arak*, or whiskey. So as soon as he bathed and fed his elephant, a stout bull, in the evening, this mahout, who was rather stout himself, was likely to ride his bull to town. At the tavern, he would buy one bottle for his elephant and several more for himself. When he eventually keeled over, the bull would pick him up like a log, wrapping his trunk around the mahout's body and resting him on his two great tusks. Then he would bear his drunken friend home. Once there, he laid the mahout on the doorstep and waited until someone came to drag him inside. Then he headed back to his corral.

They might have grown old together, those two, but the bull died suddenly of rabies, or possibly anthrax, in his early fifties. One week later, the mahout died, of causes unknown. Possibly anthrax; possibly a broken heart. Some say he went to look for his elephant. A couple of very reliable people I met in the area claimed to have known this mahout personally. Everyone seemed to know the story. Similar stories can be heard in other parts of Asia. I wouldn't claim that they are all true, but with elephants, you don't need to make up all that much.

A couple of miles down the road from Theppakadu was a subsidiary camp where the mahouts and their families lived, along with a number of elephants not currently being used at the tourist center. Just outside the grass and bamboo huts, fires smoked in the drizzling rain and playing children dashed past tethered giants. Three large bulls guarded the encampment from wild elephant groups that frequently used this same riverine area.

Another camp bull I passed had a lot of wildness and white in his eyes. He was in musth, said the mahouts; take care not to get too close. Unsure what "too close" was, I edged by him on my way to the river. From Africa, as well as my recent days in the Nilgiri bush, I expected that an elephant about to charge would kink its tail and draw in its head, bringing the trunk back in preparation for a strike. Often, the animal would even take a few steps backward before beginning a rush. But in the instant before this bull lunged at me, whipping out his trunk as he hit the end of the tether that held his rear leg, all he did was widen his eyes a fraction. Luckily, I caught that change and was leaping away as he lashed at me.

Yaaah! Missed, you ornery bugger. I gave him the finger and was backing away with a stupid grin on my face when I froze, because I suddenly felt a trunk touching my back. Turning slowly, I was relieved to find that the elephant greeting me was a three-year-old bull about my height.

As the juvenile probed, so did I, stroking its hairy head, already taking on the marked dome shape of the species, and examining the trunk tip. The little bull probed slightly harder and then placed that bristle-haired head against me and began to shove me around a little. I knew that he was testing me, but I didn't know the camp protocol for shoving back. The last thing I wanted to risk was offending any mahouts and losing their cooperation, so I led the polite tussle in the direction of one of them and raised my eyebrows in an appeal. He waved his hand at the animal and told it in Tamil to quit, and it did. Smiling, he let me know that several mahouts were Tamils who spoke their own language to the elephants. Quite a few of the giants were bilingual, responding to commands in both Hindi, the standard, and Tamil.

Near one end of camp, where several elephants were tethered together, a dozen or so men had gathered inside a bamboo building to cook the elephants' breakfast. They had made several dozen cakes and were stirring grain in a huge iron kettle to prepare the next batch while the first one cooled. Just the day before, they had thrown a party for the elephants to mark the end of the long, hard logging season and thank these animals. "They feed us all year long; it was our turn to feed them," a mahout said of the affair.

At the party, the handlers had painted the animals' foreheads, emphasizing the center, where devout Hindus paint their own foreheads with the sacred *tika*, symbol of the god within, locale of the hidden third eye that will open upon enlightenment. Next, they ceremonially thanked the giants and praised their abilities. After that, they presented them with a feast of rice, fruits, and sweets purchased with money out of the mahouts' own pockets.

Today, wild boars had come in from the jungle to scavenge leftovers, snuffling just beyond the cook shack. Perched on elephant hitching posts close by, the ubiquitous bonnet macaques watched and commented, waiting for an opportunity to grab their share of scraps. The mahouts were telling me how one man among them could work his bull elephant even during musth. Part of his secret was to wear the same clothes for a month. They were about to let me in on the rest of his secret when through the doorway came the young bull that had been testing me. He was given a cake. But when he tried to push closer for more, he was shooed away again. Apparently, he had free run of the camp up to a point, and I had just seen the point. The other part of the mahout's secret, his companions went on, was that he had worked with elephants for half a century—longer than I had been alive, they laughed.

Two other pieces of elephant information were imparted at the cook shack. I was told that the camp manager had seen a mother lift her baby up onto a ledge using her trunk, reinforcing tales of elephants lifting young over fences. And in regard to memory, a cow elephant who had spent one year at this camp was transferred sixty to ninety miles south. Ten years later, she was frightened by something and ran away. She showed up here about twenty days after that.

꧁꧁꧁꧁꧁꧁꧁꧁꧁꧁

Some say that Asian elephants were first tamed 3000 to 4000 years ago, but tribes surely kept pet elephants before that. In the

Nilgiri area, where the lifestyle of indigenous people and villagers hasn't really changed over the millennia, and where elephants mingle freely with families in the mahouts' camps while wild elephants trumpet in the distance, it was easy to envision how the human–domestic elephant relationship might have started: elephant hunters bring back a surviving calf that lingered by its mother's body; an orphaned animal wanders in from the forest on its own and is rewarded with some extra grain in a good harvest year; a juvenile is caught in a pit meant for pigs or deer and gradually accepts food and caresses from curious people.

What is unusual is that in all the centuries that the Asian elephant has served as a domestic animal, it has never been truly domesticated in the sense of being bred in captivity and gradually turned into a creature slightly different from its wild ancestor. As discussed briefly in the first chapter, nearly all Asian elephants used for domestic purposes were still captured in the wild until recently.

Two reasons for this tradition are given by most Asians. The first is a matter of opinion—namely, that wild-caught elephants become the safest to work with. Elephants raised among people from birth have no innate fear of them, they say. Sooner or later, in one of those delicate, outer-edge-of-control negotiations between giant and mahout, the giant, if it is captive-born and especially if it is male, is going to do what it wants, and the mahout is going to be hurt or killed. A matter of opinion, yet an opinion tested often enough over time to warrant respect. I spoke with quite a few elephant handlers in Asia who knew of someone who had raised an elephant from birth and found it to be a risky work partner. The usual description of the animal was "spoiled."

The second reason for working with wild-caught elephants is economic. Breeding a female means losing her from the work force for nineteen to twenty-two months of gestation followed by up to two or three years of nursing. It is far more efficient to snatch an already weaned youngster from the bush. Actually, the elephant need not be all that young. Serious training cannot begin until the animals are at least five years old, and they will not be ready for preliminary logging lessons until they are teenagers. Contrary to what you might expect, the mahouts insisted, it is not so much more difficult to train a wild adult than a wild juvenile. More dangerous, yes, which is why juveniles are preferred. But the older ones catch on just as quickly and become just as tractable.

Now that wild capture was difficult or illegal almost everywhere, mahouts still did not like to breed captive animals to one another. Instead, most preferred to tether or hobble an oestrous female out in the forest and let wild bulls come to sow their seed in her. Again, there was both an intuitive reason and a pragmatic one behind this practice. The pragmatic reason was that with a wild bull, the mahout did not have to worry about getting him back under control once mating was accomplished—and didn't have to worry about a pair of giants thundering around camp while mating was under way.

And the intuitive reason? Domestic elephants, it was feared, lose some of the vital qualities that will produce powerful, healthy offspring. Science would not necessarily agree, since genetic material does not operate quite like that. But perhaps the traditional belief was a way of getting at a suite of other, genuine cause-effect relationships. Juvenile elephants caught in the field were likely to prove robust, because they had already undergone testing by nature that eliminated the weaker, less genetically fit individuals. If they went on to survive the stressful and sometimes physically punishing process of being "broken"—confined and forced to submit to human will—their vigor was indeed good. By contrast, a mahout might invest years in raising a captive-born elephant only to discover that it was inherently frail and sickly and ultimately useless as a working animal.

An important corollary of the way Asians replenished their supply of tame elephants is that the gene pools of the domestic and wild populations have long been virtually identical and still are, for the most part. This is a rare instance of an endangered species with some 16,000 fully representative, genetically diverse members in captivity. All the animals ever needed to restock a depleted range are at hand.

Still, three problems have arisen, beginning with the fact that most of the range can no longer be restocked, having been transformed into human range.

Problem number two is that the number of captive elephants is in the midst of a steep, long-term decline. Machines are rendering the giants obsolete in the realm of transportation at the same time that the severe deforestation taking place throughout tropical Asia is throwing elephants out of work by the thousands, removing the main impetus for keeping them. Recently released studies sponsored by the United Nations show that the rate of destruction of tropical forests is more rapid than even the most alarmist broadsides of environmental organizations said it was, proceeding 50 percent faster than projected by the last report, in 1980. India was one of the nations found to be losing its tree cover on such a vast scale—ten times the previous estimate—that global forest-loss percentages had to be revised.

As native woodlands are cut and then converted to cropland or monocultures of commercially valuable trees such as coconut, oil palm, or teak, not only are wild elephants displaced, but mahouts find fewer and fewer acres on which their tame elephants can be turned loose to forage. The mahouts either have to begin buying forage or periodically go out to the nearest available habitat and cut grass, palm fronds, bamboo, and other elephant groceries themselves. Feeding a captive elephant therefore becomes a more expensive, time-consuming proposition and, in the end, a less desirable one.

During the height of poaching in the Nilgiri Reserve, the mahouts had to keep their bulls in at night and bring them food instead of letting them hobble through the jungle. Most of the tuskers survived, but they and many of the other animals at the Mudumalai Sanctuary Elephant Camp will probably wind up unemployed within a few years, since the available big timber in the sanctuary will be gone and new trees will not yet have reached commercial size.

Ironically, the elephant camp already includes elephants given to the government by an enterprise that had to scale down its own logging operations—the Bombay-Burma Trading Company. Its elephant corps numbered more than 3000 back around the turn of the century. Those were the days when rivers from the Ganges to the Irrawaddy ran thick with rafts of the teak logs cut by this colonial monopoly, and special teams of the strongest tuskers had to be sent in to pry apart logjams in the shallows each year after the monsoon floods receded.

The third problem is that population declines coupled with the listing of the Asian elephant as an endangered species have led to regular breeding of captive elephants with other captive elephants, and the gene pools of wild and domestic groups are at last beginning to diverge.

At Theppakadu, the captive-born young are separated from their mothers early, before one year of age. Prior to that, the babies are trained to enter a special stockade. One day after a baby is enticed in, the mother is abruptly dragged away with the help of two tuskers. Seven to ten days later, if the young one is faring reasonably well after this forced weaning, it is shipped off to another camp, where its dependency and, the handlers hope, its affections, are transferred to its new human tenders.

Each elephant has one mahout as its chief trainer. This man is the animal's steady human companion from the age of six months until six years. After an elephant reaches six, the mahout takes on a full-time assistant, or apprentice, called a *kavadai*. The growing giant now has two male humans devoting a good portion of their lives to it. Boys as young as ten may become assistants, and the apprenticeship usually lasts about ten years. At the outset, the assistant is mainly a hauler of chains and ropes and a shoveler of dung (no small job, with 90 percent of the hundreds of pounds an elephant eats daily being passed as manure).

In the course of his chores, the apprentice comes to know the behavior of elephants in general and the temperament of his animal in particular. At least, he ought to. The sign of his having succeeded is being allowed to take off the giant's foot shackles when it is to be moved. It means that the elephant accepts and trusts the man as a handler; some elephants never will. It also means that the mahout accepts and trusts the assistant to handle the elephant.

Up to age eighteen, elephants have it better than their keepers in some respects. While apprentices work mainly as cleaners until that age, elephants are merely doing schoolwork. Early on, the mahout begins teaching basic commands: go, back up, kneel, etc. From the age of five, the lessons become more complex and begin to include the techniques necessary to the animal's future work: hauling, sorting, loading, and stacking logs, for example, plus working in tandem with other elephants to handle the biggest fallen trees. Still, as one mahout told me, "The elephant stays like a teenager. It is jolly and likes to dance. It has a free life until eighteen or twenty. Then it goes to the working camps, and after that, it is too tired out to be jolly anymore."

Naturally, traditions vary from region to region and from one mahout to another. Some, like the mahout who rode to the tavern on his elephant's back and returned cradled on his elephant's tusks, prefer to stick with one animal through a lifetime. Others have less compunction about shifting from one animal to the next. A lot depends on the elephant as well. Like mahouts, certain elephants appear to be intensely loyal, while others are more flexible about whom they respond to. And to make the situation still more complex, there are mahouts who encourage their elephants to dislike other mahouts. You might expect giant-tamers to be a proud lot, and they are. That means they can also be highly competitive, and this is a reflection of it. The interesting thing is that the elephants can be trained to respond neutrally to visitors but to challenge anyone who tries to issue commands reserved for the mahout.

In the opinion of some observers, aggressive trainers tend to turn out aggressive elephants, and calm trainers turn out calm elephants; lazy men, lazy elephants, and so on. And every once in a while, a trainer simply ends up dead for reasons no one but the elephant quite understands. Manslaughter is one obvious reason why not every elephant has the same mahout all its life. Curiously, a potentially lethal elephant seldom lacks for new candidates to be its mahout. As I said, mahouts can be highly competitive.

"Behold: I am the mahout of the elephant that has killed a dozen mahouts."

Some of the traditional methods of handling elephants in India are extremely harsh. To restrain a newly captured, willful, or musth animal, its leg may be clamped in an iron hoop with inward-pointing spikes. The harder the animal strains against the device, the deeper the points bite. A long pole, called a *valia kole,* is used to prod the giant in the sensitive ankle and wrist joints while the handler keeps out of reach of the trunk and tusks. Some of these goads have blunt ends and are thrust so as to bruise the small bones that protrude near the surface of the lower foot. Others are actual spears but have a hilt on the blade to limit penetration.

Mahouts usually carry a *cherya kole*, a short rod with a blunt metal end, also used for walloping joints or, when mounted, the top of the skull. Close to the Indian border in Nepal, I rode on several occasions behind mahouts who whacked the top of the elephant's head with the dull edge of the large, curved *kukri* daggers men carry in that country. Crueler yet is the technique I saw of incising a wound atop the elephant's head and worrying it with a knife blade to get the animal to respond. One Nepali mahout carried a hammer expressly for pounding on his elephant's head. Whether the weapon was a hammer, knife, or *cherya kole,* the giants would stagger with a loud groan when struck.

In a modern-day version of going on a tiger shoot with the maharajah, I rode elephant-back with a scientist who shot the cats with tranquilizers in order to fit them with radio collars in Nepal's Chitwan National Park. I also rode elephants in order to observe the rare Indian rhinoceros on the flood plains of Chitwan's lowland Terai region. An elephant's back offers the best perch for viewing in the tall elephant grass—and the safest one, since even an aggressive mother rhino with a calf is unwilling to charge an elephant when surprised at close quarters. In all those trips, surrounded by the wild and lovely and unexpected, what I was most aware of was the thud of the mahout's bludgeon and the shuddering of the great beast beneath us.

Mahouts nearly always carry a *thotty,* or ankus, as their primary instrument of control. It, too, is a short stick, but with a sharp, curved, finger-length hook at the end. When the mahout is afoot, the hook is used to grab loose folds of skin along the leg to urge the animal forward or backward. If the animal is not especially responsive, the handler can easily dig deeper to get its attention. And if that doesn't work, he may hook the sensitive folds of the skin around the zygomatic arch, just below the eye. Mounted, he will use the ankus on the ear, another sensitive region. Abused elephants will have open wounds, holes through the ear, and paralyzed nerves there and around the eye.

The chief means of controlling an elephant is through nudges from the mounted mahout's toes at the base of the elephant's ear. Together with voice commands, this is sufficient to control the largest of elephants if it is paying attention. At most, an arm holding an ankus or *cherya kole* might be upraised as a threat—the equivalent of "showing the whip" to a horse. The rapport between a good working elephant and a good mahout seems almost telepathic, especially since the animal anticipates much of what is expected of it and proceeds to do it unasked. And therein lies the tragedy of a mahout who feels he must abuse an elephant to make it do his bidding.

One reason I thoroughly enjoyed my days at the elephant camps of Mudumalai was that trainers there had started phasing out the use of iron hooks by 1932, encouraged in that direction by the British. The key instrument of control now was a simple, slender switch cut from a bush in the forest. It was little more than a token, the physical equivalent of raising your voice a bit. It was also a clear sign that the psychology of positive reinforcement and bonding prevailed over punishment and the avoidance of pain. The only time I saw switches used to really hurt an elephant was when an inexperienced young one got grabby with a visitor at the tourist camp. I am not sure the animal realized that it could have hurt the person, but by the time three mahouts were done whipping it, stinging it from head to toe, it probably had a pretty clear idea that tourists were not to be bullied.

The absence of the ankus made the camp elephants gentler than elephants elsewhere, I was told, and it was one reason some of the males could be worked even in musth. This was economically important, for musth can last three months, and some bulls come into musth more than once a year.

About the time the ankus was abandoned, mahouts here also changed the way elephants hauled heavy loads behind them. Instead of putting the animal in a harness, as is done in most of Asia, they began training their animals to simply pull on a rope that they gripped in their huge molar teeth. The rope is less costly and couldn't be simpler to operate. An elephant cannot haul quite as much weight as it can with a harness, but that is the point. A harness encourages workers to overload an animal, and regularly overloaded elephants are prone to develop heart conditions, arthritic joints, and other ailments that shorten their effective working life.

When an elephant is toiling on steep terrain with a harness, it strains constantly against the burden dragging behind it. But with a rope, it can drop its load to rest while going uphill, and it can drop a load that threatens to pull it off balance, thereby avoiding injury. The only drawback anyone mentioned was that an elephant with a rope clamped in its teeth sometimes gets winded, since about 40 percent of its air intake is normally through its mouth, the other 60 percent being through the nostrils and trunk. Again, though, this becomes a check against overexertion. All things considered, the rope gives the elephant more leeway, and this becomes part of the atmosphere of cooperation between individual mahouts and individual elephants.

꧁꧁꧁꧁꧁꧁꧁꧁꧁꧁꧁

I began learning names at the mahouts' camp. A bull that had been staring hard at me with crescents of white in his eyes—not the musth male who tried to slam-dunk me soon after I arrived, but one tethered closer to the cook shack—was Ravindran, age twenty-eight. His mahout was Subbaraman, the old man who had been a trainer for fifty years and claimed to be able to handle his bull during musth. Born in 1929, Subbaraman has survived a viper bite as well as this bull. His helper, named Maringan, was not so lucky. Six years before, when Ravindran was in musth, he drove a tusk through Maringan's shoulder and neck. Although the man survived, he can do only light chores around camp now, handling what the mahouts call "soft elephants." Maringan still cannot go near Ravindran. Neither can anyone else save Subbaraman and his new helper, his son.

During that time of musth madness when he impaled Maringan, Ravindran had broken loose and was storming around camp like an animated thunderclap. He held the entire place hostage for four days until a government veterinarian, Dr. V. Krishnamurthy, arrived and climbed onto the back of another bull behind its mahout. This elephant's name was Tippoo, after Tippoo Sultan, the Tiger of Mysore. Tippoo Sultan fought British colonial forces to a standstill for years, using the mountainous Nilgiri area as a base. Tippoo the elephant ran down Ravindran, and Dr. Krishnamurthy was able to tranquilize the musth bull, shooting a drug-laden dart from a blowgun.

"A splendid example of why we prefer our elephants to be from the wild," the veterinarian told me during an inspection visit. "You see, Ravindran was born in a camp. Of course, it did not help that his first mahout was absolutely worthless. Now that Subbaraman is retiring, Ravindran is beginning with his third mahout, and he is still a problem. In musth, he fights with other bulls and causes headaches for everybody."

Dr. K—as I came to think of him—was utterly at home as he strolled among the camp elephants, putting a few older ones through their paces, coaxing a trick or two from the younger ones, dispensing treats. He said that he had lately been called upon to tranquilize two wild bulls that were part of the trouble-prone group colonizing Andhra Pradesh. These were the elephants who had been bashing the people who came to worship them. This time, they were merely ravaging a sugar-cane field. Dr. K darted the bulls, hauled them into a lorry with the help of tame bulls, and drove them some distance to a release site in the forest. They returned to the same cane plantation within days. When Dr. K went back after them and managed to tranquilize one of the raiding bulls, he didn't bother trying to transplant it again. Instead, he kept it confined and proceeded to tame it.

At least the flow of genes from the wild into captive populations hadn't dried up completely. But the capture and removal of any bull was bad news for the wild population because of its deficit of males. "Truly, we have made some great strides in conservation," insisted Dr. K, "especially in tiger conservation. I am so delighted that everyone admires this noble cat, because in its name we have saved habitats for all kinds of wildlife. But I must tell you, the actual amount of wildlife reserves and national parks in this country is still no more than 1 percent of the total land area."

I had read that India contained 68 national parks plus 367 sanctuaries, adding up to 3 percent of the nation's land area. "To be sure, forestry officials list a high number of reserves on the books," Dr. K agreed, "but many of those are in fact inhabited by squatters and are cut over. Not far from here, in Tamil Nadu, 39,000 acres of one reserve have been encroached upon by people, and the government has decided to give some of this land to them outright."

Now in his sixties, Dr. K had at various times and in various capacities been in charge of the health and welfare of the majority of working elephants in a large part of southern India. He was supposed to be retired. In reality, he was busier than ever, serving as a sort of veterinarian emeritus and general consultant, drawing upon decades of experience throughout the country. He was a fine scientific observer. To say that he was immersed in elephants was only the literal truth. His duties included making post-mortem examinations of both camp elephants and wild ones, and he performed these by climbing completely inside the body cavity of the animal, amid "miles and miles of intestines." He was able to use the forensic evidence during testimony against poachers in court. "But, you know, I never touch a dead elephant or a live one without taking a bath first in the morning. A ceremonial bath, as we Brahmins do. Then I make a brief *puja* [prayer ceremony] and put the caste mark on my forehead," he added.

In keeping with his Brahmin beliefs, Dr. K was a strict vegetarian. "I do it out of respect for the elephants," he told me, only partly joking. "More than 60 percent of Indians are still vegetarians, you know. It is why we still have wildlife. Once we all start to eat meat, like you people, there will be no more elephants, no more anything. And more and more Hindus *are* starting to eat meat." Dr. K was lucky he could chew anything, as he suffered from terrible teeth. They gave him one of the world's most original smiles, though. He used it all the time. His warm, keenly intelligent eyes would dance between those curious tusks and his bald pate, which was noticeably domed in front like an Asian elephant's, as he recounted tales of giants from a limitless trove.

Among Dr. K's physical characteristics was a scar on his shoulder from where a camp bull he knew well suddenly lunged and nicked him. The bull was slightly in musth. "Many, many have tried to get me over the years," he said. "You have to have an instinct for these things, a kind of sixth sense, to stay out of trouble." He agreed with the tracker Chenna, who stood up to elephant charges, that it was crucial to avoid showing or feeling fear in a tight situation, since elephants could smell or otherwise detect it. That understanding, too, had helped keep him alive.

"I believe the closest I came to dying was when I was walking with three other guys on a road in the park and a wild tusker began to chase us," Dr. K remembered. "We ran a hundred yards, but the elephant kept coming and was closing on us quickly. One of us almost surely would have been killed, but an automobile happened by at just that moment. It stopped very fast with its brakes squealing. That made the elephant halt. We jumped into the car and hurried away in the other direction." Once in a while, you get through on nothing more than blind luck.

Another story, again starring the bull Tippoo, was that the mahout who had handled him for many years finally retired and moved away. The man's son took over and became the only person who could handle Tippoo, especially during musth, when this bull turned extra tough. After an absence of four years, the old mahout came back to camp from retirement. He walked up to Tippoo and controlled him at once with no more than a few words. Praise Shiva that he could. During one subsequent musth period, Tippoo got so out of hand that he overturned a massive logging truck. The next day, the young mahout tried pressing against the bull's swollen temporal gland, trying to squeeze out fluid and help relieve some of the pressure. Tippoo suddenly lifted his head and sent the mahout fifteen feet through the air. Dr. K took over, trying the same gland-squeezing technique. Tippoo started to turn on him, and Dr. K couldn't get away in time due to a trick knee crushed earlier by a different elephant. Whatever might have happened next never did, because the old mahout came hurrying over and spoke a single word to Tippoo. The giant subsided.

"That old fellow, he couldn't stay away from the elephants. He was the same way I am: once an elephant man, always an elephant man. I can't retire. I will stay with them until death," Dr. K said with a shrug. I was glad he had decided to do that—glad for him, as the animals so plainly brought him joy, and glad for the opportunity I had to observe elephants through one of the most practiced set of eyes in the world.

Indians distinguish two fundamental types of conformation among tame elephants. One is called *mirgha*, which is Hindi for deer, and refers to the animal's long-legged, comparatively slender build. *Mirghas* are the elephant ectomorphs. The other type is *kumeriah*, the endomorph, distinguished by a stout, blocky build. The legs and neck may look short next to those of the *mirgha*, but the overall impression is of power and solidity. The biggest among the *kumeriahs* are considered inherently regal. They are therefore the ones chosen to carry dignitaries and lead religious processions in addition to being preferred for the heaviest hauling. *Mirgha* elephants are fine for general labor and transport and sometimes have better overall endurance than the more majestic-looking *kumeriahs*.

Along with pointing out *mirghas*, *kumeriahs*, and intermediate forms, Dr. K could identify elephants captured from the wilds in southern India. "They have more of a frontal bump on the head than northern populations," he commented. The only differences among Asian elephants I had been aware of were that 90 percent of the bulls in southern India carry tusks, whereas only about 50 percent of bulls have them in northern India, and just 5 to 10 percent of the bulls in Sri Lanka are tuskers. Also, Sumatran elephants were said to be smaller than average—somewhat like the now-extinct Javan elephant—but with relatively long trunks. I began to wonder how many other distinct variations the dwindling wild population of Asian elephants still contained.

The public is used to thinking of extinction in absolute terms: either an animal is still here and struggling to carry on, and we are absorbed by the drama of trying to save the last few survivors against eternal oblivion, or it is gone. Unfortunately, long before the brink is reached, and usually before the species's plight even starts to attract widespread concern, a substantial portion of the genes it carries will already have gone extinct. Sure, there are still trumpeter swans and bison around, and sarus cranes and Bengal tigers. But the diversity they once represented—the multitude of races, local variations, and ecotypes that were expressions of unique sequences of DNA; the potential inherent in the species; the genetic strength and flexibility that would allow the species to weather great changes in the environment; the assurance that at least some population within the geographic range would turn out to have the right combination of qualities to adapt—the majority of those creations have already ceased to exist.

My guess is that some level of homogenization has been taking place for millennia in elephants, because captives were bought, sold, plundered, and paid as tribute throughout Asia, mixing genes from different ends of the continent. For instance, the *Shahanama*, Persia's equivalent of the epic *Mahabharata*, mentions two items traded to that Middle East empire from India: elephants and swords of Indian steel. While Myanmar (Burma) and adjoining Southeast Asian kingdoms shipped elephants of their own to India, Sri Lanka was for centuries a source of working and ceremonial elephants for northern India and Southeast Asia.

No one is sure whether the tuskless trait prevalent in Sri Lanka today stems from natural genetic isolation of the population on that island or from those centuries of selecting big tuskers for trade. How about trade combined with heavy hunting by colonial Portuguese? And the Dutch, who mounted a firestorm in their quest for ivory? And, finally, the British, who combined avid trophy hunting with shooting crop-raiders to reduce damage to plantations?

I can't help thinking of the ivory-less females and young in Amboseli that Cynthia Moss and Joyce Poole called the Tuskless family. They alone might survive an onslaught of intensive poaching and pass along their characteristics. Maybe tuskless-ness offers the best chance for both elephant species to survive today's ivory binge.

Mukna, also spelled *mukhna* and *makhna*, is the Hindi term for a tuskless male. An elephant used to capture and control wild ones is a *kumkie*, Dr. K informed me. An elephant that rocks in place, as many do when tethered, often swinging the free front foot across the other one, has a special name as well: *nataraj*, king of the dancers, a reference to Shiva. You can see the pose in any one of the thousands of representations of Shiva, who swings one leg across the other as he dances to endlessly create and destroy the universe. Often, he is depicted dancing on a dwarf, who represents ignorance.

After examining the ear of a *nataraj* elephant for signs of infection from a recent tear, Dr. K pointed to another elephant and said he could see in the fallen arch of its back the results of years of carrying tourists. The giants are far better at hauling loads behind them than on top of them. As a general rule, he said, a horse can carry a 10 percent greater load relative to its body weight than a human can and an elephant 10 percent less.

From the swayback elephant, he went on to introduce me to Rathi, a cow he described as "the most beautiful elephant in camp. Very well built. Rathi is the Hindu equivalent of Aphrodite. She is fifty-eight now and has had ten calves, and I wouldn't be surprised if she had another. She will not accept any camp males, only wild tuskers. She won't always accept them either. If one tries to rape her, she grabs his penis, and he runs away

squealing. Oh, she is something. I once had a beautiful male elephant named IG for Inspector General. He was a regular Ro-
meo, the male version of Rathi. I am telling you, the cows had
eyes only for him."

🮲🮲🮲🮲🮲🮲🮲🮲🮲🮲🮲🮲

Dr. K had come to the mahouts' village camp to minister to a
male gored by wild bulls while out feeding in the bush. The
puncture penetrated two feet deep into the animal's flank. As Dr.
K worked to drain and clean the hole, the giant lay passively on
his side, and his mahout sat upon one of the tusks, watching him
carefully. The only sound the elephant made—in the audible
spectrum, anyway—was slow and steady breathing combined
with a deep, gurgling noise, almost like an elephant version of
purring. I thought I could feel a subsonic component to this
sound reverberating within me.

Dr. K commented that this was a noise of contentment. A few
camp elephants knew him as the man who brought pain and re-
sisted his approach, he said, but most seemed to be able to make
the connection between his actions and the eventual relief of
pain. "Elephants are one of those animals that realize you are
doing something good to them," he said. I was to hear almost
exactly the same words from Dr. Michael Schmidt, chief veterinarian of the Washington Park Zoo in Portland, Oregon.
"They understand you are trying to help," Dr. K continued.
"Even wild elephants seem to realize this when I am treating
gunshot wounds. The most rewarding experience with the
camp elephants is that they know me and know what I do. Even
very protective mothers of newborn calves will let me do almost
anything to the babies."

I told him I had read a news report from northern India of a
wild elephant family seen walking down a road in a refuge supporting a wounded member between them as they took it to a
ranger outpost, supposedly for care. Dr. K said he had seen
plenty of examples of concern and help for injured family members. For two days, he watched a mother and older sister guard

a baby hit by a truck on the road. They wouldn't let any other vehicle pass after that and kept trying to lift the baby. The baby died. Yet for two more days, the females stayed on to defend the carcass. Did Asian elephants pay as much attention to older corpses and bones as African elephants seemed to? Dr. K hadn't seen such a well-developed interest in the dead. Come to think of it, though, he had seen an elephant dig up human bones from a tribal burial ground. "Let me think more on this," he said.

As the good doctor dug deep into the pus-filled puncture wound and the bull let out a vibrating sigh, I stood back and clenched my teeth and, as I did, suddenly realized how extraordinary each of these beings was in his own way—the bull and the veterinarian.

Fights between wild and tame bulls are not uncommon in the Nilgiri Reserve. Being hobbled puts the tame bulls at a serious disadvantage. Some return with broken tusks, many more with puncture wounds and mangled tails, for when they turn to flee, their hobbles keep them from racing away. The victor takes their slow departure as a sign of recalcitrance and is likely to tusk them and bite their tails.

Puncture wounds heal slowly, and the animals are prone to develop abscesses once the skin heals over. I noticed several animals whose skin had weltlike bumps all over the shoulders, back, and flanks. Dr. K identified the cause as rectal flies, not wounds. Related to horseflies and deerflies, these biting members of the tabanid family transmit microfilaria—tiny parasitic worms—that make their way toward the host's top side and form the subcutaneous nodules I noticed.

Other filarial worms, transmitted by mosquitoes, also cause nodules to develop on the elephants. More worrisome to me was the fact that they cause fluid swelling in the lymph system of humans, leading to the condition known as elephantiasis. I had seen several people in the area shuffling about on baggy, saggy, giant legs as a result of this disease. A disease that causes fleshy growths to develop on the arms and legs of people goes by the name of elephant's ears but is unrelated to anything elephants suffer. However, elephants are susceptible to several other diseases that human flesh is heir to, including tuberculosis, anthrax, and rabies—and, some studies suggest, heart problems due to social stress.

A trypanosome related to the organism that causes sleeping sickness in humans afflicts elephants. Whereas African elephants host *Trypanosoma elephant*, Asian elephants host *Trypanosoma evenk*, and they often get it from domestic cattle via the bites of tabanid flies. The farther cattle encroach upon elephant habitat, the more prevalent is the spread of this disease to elephants.

One camp bull was using a stick to scratch at recent insect bites on his forehead as the veterinarian grabbed his tusk and pulled it down to show me the heavy fold of skin where the ivory inserts through the lip. This is where flies labeled *Cobbaldia elephanti*, in the oestrid family, deposit their eggs. When the larvae develop, they burrow into the sinuses, then into the stomach, where they attach to the lining of the gut to absorb food and grow. If enough of them develop there, they cause gastritis, and the elephant begins to lose condition.

To treat this section of the lip, Dr. K applied an oil made of camphor, garlic, and gardenia, the combination acting as both a repellent and antiseptic. In Kerala, elephants that lose condition are given a broth made from meat for a week or so. Occasionally, the meat is from a goat. More often, it is from a chicken. Oddly, while most elephants will ignore a chicken running by, those that have consumed broth are liable to kill the bird, he noted. In northeastern India, an elephant was found consuming a human body. Or so he had heard.

Asia has its own legends of elephant graveyards, by the way. As in Africa, this may have something to do with the scarcity of elephant carcasses—and easy-to-get ivory—in the bush. Carcasses of these beasts are so large and ought to be so obvious and yet are so infrequently found, people assume the giants must go somewhere special to die.

Asians say the giants slowly wend their way to some deep and remote valley. No, just to dense streamside cover, said Dr. K. They go there when they are hurting so they can be near hiding places, food, and water with the least amount of movement. After they die, wild dogs, hyenas, and, above all, wild boars may scatter the smaller remains until only the vultures know where to find them. The lush riparian growth covers the rest.

But the Nilgiri Reserve area is exceptional, in that carcasses do get found. Perhaps it is the result of having so many wood-cutters, herders, and other people wandering through a protected area. Another factor has been Dr. K's good contacts in the local communities, plus the fact that he has been around for so long. In any case, he has personally examined more than 350 elephant carcasses in the bush.

Nearly a third were victims of poaching or injuries resulting from conflicts around fields and villages. Of the remaining 70 percent, most of the deceased animals were quite old or calves under the age of six—a typical natural pattern of mortality for large-bodied animals. The greatest single agent of death appeared to be gastrointestinal diseases caused by parasites. Roundworms, hookworms, and tapeworms, which cause anemia and hypoproteinemia (reduced protein uptake), and flukes, which lead to cirrhosis of the liver, were the chief culprits, spread mostly from crowded waterholes. However, what made the elephants vulnerable to the effects of parasites and illness in the first place was environmental stress—hard times, the difficulty of making a living. The majority died during the dry months between December and May, when forage was the scarcest and least nutritious, and it was sometimes a long, long hike to water. Historically, drought—the periodic failure of the monsoons—probably played a key role in limiting elephant numbers on the Indian subcontinent.

Dr. K said he had veterinarian friends in Kerala who could tell me more about both elephant diseases and captive elephants in general, and he offered to drive with me to visit them. I accepted at once. I had planned to have a look at some temple elephants in Kerala anyway, but I would have driven anywhere with Dr. K for the privilege of having him continue to talk about a lifetime among giants.

On our way from the Nilgiri Biosphere Reserve to the city of Trichur in Kerala, Dr. Krishnamurthy discoursed not only on elephants but on nearly everything we passed in between. He touched upon sacred cows and cattle diseases, langur monkeys and primate psychology, cashew plantations and the strong alcohol brewed locally from these nuts. We screeched to a stop where the road crossed over the Karimpazha River. Down the broad, muddy waterway was floating one raft of teak logs after another, each ridden by a man with a long bamboo pole that he used to try and keep the raft clear of the shore around turns. Close by, elephants were hauling teak from a riverside plantation down to the water's edge to be tied into rafts and sent downstream along with the others.

Although the monsoon rains had begun, they had not yet broken the heat that builds up toward the close of the dry season. At this low elevation, they had only made a steam bath out of the air and turned the soil to mush. The value of using elephants over machinery was once again apparent, for the elephants had little impact on the muddy ground compared to the quagmire heavy machines would have created. As a result, replanting could take place right after harvesting. On the average, sixty to eighty years would pass before the new teak trees would reach harvestable size.

In this hot weather, the elephants worked from 7:30 in the morning until 12:30, took a break until evening, then put in another three hours or so. It was nearing noon when we stopped by, and I was bathed in sweat just following behind the working men and animals with my notebook. Away from the river the elephants paused from time to time and sprayed themselves with their trunks to cool off a little. Where did the water come from? There was none nearby. A common explanation is that the animals are able to withdraw water from their voluminous stomachs, but that isn't what happens. "Both the large sinuses of the head and the trunk itself produce secretions of watery mucus," Dr. K informed me. "Copious secretions. They are stored in the trunk. Its capacity is eight to ten liters—about two of your gallons—and this is what you see sprayed when there is no water about."

The hardest-working elephant was a tusker named Vetta-karan, meaning Hunter. As he approached dragging a long, muddy bundle of logs, the mahouts warned me not to get near his right side. This is the side mahouts usually mount from. They order the animal to crook its rear leg and use that as a ladder, or use a combination of a crooked front leg and the trunk, also bent to serve as a step. But for reasons of his own, Vetta-karan would thunk anyone coming from his right. Figuring out how to handle this bull had cost the lives of three assistants in the last three years.

"This is a government plantation, but the elephants are from private contractors," observed Dr. K. "Mahouts in the private sector are very much involved in this business of making an elephant a one-man animal that will not let other mahouts handle it. You could call it a form of job security. It is a problem to begin with, one man owning just one elephant. He raises it in isolation; that elephant is brought up in solitary confinement. It has no chance to be a herd animal—a normal, socialized animal. You see, it is bound to be a social-psychological misfit."

As if to emphasize his point, Vettakaran passed by looking at me like I was a stray dog—get near my path, and I'll knock you from here to the river. He was no Ganesh, no god of wisdom and success, and certainly no potbellied facilitator concerned with my ordinary complaints and frustrations. But he was a god to whom I would pray. He was an old-time god, huge and muscular and seething with wrath. He was the kind you brought offerings to in the hope that he would relent in his anger or at least take it out on somebody or something else.

Part of the reason Vettakaran had killed helpers instead of mahouts is that on contracted jobs, the helper is often the one who rides the elephant while the mahout sleeps under a tree or has a long smoke break. When the helper has problems governing the beast, then the mahout takes charge again. The helper might or might not be in one piece by then.

"In the private sector," said Dr. K, "we have no regular program to see that the animals are well cared for. Owners call in the veterinarian only after they have exhausted all their home remedies and prayers. No one wants to spend the money if he doesn't have to. But my god," he sighed, fanning himself in the midday steam, "sometimes the elephant hasn't crapped in twenty or thirty days by the time I get there. I have to remove a turd of dry fiber in two-foot-by-three-foot blocks. You get that sort of thing as a result of the elephant being marched fifty kilometers with no water in the heat. A month after the march, they kick the bucket, and the owner hasn't a clue why."

Kick the bucket? Grinning away with his curious tusks, the good doctor admitted that he was a long-time fan of Zane Grey and Louis L'Amour western novels. I was beginning to wonder. I would hear a phrase such as "That sonofabitch is plumb loco" and have to turn around to convince myself that the speaker was really this bald, bright-eyed Brahmin with a *tika* of vivid orange and red pigments painted on his forehead.

Not far downstream, we saw the other end of the logging sequence. Elephants lumbered down a steep embankment to rafts along the shore and hauled the logs back up to be stacked in a lumber-mill yard, awaiting the saws. One of the elephants at the yard was a cow called Sarasu. Her owner, a Muslim named P. Mohammed, said she was forty-five years old. Dr. K whispered that Sarasu was at least fifty, pointing to the markedly sunken temples and a strong folding over of the tops of the ears. The ear edge begins to fold at age fifteen to twenty. By age thirty to thirty-five, it has a one-inch fold; by age forty to forty-five, a two-inch fold. And over age fifty, the top of the ear shows the type of wide, loose curl Sarasu had. But P. Mohammed might get a lower daily rate for his elephant if her true age were known.

Sarasu was struggling hard to heave logs up what was almost a forty-degree slope. She would tug on the rope held in her teeth, pause to gather her strength along with better footing, and heave again with a mighty lunge of her neck, letting the rope press against her shoulder to help take some of the strain. Dr. K told me that teak weighs 56 pounds per cubic foot. A typical log consists of between 50 and 100 cubic feet of wood, or roughly 1 to 3 tons, and more when waterlogged. A good working elephant drags something like 1000 cubic meters of logs in a year. At 1800 pounds per cubic meter, that's getting close to 2 million pounds.

While the ample-bellied P. Mohammed stood talking in his clean, white robe, Sarasu continued her contest against gravity, urged on by both the mahout atop her neck and a helper at her flank. I asked Dr. K if he wouldn't mind translating what the mahout was saying to Sarasu. "But of course," he replied. "He is saying, 'Sarasu, the man is taking photos! Can't you pull this log properly? Have you no manners? Can't you lift anything? What a lazy girl you are. Dear God, what a lazy bitch. Aren't you ashamed?'"

Yet it was all meant lightly. The mahout was very gentle compared to the one who rode the bull Vettakaran. That handler wore a grim, macho, I-am-the-mahout-of-the-elephant-who-has-killed-many-men expression and used the ankus hard. Sarasu's handlers had only a thin *cherya kole* and a switch. She required, and could endure, little else. Her limitations were taken into account, and I felt none of the tension and fear, none of the potential for detonation, that was so often part of the atmosphere around big bulls. Here, it was just slow, hard work with a pleasant beast. I felt immediately comfortable around her. No one needed to warn me about where I should or should not go in her presence. Any place was fine.

When I heard the thwack of the *cherya kole*, I looked up in surprise from watching Sarasu's feet on the slippery slope. The unfamiliarity of the sound made me realize that for the past three-quarters of an hour of labor, the mahout had not touched her with anything but his feet and words. Sarasu heaved the log to the top of the bank and proceeded to haul it over level terrain toward a stack of logs. There, she dropped it roughly in place, then knelt on one foreleg and shoved it exactly parallel to the others with the front of her trunk. Finally, she swung her trunk sideways to tamp the end even with the others. The log proved slightly too heavy for fine adjustment with the trunk alone, so she brought a foreleg up behind her trunk for support and finessed the log precisely into place.

"I need to make 500 rupees a day to break even, keeping in mind what I must pay the mahouts and food for the elephant," P. Mohammed was saying. "I am barely getting 250 rupees a day here. I do this at a loss, but it is better than being idle and just spending money to keep the elephant fed." Dr. K did a quick calculation of the number of logs Sarasu would drag up from the river in a day, and the price paid the owner per cubic meter, and decided that Mr. P. Mohammed was fibbing again. He was making money with this sweet older lady of an elephant. Dr. K thought he ought to invest some of it in bigger rations for Sarasu. Her hip and shoulder bones were a little too prominent, and her back seemed broken down. But on the positive side, a sort of working vacation waited on the horizon.

"For one more month, I will work Sarasu here logging. Then," P. Mohammed said, folding his hands as if in prayer, "I go with her to the temple. We will perform religious processions and marriage processions. People will feed Sarasu rice, banana, coconut, *jaggery*, many good things as she passes. The people wish to feed Ganesh. For luck. They also give tips to the mahout."

彁彁彁彁彁彁彁彁彁彁彁

In Trichur, the cultural center of Kerala, a man could make as much money renting an elephant for festivals as hiring it out for logging. Most owners, like P. Mohammed, did both, walking their animal from the logging sites to the city in time for holidays and religious festivals, which Kerala has in splendid profusion.

Long before Ganesh worship grew popular, Hinduism still had a special place for elephants among animals, believing them to have been created by Brahma with wings and a beautiful ivory-white color. Much the same legend of flying white elephants, usually with an affinity for clouds and rain, can be heard across Asia with local variations. Hinayana Buddhism replaced Hinduism as the primary religion for several centuries, until about A.D. 400. According to its teachings, Buddha's image should never be shown directly, only by symbols: the dome called a stupa, a footprint, a tree, or an elephant. Mahayana Buddhism supplanted the Hinayana school, but the elephant remained an important symbol. As everyone knew, a white elephant had entered the side of Queen Sirimahamaya as she lay dreaming. Later, she gave birth to Prince Siddhartha, the future Gautama Buddha. By implication, Buddha was a white elephant in his earlier incarnations, and the elephant was a Buddha-to-be.

Buddhism was largely replaced by a resurgence of Hinduism later on. The apostle Thomas is said to have visited Kerala in A.D. 52 and seeded Christianity here. The Catholic churches used to hire elephants for processions every so often, having adopted this most impressive feature of traditional Hindu festivals. They were told by Rome to quit, but Kerala's Orthodox churches still use elephants in their parades. The Muslim religion was established during the seventh and eighth centuries as the Arab presence grew along the Malabar Coast. The mosques of Trichur also hire elephants now and then. In the meantime, Hindu festivals, ceremonies, and holidays continue to take up a substantial part of the calendar year.

Endowed with good ports, rich soils, lush vegetation, and ample rains, Kerala supports one of India's densest human populations. Its natural wealth and trade connections have allowed this state to maintain an enviable standard of living despite the crowding. Kerala now has the highest literacy rate in the nation, some of the best family planning, and one of the lowest birth rates. Business was flourishing during my stay there. Trade ventures between Muslims in Kerala and the Arab states were doing particularly well. Also, Indians regularly shipped out from Kerala to work as laborers for a while in the Gulf region and returned with cash in their pockets. So there was a lot of new money floating around. More money meant a rising demand for status symbols, and one of the most prestigious of all was the sponsoring of an elephant.

The practice of individuals or families arranging for the presence of an elephant in a public procession is an ancient one. As always, people who can afford it want the biggest, tallest *kumeriah* available to represent them. Sponsors even compete to see who can spend the most. Every so often, a well-to-do person may buy an elephant outright and donate it to a temple. To gain merit in the eyes of the community. To atone for a great sin. Or to make good on a promise made in prayer. And sometimes just out of the goodness of a heart. Virtually every major Hindu temple in Kerala housed at least an elephant or two.

Side by side with the veneration of elephants went the selling of ivory jewelry and sculptures. Shops sold gods' teeth all through the city. As ever, one of the favorite subjects of ivory carvers was elephants—majestic bulls or strings of females and young. A vigorous cottage industry had developed around carving elephants, rhinos, tigers, and the like from teak, rosewood, and imported ebony, partly because ivory was becoming so scarce and expensive. In 1986, a large tusk sold in Kerala for 1000 to 1500 rupees a kilogram. Now, the price was 2500. Two years earlier, the selling of a pair of 45-kilo tusks for the price of an elephant made news. At the time of my visit, such tusks would have been worth a good deal more than the animal itself.

🙵🙵🙵🙵🙵🙵🙵🙵🙵🙵🙵

Near the center of the city, I was shown to the home of K. N. Venkatadri, nicknamed Raju. His business card read "Elephant and Decoration Contractor." He is a caparisoner and broker of giants. When people want to hire an elephant to represent them at a festival, or for a marriage ceremony or an inauguration of dignitaries, for filmmaking, or just for a party, they go to Raju. He will find the elephant in their price range from his list of animals and owners throughout the area. Clients count on him to make all the arrangements for the elephant to be present when and where needed, complete with mahout and assistant. Raju takes a modest commission for his efforts, of course. Then, if the client wishes, he will also dress the elephant, and for a reasonable fee.

The traditional costuming of an elephant Kerala-style was something I wanted badly to see. But we were in between major festivals, and no one happened to have requisitioned an elephant for any other function lately. There was only one thing to do. Photographer Bill Thompson and I hired our own elephant to be dressed up and paraded through the streets. Extravagant, but it was a way to compensate Raju for opening his home and work-place to us and for the days he spent explaining the details of his operation. And his good will opened other doors to us down the line.

Raju's household included his wife and two children; his mother, Parvati; and his father, K. V. Narayan, who had inherited the business from his own father and recently turned it over to Raju. During the day, the household was joined by a host of workmen, who occupied a warren of sheds and tables in the rear courtyard. Several tapped out ornaments from copper all day, mainly half-spheres, or domes, from the size of grapes to grapefruit. Others electroplated them with gold in a little tub, where two wire leads from a bank of batteries dangled into a chemical bath. Still others sewed the dazzling metal pieces onto silk and velvet. Further adorned by richly colored brocades, one sheet of the resplendent fabric would become a hood shaped to fit down over the elephant's broad forehead. Larger sheets would lie across its back and down the sides like a colossal cape.

But this was only the beginning. Upstairs, Raju showed me the room where he stored accessories. First, he picked up harnesses of bells and shook them. Some would be strapped around the animal's neck, others around each foot. The wearing of bells is both ornamental and a requirement for traveling in traffic, like having a horn on your car. The idea is for blind people in a festival crowd always to be able to tell where the elephant is. When he turned around the next time, Raju was waving fans made of peacock feathers. Then *chamaras*, silver-handled pom-poms made of yak hair from Nepal. Next, tall, silken parasols trimmed with silver thread. And shields as high as a person, blazing with more silver and gold.

To handle all the accessories would take a multi-armed Hindu god. Instead, three, four, even five men ride the elephant. The man in the lead plants the shining shield before him and begins to rhythmically raise and lower it. Behind him, the others wave the fans and pom-poms and open and close the parasol. As our hired elephant paraded through the streets of Trichur, I was fast in the grip of two mental states involving elephants. One was *anakambam*, a fascination and love; Raju taught me the word. The other was *ananranth*, a mania, but a good one, in the sense of a fine madness. I ran down a street to view our bespangled creature head-on and realized that the overall effect of the men atop it was, indeed, that of a multi-armed Hindu god.

That was more or less the idea, Raju agreed. Following designs from long-vanished empires, the caparison transforms the elephant into a moving temple—the house of the god—and the riders become a representation of the deity itself, with fans to cool it and a parasol to shade it. Flowers and rice thrown by the crowd as it passes add to the elephant's adornments. Some elephants sway and flap their ears and trumpet in response to the music, adding to the display. "At a festival, there are no caste differentiations," said Raju. "This is especially true in Kerala and especially with elephant functions. All are equal. All are equal in front of the elephants."

I asked my imagination to help me see scores of them now in full panoply, rumbling through the streets and gathering to be arrayed in rows before the entryway to a temple. Envision the fabric and metal being thicker, with spears and bows projecting behind the shields, and you could conjure up the spectacle created by ranks of war elephants preparing for battle. Imagine the workers kept busy making and mending armor and other trappings in the days when emperors and maharajahs kept elephant corps in the many hundreds.

Different-size caparisons have to be made for different animals. A few wealthy Kerala citizens buy the whole outfit for 30,000 to 35,000 rupees. But most rent them; after all, they have to pay for renting the elephant too. A run-of-the-mill elephant might cost 2000 rupees for the festival day (the price includes two days on either side to march the animal from wherever it is being kept). But if the animal is a truly impressive tusker, the owner could get as much as 12,000 rupees (close to U.S. $1000). Three such festivals per year, and the owner will have paid for the annual upkeep of his elephant, which at the time of my visit was running between 32,000 and 40,000 rupees, including the handlers' wages; anything beyond that was profit.

Given the fees a ceremonial bull could command, coupled with the decline in logging work as forests continued to shrink, the competition among owners to rent out their animals for special occasions was intense. People bad-mouthed other owners and their animals. They even bribed other mahouts not to take a particular owner's elephants to a festival.

Some owners were tempted into renting out animals on the edge of musth or even in actual musth. Opium and marijuana could be used to mask the condition, much as temple elephants were sometimes kept drugged to make them more tractable—"a substitute for good training," Dr. K called it. Whiskey worked to slow down a musth animal, too, once it came off the high and slid into the hangover, turning dull and sluggish. Naturally, an owner didn't want to give his elephant a few belts of high-octane *arak* and send it right off to a parade. On the other hand, he might slip a competitor's elephant a few drinks just before a performance to cause problems and ruin his reputation. There was too much of that sort of sabotage going on, Raju noted.

All of which helped explain why a kit containing tranquilizing drugs and darts lay on the desk of Dr. Jacob Cheeran, to whom Dr. K introduced me one morning. Dr. Cheeran had to be ready to go at a moment's notice. In the past several years, this senior scientist at Trichur's College of Veterinary and Animal Sciences had answered 153 emergency calls involving elephants out of control.

"No females," he told me. "Not one, because they can usually be dealt with some other way. Females can be exceedingly stubborn, I grant you, but they rarely go amok. Tuskers cause the trouble. One ran amok at a festival and killed somebody just last week. It broke into a theater compound and tore up everything, including a person."

Dr. Cheeran's task is basically the same as Dr. K's when called to a disturbance: calm the animal with chemicals enough to restrain it but not to knock it out. Too bulky to be lifted and carried off, the berserker must be led away with tame elephants and taken somewhere safe to be tethered. The main problem can be the festival crowd itself, with people running in all directions, getting in the path of the animal and of those trying to control it. Everyone seems to think that the drug is going to put the bull to sleep within seconds after it is shot, Dr. Cheeran complained. In reality, at least five to seven minutes are needed for the tranquilizer to seep through enough of the massive body to begin working. That gives people plenty of time to crowd in close and get in trouble all over again.

A less pressing problem is that the elephant's penis goes loose under the influence of the drugs. Faced with an exceptional organ dragging on the ground so far that the bull is likely to step on it, the veterinarian may have to rig up a penis sling to get the stupefied animal home.

Sometimes a cranky elephant simply gathers up all its chains and ropes, its fetters and traces, and piles them in a heap in front of itself, refusing to let anyone near. It goes on strike. Then there are the cases of bulls suddenly running amok with mahouts still on their backs. The handler hardly wants to stay where he is. And yet he may be stuck there all night, for he dares not jump down either; if he didn't hurt himself, the bull would do it for him once he hit the ground. In fact, a musth elephant will often ignore women, children, and the crowd in general to chase only the mahout who did something to spark its rage. When it can't get at the mahout, it may continue ignoring other people and redirect its fury toward trees, cars, temples—any inanimate object close at hand.

A fascinating piece of elephant psychology is that while a giant might try to shake a rider loose, rub him off against a tree, or even catch his legs in the crease between the neck and shoulder and then rub him off, it will not reach back with its trunk and pull the rider loose. Such a behavioral gap seems doubly odd, because an elephant will reach back to exactly that spot on command to deliver the rider's ankus, a rope, his lunch—anything the mahout requests.

For whatever reasons, an elephant just does not use its trunk to grab people atop it—nor atop other elephants, it seems. This quirk is what made it possible for mahouts to chase down wild elephants with tame ones in the first place. The wild elephant might fight with its elephant pursuer but not with the man astride it. In fact, a mahout could ride his mount into a *keddah* full of newly captured wild elephants to sort them out and be fairly certain that he would never be touched unless he fell off during a fracas.

Besides the pit and *keddah*, Indians employed another capture method, one that might not have been feasible without the elephant's strange avoidance of, or inattention to, forms on the backs of other elephants. The technique was directed toward catching big bulls and was necessary because tuskers were so seldom taken in *keddah* drives, due to their largely solitary habits. One or more mahouts mounted on the backs of female elephants and hidden beneath dark cloaks would locate a bull and keep him awake through close contact for two or three days on end. The mahouts might work in shifts to avoid falling asleep, sometimes bringing in new females to pique the male's flagging interest. Finally, too tired to respond any longer, the bull would doze, usually standing up. A mahout would ease off his mount's back and carefully tie the male's legs, then slip a heavy rope or cable around his neck. They say that upon awakening to find themselves bound, bulls often died in a raging struggle to free themselves. Otherwise, the men waited until the bull exhausted itself, then led it away or camped right at the capture site to begin the taming process.

Dr. Cheeran had killed only four out-of-control animals in the last decade, partly because to destroy a tusker is to wipe out an investment of 100,000 to 200,000 rupees, and partly because even the crowds at risk wouldn't stand for routine killings of problem elephants. Once, however, when the veterinarian was called in to dart an elephant that had killed a forest officer, he found the other officers so upset that they insisted upon shooting the animal. "This elephant had already killed thirteen people and was looking for number fourteen, so I did not try hard to talk them out of it," he said. "Soon, I wished I had. They all stood there and shot at the poor beast with various weapons but didn't know where to hit it. They fired more than a hundred rounds before it collapsed."

"I saw police once shoot sixty-four rounds into an elephant, and it was still running around," Dr. K contributed. "I believe it finally died of sheer disgust."

回回回回回回回回回回回回

On the twenty-fifth of September, the daily paper reported lions killing villagers and livestock in India's Gir Forest. People there were too terrified to go to work in the fields. I had lots of time to peruse the paper because I was down with seriously loose bowels, most likely from a dose of unfamiliar bacteria or protozoans, but possibly from nothing more than a diet of unrelentingly spicy southern Indian food.

To cheer myself up, I went to Trichur's circus. For about U.S. $1.30, I saw so many death-defying acts, interspersed with tricycling elephants and motorcycling Himalayan black bears, that I lost count. The name of this greatest show—for the money—on earth was, of course, Jumbo Circus. Its spectacular craziness was apparently just what I needed, for my stomach and bowels felt well enough by the next morning for me to get excited about being a reporter again.

回回回回回回回回回回回回

Dr. Cheeran introduced me to two of his colleagues: Dr. K. C. Panicker, also a professor at Trichur's veterinary college, and Dr. Radrhakrishnan Kaimal, the college's dean. Together with Dr. Krishnamurthy, these elephant doctors took me to one of the main religious sites in the area, the Guruvayar Temple complex. Within its walls lived forty-two elephants, enough that the temple briefly experimented with generating power from methane gas produced by elephant dung. The temple elephants were mainly males and cared for by 109 mahouts and assistants—two men each for the majority of elephants, three for the most magnificent tuskers. There, among one of the finest collections of big bulls in the nation, the veterinarians described the details of this still somewhat mysterious condition called musth as it occurs in the Asian elephant.

First comes the premusth period, which lasts from seven to fifteen days. With his testosterone starting to shoot up to as much as sixty times the normal level—Dr. Panicker discovered that the testes enlarge to two or three times their normal size in the process—the bull begins to exhibit a restlessness that at first may be detectable only by his handlers. During this phase, the bull begins to rub his temples with the tip of his trunk. Next, a noticeable swelling appears at the base of the penis. Soon, there may be signs of disobedience to go with the restlessness—we walked by a musth male dragging broken leg chains—and the bull frequently masturbates.

Full musth follows and may last for two to three months, depending upon the condition of the bull; the healthier, the longer, as a rule. Now the temporal gland is fully engorged and leaking fluid. Ajay Desai, the elephant behavior researcher in the Nilgiri Reserve, tried putting out musth secretions in the forest to test the reactions of elephants of different ages and both sexes. Young males tried to avoid the area once they smelled the scent. Old males beyond breeding age ignored it. Cow elephants showed some signs of excitement.

The penis of the musth male is also engorged, protruding, and dribbling urine. The animal is in behavioral hyperdrive, his restlessness consuming him. In a natural setting, this might spur a male to herculean feats of travel and battle and vastly increase his chances of finding and mating a receptive female. But in captivity, he becomes a monumental challenge to control.

The classic bull in full musth is crazy-eyed, rocking and tugging at the chains that entrap him, hurling sticks, food scraps, and feces at anyone who draws near, obeying little or not at all, looking as if he is about to implode. Well fed and idle most of the day, temple elephants come into musth much more strongly than elephants worn down by work and meager rations. We found a perfect example at Guruvayar, a real hunk of chained fury. He, too, had broken hobble chains dangling on his legs. He had also broken a longer chain used as a tether. Whenever someone ventured near, he would reach down to grab the chain with his trunk and whip the free end at the intruder, or else grab a palm frond and hurl it instead. The rest of the time he placed his trunk tip in his mouth to hold it and nodded his head so that the meaty part of the trunk bounced up and down like rubber. Stark raving musth.

Finally, full musth is replaced by a postmusth period of up to fifteen days. The temporal gland regresses, its flow dwindles, the penis relaxes, and urination becomes more regular. The giant begins to respond to commands again, able to concentrate on something other than invisible chemical forces shouting in his blood and brain.

One of the odd things about musth, the veterinarians agreed, is that while it may make one bull enraged, another bull may appear to grow sleepy under its influence. And the same bull may act quite differently from one musth period to the next.

A healthy male elephant should be in musth at least once every year between the ages of fifteen to eighteen and age fifty. At three months per musth period—not counting the onset and latter stages—that's eight-and-a-half years of hormone intoxication. Eight-and-a-half years of juggling dynamite, for people trying to work with the animal. The two peak periods of musth seem to be summer (May–September) and winter (November–March), with up to 80 percent of the bulls in Kerala coming into musth during winter—which happens to be the height of the festival season.

The Trichur veterinarians keep in regular contact with colleague Michael Schmidt of Portland's Washington Park Zoo, and he has suggested castration as a solution to the interminable problem of controlling musth males. However, traditional ayurvedic medicine holds that seminal fluid is one of the vital humors of the body, produced by every organ. It is part and parcel of life in Hindu philosophy. Lord Siva himself is conceived of as an infinitely large *lingham*, or penis.

Castration for elephants would be hard to sell in Kerala. On the other hand, the veterinarians are looking seriously into another option proposed by Schmidt. He will supply them with androgen, a chemical that can reduce the output of testosterone, and they will experiment with different dosages on various males to see if they can lower the intensity of musth or perhaps suppress it altogether. Cultural opposition to this approach may arise as well, though, if it is ever put into widespread use.

One of the bulls at the Guruvayar compound had a broken tusk and was named, of course, Ganesh. Another had distinct grooves in its tusks; such an animal is known locally as a four-tusker. Bulls with four actual tusks have been reported from the wild. Closest to the temple on the grounds of Guruvayar were the grandest *kumeriah* elephants. An especially desirable trait is that the animal carry its head high—proudly, as humans see it. Ideally, the bumps on its cranium would be on a level with the top of the arch of its back. An elephant that has the stocky *kumeriah* build but carries its head in a droopy fashion is not valued nearly so highly.

Perhaps the strangest thing I learned that day at the temple was that if you measure the circumference of an Asian elephant's front foot and double it, you get the height of the elephant at the shoulder. The foot looks so inconsequential compared to the towering back of the giant that I guess this comes under the heading of Amazing But True Facts. Unlike a lot of such facts, this one seemed quite useful. After trying out the formula with an assortment of animals to confirm it, I could see how I might use it to better guess the approximate age of animals I was tracking in the bush.

Bathing time arrived, and most of the forty-two elephants were taken to a large, walled pool within the temple grounds to be scrubbed down with coconut husks. From a distance, the scene was of great indolent gods at a bath house, spouting and rolling and lolling about while being laved by human slaves. These elephants did live a pampered life in some respects. Each day, the temple provided 17,775 pounds of food for them. The staple was *Caryota aureus*, commonly called palmira, or toddy palm, richest in starch of the local palms. The bull Lakshmanan, heaviest of the temple elephants at 11,550 pounds, ate 615 pounds of palm per day. Rations often included the nutritious treat of coconut meat as well. A fat life, but not a free one. Nor was it free from cruelty.

The veterinarians had brought me to the temple in part so

they could check up on the animals' condition. As it turned out, one needed their attention badly. Some fool of a mahout had been prodding its front ankle, or wrist, with a pointed *valia kole* until it became inflamed. It went on to develop an abscess. If the infection spread laterally through the wrist, the beast could be crippled. While an elephant can hobble about with an injured hind leg, a ruined foreleg renders it all but immobile. Should that happen, this giant would have to be put down.

After the mahout ordered the elephant onto its side and sat on its upper tusk, the doctors set about lancing and draining the ulcerated area, cleaning out gobbets of dead tissue. Marveling once again at how tolerant a huge male could be, I contemplated the profound difference between this and the state of musth. Outside of musth, no elephant needed to be hurt in order to be made to obey. It only needed to understand; that much seemed clear. If someone did hurt the animal, the pain was stored away in memory and could be returned a hundredfold any time.

"If a mahout is cruel, one day, sooner or later, perhaps a decade or more may pass, the elephant will try to kill him," Dr. Panicker stated. "Especially, of course, in the time of musth. I have seen an elephant tear a mahout's carcass to pieces for revenge. An elephant may also develop a hatred for the helper, the man who ties and binds."

In Amboseli, Joyce Poole had told me she thought musth increased aggression to the point that males were driven to assert dominance far beyond their normal rank. She had recorded young herd bulls in musth suddenly taking on older, more established bulls in battle and could see how this might ultimately improve the musth animal's chances of breeding with a receptive female. Maybe attacks by captive bulls on mahouts during musth are a somewhat parallel behavior, I reflected, insofar as the mahout is normally the dominant animal in the relationship.

"But then I have seen an elephant guard the carcass of a mahout that it killed on purpose or by accident and refuse food or drink for two days, as if it were grieving," Dr. Panicker observed. A Greek ambassador to ancient India, Megasthenes, wrote of similar behavior in his fourth century B.C. account: "Some of them have been known, when their drivers have been killed in battle, to have lifted them up and carried them to burial. Others have stood over them and protected them. . . . One, indeed, who in a passion slew his driver, died from remorse and grief."

"Some of the feelings of this animal are obviously important," Dr. Panicker continued, "and complicated. And this is why I say that mistreatment of elephants at private camps and dwellings and even temples is one of our most serious problems. You can't imagine how often we see these infected legs, feet deformed with welts, and similar signs of abuse. But it is almost worse to see the cases of psychological trauma that we do among elephants."

Daphne Sheldrick had used that phrase—psychological trauma—to describe the elephant babies brought to her animal orphanage on the outskirts of Nairobi. These were infants that had seen the rest of their families mowed down by poachers. I remembered how she spoke of them having terrible nightmares and waking up at night screaming.

P. G. Menon of Kerala wrote me a letter with the following tale: "My matrilineal family have kept elephants . . . from time out of mind. . . . Once, when my grandfather had come courting, he was unexpectedly knocked down from the back by a playful baby elephant which had the run of the front yard; it had become accustomed to him and was no longer shy of him. But my grandfather had not grown up with elephants. So he scolded it angrily. It began to bawl and shed copious tears. It needed so much consoling that my grandparents could both recall the incident vividly forty years later."

Dr. Cheeran had commonly seen evidence of elephants crying. He told me of watching a mahout beat a tusker until even that enormous bull cried. He also knew of a tusker that ran away, and when his mahout of twenty years found him and hugged his trunk, the mahout began to cry, and so did the elephant. Science admits that an elephant can definitely leak tears; yet some would say that it is a reaction to stress rather than sadness. I wonder exactly what the difference is, in either humans or elephants.

In Kerala, people may work to remedy the maltreatment of

elephants by joining the Elephant Welfare Association. Its charter members include Dr. Panicker, Dr. Kaimal, and Raju. They
advocate proper treatment of elephants and comprehensive
health insurance policies for them to encourage better medical
care. They also want to cultivate more trees, especially palm, to
ensure a good forage supply. Their overriding goal is to maintain the traditional roles of elephants in Keralan culture. All
things considered, their prospects look good. Thanks to the
prospering economy, Kerala is one of very few places in the
world where domestic elephants are more in demand than ever,
at least for ceremonial purposes.

Logging is a different story. On the way out of Trichur, headed
for the ancient port of Cochin, I stopped when I spied a tusker
at the C. V. Devassy & Co. lumber yard. The focal point of the
operation was the sawmill, a nineteenth-century affair of whirl-
ing pulleys, worn belts, bands of steel teeth, flying sparks, and
plumes of sawdust—with workers, customers, and curious on-
lookers wandering hither and yon inches away from sudden
reincarnation. A forty-year-old bull worked in the yard as an all-
purpose fork lift and tractor, sorting through the timber piles
and hauling in one log at a time to be sliced apart. After all the
emphasis on difficult bulls, it was comforting to be around one
that paid almost no attention to bystanders, except when they
came forward to offer him bananas.

The big male was surprisingly acrobatic, climbing up, down,
and around on heaps of precariously stacked logs like a four-ton
goat, occasionally using his trunk like a walking stick for extra
support. Dr. Cheeran had told me that elephants were naturally
more limber than people assumed. He had timed them racing
along at twenty-eight miles per hour in short spurts. They could
maintain a pace of twenty-four or twenty-five miles per hour for
longer intervals. Although the popular notion is that elephants
lack enough spring in their columnar legs to jump, he said elephants could leap a moat or ditch with a running start.

I had heard that they would not descend a truly precipitous slope, and if they absolutely had to do it, they climbed down backward. I had even heard stories of Asian poachers taking advantage of this by planting sharpened stakes to pierce the animals' feet along the steepest part of a jungle path. But Dr. Cheeran and others insisted that elephants faced with a sharp descent would slide down forward while sitting on their rumps.

I was also impressed with the way this bull proceeded through most of his routine—from restacking logs after pulling out the desired one to placing the log inside the sawmill with the end tamped exactly in line with the conveyor—with scarcely any guiding by the mahout. Here was a thoughtful, nimble bull-dozer, operating in a cramped, 1.2-acre yard where no gas-guzzling machine could get around half as efficiently. And yet the only reason the giant was still employed was that most of the logs in that yard, like most of the logs in Kerala these days, came from outside India.

Overseer C. D. Joseph, an Indian with a Christian name, pointed out teak from Burma, mahogany from the Malaysian portion of the island of Borneo, and a species called vitex from Papua New Guinea. That was a cross-section of the world's rain-forests the bull was climbing on out there in the yard. In the case of Burma and Borneo, they were trees from fast-disappearing elephant habitat.

"All is importing now," grumbled C. D. Joseph. "From all the ports, the wood is coming. Our own state cut too much without planning. We can no longer meet the demand with trees from our own forests. Before, we paid a 50 percent import duty on foreign logs. Now it has been changed to 15 percent, as we need the wood so badly. But the duty still hurts. What to do? En-croachments on the forest reduce our timber base steadily. The loggers encroach, and the squatters and firewood cutters en-croach, and it is only getting worse."

I intended to get to some of those other places in Southeast Asia where the forests were being stripped. First, I had to detour through Lausanne, Switzerland, to a meeting of CITES that would determine the future of international trade in ivory. My touch-off point was Delhi.

🌀🌀🌀🌀🌀🌀🌀🌀🌀🌀🌀🌀

The Second Law of Thermodynamics states that things tend toward chaos. But then what? Downtown Delhi at rush hour. It is beyond the Second Law. Beyond physics. I was nearing the edge of Delhi in a hired car when I passed two bull elephants painted from head to toe, trotting between eighteen-wheeled trucks down one lane of a five-lane freeway, bound to who knows where. Once in the city, I finally found a street not choked with vehicles. It was blocked instead by a demonstration. A humane organization was trying to rouse public support for animal rights. The speaker called for a return to the Indian values of kindness and concern for other beings—a strengthening of *ahimsa*. Behold the elephant, she cried. Mightiest of all and yet a vegetarian.

Two days later, another group of demonstrators took to the streets to protest the awful behavior of people toward other people, referring mostly to the growing violence and unrest plaguing Delhi in recent months. Bombs had been going off in the city, killing and wounding innocents. Animals are not so heedless and ruinous of their own kind, said this day's demonstrators; let us be more fair.

India would have little wildlife if its people did not take the concept of *ahimsa* very seriously, which is a rare and powerful thing. In the majority of other cultures, a highly developed sense of tolerance is likely to be construed as a sign of weakness. How many wild creatures would be roaming the United States if we had about four times our current human population on one-third the land area? Can you imagine North Americans or Europeans putting up with elephants in their fields nightly? With elephants killing between 150 and 200 people yearly?

But to Hindus, Buddhists, and Jains alike, the soul is not an exclusive possession of each person nor an exclusively human possession. It is a vital force that cycles through different lives, animal as well as human. *Namaste* is the usual greeting in much of India and Nepal; it means "I salute the god within you." God is within the giant, too.

In crediting other species with souls, people are acknowledging the animals' commonality with humans. They, too, have eyes, ears, glands, muscles, hands, and feet. And brains. They, too, have families and show emotions. They, too, have needs. Why would they not also have souls? Not as advanced as ours, say the sages, but nonetheless sacred. After all, the soul animating that beast may have animated a human in a former life. This is not too far a leap from saying that the vitality of an ecosystem that sustains other species is one and the same as the vitality that ultimately sustains us.

Jainism diverged from Hinduism at about the same time as Buddhism and took the practice of *ahimsa* to what some would consider an extreme form. Aren't Jains the folks who went around with cloths over their mouths because they were afraid they might accidentally inhale a bug and kill it? Yes, their monks and nuns did—and still do. And Jains eat before dusk, when so many insects emerge to fly about that some are likely to land in the cooking pot. Yet the point is not wholly to save insects' souls. It is in good part to purify one's own life and increase one's own awareness through concern for the lives of others, and that seems to me a point well worth considering.

Even though it has been said countless times in countless ways, it bears repeating: The way in which we treat other species cannot finally be separated from the way we humans treat one another, and vice versa. That's what the demonstrators were saying in the streets of Delhi.

Beyond what I learned about elephants, India taught me about the power of a moral belief, seriously applied, when it comes to coexisting with wild beings. It made me realize that establishing wildlife reserves was only part of the solution. There is a tremendous amount of moral habitat left to work with in most countries in order to achieve the conservation of kindred beings. Neither approach—admirable sanctuaries or enlightened acceptance of the right of other life forms to exist—is going to work alone. Together, they can work miracles.

At the same time, India taught me that even the most promising combination of nature reserves and tolerance cannot with-stand for much longer the unrestrained growth of human numbers under way at the moment. Without population control, all the best intentions in the world to preserve and learn from nature are probably going to prove futile. All the miracles will have been for naught.

I used my short time in Delhi to visit ivory shops. One of the first I located was an ivory boutique in an expensive hotel. Ironically, the owner assured me that he was a Jain opposed to harming any animals; that was why I should consider buying his wares. The sign in his window proclaimed: "All ivory articles are from mammoth tusks—a prehistoric animal—and are not included in SITES [sic] in the world. At least 10,000 years old."

The carved articles were mainly large statues. Part of the rind, or exterior, was generally left on to show the tusk's age by its cracked and discolored quality. Yet the interior was the same exquisite pearly white as modern ivory, right down to the cross-hatched moire pattern of reticulation. A fossil rind can be mimicked on modern tusks by a combination of baking and staining, but the carved tusks in this shop were so big that they would have been worth a fortune if they were really modern ivory. One statue of an entwined Siva and Parvati was hewn from a tusk whose likes hadn't been seen since the Great White Hunters pursued 150-pounders in British East Africa. It was mammoth ivory for sure.

In most of the other ivory shops, I found plenty of the usual items carved from recent tusks: gods, elephants, lamp pedestals, and gee-gaws. I also encountered ivory plate fashioned into virtually anything you can imagine, from model railroad trains and village scenes to book covers. Still thinner sheets of veneer had been shaved for miniature painting in oil and gold. Once again, every dealer assured me that he handled only legal ivory. Better yet, each swore that it was old Indian ivory, from tusks bought long before CITES even existed. And only two dealers out of dozens admitted that I would be violating the law if I tried to take any ivory into the United States, but both cheerfully showed me how I could slip sheets of painted ivory veneer into a book and carry that through customs.

Thus I spent my final hours in Delhi listening to little white lies and a couple of whoppers. I considered that significant in view of the impending CITES meeting. As a result of existing bans by individual countries and a growing boycott by consumers, the price of ivory had tumbled by 50 percent in places such as Zaire. Middlemen no longer gave advances to poachers. The business of illegal killing was on the skids, and poachers were reportedly stockpiling tusks by burying them in the forest, awaiting better market conditions. Another report claimed Hong Kong was still obtaining and stockpiling ivory, too, even though its "legal" total, accounted for in recent CITES inventories, now exceeded 700 tons.

Zimbabwe and South Africa were still utterly intent upon sabotaging any unanimous ban, claiming that they needed to sell ivory to support conservation. CITES Secretary-General Eugene LaPointe was pushing their "Buy ivory—save an elephant" position even harder than before, despite criticism of CITES for accepting donations from ivory dealers. One of LaPointe's chief arguments was that the ivory trade could be controlled and all aspects of it conducted legally.

As I said before, I met only a handful of honest ivory dealers in all my travels, and they were the ones who openly advised me to smuggle the stuff. Another thought I carried with me to the meeting concerned how many hundreds and hundreds of thousands of dollars were going to be spent on airplanes, hotel rooms, meals, and drinks—not to mention the pro-ivory propaganda being produced at CITES' expense by LaPointe—so bureaucrats from around the world could huddle in one of the most costly of nations to decide the fate of elephants. Meanwhile, Kenyan park rangers continued to risk their lives against poachers for about U.S. $2.50 a day—the price of a beer in Lausanne. In Corbett National Park, north of Delhi, I had just met trackers assisting in crucial scientific studies of elephants for U.S. $40 per month. Why was it that the money never seemed to make it all the way out to where elephants needed to be saved?

ELEVEN

SWITZERLAND

🗗🗗🗗🗗 WILDLIFE IS THE second-most-lucrative illegal trade item in the world, exceeded only by drugs. That this sordid use of our fellow creatures should continue heralds grievous ecological damage and "the moral impoverishment of us all," intoned Prince Bernhard of the Netherlands, leading off the October 1989 meeting of the Convention on International Trade in Endangered Species (CITES), the primary international body governing the import and export of wild animals and the products made from them.

Gathered at the Palais Beaulieu in Lausanne, Switzerland, on Lake Geneva's shore, the 100-odd member nations of CITES had many subjects on their agenda, from vanishing crocodilians to the farming of rare butterflies. But everyone knew that the heart and soul of this meeting was to review the official status of the African elephant. Would it remain on Appendix II of CITES regulations, the threatened species category, which permitted continued trade in ivory? Or would it be declared truly endangered and placed on Appendix I, under which further trade in ivory would be universally banned? Every hallway and room buzzed with opinions, rumors, and negotiations regarding the elephants' fate.

In addition to delegates from the member nations, the palace held selected advocates from both the ivory industry—I recognized Kageo Takaichi, the ivory importer and *hanko* manufacturer I had visited in Osaka—and conservation organizations. Representatives of the press were present as well, but had been screened and winnowed down to a few in order to avoid what delegates feared would become a media carnival. Although, as a representative of the National Geographic Society, I was among those chosen, I thought it unfair that CITES did not permit more open coverage. Too few members of the public even understand what CITES is, much less how its decisions affect their world's living resources.

The more coverage, the better, for wildlife. It was because the plight of elephants had been so well reported lately that these animals were now the subject of global concern. In many respects, elephants had come to symbolize the world's fauna as a whole. The giants' fate reflected the fate of countless smaller species being hounded toward oblivion. At the same time, the type of frenzied commercial onslaught associated with ivory reminded people of what had happened to the one group of living animals larger than elephants: the great whales. Accordingly, this somewhat technical issue of whether *Loxodonta africana* should be listed on Appendix I or II had become something of a crossroads for modern conservation, a test of our will to coexist with other life forms.

CITES officials said they did not want a carnival atmosphere, but that was exactly what glimmered in the plaza just outside the Palais Beaulieu. Nearly a thousand schoolchildren wearing elephant ears paraded about and at one point dashed up the imposing palace steps and completed a singing, chanting circuit of the building's interior. An African band played in the center of the square. Above the whole scene floated a gargantuan hot-air balloon replica of an elephant, costumed as if for a procession in India. Not only was this plaza scene a lot more fun than the tense, suited-up-for-business climate inside, it touched more directly upon what elephants really represent to the populace at large: Awe. Wonder. Fascination. A sense of kindred needs and consciousness. I had been in India long enough that I could squint up at the great balloon and imagine Ganesh hovering there, reminding us—amid the discussions of biology and economic trade-offs heating up inside the palace—that elephants are irreplaceable resources of the spirit.

Overall, the news from the ivory war front continued to be mixed. Iain and Oria Douglas-Hamilton greeted me with accounts of continuing improvement of protection in Kenya. "It's quite amazing," Iain told me. "Our parks are patrolled by wild-life department guys who actually have guns and *cars* and *radios* that *work*! Young, able, dedicated guys. The department finally has the money it needs from the government, and outside con-tributions have added to the kitty. We've managed to seriously knock down poaching in the past few months."

The price of raw ivory continued falling in Africa due to the recent U.S., European, and Japanese bans on imports. How-ever, poaching was still reportedly heavy in some regions, in-cluding parts of Angola, Mozambique, and Zambia (and parts of India, Burma, and Thailand as well, I knew). Ivory sales re-mained brisk in Far Eastern countries such as North Korea and Taiwan, and tusks were reportedly selling for an all-time high in South America. Several conservationists with whom I spoke saw this as a sinister development, given the involvement of cer-tain South American nations in the number-one illegal trade item, drugs. Prince Bernhard had pointed out in his opening re-marks that the same people were increasingly dealing in both commodities.

It seemed clear from straw polls that the majority of dele-gates, reflecting world opinion, favored stronger protection of the African elephant. Nevertheless, representatives from Zim-babwe and South Africa were desperately marshaling support for the pro-ivory cause. They maintained that elephants in those countries were overpopulated and needed regular culling, and that there was no good reason why sales of culled ivory should not be allowed to continue, especially since the money was used to support other vital wildlife management programs. More-over, fees from trophy elephant hunts could be channeled back to local tribal groups to encourage them to protect the animals and their habitat.

While not so adamant about continuing to sell ivory in the fu-ture, a few other nations complained about being stuck with substantial stocks of ivory at present. For instance, a delegate representing Congolese traders told the assembly that three ma-jor ivory shipments to Japan had been caught in transit by that country's latest ban and were now gathering dust in customs, doing no one any good. The Congolese would not have engaged in the trade if it had not been legal, he said, but we did it because CITES approved. He asked that they at least be allowed to sell the ivory they were holding.

Not surprisingly, that was Hong Kong's plea as well. But the subject of legalizing ivory stocks was a sore one. Eugene La-Pointe, head of the CITES secretariat, had been doing that for years—declaring a kind of amnesty for accumulations of tusks that everyone knew had been obtained mainly by hook and by crook. All right, he was saying in effect; the elephants are already dead, so you might as well sell off the stuff. But just this once. You better not buy any more illegal tusks, because this is absolutely, positively the last time I'm going to let you do this.

And then LaPointe would do it again. It was difficult to see what the legalizations had accomplished other than further profiting poachers and rich ivory dealers at the elephants' expense. The following passage from Marc Reisner's terrific book *Game Wars* sums up the situation:

"In 1986 . . . acting on the paid advice of Ian Parker, a former professional elephant hunter who has killed thousands of the animals in his lifetime, LaPointe issued CITES permits to eighty-nine *tons* of ivory stockpiled in Burundi. Because Burundi's elephant population is completely extinct, every one of the eight thousand elephants sacrificed to the charnel pile is likely to have been poached. LaPointe did the same thing again in Singapore—where he unilaterally 'legalized' *three hundred and fifty tons*, most of which was again poached—and again in Somalia, Djibouti, and several other countries. The secretariat's argument, then as now, was that a legal ivory market must be allowed to exist; if the trade were to go completely underground, as in the case of cocaine, prices would skyrocket and things would get even worse. But Ian Parker later admitted that he had taken a seven-hundred-fifty-thousand-dollar bribe in Burundi in exchange for including, in his 'amnesty' recommendations, several huge shipments of poached ivory then about to be added to the stockpile (it came from Zaire, Tanzania, and other African countries)."

The private, London-based Environmental Investigation Agency estimated that select Hong Kong dealers garnered on the order of $20 million in windfall profits from LaPointe's "legalizations," which made those dealers' contributions to CITES over the years of LaPointe's tenure, at best, unseemly. And elephantless Burundi had accumulated yet another ivory hoard that it was requesting be legalized.

Improprieties and innuendoes of criminal mischief aside, the inescapable fact was that since 1976 CITES had tried one scheme of quotas and trade controls after another—eight all told—to get a handle on illegal ivory dealings. Each in its turn had proved naive and wholly ineffective. (Some said that was the whole point of the exercise.) Poaching and smuggling had only increased, and the African elephant population had collapsed. And now, here in Lausanne, LaPointe and the southern African contingent were once again promoting the idea that with a new system of quotas and controls, ivory could still be traded without harming the African elephant. Why? Because, this time, the illegal side of the business was really going to be shut down. This time, they were absolutely, positively going to find a system of quotas and controls that worked.

It was not an easy argument to sell. Yet it was being taken seriously.

In addition to being a professional elephant hunter and ivory trader, Ian Parker was known as a game management specialist. He had carried out research on elephant populations in Uganda and other African countries over the years and worked for international agencies as a scientific advisor. Together with Rowan Martin, another well-known game biologist and current head of Zimbabwe's parks and wildlife department, and South African wildlife biologist Anthony Hall-Martin, Parker had long been in the forefront of those in the wildlife fraternity opposed to stricter protection for *Loxodonta africana*.

These men maintained that the problem in a number of areas was not too few giants but too many; that instead of being coddled, they needed to be controlled to keep them from damaging native habitats and other species of wildlife dependent upon those habitats. When Parker and Martin asserted that there were far more elephants left in Africa than the figures put forth by Iain Douglas-Hamilton suggested, respect for their opinion was such that many people assumed the question of how elephants were really faring was still wide open. Maybe things aren't so bad after all. You know how those animal-lover types are always screaming that the sky is about to fall. Let's not get too excited here. It takes a professional game manager to stand up for the rational perspective and point out the harsh reality that we sometimes have to shoot animals for their own good.

So the elephants and their specific problems got lost to some extent in the ongoing philosophical battle within the conservation community. Finding the emotional protectionist approach distasteful personally, a number of wildlife professionals sat back to await indisputable population data showing that the elephants were in trouble. The protectionists felt that the burden of proof should be on those who believed elephants were doing fine.

No shortage of accusations existed on either side. As often happens, what started as a disagreement over ideas had deteriorated into an intense personal battle between key players. I had met Ian Parker in Nairobi and spent an afternoon talking with him at his home. He felt so personally maligned by others at that point that he didn't even want to talk about elephants at first. Once he did begin to present his viewpoints, however, he arrayed them before me with a quickness and grasp of biology that revealed a formidable intelligence at work. I understood why his had been such a persuasive presence over the years.

⁂

Yes, the southern African states make a strong argument for ivory, said the representative from Gambia as the formal debate proceeded on the floor. But we in Gambia see death instead of economic benefits. We see poachers killing not only elephants but people—most recently a twenty-four-year-old park guard, who left behind a wife and newborn child. As for the ivory stockpiles, they represent illegally, immorally obtained tusks. If certain countries are left holding them, too bad. It is not our responsibility to bail them out.

Ninety-four percent of the ivory taken in Tanzania is poached, said that country's delegate, wildlife department director Constantius Mlay. That leaves only 6 percent yielding money for government coffers. So why should the killing be allowed to continue? Tanzania had 100,000 elephants in the Selous Game Reserve area alone in 1976. A decade later, in 1986, there were just 55,000; and in 1989, only 27,000—halved again, this time in just three years. Poaching on such a scale encourages lawlessness in general. It breeds social instability. If you like the idea of keeping ivory legal, wait until your countries are invaded by paramilitary forces with automatic weapons. This is too great a price to pay. Besides, he reminded the audience, the CITES gathering is supposed to be about saving species, not about saving businesses, not about saving face.

Zimbabwe, represented by Rowan Martin, countered with its argument that banning trade in rhinoceros horn hadn't slowed the killing for a minute; in fact, it had made rhino horn more valuable than ever and increased pressure on both black and white rhinos. But, he added, we have rhinos aplenty in Zimbabwe. Antipoaching efforts work in our country because we back them up with dollars, as Kenya is finally coming around to doing now. Zimbabwe spends U.S. $12 million annually to counter illegal killing, and it is worth it, because revenues from wildlife come to almost U.S. $100 million, including more than U.S. $10 million from ivory sales. Ivory alone pays for most of the protection for all species. If the elephant is removed from international trade, it will be devastating for Zimbabwe. Why should we be made to suffer and give up a proven system because of the inability of other nations to control poaching and practice sound wildlife management within their borders?

South Africa said little and worked mostly behind the scenes, perhaps aware that it would not help for a delegate from the white-ruled political pariah of the continent to tell other African countries what to do. The mystery was why South Africa was fighting so hard for continued Appendix II status when it had fewer than 8000 elephants and made a relatively insignificant amount of money from sales of legally culled ivory. Safari hunting was big business in South Africa, but Appendix I status wouldn't change that. My guess was that the country was in the fray chiefly on principle, being a leading practitioner of intensive game management.

Explaining why it had finally decided to support Appendix I listing, the World Wildlife Fund said that despite the good conservation records of Zimbabwe and South Africa in recent times, the illegal trade spilled across international boundaries and defied all efforts to regulate it more closely.

The U.S. delegation observed that it agreed in principle with the southern African position of culling elephants on a sustained yield basis. But, added the spokesperson, forces beyond the control of any one nation clearly placed the African elephant in serious danger. Since all efforts to cut off the illegal supply had failed, it was time to try ending the demand for ivory by banning it outright.

Someone speaking for the IUCN (the United Nations–sponsored International Union for the Conservation of Nature and Natural Resources) refused to even call the elephant killers poachers. We must call them what they truly are, he declared: well-organized, ruthless criminals involved in the destruction of an African asset and a world asset. He then proposed a sort of compromise that had been the subject of much private discussion: first, Appendix I listing for most African countries but Appendix II for those such as Zimbabwe, South Africa, and Botswana, which had proven management programs and evidence of stable or increasing elephant populations; second, a moratorium on ivory trade for at least a year until a criminal-proof system of collecting and trading ivory was established.

Hold, said the delegate from Israel. Some countries have been implying that they could no longer manage their elephants if there is a change to Appendix I listing, but this is deliberately misleading. An Appendix I listing in no way stops countries from killing elephants to protect crops, culling them to protect habitats where the giants are confined and overcrowded, carrying out trophy hunting, or taking a certain number for meat to provide protein to local people. Appendix I stipulates only that the tusks of the animals will not be traded. Yet now I hear a call for compromise. CITES has compromised for years and years and is compromising the elephant out of existence. The ivory dealers have demonstrated time and time again that they can exploit every loophole, and a brief moratorium will only stimulate the stockpiling of ivory during the interim. South Africa, a chief proponent of continued trade, suffers from illicit ivory dealing. It is known that South Africans have been involved in laundering tusks poached in Angola and Botswana. Forty tons of poached ivory have lately exited South Africa despite their best protection efforts. How can they, of all countries, claim that CITES will now be able to control trade internationally?

Similarly, although Rowan Martin stated that he doubted the number of elephants poached in Zimbabwe of late had reached double digits, the Environmental Investigation Agency stated that some 1000 elephant carcasses lay scattered in Zimbabwe's Gonarezhou National Park. The culprits were said to include rebels from neighboring Mozambique, the Zimbabwean army, Zimbabwean park personnel, and the relative of a ranking government official; among them, the park superintendent and the relative of a top-ranking minister. Also, argued various parties, the high number of living elephants claimed by Zimbabwe very likely included animals fleeing from heavy poaching in nearby sections of Zambia and seasonal migrants from bordering areas in Botswana. Zimbabwe was cooking its census figures. Not so, Martin replied. Zimbabwe keeps revising its estimates upward—they seem to show elephants increasing faster than the species' reproductive capacity—because techniques for surveying the animals are improving.

India had lately been claiming that it had 7000 to 10,000 ivory carvers, though Esmond Bradley Martin's updated figures showed only 2600 to 2700 still in the business. I was curious as to what the Indian delegate would say. What he said was that India did not want its ivory industry to survive at the expense of the African elephant. Though saddened by the fate of its carvers, India would go along with Appendix I.

And so it continued through one day and into the next. And the next. I took long walks along the autumn-colored shores of Lake Geneva, smelling fresh snow from the distant peaks on the wind and getting homesick for Montana. I covered many miles, striding off the tension and mulling over the latest facts shot into the debate. For example, in 1979, it took 54 elephants to get a ton of ivory. Now, with mature tuskers all but nonexistent and females the prime target, it took 113 elephants and left an average of 55 orphaned calves and young juveniles to die later. All this, I thought as I hurried on—all this killing, the corruption, the years of controversy, the meeting itself—and they're only teeth. Calcium phosphate. The dentine from incisor teeth.

Back in the building, I bumped into game-warden-turned-wildlife-cinematographer Simon Trevor from Tsavo. He told me that while filming in Zimbabwe, he came upon an elephant hunting guide with a downcast face. It turned out that the man's client, a shooter from the United States, had just quit following a phone call from his wife. This was not long after the U.S. ban on ivory. The wife had said something like: I just heard about what's happening to the elephants over there in Africa. You get a trophy elephant, husband dear, and you get a divorce from me.

Simon had no sympathy for Zimbabwe's practice of large-scale culling of elephants. What kind of men, he asked, can shoot down a herd and tie the surviving babies to their mothers' carcasses to be saved for later export to zoos and circuses, knowing what they do about elephant intelligence and social behavior? Simon knew perhaps more than most. He also lived next door to Eleanor, the elephant matriarch who acted as surrogate mother for the orphans reared by Daphne Sheldrick and released back into the wild in Tsavo.

I hope I have conveyed a sense of the emotions invested in this debate. I don't know how even-handed I've been. Probably not very. My own feelings regarding elephants must be fairly evident by now. I did not start out favoring the southern African position on ivory trading, and the more I saw of the elephants' situation in both Africa and Asia, the less I cared for the pro-ivory stance. To state it as plainly as possible: at this stage in my elephant travels, I was nowhere close to being an objective reporter.

The examples I selected to illustrate the debate in the Palais Beaulieu are weighted heavily against the Appendix II forces. That reflects my own bias, but also the way things stood among the delegates. The final vote was seventy-six to eleven in favor of moving the African elephant onto Appendix I, with a ban on all further trade in ivory and a resolution that all existing stocks of tusks be destroyed within months. Through the auspices of Great Britain, an exception was made for Hong Kong, which was given a six-month window in which to dispose of its stock. Also, the import and export of tusks from trophy hunting would still be permitted. But beyond that, the African elephant won a sort of restraining order against humans afflicted with ivory madness.

Contrary to the southern African group's predictions, the price of elephant teeth did not soar as soon as the commodity became outlawed everywhere. On the contrary, the price plummeted at once and continued to sink by degrees for months afterward. Despite their earlier threats to exercise the right of any nation under CITES to take an exception to the ban and continue ex-porting ivory, Zimbabwe and South Africa refrained from trad-ing tusks, much to their credit.

The public was just starting to get the message: Don't buy ivory. I thought it important that they not be sent a confusing follow-up to the effect that some ivory is "good" and you should buy it and wear it with pride. I also subscribed to the opinion that as long as any countries continued to trade in ivory and en-courage its consumption, this would hold the door open to abuses and jeopardize the greatest creature walking the earth.

But it was at the CITES meeting that I made arrangements to visit Zimbabwe toward the beginning of the next summer.

Seeing as how I had such a strong opinion about the southern African approach, it wouldn't hurt to go gather more facts first-hand. Just now, I was going home to my family. Then I was going to stop off in Southeast Asia to finish my investigation of the most endangered species of elephant. Eventually, my course would lead to Zimbabwe and beyond, to Botswana, where it would intersect the paths of southern Africa's greatest remaining elephant population. At the time, I knew Botswana was considering a program to begin culling its herds, estimated to total between 60,000 and 90,000 animals. What I could not have guessed is that by 1991, Zimbabwe and South Africa, this time joined by Botswana, Malawi, and Namibia, would be asking CITES to downlist their elephant populations and that of Zambia to Appendix II, and the whole debate would be in full roar again in preparation for another tumultuous meeting of CITES in 1992.

TWELVE

THAILAND

🔲🔲🔲🔲 A THAI ZOOLOGIST, Dr. Boonsong Lekagul, notes a report of pygmy Asian elephants living along the shores of a lake at Songkhla, near Thailand's southern tip, within the past century. He said they were less than five feet tall at the shoulder. Were these juveniles with exceptional tusks? Adults whose growth was stunted by poor forage or certain chemical compounds in the area's plants? A genetically distinct subpopulation? Whatever it was, the Songkhla elephants have disappeared in more recent times.

Nevertheless, some interesting physical variations remain within *Elephas maximus*. I've mentioned tusklessness in India and Sri Lanka, where bulls with that trait are known as *mucknas*. In Thailand, they are called *sidor*. Conversely, female Asian elephants with full-length tusks are found on rare occasions. Some bulls have tusks shaped like banana flower buds. As part of this apparent genetic trait, the same animals tend to have deep black skin and blackish nails. And then there are the white elephants.

Among the predominantly Buddhist kingdoms of Southeast Asia, white elephants are seen as descendants of the original winged elephants that roamed the cloudscapes above Earth and as avatars of the Buddha. The finding of a white elephant during the reign of a monarch was considered the most auspicious event imaginable. The peasant who located the beast might be brought before the ruler to have his ears and mouth stuffed with gold as a reward. As the white animal lumbered through its new home at the palace compound, attendants shaded it with silk umbrellas, offered platters of delicacies, and burned incense to sweeten the air while musicians played soothing music. The youngest were said to be suckled by twelve human wet nurses.

It is hard to know whether treatment so luxurious took place on a daily basis or was part of the display laid on for special occasions and visiting dignitaries, who penned some of the surviving accounts of such fabulous pomp. The maintenance of a white elephant was never cheap in any case. According to the stories, a king might make a gift of several white elephants to a powerful upstart noble, knowing that care of the creatures would be a serious enough drain on the man's treasury to keep him from raising an army instead. This is one of the explanations for how the term *white elephant* came to stand for something large and costly that you find yourself stuck with.

A long struggle between the Khmer and Sukhothai states in this part of Southeast Asia was finally won during the thirteenth century A.D. by the Thais, whom the Khmers called *syams*, from a Sanskrit word for dark, referring to their skin color. Hence the early name for Thailand: Siam. After a major invasion mounted by the Burmese in 1549 narrowly failed, the Thais decided to round up 300 more wild elephants to train them for battle. As men scoured the forests for war elephants, seven white ones were found and sent off to the Thai monarch. When Burma's King Bayinnaung heard of this, he was supposedly so overcome by jealousy that he prepared another invasion.

This one succeeded. The Thai capital was sacked in 1569 and a vassal king installed. But fifteen years later, that king's son, Naresuan, struck back and liberated Thailand. Popular tales still recount the epic battles between Naresuan's elephant-mounted forces and those of Burma's Prince Phramaha U'paraj. I heard more than one person say that Thailand won its freedom on the backs of elephants, which the Thais call *chang*. During the early years of the current Chakkri Dynasty, founded in 1782, the Thai flag bore a likeness of a royal white elephant. Insignias for the Thai navy and embassy incorporate a white elephant in their design. Various awards for government service do the same. Bronze sculptures of white elephants stand by memorials for the Chakkri kings buried at the old royal palace. The elephants' features have been blurred over the years by untold thousands who came to pay their respects and paused to rub the sculptures for luck.

Few real white elephants exist, and almost none of them are literally white. I never saw anything like a true unpigmented albino, though I was told of a strikingly pale animal kept in a zoo in Vientiane, Laos. Most of the so-called white elephants of Asia merely have coloring that is slightly lighter than normal. This is usually most noticeable in the eyes, toenails, the hairs on the body, the long hairs of the tail, and, if you stretch out the skin and look closely, in the creases between thicker parts of the epidermis. Other light areas are the palate and testicles, making seven traditional measures of whiteness altogether.

You or I might find it hard to tell a white elephant from an ordinary one. But there are men who specialize in determining grades, or degrees, of elephant whiteness. They are called *gajajeeva*, to use the Hindi term for elephant expert—or perhaps elephant metaphysician would be more appropriate. The seven measures assume great importance in their work, and so do such qualities as an elephant's gait, carriage, and overall conformation. *Gajajeevas* can discourse for hours on the way a giant's tail hangs in relation to the hindquarters and what that reveals about the animal's vigor and what sort of luck it will bring to the people around it. They know how an elephant with an "uncouth" stance or a crooked tail is a harbinger of misfortune. *Gajajeevas* can tell you all this and more—that is, if you can find any. Such men have always been scarcer than white elephants.

I met a *gajajeeva* in mid-April of 1990. The arrangements were made by Dr. Mom Luang Phiphatanachatr Diskul, nicknamed Pony, veterinarian to His Majesty Bhumibol Adulyadej, King Rama IX of Thailand's Chakkri Dynasty, at the royal palace in Bangkok. A visitor does not pass easily through the palace gate in this country, where at least twenty-six coups and countercoups have taken place since 1932. But Pony, who is of royal blood himself, ushered me speedily past the guards and militia toward the green palace grounds, where he oversees the health and welfare of the animals kept there. These include horses, dairy cows, and, at last count, four male and six female white elephants, the oldest of which was sixty-three when I arrived. Thirty royal mahouts attended to the giants. The elephants lived in special houses with gilded pagoda roofs and dined on grass, sugar cane, papaya, banana, and mineral supplements. And when they bathed, they splashed about in a tiled pool set within a courtyard of mowed grass. As several showered themselves beneath a flowering jacaranda, Pony introduced me to Sanet Thanapradit, an overseer of royal ceremonies and long-time official connoisseur of white elephants. A true *gajajeeva*.

"We have entire books on how to certify a white elephant, but a person must rely upon his own judgment as well," he said. "I started in the royal ceremony division at age eighteen, and I would tag along on trips through the country with people who were quite expert at checking the qualities of elephants. Now I know more than they did. After all, I am eighty-four years old, so I have been sixty-six years with white elephants. Memory and experience; how else does a man learn?"

I told Sanet Thanapradit that I thought he looked at least two decades younger. I meant it.

"Thank you. I attribute my longevity to my use of bee pollen and ginseng. I don't smoke or drink. Or have a wife—ha! Now, we must get on to this business of elephants." And he proceeded to talk practically nonstop for the rest of the afternoon.

Whenever someone catches an elephant in the forest, said Sanet Thanapradit—who sometimes tended to overlook differences between the present and past, as if the current difficulties with endangered species and bans on any capture of wild Asian elephants might blow over and things return to normal in royal Siam—that person is supposed to register the animal with local authorities. If any among them observes the seven signs of whiteness, he is obliged to notify the royal office. A *gajajeeva* such as himself will be dispatched at once to examine the beast for further desirable traits.

Not only must the nails be white, the elephant metaphysician elaborated, but in the best elephants they should be smooth as well, and clean near the origins. The cuticle should be white, too. Although the hairs of virtually all elephants are black at the base, those of white elephants lighten markedly toward the tip. Just as important, whereas normal elephants have a single hair coming out of a pore, or follicle, white elephants tend to have two or even three hairs per follicle.

Sanet Thanapradit indicated those on the side of a resting animal. From there, his hand swept back toward the long, clublike tail. "The long hairs here must grow in a nice fan pattern and be visibly whitish, at least near the tip," he informed me. "The whole tail should give the impression of curling upward at the end, like a bodhi leaf." His hand continued downward, cutting curves to show the proper relationship between the tail and rear legs. "Don't forget how important are the length and shape of the ankles." Certainly not. Nor would I forget how he pointed out the way the animal's long chin hairs should take on at least a hint of a true beard shape as well as being white. Finally, the voice during trumpeting ought to be high and resonant, its tone reminding listeners of the sound of a conch shell, widely used in Buddhist ceremonies.

If the majority of these additional characteristics are present, the elephant must be turned over to the king. The finder will be suitably rewarded—these days, perhaps with a medal. An official is sent to the province to oversee construction of a special stable and initial training of the animal. "Before setting out," noted Sanet Thanapradit, "the trainer must conduct his own ceremony and pray to the angel of elephants for success in his undertaking." (Thai Buddhism generally includes a strong infusion of Brahminism. Consequently, while elephants usually symbolize Buddha, they may also be associated with the Hindu deity Ganesh.) "For this ceremony, he must bring a new rope for the elephant plus an old rope from the National Museum. We Thai people pay respect to our ancestors and teachers before we undertake anything. It brings luck and makes things work."

The goal of the initial training is to teach the elephant the correct way to approach and mount a teak platform and accept certain ministrations. Once the animal has learned to do that, it will be brought to the royal palace grounds and there take part in a three-day ceremony, during which it is given its name by the king. Once the elephant is standing upon the teak platform, the king, who has mounted still higher, pours holy water over it.

Then the king descends and, accompanied by the chanted blessings of assembled monks, feeds the elephant its name; that is, he gives the animal a stalk of sugar cane with its name carefully carved upon it in delicate script. Ideally, the elephant shows no trace of nervousness as the king approaches and performs these acts, and this is taken as proof of the natural kinship of the king and white elephants.

The name fed to the elephant is a long title that includes its rank. There are four classes, or castes, of white elephants, and much of the examination by elephant metaphysicians is to determine exactly which one the particular animal belongs to. All of them are roughly equivalent to a member of the royal family. In fact, the whole naming ceremony differs little from that used for princesses and princes. And when a white elephant dies, it is given the same burial ceremony as a highly regarded human, complete with the presence of a Brahmin priest.

Pony and Sanet Thanapradit took me to see the grandest of the king's white elephants, a bull called Pra Barom Nakkot. He is one of the highest-ranking white elephants ever captured. On the outside of the pavilion where he lives alone, his name and rank are etched onto a plaque. The title is four full lines long and written in old-style Sanskrit. The translator with me had a difficult time putting the meaning into English.

"Carrier of Vishnu," the translator began, "he who will progress much among the elephants . . . One who has foremost prestige. Oh, this is very complicated. Highest of the highest of the elephants. It goes on to say he comes from heaven as a gift to the king. Belongs to the king as a gift from the Siamese people, too. He is so rare and strange, the most beautiful of all . . . with the color of water lotus. That is between pink and white, you know. Let me see . . . The big lotus that is pure; lotus from a pure, clean source devoid of all evil, . . . all the good characteristics that emanate from its own self. Happy to offer all this to his majesty, to augment his majesty's power with his own. . . ." The translator suddenly turned to me, a sheepish smile replacing his earlier look of bewilderment mingled with frustration, and whispered, "Do you know this elephant outranks me and everyone else here by many miles? It is like the highest of princes. I really ought to bow to it to show my respect."

"Its toenails and cuticles are perfectly white," the overseer of ceremonies said in a hushed voice. "They also"—and here he paused for effect—"number twenty." That was two more than other Asian elephants have, the norm being five toes on each front foot and four on each rear foot. According to Sanet Thanapradit, twenty-toed elephants are one in a thousand. The chances of one also being a white elephant are nigh miraculous.

"This is the first white elephant since the first king of this dynasty to have twenty nails," he went on. "You must look at them carefully." But now that my eyes had adjusted and I could better see this figure looming in the pavilion's darkness, I was transfixed by its entire presence. Pra Barom Nakkot, king-fed prince of princes, seemed to throw off a faint, pale aura. He was quite tall and unbelievably wide. Not lumpy wide or fat wide, though he was overfed—just thick wide, adding to the impression of strength. His tusks were huge and asymmetric. But the most startling feature was his eyes. They were pale green one moment, pale blue the next time I looked, and wide open all the time, holding some unsettling message in them.

And he rocked, constantly, tugging on chains that bound his legs to the slightly raised platform on which he stood. Pony explained that this bull was never let out of the pavilion. He received a bit of training as a youngster but none thereafter. Before Pony arrived, all the elephants had been somewhat neglected, because their traditional use in ceremonies had all but ceased in rapidly modernizing Thailand. Pony managed to reestablish programs of exercise and training for all the other white elephants. But the great bull had grown too big and wild and strong over the years. No one could regain control of him.

So for decades now, he had been here on his raised dais, rocking, straining, surging back and forth with unfathomable power, as if someone had finally harnessed the tide. Surging, swaying, pulling this way and that, forever and a day—the heaven-sent king of elephants, born of clouds and rain, colored like the sacred lotus, a captured god but now an obsolete one, something out of a distant time and kingdom, his purpose all but forgotten. Swaying, surging, alone in his dark, golden-spired pavilion. Forever alone. Colossal. And very likely insane. That was the message in those eyes: madness.

Divine madness. Thrice, I was told, this great mad elephant has trumpeted wildly in alarm. Each time, the king was in grave danger. Nobody wanted to talk about the specifics, but one threat was physical illness and another an attempted military coup.

Sanet Thanapradit gave me all manner of details about what he considered to be the natural history of white elephants in their native forest habitat. He spoke of how they were stouter and stronger than any other elephants and destined to be leaders of their herds. Just as he said this, several elephants began roaring from their pavilions. The elephant metaphysician nodded knowingly and, without missing a beat, added that even the mother and father of a white elephant were in awe of it, a little frightened. "They can see its natural dignity and leadership ability just by looking at it, and so can we. It should mate only with the same caste of white elephant and only in the forest."

The elephant metaphysician went on to tell me that "the Asian elephant has smaller features than the African elephant, but they are in balance—more *harmonious*." Asian elephants are smarter than African ones, too, he thought. His loyalties even led him to insist that Thai elephants are more intelligent than Burmese elephants. I had recently read a book about elephants by a noted Thai expert from the forestry department. In it, he informed readers that elephants live an average of 100 years, which is the same antiquated misinformation Sanet Thanapradit passed along to me. Just as he tended to speak of white elephants as natural kings in the wild, the forestry department expert spoke of how elephant society relied upon "the strongest bull to defend and provide for the family by leading the search for fodder, water, and shelter." In another passage, the expert asserted that "a female is shorter, sleeker, with a bony face and a wee bit less dignity than the opposite sex." All of which reveals much about the psyche of male *Homo sapiens* and nothing about the ecology or behavior of *Elephas maximus*, whose leadership is distinctly matriarchal.

🔲🔲🔲🔲🔲🔲🔲🔲🔲🔲🔲🔲

Following the course of countries such as South Korea and Taiwan, the constitutional monarchy of Thailand has lately metamorphosed into one of the new economic tigers of Asia. Beginning as a source of cheap labor and raw materials, it rapidly developed its own manufacturing base and attracted still more foreign investment. With Japan as its primary trading partner—Japan accounted for 53 percent of the total foreign investment as of 1990—trade has grown prodigiously. For much of the last decade, Thailand's annual increase in gross national product has been between 20 and 30 percent, the envy of any nation. The country has further prospered by developing a very savvy and efficient tourist industry.

There was a parade grounds behind Parliament in Bangkok where the king used to view all his white elephants every year on his birthday. Special songs were sung to his majesty. Dressed in traditional finery, the elephants screamed and trumpeted along—with some cueing from their trainers. When foreign dignitaries came to pay their respects to the king, his white elephants might be assembled for their viewing pleasure as well, just as in the old days.

The annual viewing of the elephants ended in the mid-1970s. Bangkok's traffic became too nasty to allow the giants to walk the three miles from their compound at the current royal palace to the old palace and Parliament area, where public events take place. Since nearly all their other ceremonial functions had already gone by the wayside, the elephants' training had slipped as well, which made it all the more difficult to get them past traffic and crowds.

The last time the royal white elephants left their compound was in 1982, for the 200th anniversary of the Chakkri Dynasty. The last time a white elephant was found in the forest was in 1978. The last naming ceremony took place that same year. Four of the elephants at the compound have never been through the ceremony and perhaps never will. Pony, who seemed vaguely embarrassed by all the trappings of the ancient white elephant tradition anyway, thought the best course for the future might be to release the animals back into the forest in a reserve. Princess Serinthon loves to visit the white elephants, though, he said with a smile. How often? Well, once in a while. How often? Well, it had been a couple of years. Unwanted, unused, and costly to maintain, the giants had become figurative white elephants.

The challenge of moving elephants through Bangkok is immediately apparent on almost any street. The routes have become a near-gridlock nightmare compounded of cars, buses, three-wheeled motorcabs called *tuk-tuks*, and motorcycles all snarling in a brown diesel haze. It takes longer to drive many places than to walk, but the air is so foul that you don't care to go by foot. You should not try to meet with more than two or three people in any one day in Bangkok, because, given the traffic, you cannot possibly reach more than two or three different destinations.

What has happened is that the economic boom has greatly increased car ownership and also lured tremendous numbers of rural people to this capital city. High-rises proliferate. So do enormous slums, many of them resting on toxic wastelands next to industrial centers, where packs of homeless street urchins escape their bleak surroundings for short periods by sniffing glue. No plan to coordinate growth with transportation has ever been effected. Speculators build willy-nilly. But who can wait? Bangkok real estate continues to double in value almost yearly. Business of every kind is coining money. For the sake of efficiency, developers have taken to having competitors assassinated. Murder is a surprisingly common business practice in modern Thailand. The usual technique is a drive-by shooting with the hit man mounted on a motorcycle. Prices run from a few hundred U.S. dollars for a relatively unimportant person to $40,000 for an influential businessman. You could buy a child outright for around $200, which is ten times what one costs in Sudan, but still less than a fancy watch. This is the other side of the nation known as the Land of Smiles, whose people are so unfailingly warm and gracious in everyday encounters.

Only a few years ago, mahouts used to ride their elephants to Bangkok during the premonsoon season of boiling heat, when they were out of work in the fields and forests. Once in the city, the animals strolled the streets, acting as what could be called doctor elephants. They allowed people to walk under their bellies three times for luck. Women walked underneath to improve their fertility; pregnant ones did it to make childbearing easier. Meanwhile, the mahout collected fees and sold ivory trinkets such as little carved Buddhas and rings or bracelets made of elephant hair, also to bring luck.

For 200 to 400 bhat—about U.S. $8 to $16—the mahout might let someone pluck a fresh hair from the tail. The elephant would quiver, and the pore would bleed, but this, too, was supposed to bring luck. Sometimes the mahout remained mounted and gave people rides while an assistant sold the baubles and charms. Although doctor elephants may still be seen in the countryside, they can no longer navigate the traffic of Bangkok any more than the sacred white elephants can. Besides, the nearest forage is now too far from the city center. And city hustlers have taken to robbing the mahouts who ride doctor elephants, knowing they are likely to be carrying a fair amount of cash.

About the only elephants seen in Bangkok other than those trapped at the palace are several at a park called the Rose Garden, where mini-re-creations of battles between Burma and Siam are carried out daily for tourists by the giants and their riders. And young elephants act as greeters at a couple of Bangkok's myriad massage parlors. Poor rural villages in many parts of the country are all but empty of women between the ages of fifteen and thirty, because they have gone to the cities to work as prostitutes. Their services are arranged with families through brokers, and the pay scale is such that the practice amounts to indentured servitude, barely a step above slavery. It was recently reported that, in order to meet the ever-growing demands of the Thai sex trade, young women were being bought by the thousands from neighboring Laos, Burma, and southern China. On the way back from the royal palace, a Thai friend tried to talk me into going for a B-course—a body massage in which the girl oils all of her own body and uses that to rub the client's skin—at one well-known high-rise parlor. The place has 500 rooms and a prostitute in each one, giving new meaning to the term sex industry.

I tried to imagine the great mad elephant from the palace breaking loose and smashing his way out of this city, clearing a path through traffic with his mighty trunk and trampling feet, and making his way back to the quietude of the woodlands where he grew up.

But the highest of the highest of white elephants would be in for a grim surprise. The old woodlands are gone, having been swept away in an unbridled spasm of logging. The majority of the timber went to Japan, which was buying raw hardwood lumber as fast as Thailand could cut it—U.S. $88 million worth in 1989 alone. Fifty Thai companies made or exported hardwood furniture, for which the United States was the major client, taking about a third of the production.

Thailand still has some forests, but they are a far cry from the original jungles. They are cutover lands with brush and spindly second-growth trees that seem lush only to foreigners from temperate countries. Many logged hillsides lack even a second-growth forest. Some burn too often, either in fires that escape squatters practicing slash-and-burn agriculture or in dry-season blazes set by poachers to drive game. On thin or stony soil, repeated burning can eventually lead to a monoculture of scraggly, fire-resistant dipterocarp trees with an understory of annual weeds. Other hillsides lack second-growth forest because they are so steep that, once laid bare by cutting, they keep eroding away in monsoon rains. Elsewhere, the complex native forest has been replaced with a monoculture of commercial tree species such as pine, teak, eucalyptus, or rubber.

With encouragement from the World Bank, Asian Development Bank, and other international organizations, eucalyptus, an exotic from Australia, has been widely planted throughout

Asia's tropical areas. Planners see it as a fast-growing, hardy source of small lumber and fuel for cooking and heating. Eucalyptus does thrive on tropical soils and proves highly resistant to diseases and pests due to its volatile oils. About the only creature that can digest eucalyptus leaves is the koala, which evolved along with the plant. Decaying leaves virtually sterilize the ground underneath the tree. As far as native Asian wildlife is concerned, a stand of eucalyptus is about as useful as an arctic ice pack. Thai farmers have protested against widespread eucalyptus introductions and started hacking the trees down because nobody can grow crops or graze livestock in association with such stands either. Yet the government keeps planting more eucalyptus. When the bureaucrats tote up board feet of wood produced per acre on marginal soils, eucalyptus looks good, and that is as far as they seem able to figure.

Again with the help of the World Bank, a consistent promulgator of inappropriate technology and misguided development schemes, Thailand's annual rubber production increased roughly 400 percent—from 270,000 tons to more than a million tons—between 1975 and 1990. Once established, a rubber plantation covers the hillsides with a robust green cloak. The trouble is that this canopy of closely planted trees is so dense and unvarying that little grows underneath in its shade. What does pop up is knocked back by herbicides. Here again, the soil has no ground-cover to anchor it and, thus, remains vulnerable to erosion in heavy rains.

In 1989, a series of heavy monsoon storms swept across the recently denuded Thai countryside, causing floods and mudslides that devastated villages (40,000 homes destroyed) and killed hundreds of people. The toll was high enough and widespread enough to finally shock the government into action. A hastily passed law banned all logging throughout the nation.

A strong measure indeed. However, by the time it went into effect, few trees of commercial size were left to cut anyway. Anticipating the ban, logging companies had sent men with chain saws to work seven days a week getting out almost every last tree. Some worked through the night under lights. A few Thai logging companies then shut down. Others moved on with their heavy machinery and the biggest working elephants into Burma. Eighteen Thai companies had set up concessions with the repressive military regime there to begin stripping the jungles, believed to harbor anywhere from 3000 to 10,000 wild elephants. This wild population was already heavily exploited for ivory and to replenish Burma's elephant work force, estimated at 5000 to 6000, the largest of any Asian country.

In some areas of Burma, the Thai timber companies found they had to pay bribes not only to military officials but to rebel ethnic groups, such as the Karen tribe—not to mention the local warlords who control the drug trade. The real cash crop in many parts of this region—the Golden Triangle—is the poppy, tapped to produce opium and heroin. Just the same, ivory fever was high, and teak fever had begun to resemble it. One logging truck rumbling back across the border from Burma toward a mill in Thailand would be laden with logs worth tens of thousands of U.S. dollars in retail lumber. A logging company executive near Lampang in northern Thailand was blown up by anti-personnel mines in a hit thought to have been arranged by a rival timber baron.

The Thais were also arranging timber deals with relatively undeveloped Laos. Formerly known as Lane Xang, Land of a Million Elephants, it harbors somewhere between 2000 and 4000 wild elephants and fewer than 1000 domesticated ones. Wildlife trade expert Esmond Bradley Martin reports that 1.2 guns per square mile can now be found in Laos, and the illegal wildlife trade is burgeoning. Markets openly display elephant meat and ivory, horns of Sumatran and possibly Javan rhinos, and an array of products from other rare species. Hunted year-round, the once rich community of birds and mammals is becoming increasingly depauperate. The 1990 World Resources study, prepared with United Nations support, found eleven countries responsible for 82 percent of the world's tropical deforestation. They included India, Indonesia, Thailand, Burma, Laos, and Vietnam.

While in Bangkok, I kept pursuing applications to visit both

Laos and Vietnam. Neither country looked as if it was going to grant me access before still more months went by, so I would probably have to skip them altogether. In the meantime, though, I learned some interesting information from a sixty-year-old Vietnamese entomologist named Vo Quy. In the early 1940s, before fighting began with the French, Vietnam's 128,000 square miles were 46 percent forested. By 1975 that figure had fallen to 29 percent, and it was currently 20 percent. But the really astonishing statistic was that 40 percent of the countryside was essentially barren wasteland.

The chief causes were the spraying of Agent Orange and other defoliants and saturation bombing by the United States during its war against Vietnam. Twenty-five *million* bomb craters pattern the Vietnamese earth. Some are at least big enough to be useful as fish ponds, said Vo Quy. About 715,000 acres of forest had been knocked down by U.S. bulldozers, which cut swaths along roads and canals to minimize the chances of ambush.

Some of this landscape simply was not growing back. Other sections grew coarse *Imperata* grass that, ungrazed, turned rank and unpalatable and choked out all other growth. In addition, Vietnam was itself cutting 450,000 acres of forest per year. Vo Quy was leading a campaign to replant at least as much as was being cut and seeking international support to help restore the torn and poisoned forests of his country. I have talked to American veterans of that war who bombed or machine-gunned elephants on sight, because they were used by the enemy to transport men and materiel. Today, Vietnam is thought to sustain perhaps 1500 to 2000 elephants in the wild and another 500 to 700 in captivity.

In Thailand, domesticated elephants numbered in the tens of thousands around the turn of the century; one source puts the figure at 100,000, but that seems inflated. Most tame elephants in the ancient kingdom served for transport and as draft animals for the fields. They were always available for hauling logs when needed, but the formation of a massive work force for timbering was mainly a consequence of the colonial era, as epitomized by the Burmese tales of Colonel J. H. Williams, who wrote *Bandoola* and *Elephant Bill*.

By 1965, the figure for domesticated elephants in Thailand—reasonably accurate since all such elephants now had to be legally registered—was just over 11,000. Current figures are between 4000 and 5000, and, with the logging ban, the majority are unemployed. Once again, elephants were used to help bring about their own demise, both in the wild and in the logging industry. By contrast, Thailand's human population had increased tenfold since 1850, from 5 million to more than 50 million.

The deadly floods and mudslides that prompted the ban were over by the time of my visit. Instead, while I was traveling the countryside, it was suffering from one of the worst water shortages in its history. Yet the cause was the same. Without intact forests and humus layers in the soil to sponge up rainfall and release it later in a steady flow, all the monsoon precipitation had rushed off the hillsides at once and continued on to the sea, leaving nothing for later on. Crops as well as lives had been lost in the floods. Now they were being lost to drought.

This pattern of aridity and falling water tables in the wake of deforestation was becoming evident throughout much of Asia. According to the Asian Development Bank, the forest cover of the region as a whole had been reduced from 52 percent of the total land area in 1944 to 19 percent in 1990 and was shrinking faster than ever. Another pattern seen across Asia was an attempt to solve the crisis not by controlling logging but by building more dams to store water. Flooding of rich, vital lowland habitat and disruption of migratory patterns due to dam construction had become one of the leading threats to wildlife.

The results of a fast profit for the timber companies in Thailand were hunger and thirst for thousands of people. Plus social unrest as groups fought over rights to what water was left and accused one another of ruining stream flows through upstream diversion. Plus the cost of dam-building sometime in the future. Plus the cost in terms of wildlife habitat and arable bottomland lost to reservoirs.

And illegal logging openly continued inside forest reserves.

Like many of Thailand's corporations, the timber companies are controlled by a web of high-ranking military officials, aristocratic Thai families, and Chinese banking and merchant families. This elite in turn holds sway over civil authorities, and, as a result, true reform is not easy to enforce.

It was discovered that the company awarded a major tree-planting contract, Suan Kitti Reforestation, had been cutting down the remnants of forest instead, profiting from timber sales at the same time that it took money for nonexistent replanting work. Newspapers reported that Suan Kitti had been hired because its owner was a friend of the minister of agriculture, Major General Sanan Kachornprasat, who oversaw the forestry department. If the press becomes too diligent in exposing such schemes, military leaders begin talking about shutting down newspapers in the interest of maintaining national pride and national security.

Thailand has dozens of wildlife sanctuaries and national parks, the oldest of which was established just two decades ago. But they are rife with illegal timber cutting, encroachment by squatters (between 1 million and 1.5 million of them occupy slightly more than 1 million acres of forest reserve land), opium growing, and poaching—the primary cause of elephant deaths in the country. Bull elephants are shot for their tusks. Cows are sometimes shot so the poachers can catch the babies. The young animals are sold through the illegal market to zoos, circuses, and private hobbyists who, increasingly, want to keep elephants as a status symbol. Thailand has also become the main market for baby elephants caught in neighboring Burma, Laos, and Kampuchea and smuggled across the border. Some hill tribes hunt the giants for meat. People growing crops in or around the reserves also kill elephants to keep them from damaging fields. And wealthy young Thais from the city sometimes go shooting in the reserves for sport, knowing their family connections will keep them out of serious trouble if they get caught.

Wardens who interfere with Thailand's lucrative illegal wildlife trade have been harassed and murdered. They are poorly paid and equipped to begin with, averaging about U.S. $80 per month in pay. In keeping with the pattern seen in so many countries, money generated by conservation through park visitation and other forms of tourism does not go back into conservation. It is not used to benefit and encourage wildlife or wardens or local people in any substantial way. The agencies charged with protecting beleaguered wildlife continue to receive only token support from the government. At best. Saving the living world is simply a low priority. Its relation to the quality of human existence is not clearly perceived, in part because the true profit/loss figures for certain types of development are never factored in. Which is why the Thai government has lately shown an interest in opening some parks to logging and to more hydropower projects.

Even if the reserves in Thailand were splendidly run, they are much too small and isolated to be effective in conserving large animals over the long term. Estimates put the number of wild elephants in Thailand at just 1300 to 2000. Most of them are already focused around areas listed as protected, and not one of those areas is sufficient to sustain a genetically viable elephant population through the centuries.

Perhaps the nearest to being an effective habitat is the Huai Kha Khaeng Wildlife Sanctuary in western Thailand. Though just 1000 square miles in size, it is the largest stretch of protected wildland in all of Southeast Asia. Situated near undeveloped lands in Burma and buffered by adjoining Thai national forest lands that are still somewhat intact, it supports a varied fauna from wild water buffalos and Malayan tapirs to tigers and marbled cats. At the opposite end of the scale is the Khao Chamao Reserve, which had exactly seven elephants at last count. A few protected areas are barely big enough to picnic in, much less harbor giants, and picnicking is in fact what they are mainly used for.

The concept of wildlands as key elements in the struggle to preserve biological diversity and functioning ecosystems has not yet penetrated very far into the consciousness of the Thai public. Exactly where their consciousness stands in regard to nonhuman species to begin with is something I would not venture to guess.

Sections of the Thai countryside have terrible problems with rodents, in part because the areas are almost devoid of snakes. The reason they are devoid of snakes is that people catch and sell every one they see. And the reason they do that is because the blood of live snakes, mixed with other potions, is considered a good tonic and aphrodisiac. Live snake blood is a favorite drink for those on their way to visit the local massage emporium. Large quantities of snakes are also exported to China and Taiwan for the same purpose.

In Bangkok, people can still order a feast with an Asiatic black bear or a sun bear as the centerpiece, bawling and screaming as it is slowly roasted alive over coals before the assembled guests. Or a restaurant will cater one of those affairs, known throughout much of the Orient, at which the top of a live monkey's skull is removed and the primate watches the diners scoop out its brains to eat. We are talking hard-core gourmet fare here in the Land of Smiles. Some Chinese dealers had orders out in Thailand for elephant penises. Shooting elephants for their tusks seems almost wholesome by comparison.

In every major town, and Bangkok in particular, ivory shops are a common sight. During my visit, sales were off by about 50 percent, as they had been shortly before the CITES ban, but the goods were still moving. Dealers were keeping the prices fairly high, though they were more than ready to negotiate. A lot of sculptures and jewelry that looked like exceptional bargains were actually carved from bone; some were made of a more sophisticated fake material concocted of ground fish bone and animal bone in a plastic matrix. Ivory advertised as legally obtained from Africa before the international ban was coming from elephants poached in Burma and smuggled in along with animal skins, gold, and drugs. Carvings advertised as traditional Thai pieces supporting local artisans were clearly mass-produced Hong Kong products: cut-rate netsuke, Buddhas, Shiva, potbellied Chinese gods of luck, and copulating figurines. And as ever, when I asked dealers if I could take any of these ivory wares back into the United States, I was told: No problem, my friend.

Only one fellow strayed from the standard lie that customs

would let me take everything through except the largest tusks. He assured me that I could take them as well. Foreign buyers were wary, but European tourists still took plenty of small pieces, the dealers said. Much of the consumption of larger ivory work in Thailand was domestic these days, fueled by the new wealth washing around the country. Rich Thai business-men wanted whole carved tusks. Ivory handles for pistols were all the rage among the military-industrial elite.

When a new business is established in Bangkok, the owner may set aside a small space nearby and build a public shrine in the hope that it will bring blessings upon the enterprise. There is one between the 7–11 and McDonald's stores in the heart of town. Farther down Rama I Avenue, past the banks, the trading company offices, the boutiques selling boots and belts made of elephant hide, the ivory shops, and the venereal disease clinics, the owners of a department store built a shrine on a corner by a busy intersection. The miniature pagoda roof houses an image of Brahma, with four faces and six arms. But people call it the Erawan shrine, Erawan being the Thai version of Ganesh.

The shrine's name apparently comes from the custom of leav-ing offerings of carved elephants as thanks for answered prayers. This shrine's reputation for bestowing boons upon worshippers must be well deserved, for there are herds of assorted elephants crowded into its courtyard: huge pachyderms of stone or wood left by wealthy donors and countless small wooden elephant fig-urines, which are collected from the shrine after a decent interval and sold again by vendors outside on the streets.

What made the place special to me was the practice worship-pers have of pressing inch-square pieces of gold foil onto the larger elephant statues. In gilding the elephant, each person gains a touch of merit. Nothing holds the thin foil on except friction and oils from the donor's fingertips. After a while, the foil begins to loosen at the edge and then come free. Yet instead of falling to the ground, it often wafts slowly upward, carried along like a seed pod on a rising air current generated by rows of burning candles and incense in the courtyard. I remember watching the golden offerings to the elephant go floating past a troupe of tra-ditional Thai dancers performing in full golden regalia—another form of thanks from a wealthy worshipper—and the wreaths and necklaces of marigolds hung from the shrine; past the hurrying pedestrians, who paused to fold hands against forehead and make a brief bow toward the shrine, and the traffic jamming by in its wreath of acrid brown fumes; up past the department store's concrete sides, past the steel skeleton of the higher tower being constructed across the street, and finally into the dazzle of afternoon light filtered through smoggy, humid, 105° F air to make their way alone to the heavens.

And I kept wondering: What do all these people praying think about live elephants and jungles and the miraculous natural world out there somewhere? Urban, rural, or wild, survival or extinction—I suppose it is all one to Brahma, and that is a point I should probably consider more often in my musings. Maybe things are supposed to turn out the way they are. Maybe whatever happens is natural; I've heard that argument often enough. But it strikes me as too fatalistic. If we are supposed to be content with events as they unfold, why are so many people stopping to beg Brahma to intercede in their fate?

Richard Lair, an American biologist, lived for years in Thailand and collected a great deal of information throughout Asia on both wild animals and cultural attitudes about them. He told me of visiting a part of Laos where the people, being serious Buddhists and therefore opposed to killing, justified catching fish by saying they were saving them from drowning. Richard even saw a man lay his catch carefully upon a clean white cloth and then, unable to bring himself to club them on the head and end things quickly, begin playing a flute to ease their suffering as they flopped and gasped their life away.

While the glittering foil floated upward in the evening air, I kept mulling over such things, and the harder I tried to find meaning in them, the less sense they made. Billboards along the avenue advertising current Thai movies showed warriors brandishing guns and heroine/sex goddesses wearing bandoliers across their nearly naked chests and bodies being blown up and flying through a sky full of flames. In a way they seemed little changed from pictures made a couple of thousand years ago to illustrate religious epics.

Whenever I returned from the Thai countryside to a hotel that had a television, I usually flipped through the channels to look for a news station. Sooner or later, on my way around the dial, I would turn to a scene in which a defenseless woman waited alone in a darkened house or alley while some menacing figure approached to maim and murder her. This would almost always be a show made in America. Back home, this sort of program was so pervasive that I scarcely paid attention. But here, seeing it through the freshened eyes of someone who had been traveling in faraway places, I would start wondering about the cosmology of my own culture.

I am trying not to be a tiresome moralist. My purpose is to remind those who want to save species that we are dealing with some terribly contrary impulses deep within ourselves. Somehow, we have to come to terms with this dichotomy, this mixture of destructiveness and compassion in the human soul, and figure out a way to strengthen and expand the nurturing side.

The fact that Buddha delivered this message an awfully long time ago does not seem to have interfered with Thailand's current transformation into a society that is consuming its wild places and creatures. It gets back to the unsurpassed ability of humans to see what we want to see, I decided at the Erawan shrine. The only reality I know that is not highly relativistic and fickle, because it is not fabricated from human cultural needs, lies in the workings of natural systems. I lit a candle and made a few prayers of my own. I left a couple of small carved elephants as a sort of advance thanks, then took off for the north of the country to see for myself what remained of those systems.

〰〰〰〰〰〰〰〰〰〰〰

A century ago, claims one source, northern Thailand had 20,000 tame elephants working just to transport materials, plying major trade routes and village trails alike. Brahma alone knows how many wild ones dwelled in the thick forests. When I thought of the region, I envisioned *wats*, or spired temples, poking through the jungle vines and mists. One of the most famous *wats* is Suan Dok, founded in the sixth century A.D. upon a site where an elephant bearing the remains of Buddha supposedly stopped to sleep. Buddhist monks at some *wats* still ride to their ordination ceremony on the backs of elephants. The city of Chiang Mai, Thailand's ancient capital, plays a prominent part in the northern region's remote and exotic allure. Travel agents promote it as a world half-forgotten by time.

They promote it so well that more than 2 million tourists are funneled through Chiang Mai every year. Among the most memorable sights and sounds are those of commercial jetliners landing or taking off almost continuously. Televisions in the hotels blare Thai game shows, and lounge singers offer renditions of Frank Sinatra and Barry Manilow. The downtown area is less a rural market than a mall, offering the standard assortment of cheap watches, jewelry, imitation designer clothing, tennis shoes, rock 'n' roll cassette tapes, cameras, Fuji film, and portraits of Buddha and Elvis. Only on the periphery can you sometimes find more traditional offerings, such as tethered monkeys and pangolins awaiting execution to provide a meal.

Ads such as one I noticed in the *New Yorker* for furniture made of wood "from the mountainous jungles of northern Thailand" foster the myth that plenty of steamy, untamed rainforests can yet be found around places like Chiang Mai. But the mountainsides I walked were all second growth, and the second growth was being cut down and burned and tilled to produce fields. People and traps and snares and pits and trip wires tied to the triggers of guns were everywhere, and the countryside was virtually devoid of wild animals.

The Woodland Zoo in Seattle has a Southeast Asia Tropical Forest exhibit with 750 trees, 2300 shrubs, and 600 clumps of bamboo within 4.6 acres. It also has a re-creation of a Thai elephant logging camp, complete with classic peaked pagoda roofs on the buildings. As the elephants pull, lift, and sort logs, zoo-goers get a sense of their great strength and intelligence, while the captive giants get a bit of physical and mental exercise.

The interesting thing is that tourists who go all the way to northern Thailand will see the same simulation, only with less diverse vegetation. Elephant camps that put on displays for tourists have proliferated around Chiang Mai. Visitors pay to watch mahouts go through an abbreviated version of a working day at a logging camp, bathing and feeding the animals and then putting them through their paces in a log yard. In their brochures, several of these businesses suggest that they are actually training centers for elephants that go on to work in logging. But the truth is that the only job available in northern Thailand for an elephant that used to work at real logging, back when the hills had real forests, is at a tourist camp.

"It is better than logging. The pay is good, and the work is much easier—for me and for my elephant," I was told by a mahout named Dang at the Young Elephants Training Center. He and his assistant, a Karen boy called Song, were on a break from giving rides to tourists after the logging show. More visitors, mostly French, German, and Japanese, were lining up for the next performance. Dang's enthusiasm reflected the fact that his elephant was a female in her fifties. She would not have brought in money hauling heavy teak much longer, but she was gentle and perfectly suited for giving rides.

Manas Yaviraj, manager of the camp, came over to join us. "Where else can you put your old granny elephants and gay ones and find work for them?" he joked, pointing to a *sidor*, or tuskless male, nearby. Although he referred to the animal as a homosexual male, he noted that it never actually tried to mate and never came into musth.

It was a pleasant camp. The more adventurous tourists were given pith helmets and taken for a ride through the surrounding woodlands and along a stream so that they really did get a feel for the elephant-back life of old Thailand. Other camps in the area took the experience a step further, providing trips of several days by elephant through the hilly countryside, a challenging and stimulating experience. So I know I run a risk of sounding like a killjoy by pointing out how artfully people were being sold an image. They expected a frontier with jungles where tigers still stalked and logging elephants still toiled, and Thai entrepreneurs quickly arranged one—minus the tigers.

I have nothing against illusions, but it would have been far simpler and saner—and ultimately just as profitable, if not more so—to have perpetuated the real jungle, which was right there at hand such a short while ago. At the very least, some of the money being coined by the tourist industry could be channeled back toward conservation.

From the limited field research on wild elephants in Southeast Asia, it appears that, somewhat like Africa's forest elephants, they prefer monocots in their diet, seeking out certain families of herbaceous plants, palms, and grasses, including bamboo. And as in African jungles, the elephants both create openings within the forest canopy through their feeding and enlarge existing ones, such as around salt licks. Wild bovids, various deer species, pigs, primates, and a number of birds qualify as secondary feeders. They rely to some extent upon elephant-made openings dominated by monocots and upon seeds, branches, and leaves dropped by feeding elephant herds. At the same time, the elephants act as key dispersers of a significant number of tree species, from wild mangoes, with their lozenge-shaped seeds, to certain figs and members of the Irvingiaceae family.

Southeast Asia's native forests contain some of the highest measures of plant diversity recorded anywhere. Portions of southern Thailand and neighboring Malaysia are matched only by sections of the Peruvian Amazon. Some measure of that splendor and variety is the result of having elephants in the wild-land community. As in India, indigenous forest-dwelling people are part of that community and equally at risk. Thailand's Semang people, who hunt with blowpipes and spears, are one example. Laos, which has a relatively small human population, harbors from eighty to ninety distinct ethnic groups.

🙚🙚🙚🙚🙚🙚🙚🙚🙚🙚🙚🙚

I traveled through mile after mile of cutover, burned, and beaten-looking landscapes east of Chiang Mai with Choowit Mahamontri of the Forest Industry Organization (FIO). He used to work in a cooperative project with the Japanese, who set up an agency to instruct Thais in methods for building roads and logging by cable on especially steep terrain. But the Japanese pulled out as soon as the logging ban went into effect. Choowit's new job was to round up squatters on forest lands.

Choowit summed up a pan-Asian problem with this observation: "Whenever you build a logging road, you build a pathway for colonization by migrating farmers, who clear the land for their plots." Northern Thailand has more than a dozen ethnic groups of hill people: Meo, Lissu, and Hmong in their colorful traditional dress, Wah Chinese, Karen tribals, and so on. A large percentage of them are homeless, displaced by political upheavals in the region, by overpopulation, and by deforestation and soil depletion on traditional lands; needless to say, all three factors are closely related. The upshot is a massive increase in squatting by a floating population drawn to whatever unclaimed land is most accessible at the moment.

"The first time we catch squatters, we just warn," Choowit said. "How can you throw them away in jail? These are families with children. Many are refugees. They are very poor. We have a new program to try to keep them in one place by offering housing and schools. Also a job. The job is replanting the forest." But they don't plant forests, really. They put in those orderly, fertilizer-dosed, pesticide-laced rows of teak, exotic eucalyptus, and fast-growing pines that are the antithesis of the tangled natural richness nature once fashioned on the same spot.

A practical strategy for at least getting the maximum use out of a cutover area is to let local villagers or squatters cultivate crops such as maize, soybeans, squash, and tea beneath new plantations of trees for the first three years or so, until the canopy begins to shade out the understory. The problem is that squatters come to view whatever property they till as their own. They may organize and lobby to win legal title to part or all of it. Where there are enough of them to represent a political force, they are frequently successful.

On occasion, the FIO program that Choowit helps administer gives squatters a small plot of forest reserve acreage outright to call their own. It is part of the inducement to settle down and husband land properly. But Choowit acknowledged that the squatters sometimes turn around and sell the piece off to wealthy landowners. For that matter, he admitted, influential people encourage peasants to squat on forest, park, and wildlife sanctuary lands, agitate to win title to the land, and then sell it to the well-to-do and well-connected. Landless peasants become pawns in their schemes to dismantle reserves and privatize what were intended to be public resources.

Approaching the hillsides near Lampang, we stopped to eat at a roadside restaurant and learned that a local man had been caught logging illegally within a forest reserve just the day before. The police confiscated the working elephant, but the animal's owner somehow got the mahout to take sole blame for the log poaching. So the police sold the elephant back to the owner. The cops were 50,000 bhat—U.S. $2000—richer, the owner was free to try stealing timber somewhere else, and the mahout, a low-paid wage earner, was in jail.

After lunch, Choowit took me to meet Dr. Preecha Phongkum, chief veterinarian for 128 elephants maintained in the Lampang district by the FIO. The animals were a legacy from the days just past when the government both contracted out timber sales to private companies and did some logging with its own employees. Despite the countrywide logging ban, a small amount of work remained, such as cleaning up fallen trees before annual fires burned them, clearing old logging waste prior to replanting, and some very selective cutting of trees. It was nowhere near enough to keep all the elephants busy, but it was something to do until Dr. Preecha and the FIO figured out the future of their working elephants and the associated elephant training school—the real training school, not the tourist replica.

Confirming what I had heard from several sources in Southeast Asia, the FIO mahouts said that an elephant mother is assisted at birth by another female, who acts as a midwife, helping lower the newborn infant to the ground and tearing the amniotic sac with her trunk and forefoot. Thais have been practicing a good deal of captive breeding since wild capture was outlawed during the early 1970s, so they have had plenty of opportunities for direct observation. Still, I am not certain whether or not elephant midwifery is the norm or an occasional act that has some-how been interpreted as standard behavior. Nor have I any idea whether or how often it occurs among wild Asian elephants. To the extent that it does occur, it represents a rare relationship among animals and yet another similarity between elephants and humans.

At the FIO training center, a youngster was allowed to nurse for three years. Sometime during its fourth or fifth year, de-pending upon how well the mother accepted the change, it was separated from her and put on a diet of grass. Beginning at age five, then, the youngster learned to associate with its mahout in-stead, accept a chain, and obey fundamental commands. Oddly, Dr. Preecha insisted that baby elephants have no innate fear of snakes and have to be taught to avoid them, even though snake-bite is a noteworthy cause of death among young elephants. This contradicted the observations of other Thai mahouts, who told me elephants naturally fear both snakes and the foot-long millipedes seen in the forests.

By age ten, the elephant was practicing dragging logs, and by age fifteen, it was ready to work with a mahout. Some began to learn how to work in tandem as well. Yet, as in India, the ele-phants would not begin really laboring hard until age twenty-five, by which time an animal was expected to understand and execute about twenty-four specific commands with little urging by the mahout. After age forty, it started to get less demanding physical tasks, and after age fifty, it was headed for retirement.

Anthrax used to be a scourge before regular vaccinations were available, noted Dr. Preecha. The disease is transmitted by a bit-ing tabanid fly, which also infects elephants with *surra*, a try-panosome that causes a high, often fatal, fever, somewhat similar to malaria in humans. The main health problem on a day-to-day basis was simple wounds caused by thorns, broken branches, and mahouts' hooks penetrating the elephants' skin, which is rather thin in many places. The skin surface heals over, encapsulating a wound, which ferments and develops into an abscess.

I watched several large males put to work hauling trees that had been felled earlier. Each had a harness padded with a sort of saddle made from the soft bark of the bombax tree, *Tetrameles nudiflora*, mainly to protect the area over the spine, which has little natural cushion. A good elephant man works his elephant three days on and two off, the mahouts told me, and in 100° F or hotter weather like this, they worked only in the mornings. The elephants sweat, of all places, around the cuticles by their toenails, they said. Only a man badly in need of money would try to work his elephant any longer. Besides, it was so hot and dry just before the rainy season that any tree cut would likely crack and split upon hitting the ground.

Because of the elephant's need for rest, it could no longer compete with the ever larger and more efficient bulldozers and mechanical log skidders available. Besides, an elephant can haul only about half its weight in the first place, comparatively less than a human. When handling a lot of huge trees from a pristine jungle, as elephants still were in Burma, they had to operate in tandem or in threes, whereas one modern megamachine could do the job. Still, nothing could match an elephant for operating on steep slopes. Perhaps that was the working elephant's future, mused Dr. Preecha—to specialize in difficult terrain. But for the past five years he had undertaken a program to breed elephants specifically for a different purpose: working on the plantations of teak and other commercial trees that are replacing the natural forest in region after region. His goal was to create smaller elephants. They could maneuver more easily between the plantation rows during cutting and thinning operations, he reasoned. The cultivated trees would never grow very large before they would be cut, so the elephants did not have to grow big either. Better yet, reduced size made them easier to control, and they required less feed, the veterinarian explained.

A human-bred pygmy elephant—what a remarkable state of affairs. Oh, yes, added Dr. Preecha: the elephants he was breeding would also be tuskless. Ivory-less, pygmy plantation elephants.

The FIO camp turned out its elephants to graze at night dragging an eighty-foot chain and wearing a collar with a bell, traditionally made of resonant wood. Mahouts told the same stories as I had heard in India of an elephant occasionally coiling up the chain and throwing the thing over its back so the chain would leave less of a trail and of stuffing the bell with mud or clasping it with the trunk to keep from making noise. Usually, though, the giant was easy to find. For the past several years, Thai elephant owners had experienced a growing problem of thieves tracking down animals in the dead of night. After chaining the animals and binding them tightly to a tree, or stunning them with electric current from a portable generator, they sawed off the tusks—usually as close to the jaw as they could. This severs the tooth nerve that extends roughly a third of the tusk's length, and the resulting infection can travel back along the nerve into the brain, killing the elephant. Some poachers killed the tame bulls outright to get at the ivory.

For a while, the FIO mahouts took to keeping their elephants company twenty-four hours a day, sleeping out in the bush with them. But this was a demanding chore, for elephants sleep no more than three or four hours nightly and spend the rest of the time feeding and traveling. Even when hobbled, they can cover a fair amount of ground. And mahouts are not that dedicated to their animals, Dr. Preecha pointed out—not in this day and age. In olden times, being the mahout of a war elephant was a respected role; but a logging mahout never enjoyed particularly high status, and the job had been less desirable than ever in recent years. Hungry young men from the hill tribes made the best candidates; educated Thais had little interest.

"Our mahouts have motorcycles and a house some distance from the forest camp. They want to go home at night and watch television and videos and be closer to the action in town," shrugged the veterinarian. "Mahouts don't know their animals as well as mahouts did when everyone lived in one camp out in the forest. Our men cannot read the nuances of their elephants' behavior, and they are more likely to get killed as a result. With 128 elephants, we average three deaths of mahouts per year and many injuries. One elephant in our camp has taken the lives of three mahouts by itself."

I had heard of one in Burma that killed seventeen men. Another, in northern Thailand, was said to have killed thirty, probably making it the record-holder as serial murderer elephants go. Some elephants, it seems, just cannot be tamed. The toughest bulls in Burma are reportedly worked with a spear man walking along on each side, brandishing the Southeast Asian equivalent of the Indian long pole, or *cherya kole*. "Once in a while, accidents happen despite all precautions, because females are giving off infrasound, saying 'I am sexually receptive,' and the males begin ignoring the mahouts," noted Dr. Preecha.

Given the various difficulties of staying with elephants round the clock, the final solution to the problem of tusk thieves for the FIO and private owners alike has been to cut off the tusks of tame bulls before the outlaws do. This may save the animals' lives. And, once the owner gets used to the idea, he realizes he has a small fortune from ivory already in hand, as well as an elephant that is still a valuable piece of property. If patient, he will have another opportunity later on, for the tusk regrows at the rate of an inch or two a year in mature animals. Fewer than one in ten domesticated bulls left in Thailand still carried its tusks in 1990.

As in much of northern Thailand, the elephants of the FIO camp respond to commands in three main languages: Thai, Karen, and a jargon derived from ancient Khmer, used for certain commands and for traditional ceremonies. The Khmer people of eastern Thailand and Cambodia were the foremost trainers of elephants in the old days. Most renowned of all were the Suay people, an indigenous ethnic group related to the Khmers. *Suay* actually means taxes and refers to the fact that these people were allowed to pay taxes rather than provide forced labor as their tribute to the king of Siam. It was a measure of their status as capturers and trainers of *chang*, or, to use the Khmer and Suay name for elephant, *thum rai*.

For centuries, nearly all the mahouts chosen to work with Thailand's royal white elephants have been Suay. The mahouts I met at the palace were from the main area inhabited by this group, the part of eastern Thailand around the city of Surin, close to the Cambodian border. Before I left to visit it, Richard Lair instructed me to keep an open mind about the natural habitat of the Asian elephant. The Suay, he said, captured elephants by chasing them down on the back of tame mounts and noosing them around the foot with a rope dangling from a pole. They could do this, he argued, because so much of the region around Surin and adjoining portions of Cambodia were open grasslands, part of a savanna ecosystem that supported great herds of elephants. By the same token, the Assam region of India, which supports one of the largest remaining wild elephant populations, is also more of a grassy plain than a jungle.

So do not conclude that the Asian elephant is basically a forest-dweller, Richard cautioned; the species is more variable and widespread than that. Or was. "Half a century ago, the Surin area was a wildlife paradise," said Richard. "Along with elephants, you would have seen a large population of ungulates—Indian, or two-horned, rhino; Sumatran, or one-horned, rhino; gaur; wild water buffalo; and two more rare bovids, banteng and kouprey—all feeding in what was a mixture of knee-high grasses and copses of trees. Now, I'm afraid, it is all rice fields and brown, weedy plain, semiarid and terribly overused."

So it was. I stopped in Surin long enough to note a number of stores selling ivory along the main street, army trucks disgorging troops into the whorehouses in the hotels, and refugee relief trucks resupplying for a run toward the Cambodian border, just seventy miles distant. I picked up translators so that we could work from Khmer to Thai to English and then drove out to the Suay village of Tha Klang. I had heard that generation after generation in such outlying villages has lived in thatched-roof houses with elephants in the yard. Popular stories tell of elephants in the Surin area walking children to school, and Richard Lair saw photographs of elephants that the accompanying text said acted as nannies, caring for children while the mother was occupied or temporarily away. Those claims may or may not be valid, but in many a Suay home, a young boy and a young elephant would grow up together and form a lifelong bond, with the boy taking responsibility for the animal as its mahout by the age of ten.

Before any such relationship, however, came a much less charming period of breaking the young wild elephant. After tying it to a tree, men would poke and prod and beat it with sticks for days on end—singing traditional songs the whole time they tortured it—until the youngster quit lashing out at its tormentors and stood dazed and exhausted and wholly subdued. Once the animal stopped reacting, the men would start touching it with their hands rather than sticks, and, rather quickly, the animal accepted their dominion and became receptive to their demands. If it did not, it might have wounds inflicted in its neck and salt rubbed into them, then a rattan collar with embedded thorns placed around the neck to make the animal more responsive. I have heard stories of elephants committing suicide by stepping on their trunk, though I don't think there is much truth to them.

The way to Tha Klang led across miles of unrelieved rice paddies, looking browner and drier than ever in the 105° F days before the summer rains. Scarcely a bird sang in the scrub. If one had, it might have been shot by locals like the young men who passed me on motorcycles, each with a shotgun strapped to his back. On a corner of the road, a boy no older than five or six stared back at me with expressionless eyes, holding a slingshot in one hand and a small, dead songbird by its feet in the other. On ground too sandy or rocky to grow rice, the villagers had planted a hardy weed: hemp. Most would be made into fiber, and some would be mixed with tobacco and smoked.

The young son of an interpreter rode with me in the back of a pickup through the brown, bald contours of rice paddies that stretched away toward the horizon. His fingernails were painted bright red. Northeastern Thailand was experiencing a rash of what were called widow ghost deaths. Perfectly strong, healthy-looking young men were suddenly dying in their sleep. By the score. In desperation, males had taken to painting their nails like a woman to fool the widow ghost. After a young man with painted nails died, some men tried a new prophylactic measure—hanging huge phallic symbols outside their homes, hoping the man-hating widow ghost would attack those instead.

No one was able to pin down the cause of the deaths. Some health officials suspected environmental contaminants, perhaps combined with the stress of hard physical labor. Pesticides were a likely candidate. An astonishing proportion—on the order of 50 percent or so—of Thai farmers suffered medical problems from excessive exposure to pesticides. While working in their seasonally flooded rice fields, they were standing day after day in what amounted to a chemical soup. More than a third of all the farmers afflicted experienced severe ailments, ranging from tremors and nerve damage to liver failure.

When I reached Tha Klang in midday, I found families sitting on hammocks in the shade of their traditional wooden houses. The old men were smoking and talking; the young men were hanging out, tattoos of *wats* and flying tigers emblazoned across their bare chests; the women were weaving on looms or preparing meals; and the elephants came and went along the streets. A fifteen-year-old bull elephant stood tethered nearby, and as I struck up a conversation with some people, he thoroughly worked over itchy parts of his skin with a pencil-size stick grasped in his trunk. Behind his ears was a delicious bit of scratching; I could see the lids half-close over his eyes as he hit certain spots. Then the underside of his trunk got a going over with the stick while he simultaneously rubbed his rump against a eucalyptus tree. I was beginning to itch just watching him. Next, he turned to the callused and tether-chafed sections of his forelegs. Finally, the bull got at an irksome section on his broad side. The delicate pattern his stick made in the brown dust caked there reminded me of the paintings I saw Ruby the elephant make at the Phoenix Zoo.

I was introduced to a former elephant catcher named Bhan Kanin.

"I went with thirty other men, and each of us had two elephants. On some trips, we would be gone three months into Cambodia," the fifty-six-year-old remembered as we sat in his packed-earth courtyard. "We would go out until we found footprints of elephants and follow them, then ride and try to get our rope around a front or rear foot." To be more specific, the men used three categories of elephants: swift trackers, or chasers, which tired out the animals being pursued and prevented them from escaping into thicker forest; captors, which pressed against a wild elephant's side or rump with their heads while the mahout tried to lasso a leg; and fighters, the largest of the domesticated animals, used to help subdue a new captive once the rope around its leg was tied off to a tree and it began to panic and try to tear itself loose. Of course, the animal being sought or its relatives might turn to battle the pursuers any time before that.

"Dangers awaited us always, especially from the fighting between wild elephant families and our mounts," Bhan Kanin continued. "So before we started from the village, we brought the *pakam* [catching rope] from its resting place and made offerings to it to prevent accidents."

Other means of tipping fate their way were put in motion as well: "The wives could not cut their hair or clean the house, speak to strangers, or sleep in any other house but their own while the men were away," Bhan Kanin went on. He said it was for luck, but with the elephant-catchers gone for three months or so, it was also surely for marital fidelity. No guests or even relatives were to sleep in a mahout's house either. Family members were to dress plainly, and dirt was to be swept into a pile inside the house rather than out the door. "We spoke only in a ghost language to bring luck and not let the elephants know who was coming." And the men never used their own names.

They tried to catch elephants about three years of age— "chest-high elephants," Bhan Kanin called them—and each man might take three or four or even five of them before the expedition ended, at least in his father's day. Bhan Kanin began going on elephant hunts into Cambodia at age eighteen and continued for fifteen years. He quit, along with most other villagers, in the late 1960s, when soldiers in war-torn Cambodia began sowing the hillsides with mines and booby traps and shooting at the Suay and their elephants.

At least 2 million people have died in the war that has run on for more than twenty years in Cambodia. One of the few growth businesses in the devastated economy is the production of artificial limbs; the countryside is so thickly laden with anti-personnel mines now that humanitarian agencies report a minimum of 300 amputees per month among the rural populace. Elephants and people tend to use the same trails through the forest, which makes me wonder what percent of the remnant wild elephant population is lumbering about on three legs in the hills past villages full of one-legged and legless children.

The rumor was that, mines notwithstanding, the Suay still stole across the border into Cambodia and even into the Champassak area of Laos to snatch a few baby elephants and bring them back to Thailand to sell or raise for themselves. While the shutdown of logging made working cow elephants worth less than before, hobbyists were still paying 150,000 to 200,000 bhat (U.S. $6000 to $8000, several years' wages for an average Thai) for a handsome and well-behaved male. So the Suay were still somewhat in demand as trainers.

The Suay had always sold elephants to be used in the logging industry but seldom participated themselves, saying they did not like to see elephants worked so hard. They had always had months when they rode their elephants into villages and towns, and sometimes on into Bangkok, to do stints as itinerant doctor elephant men. Presently, many depended more upon their rice crops than upon their skills as elephant handlers. Yet the Suay were still busy raising and breeding elephants and still finding ways to profit from them.

"I got 6000 bhat for one tusker who was thirty-two years old back when I was catching them. It was a big price then," Bhan Kanin recalled. "Now we cut the tusks, carve ivory a little, and go around being doctor elephant men. We can first cut the tusks at age twelve to seventeen. They sell for 6000 bhat per kilo"— the same price he got for the whole elephant a few decades ago. Prime-quality ivory sells for three times that much. And the villagers can rent out their elephants to circuses and tourist shows for 6000 bhat per month as well. Elephants from Tha Klang work as entertainers and billboard carriers in Surin, Bangkok, Chiang Mai, and the southern coastal resort area of Phuket.

Villagers *have* to rent out a fair number of their elephants, because there is no longer enough forage for them near the village except during the rainy season. Bhan Kanin had six elephants rented out when I met him. His son owned another; I met it along the road as it was carrying back a load of bamboo fodder to the village. It had to be kept in the family yard at night to discourage ivory thieves.

Some village elders took me to the edge of the fields to meet Boon Peng, a sixty-year-old retired logging elephant whose long tusks were worth 100,000 bhat and still growing at the rate of an inch per year. Captured long ago in Cambodia, he lived out his days here attended round the clock by a herder of about the same age whose wage was paid in part by the district government. Upon hearing that a bull with such tusks still wore them, the governor himself apparently helped arrange special protection for Boon Peng. I looked upon him as the counterpart of renowned tuskers in parks of Kenya and South Africa who had full-time guards assigned to protect them.

As evening descended during one of my visits to Tha Klang, elephants traipsed by, bearing home more fodder, while monks in saffron robes tied strings from a lovely, glittering *wat* to every house in the village, symbolizing the flow of spiritual power. Oil lamps winked on from porches. The onrushing darkness seemed to restore a touch of magic to the brown and blasted land. A party with dancing was planned that night, for Buddha was coming to look in on every household and bestow blessings. I couldn't help wishing that the strings ran on to encompass the homes of all the wild creatures native to the area. Instead, the monks cranked up a generator to run two loudspeakers turned to full volume, and a lot of the magic suddenly withdrew to alight at some more distant site.

The Suay still perform *riak kwan chang*, the blessing ritual for a newborn elephant. A dignitary, or special teacher, known as the *moh riak kwan chang* presides over the affair. Offerings of chicken, rice, bananas, candles, incense, and alcohol are made. In this ritual, the sacred white cord does link human and beast. It is held by those in attendance while Buddhist monks chant and a piece of white cloth is placed upon the elephant's back. Various wild grasses are presented for the baby to eat, though it is still nursing. Then the grasses are tied in a bunch and used to flick sacred water over the young animal's back. May strength and fortune and happiness be yours, little elephant. Having been born in captivity, you are no longer *chao pa*, lord of the jungle, so we call the soul of the jungle here to enter into you. Newborn elephants are all called by the generic name Aphawk. As with infants in a number of human tribes, they are not given their true names until they have survived a while and grown a little older and stronger.

On the edge of Surin is a soccer field where, once a year, as many as 150 elephants are assembled to put on shows, including a soccer match. Another feature is a tug of war between an adult elephant and an army troop of about 120 men. The elephant is invariably the victor, which, if you think about it, makes the ability of a mahout to control such a giant with a single soft word all the more amazing. The Surin festival has become one of the largest gatherings of domesticated elephants anywhere, and it draws so many tourists that the town bulges at the seams. Townspeople still talk about an elephant that got roaring drunk in the streets after a tourist gave it a couple of bottles of booze.

Ten years before I arrived, a Chinese businessman in the construction trade, Mr. Sinchai, and his Thai wife, Mrs. Pranee Thanasamut, bought elephants from various sources and started a full-time elephant show in Surin. "Suay people are definitely the best trainers," Mr. Sinchai told me. "They have a special rapport with the animals. They are good Buddhists and can make an elephant stop walking just by reverence, by thoughts. They understand elephants in their hearts."

As he rhapsodized, we were on the open second story of his construction yard, surrounded by heaps of concrete bags, sand, cables, paint cans, and the like. Mrs. Pranee Thanasamut and a couple of young women were counting thousands of coins on an abacus and stacking them in neat rows. Mixed in with the supplies were rows of *yang chang*, elephant riding chairs, the Thai equivalent of the Indian *howdah*, for Mr. Sinchai and his wife also rent out elephants for Buddhist ordination ceremonies.

He could make money simply by buying elephants and holding on to them while their price rises, then selling them and their ivory. In fact, he does that. He informed me that although the price of cow elephants did indeed sink after the logging ban, it was on the upswing again, because more people were getting into the business of commercially breeding elephants.

"Before, I owned just four elephants. I thought of them like ducks or buffalo," Mr. Sinchai admitted. "Then a Japanese man came and gave us the idea: Why don't you do a show?" He did. At the moment, he was arranging another show with twelve elephants, this one to be sent over to Japan for six months.

From the construction business, I went to Mr. Sinchai's elephant stables and yard. A particular baby elephant there caught my attention. It had been shuffling about with a handful of other orphans on a concrete slab. Tears trickled down from each eye to streak its dusty face. A mahout who came by said it was close to feeding time, and the little ones often cried when they were hungry. He brought plastic buckets of milk mixed with supplemental food, which the babies had been trained to drink with a section of hose cut to make an elephant-size straw. But the youngster, I noticed, was crying again after it had finished eating. I don't know where it came from or where it was bound. I don't think it knew where its home was either. But that wasn't why it was crying; at least, I don't think that was it. Nor was it crying because the forests were gone and elephants had been reduced to a sort of side show. That was just my projection of how discouraged I felt now and then. It was crying for reasons all its own. For some reason, it brought to mind all the stories I had heard of elephants dying of grief.

I went to take in the nightly fare at the Elephant Gardens, where Mr. Sinchai had developed an entire entertainment complex featuring a swimming pool, billiards, live bands, food, and plenty of drink. The highlight was the elephant show, which was basically a circus act, with young elephants doing silly hat tricks, playing a harmonica, walking a balancing beam, walking over inebriated members of the crowd who volunteered to lie prostrate on the ground, and so on. These were the warm-up acts for the Thai kick-boxing match featuring a mahout clad in red silken shorts and red boxing gloves and a juvenile elephant of about five or six with a boxing glove tied to the tip of its trunk.

Both man and elephant jogged into a ring to perform bows and traditional prayers, as kick-boxing contestants do prior to a match. Then the kicking and slugging began. Between each round, baby elephants paraded through the ring carrying placards announcing the number of the round to come. Another baby trotted out and showered the contestants with water. The fighting elephant was trained to unleash some forceful side kicks with its rear leg and unfurl its trunk in straight-on punches. The mahout had to take care to anticipate them. If, like a stunt man, he began leaping away the instant before the elephant struck, then the effect was of a mighty blow lifting him through the air for several feet. But if he missed his timing, he received a thrust that knocked the wind out of him. After several rounds, the mahout would deliver a flurry of blows and appear to be gaining ground—and then the elephant would K.O. him.

It was nice to see an elephant win something, even if the fight was fixed.

THIRTEEN

MALAYSIA

🔲🔲🔲🔲 IN EARLY MAY of 1990, I was back in Bangkok from the Thai countryside, catching up on newspapers and magazines while waiting to depart the country. Three news items stood out. The first was from Kenya, where illegal killing of elephants persisted despite that nation's beefed-up antipoaching efforts and despite the ivory ban. Although many Kenyan poachers had been arrested over the past several months and some were said to have actually turned themselves in, those who remained were becoming, if anything, tougher and crueler than before. They killed at least fifty-seven elephants in Tsavo during January alone. They also shot three teenage boys as suspected informants. And they were taking hostages from villages, both to discourage informing and to serve as porters. Even Wakamba tribesmen, among the most skilled of trackers, had been fooled by poachers willing to walk backward for ten miles to throw off pursuit.

The second news item was from closer to where I had just been. Burma's military rulers were not only suppressing democracy and human rights in a general way but had specifically targeted the rebellious Mon and Karen ethnic groups for destruction. They were buying the weapons and supplies for their campaign with millions of dollars' worth of Thai money, gained from the sale of logging concessions. Recently, the Burmese had doubled the concession price. All but a few Thai companies paid it without argument; they wanted the timber that badly. As a further gesture of good will between business partners, the Thais were looking the other way when Burmese troops crossed into Thailand chasing Karen guerrillas. These arrangements were made public by U.S. Senator Patrick Moynihan, who eventually persuaded the U.S. Senate to impose economic sanctions on Burma and ban the import of tropical hardwoods from Thai companies doing business there.

The third news item came from closer to where I was going. It was an update from the Malaysian state of Sarawak on the island of Borneo, where loincloth-clad Penan tribespeople had been standing in front of bulldozers sent to raze the jungle on which they depended. Officials bent upon selling off the rainforest trees and putting in plantations were not impressed. They jailed the Penan demonstrators and moved whole villages out of the forest into settled lands, stating that this was for the Penans' own good. Strange. The old white colonial mindset about civilizing savages seemed to have been adopted wholesale by Malaysian authorities—right down to the part about how those poor jungle-dwellers suffered from disease and ignorance out in that green hell and needed to be saved from themselves. Instead of the white man's burden, call it the Malay businessman's burden. Just as in the heyday of the white colonials, most of the rhetoric was a thinly veiled rationale for shoving native people aside to get at the resources they were sitting on.

Malaysia was my next destination, but not the island of Borneo, estimated to support 500 to perhaps 750 elephants. I was off to the mainland peninsula and its last elephant range, inhabited by 1000 or so of the giants. Nearly all of them are "pocketed," to borrow the expression I heard when I arrived to meet with wildlife officials in the capital city, Kuala Lumpur. Pocketed is merely one more way of stating the usual: isolated in remnant patches of forest amid fields and plantations; trapped on habitat islands in a hostile sea of development. Stuck. Surrounded. Cut off. Pinned down. . . . Pocketed. Some herds had already been that way for more than twenty years.

In addition to the spread of village-based agriculture, Malaysia has seen the conversion of rainforest to monoculture plantations on a tremendous scale, a process begun by British colonial interests and greatly expanded after independence in 1957. This country now ranks among the world's top producers of rubber and palm oil as well as tin. Secondary commercial crops include coffee, cocoa, coconut, banana, durian (an unforgettable experience in fruit, rather like a cross between a mango and Limburger cheese), other fruits, and tapioca. Conflicts between elephants and farmers or plantation owners have been pervasive, continuous, and bitter. Ironically, elephants and other threatened large mammals, such as rhinos, tapirs, orangutans, and gibbons, helped distribute the seeds of fruits and nuts now importantly commercially. And among the chief pollinators of key plant products—avocados, figs, mangos, guavas, durian, cashews, bananas, dates, and kapok—are bats, which are threatened by pesticide accumulations and the destruction of mangrove swamps that serve as their key nesting grounds.

Elephant management in mainland Malaysia used to consist chiefly of shooting any animals that caused problems on cultivated lands. In the 1960s, officials started experimenting with an assortment of nonlethal techniques to discourage raiders. Trenching failed. As in India, maintaining steep-walled ditches through the monsoon rains proved too demanding a chore, and the giants tended to kick down the sides anyway. Once again, I heard how a large elephant was seen going down into a trench to let others walk across its back; this report was supposedly from a reliable wildlife warden.

Electric fencing proved reasonably effective. More than 350 miles of it now ran along property borders on the mainland. However, the common shortcomings were also apparent. Elephants pulled up support posts or threw trees down across the lines to get past them. Small farmers lacked the money to install such fencing themselves. When big plantations successfully used electric fencing, the result was often that the elephants focused harder on the plots of small farmers next door.

The wildlife department used to gather men to act as beaters and try to drive problem elephants to new areas. It still does, in some situations. But in the early 1970s, Malaysia initiated a new method: capturing and translocating wild elephants with the help of tame ones. Brought in from Thailand and India, the tame elephants were already fairly well trained. The challenge lay in training a band of wildlife department personnel to handle them. Malaysia has only a very limited tradition of working with elephants. Ruling sultans kept a few tame elephants as status symbols. British overlords sometimes used the giants for personal transportation and, as in Thailand, for hauling tin from the mines. But that was about it.

Being predominantly Muslim, the citizenry had no particular reverence for the beasts either. Villagers had few qualms about putting arsenic or battery acid in fruit along elephant paths. Now and then, they laid naked wires connected to high-voltage lines across the paths instead. Not many would hesitate to shoot at elephants with whatever old shotgun or homemade rifle they could get their hands on. Plantation owners and other big landholders surreptitiously hired gunmen to deal with raiding elephants. Poaching would surely have been far worse had Malaysia not outlawed high-caliber rifles for fear of insurrection. After the government handed out modern semiautomatic weapons to villagers near the northern border to use against communist insurgents, the area immediately underwent a terrific increase in the poaching of large mammals.

Oil palm plantations are popular among both economic planners and elephants, which naturally find young palm heart a delicious and nourishing food. The capture teams' first test involved a World Bank–sponsored project that had replaced tens of thousands of acres of native forest in one area with oil palm and was experiencing serious elephant munchdown. Then, in 1984, the teams were sent to rescue elephants trapped on an island by the water rising behind a new dam. Once more, they were successful. The effort was quite popular with the public, and the wildlife department won funding for further work.

Capturing and translocating pocketed bands grew to be the main thrust of elephant management. Though expensive and time-consuming, it works. The main question has become where to put the giants once caught. There are really only two secure wild spots left now on the entire mainland. One is protected as Taman Negara National Park. Established in 1938 by the British, it is still the mainland's sole national park. At 1680 square miles, it holds, at most, a couple of hundred elephants and is probably already close to carrying capacity, given the amount of steep and rugged terrain within its boundaries. The teams had been relocating some of the captured elephants there nonetheless.

The rest were released in a different stretch of mountainous terrain in the extreme north, near the border with Thailand. This area's forests had largely escaped cutting because the government recognized their value in flood control and water storage; thus ran the official explanation. The fundamental reason was that this rugged terrain had been a no-man's land in a long, desultory war between the government and two rebellious communist forces: Malaysian communists and Thai Muslim separatists.

Mr. Mohammed Khan bin Momin Khan, director-general of the wildlife and parks department, kindly arranged for me and photographer Bill Thompson to take part in a translocation to the northern frontier region from a developed district called Sungai Siput in the state of Perak. Accompanied by wildlife officer Zaaba Zainol Abidin, Thompson and I set off driving along Malaysia's main north-south highway.

Whenever I talk with people about my travels in exotic-sounding places, they want to know: Weren't there snakes? Man-eating tigers? Crocodiles? Virulent parasites? Didn't you get chased by rhinos? Lost in the swamps? No one ever asks about the most dangerous thing I do, which is hop in a car with strangers and drive hour after hour under the insane conditions that pass for normal in so many countries. Sudden confrontations, surging adrenaline, screams and shouts and hair's-breadth escapes—these outings in automobiles have it all, all the damn time. But everybody wants to know about snakes and tigers.

The north-south highway was a narrow, two-lane artery originally designed to carry a smattering of vehicles. Now that Malaysia was more populated and prosperous and car ownership was more common, the route was hopelessly overloaded. The constant game of trying to gain a few minutes by passing at high speed under doubtful circumstances made this ribbon of asphalt one of the most conspicuous causes of death in the country. I would rather have danced with wild elephant bulls in musth. Seriously. Once you have made it out to where the snakes and tigers and rampaging elephants are, you are relatively secure, having left the paved highways behind.

In Sungai Siput, we met wildlife biologist Mohammed Shariff Daim. Shariff helped put together the elephant capture teams and oversees most of their operations. His men had already tracked down a wild female that belonged to a band of crop-raiders and immobilized her with drugs from a dart gun. Of an estimated 170 elephants in the state of Perak, about 40 remained in this particular district. She was the eleventh to be caught so far. The capture team had her tethered by a cable to a tree up in the nearest hills.

To its credit, Malaysia protected habitats above 1000 meters (3280 feet) in elevation from heavy logging, a rule intended to aid water and soil conservation. But steep, hilly country was not the elephants' prime habitat and never had been except seasonally. The best forage and most biologically diverse forests grew in the lowlands, and those were typically the first areas to be preempted by human activities. In Sungai Siput, five dams had flooded out traditional lowland elephant range and forced the herds closer to existing fields, intensifying conflicts created by the loss of other lowland habitats from timber cutting and agricultural expansion.

The hills were what was left for the giants—their refuge, where they retreated after making a raid. A spine of rugged terrain running north and south through the peninsula, the hills also served as a wildlife travel corridor. We were originally going to camp up there with the captive elephant, but the army forbade it, because guerrillas occasionally used the hills as a travel corridor as well. The area was still lousy with land mines. Shariff said he had seen a number of elephants stumping around with a leg blown off.

We ended up on the outskirts of a village, welcomed with a speech by the local political dignitary, Meor Osman bin Imam

Pinawa. His grasp of resource and wildlife issues in his baliwick was admirable, and he went on for some time about how everyone wanted to have more industry, more agriculture, and more wildlife, too. Since 1960, elephants had caused some U.S. $12 million of damage in this district. Alas, he concluded, they just had to go. I slept on the concrete floor of some official barracks, listening to mosquitoes try to drone their way inside my net while a hard rain began outside.

We arose early and drove as far as we could on the muddy roads, then hiked up the mountainside toward the captive female, with the sun lifting steadily higher and the forest all around us beginning to steam. We found her in an arena of churned, yellowish mud, caked with it from trunk tip to toe. When she stood still a moment, she resembled a pottery statue left in the forest as an offering. She was relatively small and young, perhaps thirteen or fourteen years old, and thinner than she ought to have been. Though somewhat weak and dehydrated as well, and constantly giving out frightened-sounding squeaks and squeals, she was still feisty enough to hurl back the palm fronds that the men tossed to her for food. At one point, she grabbed an overhanging liana and tried to whip that into us. She was hungry, though, and finally began to eat some of the food offered her. Tracks showed that a bull had visited this female during the night. What brought him to her side was anyone's guess, but it was probably to see if she was sexually receptive. However, it was plain from her enlarged mammary glands that this cow was already pregnant.

She also had a bullet wound festering near her left temple. Drawing closer, I noticed a second wound on her left rear leg. Shariff told me that since 1972, his teams had translocated more than 240 elephants—which amounted to one of every four elephants left on the mainland, I realized. And roughly one in every five that they handled had serious injuries caused by shotguns and small-caliber rifles or snares: suppurating bullet holes, blinded eyes, legs and trunks turning gangrenous from the unforgiving wire nooses tightened around them. The snares were set for deer, wild pigs, and other smaller game, but they caught tigers and elephants too. There is nothing more disheartening, Shariff said, than watching an elephant whose snare-constricted trunk has rotted off crawl around on its knees trying to get at low-growing food.

Pit traps catch a few elephants as well. Director-general Mohammed Khan described a mother toiling all night to free her infant from a deep pit by kicking down the sides. Unsuccessful, she stayed on through the day, facing down men who came to scare her off by firing rifles and shotguns. She kept charging the men, returning to break down the edge of the pit, charging again. And by two in the afternoon, her young one was free.

I sat a short distance downhill from our captive, wringing out the sweat from my shirt and picking off leeches. Broadbills belled in the nearby branches and simian monkeys toured the treetops, carrying on loud conversations on their way toward other parts of the hills. Mr. Pinawa, the village politician, had arrived with a small entourage and bustled about collecting a plant called the *tongat ali* tree, which he said had a tonic effect like ginseng. After a while, even this energetic fellow came to a stop and hunkered quietly with the rest of us in the hot jungle air.

We were waiting for the tame elephants. They arrived in mid-morning: the big bull, Bahadur, whose name means Powerful and who came originally from Assam, and one of two cows the department got from Surin, Thailand. Carrying two riders, Bahadur approached the little female and smelled her vulva. Only a week out of musth, he still had considerable interest in feminine scents. Once satisfied about her condition, he began his work of positioning himself against her, calming her slightly, and helping to keep her from lunging about.

Then the tame female moved in, carrying her mahout, and greeted the captive with an exchange of trunk tips in the mouth. The extra calming effect on the younger cow was immediate and most welcome, for too much more stress combined with her weakened state could tip her over the edge into shock or death. Zaaba commented that in the early days of the program, losses among elephants being chased and handled ran as high as 20 percent, and stress was a major factor.

Wildlife wardens also had to kill a few elephants when faced with animals that unexpectedly charged. One wild tusker held fast by a chain wore the metal through over a period of several days. When a warden came to feed it banana leaves one morning, the bull snapped the fetters and smooshed the man. Other rangers arrived to find the bull standing over the body, refusing to budge. They put seventeen shots into him before he finally went down.

"It is a pitiful thing to have to shoot an elephant," Shariff muttered, shaking his head. "I myself have never done it in all the years I have captured elephants. I cannot. The animal is so sad, so afraid. Sometimes there are tears streaming down the face. One time, an elephant killed a villager, so I am called in to kill it. We have to recover the person's body. Ooohf! The body has been rolled up, then stretched out flat and trampled, and then rolled up again like a newspaper. All the bones have been smashed. The villagers formed a vigilante committee and shot the elephant with shotguns. We found it standing and waiting, knowing we were all around. One eye was shot off. It was bleeding from new wounds and abscesses from old ones all over its body. We dropped it with two shots. The next morning, two vigilantes went out to see the results of their shooting. The bull was up again, waiting, bleeding all over. It grabbed one of the villagers and flung him around like a palm branch, killing him. I don't think elephants are always dangerous. But once you disturb them, they become very dangerous."

Drug overdoses were a common problem during capture. Animals' systems suddenly shut down and never started up again. Shariff had seen elephants swallow their tongues and choke to death. These kinds of reactions had been dramatically cut back with more experience and new compounds with better tolerances and surer antidotes. Nevertheless, a capture team often faced the possibility that, after being darted, an elephant would keep running until it finally staggered into a pond or swamp, where it might drown before it could be revived. A few had fallen on steep slopes in such a way that they broke a leg or even the spine. Others fell with their trunks pressed beneath them and died for want of air. And due to the proboscideans' unusual breathing mechanism (having lungs directly attached to chest muscles instead of being inflated when the diaphragm creates a vacuum), any animal that collapsed onto its chest and stayed in that position—termed sternal recumbency—for more than half an hour risked suffocating from its own tremendous weight. It might be saved if its captors could somehow push it over onto its side.

While Zaaba and Shariff were explaining such risks, one mahout leaned over Bahadur's grey side and injected tranquilizer into the wild female, now squeezed between her two tame companions. The dosage was calculated to keep her calm but fully mobile. But it wasn't long afterward that she crumpled into the muddy, trampled clay. She was apparently weaker than anyone had realized. Wearing a grim expression, Shariff ordered the mahouts to have their mounts lift her up off her sternum. They did, and the female began to revive.

It was important to keep her moving. Quickly, the mahouts wrapped ropes around her, fashioning them into a harness. To the harness were attached more ropes and chains so that she could be marched down the trail between the two tame elephants, the lead one pulling and the other following, sometimes nudging her from behind. Our captive went down twice more in the mud before we got under way, then collapsed again in a shallow stream, where our cavalcade had paused to let her drink. Each time, the tame mounts urged her up and then on, and before long we were down in a mature rubber plantation at the base of the hills.

Word of our enterprise had spread with the inexplicable speed at which messages seem capable of traveling in the bush. A crowd made up mainly of rubber tappers and their families began to accompany us down the lower part of the trail. By the time we neared the waiting trucks, people were racing our way on bicycles and motorcycles. Someone had even shown up wheeling an ice cream cart. No wonder this elephant and her family had gotten in trouble. Though comparatively remote, this countryside was plainly far more crowded than I had realized.

Seeing my notebook and Thompson's cameras, tappers Tasu

bin Jusoh, Ismael bin Sood, Mohammed Alwi, and Mohammed Samad crowded around to tell us of their experiences with wild elephants. "Two people we know have been killed by them. Two tappers," said Tasu bin Jusoh. And one logger and one member of an aboriginal tribe in the area, I learned. "We used to make noise to scare the elephants. But now we just keep quiet and run away, because now the elephants get angry." With at least one in five bearing severe injuries from humans, that wasn't very surprising.

"One is in my lot right now," said Mohammed Alwi, referring to the section of the plantation he was assigned to tap. "Every morning when I go to work, I am interfered with because I must worry about elephants. I worry about my family— wife, children—each time they go to the stream to wash. The elephants chased one man here very much."

How many times had he actually encountered elephants lately?

"Ten times this year," he replied.

"We ask you to help us move away the excess," another man broke in. "Tigers are not a hazard to us. They don't bother. Elephants bother. I am glad to see this elephant go. We don't want them back."

"Tigers don't eat us. I don't know why," added the politician accompanying us. "Maybe it is because if they do eat us, their brains get damaged, and they want to go into politics."

Mighty Bahadur and the tame female finally walked the captive up a ramp onto a massive truck, where she was firmly shackled. Then the two tame elephants loaded themselves into a second truck, which became stuck in the mud but finally pulled out to bump along behind the first. Jasmi bin Abdul, the wildlife department's director for the state of Perak, also along on the expedition, smiled and said, "One wild elephant safe."

Sort of.

We still had a trip of about 120 miles ahead of us to Lake Temenggor by truck. For much of the way there, we passed an almost unbroken canopy of trees. But they were rubber trees. In the intense gloom beneath them, the soil contained little but residues of paraquat and other herbicides mixed with fertilizers. Streams issuing from the rainy slopes were laden with silt. Some were the color of yellowed cream, while others looked almost like old blood. Whenever we passed marshes and swamps, I scanned the shores, looking for wading birds. I saw none—not floating, not feeding, not diving, not flying. Nothing, and it was eerie. Nor did the rubber tree forest seem to hold any. No color, no wings, and, most unsettling, not even song. The chemicals seemed to have burned the heart out of the country.

As we neared Lake Temenggor, the altitude increased. With great relief, I began to see stands of tall native vegetation on the slopes. Farther on, there was even a highway sign warning of elephants crossing. We arrived late in the evening at an army base at Banding Island, close to the huge dam on the southern shore. The air was still hot and filled with minuscule biting gnats. As the tame elephants were unloaded and put to work unloading the captive, I was surprised to see different mahouts riding the giants. In a system unusual for Asia, all of the department's capture team had been trained as mahouts, Shariff pointed out, and the elephants were conditioned to accept them equally.

Instead of rubber tappers, we now had an army camp's worth of soldiers for an audience. They were familiar with wild elephants, whose paths could be found throughout the encompassing hills; it was tame elephants that they found unusual. I went for a cold drink before bed. At the tavern, I met an officer who told me that a big bull had killed a soldier at this camp. "We still keep the elephant's foot," he laughed and then pointed toward the peak of the thatched roof, where night-flying insects hovered around a bare bulb. "I was chased by one five meters tall— taller than this restaurant, taller than our biggest troop carrier!" he announced. Wow. Five meters. No one else had seen an elephant that tall since the imperial mammoth went extinct. But he was a major, and as far as I am concerned, pistol-packing majors in bars in the middle of the night in their country are right every time. I bought him a beer and wished him pleasant dreams.

The following day, we loaded the captive female onto a raft made of thick wooden decking upon fifty-five-gallon petrol drums for flotation and chained her in the center. Shariff sprayed her bullet wounds with disinfectant, and we shoved off as a small flotilla. Four army motorboats full of rifle-bearing soldiers pushed against the rear of the raft, and a couple of others cruised alongside as escorts, carrying assorted park bureaucrats, biologists, and dignitaries, including the indefatigable politician from Sungai Siput. The lake's shimmering surface reflected ever thicker jungle on ever taller hills. Men sprawled or sat all around the raft's edge. And in the very center, legs stretched out by tethers but towering above all the rest, stood the female, waving a palm frond from her food pile high in the air with her trunk. The pageant took on the aspect of bearing a sacred white elephant or some great personage toward a new kingdom. Or of Lilliputians taking Gulliver for a cruise.

I rode with Zaaba, Shariff, and the mahouts aboard the big raft. Before noon, men were improvising tents from tarps set on poles and crawling under them in search of shade. The day was windless and, with the sun reflecting off the satin surface of the water, growing insufferably hot. I hunkered under a parasol I had brought, but the sun seemed to burn right through the thin cloth. My urge to jump overboard and drift along hanging onto the raft was quelled when the men told me the lake was full of snake-headed, snaggle-toothed fish that would bite chunks out of my limbs and probably tear off my genitals. I tried to tell whether they were kidding me or not; maybe these ferocious fish were like five-meter-tall elephants. But nobody else jumped in, and the size of the fishy backs I saw roiling the water here and there was intimidating in itself. I later saw a picture of these fish on a poster, and their teeth were enough to give anyone pause.

The farther north we went, the more the elephant seemed to revive. Shariff continually doused her with a hose from a portable pump. I was interested to see how quickly she seemed to learn that the hose represented a source of drinking water. She kept trying to grab it and bring it closer. The more chipper she felt, the more she took to whipping palm fronds toward the men encircling her. Soon, we all were huddled at the very corners of the raft while she strained against her leg chains and shot out her trunk, trying to reach someone. She did reach a shade tarp and ripped that. She got hold of the hose, too, briefly; Shariff managed to jerk the smooth plastic free from her trunk. Next, she ripped loose a thick length of mooring rope and started whipping that around while men dove and ducked. Then a leg chain snapped. This could get interesting fast, I thought, and I started edging toward one of the motorboats at the stern.

Shariff had told me about a raft trip during which an elephant broke a chain, got hold of it with her trunk, and literally cleared the decks. Some elephants are right-handed and some left-handed, he reminded me. I thought Shariff was referring to the way they favor one tusk, often called the master tusk. But he meant that certain elephants have a tendency to swing their trunk in one direction. They also favor one rear leg over the other for sudden side kicks. Having learned from bloody experience, the capture teams were careful to observe an elephant closely for such tendencies before moving in to begin chaining or unchaining it.

At last, the northern shore where we planned to release the female came into sight. As we nudged against the muddy shore, a heavy gangplank was put out to reach the bank, and the mahouts carefully began loosening the bolts that held her chains. This was a touch-and-go part of the operation under the best of conditions. The idea was to free one rear leg and one front one at the same time, keeping the other two restrained until everyone was clear, then simultaneously release those two. But with one leg already free, our captive turned the rest of the sequence into a rodeo. One mahout got kicked all the way from the raft up onto the shore. I was out there stretching my legs when I saw a body come flying through the air. I looked over to see how he was, and when I looked back toward the raft, the first thing I saw was the female trotting down the gangplank toward me. I started racing away to one side, slipping on the muddy clay embankment. But I was flattering myself that she would seek me out for punishment. All she wanted to do was get away into the embracing jungle.

Now, as the state's wildlife director would say: one wild elephant safe.

Sort of.

Back by the army camp, I ambled off through the hills, and, in the space of a couple of hours, encountered a large python, a four-foot-long monitor lizard, soft-shelled turtles in little pools along a streambed, and the tracks of wild elephants, pigs, and deer. But when I asked permission to go hiking farther in this animated rainforest, I was told that it was out of the question. The terrain was still a guerrilla stronghold, chock-full of mines and booby traps. Talks had brought about a truce, though, and the rebel forces would soon help the government find and disarm the mines. However, that was no sooner agreed upon than the government started talking about selectively logging the region, which was intended to serve as watershed protection and had been proposed for national park or game reserve status.

Some cutting was already occurring along the lake's southern end, near the army camp. We stopped to visit one site where the largest hardwoods had just been plucked. Shorea, or sal wood, and dipterocarps called maranti and merbau were the prize sources of lumber. Altogether, thirty-one different tree species were taken in "selective" logging here, said the man supervising the loading of stacked logs onto trucks. These were bound for Saudi Arabia and the United Arab Emirates.

Zaaba observed that truly selective logging is difficult to enforce. Companies generally cut more than their allocated quota. They also tend to build big, meandering roads so that they can take still more trees on their way in to a logging unit. Once the roads have been punched through and parts of the rainforest opened up, this draws the usual squatters and poachers. Then, when enough people populate an area, the government is likely to give them ownership of private plots within the forest. Not just likely, but eager. If colonists—squatters—do not arrive in large numbers, FELDA, the Federal Land Development Authority, is likely to bring them in, subsidizing a rubber or oil palm plantation and translocating farmers from elsewhere to work on the project, giving each five to ten acres to tend. After twenty years, a settler gains title to that private plot free and clear.

This modified homesteading program is part of Malaysia's plan for opening up its last frontiers. Apparently, the political leadership looks toward Japan and Taiwan as models, believing that such nations are economically successful because they are loaded with people. While Malaysia has done very well exporting raw materials, it needs to stimulate domestic demand, and at the moment, it lacks sufficient consumers to do that, the government has stated. Accordingly, the prime minister has called for increasing the country's population from 17 million to 70 million by the year 2095. As an inducement, the tax law was rewritten to give people with large families a substantial break. I had not stopped to think about the concept of breeding citizens to create more consumers. I do not want to stop to think about it now.

Hard-pressed to save wildlife under current human densities—realistically, the chances of sustaining a minimum viable population of 500 breeding elephants in mainland Malaysia were slim—most of the Malaysian biologists with whom I spoke were less than enthusiastic about a call from the head of state to quadruple the human population. Still, they were cautious not to criticize government policies outright when I opened my notebook. Here was a potent reminder of what some would say is a simple and obvious fact: wildlife agencies cannot be counted upon to do what is best for wildlife. That is not their primary purpose. They are instruments of government policy. Their real job is to try to fit wildlife into prevailing social and economic plans. Sometimes their job is to see that wildlife is destroyed as benignly as possible.

Although the southern area around Lake Temenggor was classified as permanent forest, a number of places with the same classification have been opened up to agricultural schemes. Meanwhile, the more remote northern portion of the forest, where we had dropped off the elephant, was close enough to Thailand that it held not only Thai Muslim separatists but Thai poaching gangs after ivory, meat, other animal parts, fruits, and sandalwood, which went to make incense, carved Japanese boxes, and Middle Eastern furniture. The upshot was that none of the forest in northern Malaysia could safely be considered permanent elephant habitat.

Being this close to Thailand caused other problems as well.

Some of our large crew kept disappearing off to the whore-houses across the border and returning with serious hangovers, which Muslims are not supposed to have because they do not drink. One reason the rubber plantations continued to expand, I had been told, was the dramatic worldwide increase in the use of condoms and rubber gloves due to the AIDS epidemic. But condoms were for other countries. No one believed the virus was common in Thailand yet. Why? Because no one wanted to believe it. Tests conducted not long afterward in Thailand showed 20 percent of the prostitutes and almost 5 percent of the military to be HIV-positive.

Shortly after we finally rounded up everyone and started back toward Sungai Siput, we stopped at another army camp. A huge, old, wild bull included the barracks there within his home range. He occasionally caused problems, but the soldiers let him be, partly on the theory that if this dominant male were re-moved, even more troublesome younger males might replace him, and partly because he had become a sort of mascot. How-ever, the bull was in a bad way, the soldiers told the biologists.

Shariff and several helpers went off to deal with the animal. The rest of us met them near dusk. Still groggy from drugs, the bull was standing in a deep, leafed-over ravine, where Shariff had cleaned and disinfected his wounds, climbing a ladder to get at them. Just over a week ago, the bull had been gored in the head by another male. I could see a gaping hole on the top of his skull. Apparently, the hole continued all the way through the tis-sue into a sinus, for the elephant was spraying mucus from the top of his head. He looked like a whale spouting water. He sounded like one, too, down in the darkening grotto.

The bull's right eye was blind, lost in an earlier fight. Yet the cruelest wound was one made just days before we arrived. When the bull wandered too close to a nearby village, someone climbed a tree and dropped acid onto his back. The chemical had eaten deep down through the flesh, leaving a gaping white trench that appeared to glow in the fading light. Shariff said the bull was at least sixty years old. The tops of his ears confirmed the estimate, as they curled over and flopped loosely when the animal moved. I could not fathom much else about this massive creature and the turbulent years he had weathered. Night sealed him off from view. We left him there, snuffling and blowing, giving off land whale sounds, an animal that stood as its own monument to the will to endure.

Once back at Sungai Siput, the politician honored us with an invitation to dine at his house. As it turned out, Thompson and I were seated next to him at a head table before an assemblage of dozens of other guests and honored further in the traditional way by the host feeding us select morsels from his own hands. We dined exceedingly well on course after course of piquant Malaysian cuisine and grinned our way through speeches that we could not understand, though our host tried valiantly to translate from time to time. I enjoyed myself but could not escape the realization that, upon awakening the next morning, we had to repeat the whole translocation procedure with a different female. I drifted toward sleep tasting the spicy beef called rendang and smiling at the memory of going to McDonald's in Kuala Lumpur my first day in Malaysia and ordering a McRendang to see what in the world that was.

Come morning, we hiked through a countryside of rubber trees and secondary forest to where the second female was chained. Larger than the first, she had barely escaped drowning in a swamp when she was darted. The capture team managed to haul her uphill from the reeds and get her chained to a tree on a steep slope just above the water. A wide swath through the swamp showed where an entire elephant family had come to visit her during the night. I wished that instead of listening to speeches at the politician's home, I could have been out here trying to understand what those animals had to say.

Like the first female, she had churned the soil around her to mud, and when the tame elephants arrived, they had a lot of difficulty working around her to secure a harness and chains. Once they started to move uphill, it became apparent that she could scarcely handle the slope at all. Shotgun and small-caliber rifle wounds formed pustules along her left side, but her basic problem was that her left front leg was horribly swollen and abscessed from a snare wire embedded within it. She was unable to put much weight upon it at all.

As she struggled to get up the slippery hillside, she used her trunk as a crutch. She fell to her knees many times and twice onto her side. With a great deal of lifting and hauling, the tame mounts and their mahouts finally got her to the top, and we started off through the secondary forest. She grew less and less groggy as we ambled along. She even proved able to muster a couple of charges, breaking a loosely secured rope. During the second charge, a Malay and I, each looking over his shoulder at the female, smacked into each other at a dead run. Being heavier, I knocked him flat. By the time I helped him up, it was all over; the female had been jerked to a stop by a longer chain attached to the elephant bringing up the rear. We probably could have dodged her anyway, given that infected foot of hers.

Shariff had neither the time nor resources for performing major surgery to cut out the wire and arranging for her to recuperate somewhere. Our plan was to spray disinfectant on the abscess and hope that it didn't turn gangrenous, then release the female out among the minefields and Thai poachers of the northern mountains, which would probably be logged and turned into plantations before too much longer.

༺༻༺༻༺༻༺༻༺༻༺༻

There comes a point, I realize, when it seems as if all I am doing is chanting the same old litany of problems and complaints. But I am reporting exactly what I observed in my efforts to see and learn about elephants. The Malaysian biologists said one in five elephants they handled bore grave, human-inflicted injuries. I happened to go three for three. The biologists spoke half-heartedly of plans on paper for more nature reserves and corridors between them. I could not see any sign of such a program becoming reality anywhere. Rather, I saw clearcuts of 20,000, 30,000, and 40,000 acres—clearcuts as far as the eye could see, completely leveled and burned, to be seeded with nothing but new rubber trees.

I met Negrito aborigines who still hunted with blowpipes and poison-tipped darts, their villages surrounded by logging operations now, who told me they had to go farther all the time to find game. Like pygmies I had met in the Congo, they had long traded honey, wild meat, and medicines derived from jungle herbs with villagers, but their irreplaceable knowledge of the forest was dwindling along with the forest itself. (They were the only folks I encountered who weren't afraid of elephants. "We're used to them. We chase them out of the fruit trees and vegetable gardens with noise and firebrands," headman Baning Adik told me.) A forester informed me that one reason the native woodlands in that area were being cut and the Negritos rounded up and put in settlements was to help control the communist threat. I read a proclamation by one state official telling people to get busy and develop an "idle" tract of wild land or it would be given to someone else.

I met a Canadian consultant for a logging company working on Borneo in the state of Sabah, which is where most of the last five hundred or so elephants on the island live. He told me of new fifteen-ton skidders that could carry ten tons of logs and described logging operations running twenty-four hours a day. His comment was, "It's a war of attrition being fought on Sabah. Only now the enemy is the forest." The Amazon Basin got most of the attention when people spoke of massive deforestation, but the cutting was slower there than in this part of the world. In addition to the settlement encouraged by the Malaysian government, land-hungry Filipinos were showing up to squat in Sabah's newly opened forests.

One place keeping pace with Borneo's transformation was the other huge island nearby—Sumatra, which is part of Indonesia. Like Borneo, it was probably colonized by elephants via an Ice Age land bridge, although the possibility remains that neither island had elephants until some escaped from captive groups brought in by people sometime during the last few centuries.

A rare bright spot in the Asian elephant's status came just a few years ago when surveys by Dr. Charles Santiapillai and his Indonesian colleagues revised the number on Sumatra upward from perhaps 1000 or 2000 to between 3000 and 5000. However, a satellite map would quickly reveal that Sumatra has become, almost overnight, a textbook illustration of habitat fragmentation. Only five separated areas of natural forest big enough to hold elephant populations larger than 200 remain.

Due to the thickness of the canopy and the corresponding scarcity of palatable vegetation underneath, it takes a fair amount of Indonesian rainforest to support an elephant or any other heavy-bodied ground-dweller. The dominant large mammals in this ecosystem are primates—monkeys, gibbons, and orangutans. Taking advantage of the sunlight-washed canopy itself, primates can reach densities of up to 466 per square mile, compared to 1 elephant for every 3.9 square miles. When the forest is opened up by logging and converted to crops, the elephants' abilities to home in on the most nourishing food source soon lead them into the nearest fields.

Dr. Santiapillai, whom I met in Lausanne and again in Bangkok, carried out studies showing that, as in India, females and young elephants stick to the forest edge and do far less damage in raids than bulls. He was instrumental in establishing an elephant training school in Sumatra to convert wild giants caught pillaging coconut or oil palm plantations into tame mounts. His hope was that they could then be used for selective logging in steep terrain, thereby minimizing soil damage and demonstrating the value of saving elephants to a public that has no particular use for them—a public in many cases translocated to the island by the government from more crowded parts of Indonesia. Thai mahouts were brought in for the training school, and public relations information was sent out. Given the round-the-clock pace at which most of the logging is conducted, though, it will be largely finished by the time the elephants are fully trained. The program has deteriorated into teaching the elephants stunts, such as playing soccer and doing handstands, for Thai-type side shows.

According to the Worldwatch Institute, in 1990 Japan imported 45 percent of the globe's tropical roundwood, or unprocessed logs, 89 percent of which had come from Malaysia and Indonesia. Throwaway concrete forms. Throwaway lunch boxes. Throwaway chopsticks. These are the top three uses of tropical broad-leaved hardwoods—the softer, more porous-grained hardwoods—in Japan. I'll repeat that: disposable concrete forms, disposable lunch boxes, and disposable chopsticks. While I'm at it, I'll repeat the main uses of elephants in the world: signature seals, jewelry, and tourist trinkets.

🔲🔲🔲🔲🔲🔲🔲🔲🔲🔲🔲

"It's simply the end of a million-year epoch," said Mikaail Kavanagh of the World Wildlife Fund–Malaysia at his office in Kuala Lumpur. "I get that feeling at the leading edge of those vast cutting zones. Look at the scale of land-use change here. This is a very successful, prosperous country. You can't say it shouldn't be done." Isn't it exactly what the United States did to build its wealth? "After all, here we are chatting in this nice, air-conditioned high-rise." And in a handsome, modern city. "We don't oppose development. We advise on sustainable development. The crunch in resources is going to come, and it will affect the standard of living. People will be hurt. Right now, the outlook for connecting up specific isolated elephant populations is bleak."

But the elephant rescuers carry on regardless. They catch the animals on the mainland and move them to the last wild niches, knowing that the effort is futile at one level and probably absurd. But they also know that it is the best chance the animals have. You, the observer, tell yourself this is how things are in our age; this is the sort of thing we do to save the world. And you try not to think about it so much that you become paralyzed with despair.

I was not doing well, though. I had nights when I wanted to quit the story. The accumulation of international capital and technology is so immense today and becomes such a juggernaut once launched at a target that the lag time between when a primeval area begins to be noticeably affected and when it has been devoured is getting down to a few years. Kavanagh was right. It is the end of an epoch. We are entering an entirely new stage of human and natural history.

"I have a friend working in America," a Malay man told me on the street. I asked how his friend liked it. "Ah, very fine. Very fine. *Big* car. *Big* watch."

"Elephants don't vote," shrugged a Malay biologist I met in the capital city. "Where they conflict with people and progress, the government attitude is you ecologists and your elephants can go to hell. As for habitat preservation, the government cares only what will benefit people, people, people. Right now. The future is all development-oriented. Elephants must fit into the make-money schemes or disappear, and all the rest is talk."

An interesting observation. It was precisely what I had been told at the CITES meeting in Lausanne by wildlife biologists from Zimbabwe, my next destination. On my way out to Africa through Singapore, I did my habitual sampling of ivory shops and heard the habitual lines about how I could take everything back into the United States except the largest tusks. One Chinese shop owner thoughtfully unscrewed pieces of the pedestal supporting a classic magic balls sculpture to show me how easily the parts could be separated and concealed in luggage.

Tiny Singapore has no wild elephants of its own, but for a short time during my visit, it actually had three. They swam across the Johore Straits from the Malaysian mainland to a small Singaporean island called Pulau Tekong. The daily newspaper *Straits Times* reported: "It is believed that logging and the clearing of forests had caused the herd to flee their home, forcing the three animals to swim across the straits to find refuge on Pulau Tekong." Unluckily for them, the island happens to be a Ministry of Defense training ground complete with live firing exercises. Shariff's team was called in to capture the bulls and take them back to Malaysia. They should have been caught in their fast-shrinking Malaysian homeland and translocated before this ever happened, I was told, but the Sultan of Johore was very fond of having wild elephants in the woodlands and hadn't wanted them taken away yet.

FOURTEEN

SOUTHERN AFRICA: ZIMBABWE

🬀🬀🬀🬀 ANCIENT AFRICA HAD two main gold fields. One was in West Africa, centered in what would become modern-day Guinea. The other, the Monomotapa field, was in the southern African kingdom of Zimbabwe. While Europe drew inward at the onset of its Dark Ages, Karanga tribesmen were smelting gold from ore at their capital, a stone fortress-city called Great Zimbabwe, and trading it through Arab middlemen for treasures from around the globe; Indian ornaments, glass beads from Indonesia, and the finest Chinese porcelain have been found among Great Zimbabwe's ruins. The Karangas also exported ivory. They, themselves, did not make much use of elephant teeth, though *ngangas*, or shamans, tossed ivory "bones" into the air and, from the patterns in which they fell, divined the future.

That future included a period of British domination, during which Zimbabwe was renamed Rhodesia. With independence, in 1980, the nation became Zimbabwe once more. It covers an area of approximately 151,000 square miles and has a population of about 8 million humans and an estimated 40,000 to 60,000 elephants. Most of the central highlands have been converted to agriculture, producing such commodities as cotton and maize. But around the periphery of the country, where rainfall is less generous, a fair amount of intact woodland interspersed with scrub and savanna remains, along with the wildlife communities that depend upon such habitats. They owe their existence in large measure to what conservationists like to refer to as the best damn wildlife warden Africa ever had: the tsetse fly.

People in this part of the world have a heavy cultural investment in cattle. Unlike native ungulates, cattle never developed a resistance to the trypanosomes that cause sleeping sickness and are transmitted by these biting flies, which flit around your exposed flesh buzzing *tsee tsee*. Human numbers therefore remained sparse in many portions of Zimbabwe, and the white-run government took the opportunity to establish a number of game parks.

Other African countries have intact savanna-woodland ecosystems and a system of reserves, too. Yet in recent years, they had been fast running out of elephants, while Zimbabwe's herds were not only large but actually increasing. Why? And why were they not only increasing, but growing so fast that the government of Zimbabwe was culling its herds to prevent overcrowding? I had heard a variety of explanations. I came to see for myself how accurate they might be.

In late May, after making contact with biologists and planners in the capital, Harare, I flew to Bulawayo in the western part of the country to meet with Mark Butcher, a young biologist working for the Forestry Commission. His area of responsibility included both government-controlled forest lands and tribal, or communal, lands adjoining 5000-square-mile Hwange National Park, and he wanted to give me a thorough introduction to both. To that end, we drove and hiked through his territory for days at a time, having what he called a jolly runabout through the bush, and he filled me in all the while.

Butch, as everyone called him, was a top-notch field man as well as a fount of information. I listened. I wrote everything down. But I was not quite with him. My attention was too easily distracted by flying hooves, the curve of sunlight along horns, the musks of animals constantly in our nostrils. I was overwhelmed by being back in the African bush.

On the first day out, we followed a large elephant bull into a clump of thornbush, trying to get a closer look at a wicked-looking scar on his side. Just as he was stretching to take a bite, the big creature froze. All at once, he was coming back my way, fully alert. How? . . . The wind was still in my favor, and I had been dead quiet. Then I understood: he hadn't sensed me—not yet—but another bull nearby had and was sending out an alarm in frequencies too low for the human ear to detect. We scuttled into the shadows of another thornbush while he trotted past, sweeping the air for clues with his upraised trunk.

That night, the sky was fluorescent yellow and laminated with red. Three bull elephants loomed against it, drinking at a waterhole. Jackals sang and mewled in the distance. Behind the elephants moved the silhouettes of roan antelope and a long file of wildebeest. Then impala, so small by comparison with the giants that they appeared to be walking under their legs. After them, Cape buffalo, trotting darkly and heavily through the tall grass, three and four abreast, more than a hundred all told.

We watched while hidden behind the trunks of *ilala*, the local name for the wild palm *Hyphaene natelensis*. Its English common name is ivory palm, as the hard nuts can be carved to produce vegetable ivory. The species flourishes around springs and in meadows with underground water. Tall ones loomed everywhere around us, heads bursting with fronds and fruit. But young palms were scarce. The elephants considered them a delicacy and, just as in Malaysia's oil palm plantations, sought them out and gobbled their hearts. Palm swifts darned the purpling air around the trees, taking insects and then returning to nests on the undersides of fronds. A nest is built of the bird's own feathers, Butch said, and stuck to the leaf with saliva—swift spit—creating a pad just large enough to rest two eggs upon. The parents must hang almost vertically to incubate them.

While I was watching a mixed flight of swifts and bats, something screamed, then suddenly went quiet. Butch whispered, "Life's a bitch at the bottom of the food chain. There's a lot of Bite-You's out there." Soon, the first lions began to make territorial pronouncements somewhere in the grass. A troop of chacma baboons took refuge in a big combretum tree. We camped upon a small knoll nearby, our back against a tree that had a termite mound packed around the trunk. In front of us, a little fire sizzled and smoked, helping to mark out our space against the rustling night. The field of stars was limitless and, in the dry air, pulsed with a strong, clear light. I felt as if I were receiving some sort of current directly from it. My whole being tingled and then began to trill. The more the night deepened, the more awake I became. And the more I awakened, the more I began to realize how much I had sealed myself off in order to cope with Asia.

Unconsciously, I had erected baffles against the all-consuming tidal wave of human culture until, by imperceptible degrees, I had grown numb. I had forgotten what it was like to be wholly immersed in the sensations of wildness. As a result, I had all but lost sight of why this story was so important to me. I seemed to have been rolling around the world saying good-bye to its giants without comprehending why I was doing it any longer. All this effort toward saving untamed places and things had come to seem quixotic, an indulgence in nostalgia for a world that could never be brought back. Never—not a chance of it, not given the pace of change I had seen. What had attracted me to this lost cause to start with?

But no; this cause wasn't lost. Suddenly, I could feel it in the hoofbeats traveling through the ground beneath me as I lay under my blanket. It was as real as the red and gold eyes that sometimes circled in toward the campfire, and the singing in my blood said that it was within me, too. It could be kept real. It had to be; I could not imagine my own life without the deep currents of nature flowing close by. That was why I worked in conservation. It was why I had undertaken the elephant story. I remembered.

I would come back to spend time with Butch, but I knew now what I really had to do. I needed to go off by myself and get right. I couldn't recall the last time I had spent more than a few hours in the field alone. Asia had all felt elbow-to-elbow, even in the last refugia. I needed to stay by myself in the bush until I felt strong and connected and could hope again. Maybe then I could come back and really concentrate on what people were telling me.

I drove fast and straight through Zimbabwe, westward past Victoria Falls, where the Zambezi River explodes into prismatic clouds, and on across the border into the northeast corner of neighboring Botswana. There, I pitched my tent along a tributary of the Zambezi—the Chobe River, at the edge of Chobe National Park. Although less well known than the game parks of East Africa, Botswana's reserves offer perhaps an even better glimpse of primeval Africa. When combined with the Okavango Delta and Savute Marsh, two other wetland oases within the arid scrub of northern Botswana, 4500-square-mile Chobe National Park, established in 1968, and its surroundings comprise one of the grandest wildlife spectacles left on the earth.

Botswana is exceptional among African countries in that it enjoys a strong economy, fueled by seemingly bottomless reserves of diamonds. Almost exactly the same size as Kenya, it has fewer than 1.4 million people, compared to nearly 25 million in Kenya. Most of Botswana's landscape is just too dry to support a high density of humans. In this country, the word for rain, *pula*, is also the name for the official currency. Botswana includes the Kalahari Desert and similar arid terrain long inhabited mainly by scattered Bushmen tribes. The marshes and pans and riverine plains that offer green abundance are given over to native wildlife rather than to human tribes. This is not the result of any plan. It is, once again, largely the work of the tsetse fly.

During the November-February rainy season, wildlife can use all but the most arid zones of the countryside. Then, as the dry season progresses, animals contract toward the fly-loud Okavango, Savute, and Chobe. Canadian researcher George Calef, who has tracked elephants in Botswana for several years, recorded some herds moving about 300 miles on a round trip that took them from the Moremi Wildlife Reserve in the Okavango Delta area to the Sibuyu Forest Reserve on the east, near the Zimbabwe border, and back again. Tracks and trails had always suggested that some herds continue on from northern Botswana into western Zimbabwe as well. Calef confirmed this, locating an elephant he had radio-collared in Chobe traveling through Hwange National Park. To the animals, it is all one range, and they are still able to use it that way. That is what makes this ecosystem so vital and such an increasing rarity in the world. It simply has room for the creatures to live much as they always have, migrating over tremendous circuits with little but wildness in their path.

By October, the height of the dry season, elephants and a host of smaller creatures would overrun the banks of the Chobe seeking water. Already, in early June, they were beginning to arrive in considerable numbers as water evaporated in the shallow pans and seasonal streams elsewhere. I stopped a solitary bull in his prime as he made for the river. He didn't have far left to go when I swung my Land Cruiser in front of him for a better look at some odd streaks of green pigment on his head. He strode away on a diagonal, and I cut him off again, still trying to get a glimpse of his forehead. He backed up. I pressed forward. It was a dumb move—I was still feeling unfocused and, I guess, a little crazed—and he took it as a challenge. I got a full-on, ear-flapping, kinked-tail, raised-trunk, trumpeting, dust-billowing, ground-quaking, O-&*%#@!-look-at-the-size-of-this-animal charge. His eyes were reddish brown in the late evening light, and so wide, so focused on me, that I thought he was going to carry through and slam into the car, leaving me with "Cheap thrills aren't worth it" as my dying thought. He stopped a couple of trunk lengths away.

The pigment on his forehead was plain old chlorophyll, probably from streaks of greenish bark he had rubbed or crashed against earlier. I was feeling grateful to be alive even before I met him; it had been a fine day. After the giant let me go, I gave thanks aloud. He had treated me better than I had any right to expect.

For the next morning, June 6, long sections of my notebook that simply record the species I observe seem like an invocation performed at the water's edge, manifesting beautiful things by calling out their names. Yellow-billed stork. African fish-eagle. Grey heron. White-faced ducks standing in flocks that jut out into the shallows like a sandbar. Wedges of Cape teal flying past. Egyptian goose gaggles. Squacco herons everywhere along the shore. Blacksmith plovers everywhere, too. Orphaned water-buck calf, jumping at each shadow in the bushes. Hippo families grazing out of the water, groaking and grunting. Crocodiles gliding past the ducks. African jacana, the lily pad walker. Helmeted guinea fowl, raising puffs of dust with their scratching.

And kudu, browsing inside bushes, striped by sunlight and their own patterns of white on brownish grey fur. Chobe bushbuck. Reedbuck. Reed cormorant. Black-necked stilt. Long-tailed starling. Fork-tailed drongo. Sharp-tailed starling. Yellow-billed hornbill, picking through elephant dung. Grey lourie. Banded mongoose troop, common near the water's edge, also picking through elephant droppings. Impala drinking. Bull elephant coming out of the bushes. Glossy starling. Little bee-eater. Blue waxbills. Giant kingfisher. More elephants. . . .

By then it was nearly midday and hot. From that point on through the afternoon, elephants would emerge from the surrounding scrub and open forests by the hundreds and hundreds. By August, it would be by the thousands and thousands.

For June 7, the notebook describes: On one side of me, a dominant male impala running off bachelors from the herd. On the other side, wart hog females posturing and briefly fighting over a site where one had been rooting. On yet another side, chacma baboons, the young tussling and older animals grooming or napping in the dawn after a wakeful night of listening for lions and leopards. On another side, white-rumped babblers noisily convened in a bush that my field guide calls Transvaal gardenia. Other kinds of languages with things to say about this business of living. Other kinds of minds at work. The old feeling returned of being among not just animals but animal tribes and nations.

A young bull elephant and two adult baboons have a screaming match at the riverbank, seeming to entertain one another. With more or less the same intent, two teenage bulls who have been feeding together on river-edge brush try to intimidate a band of buffalo. All the buffalo give way, except one. This hold-out seems to take the challenge more seriously. He digs in his front feet and lowers his head and absolutely refuses to budge, despite false rushes by one of the bulls, who is easily twice as large as the buffalo. The other bull leaves. After a long stare at the buffalo, the remaining bull flips up his trunk, gives a violent shake of his head, and follows.

Elephants wade and shower, multicolored with dirt and patterned with streaks and bands of wetness. Elephants swim the Chobe, with only their trunk tips exposed above water, and go on to forage in the lush expanse of papyrus reeds on the river's far side. On the near shore, an elephant family is grazing on *Cynodon dactylon*, a tough, rhizomatous grass adapted to trampling and heavy grazing. Another family stands in the shade. The matriarch is an attentive mother with a very new baby looking out from beneath her legs. While waiting there, her group is approached by another family on its way to the river. The matriarchs exchange greeting with their trunk tips, then each wraps her trunk around the other's until the two proboscises are entwined along most of their length, like a double helix. Other females keep the juveniles together in a huddle toward the group's center, where they trunk-wrestle and mount one another in play.

Overall, the most prominent behaviors displayed by the groups are solicitous—expressions of care and concern, all emphasized with ministrations of the trunk. These are hugely affectionate beasts. With the overwhelming concern of the individual for the group and of the group for the individual, elephant families strike me as more closely resembling the primates—chacma baboons and vervet monkeys—than any other species in the wild menagerie of Chobe. Small wonder we humans naturally develop such a strong sympathy for the giants. A skeptic might ask for proof that elephants actually possess the so-called higher emotions. I would say, watch a family on a morning like this and prove that they don't.

For years, Botswana citizens were allowed to hunt elephants under a permit system, much as Americans are entitled to hunt deer, for example. Inflated ivory prices caused the one elephant per person quota to be abused, and a nationwide ban on elephant hunting went into effect in 1983. Subject only to relatively minor poaching since then, Botswana's elephant population numbers at least 60,000, and estimates run all the way up to 90,000. These may be the most free-ranging and least disturbed herds in Africa, at least among savanna elephants.

As much as I wish I could leave the subject on that note, I have to point out that Botswana and its wildlife sanctuaries are on the threshold of major change. Improved health care has boosted the number of people in the nation. Meanwhile, tsetse fly eradication programs are opening more and more wildlands to the expanding human population and its cattle. (Carried out mainly from airplanes, the pesticide-spraying programs have broadcast DDT into the food chain, and the chlorinated hydrocarbon residues are now showing up in the milk of human mothers.)

The northern shore of the Chobe River is not included within the park. Where it used to serve as a buffer zone, growing numbers of livestock mix with the wildlife these days. I saw herders burning the papyrus to create meadows with short grass for their cows. At night, elephants sometimes continued from the swamps on into nearby fields and the village of Kasane. Illegal killing by farmers and herders was on the rise.

A long, stout veterinary fence intended to keep wild buffalo from transmitting rinderpest to cattle hinders the movement of elephants and other wildlife in the southern reaches of the ecosystem. Plans to dredge and channelize major waterways for large-scale agriprojects and to provide hydraulic power to diamond mines threaten to begin unraveling the entire delicate wetland complex. And there is a growing demand to open the green expanses contained within reserves themselves to grazing and farming. The era of untrammeled freedom for the elephants here is clearly coming to a close.

Botswana's high elephant population may include refugees from bordering countries. Some come from the politically troubled, heavily poached part of Namibia called the Caprivi Strip, which lies to the north. Others are thought to arrive whenever Zimbabwe begins carrying out another round of culling operations in its western region. Ironically, at the time of my visit,

Botswana was contemplating whether or not it should begin culling operations of its own. It has since decided that it will. Following the lead of Zimbabwe and South Africa, it plans to begin shooting a percentage of its herds to limit their numbers. One of the main justifications for this has been the impact of elephants along the Chobe River.

The local Tswana people say that if you drink a brew made with baobab seeds, you can swim the river without trouble from the crocodiles. Who knows? Elephants sometimes tear into the moist, spongy core of baobab trees for food, and observers have remarked that it seems to make them excited and unusually aggressive, as if some chemical in the wood were an intoxicant. As they gather along the Chobe during the dry season, especially in times of drought, the giants hit the baobabs pretty hard, occasionally tusking and chewing their way through the pulpwood until the tree collapses.

During the hot season, the elephants turn more and more to stripping bark for food, particularly since certain acacias and other species are moving nutrients in preparation for flowering just then. Some of the riverside acacias have been killed outright by girdling, as have some of the large Zimbabwe teak (*Baikiaea pluijuga*). Other damaged trees along the Chobe include *Albizia* and Kalahari apple-leaf (*Lonchocarpus nelsii*), often called the raintree. Smaller trees such as the croton, along with shrubs such as *Ochna*, *Berkia*, and terminalia, have been splintered and stripped of limbs. Sections of the river's edge consist of little more than the bleached skeletons of wood standing or lying on bare, sandy ground. The transformation extends some distance back into the adjoining terrain.

Unfortunately, no one really knows what sort of cycles a heavily used riverine forest in elephant country normally goes through. How does one sort out the results of periodic severe drought that concentrates animals near water from the consequences of elephant overpopulation? Or the effects of frost and fire from too much foraging pressure? What's "normal" in this ecosystem? What are the banks of the Chobe supposed to look like? Haven't the elephants changed its forests before? This is much the same puzzle that faced managers decades ago in Tsavo, before the herds that many thought to be too crowded were decimated, first by drought, and then by poaching.

The only way to answer the question of how nature works over the long term would be to stand by, record, and document. Culling can help maintain an ideal standard of elephant density. But how can anyone yet be sure what the ideal is? I would pursue the subject when I returned to Zimbabwe. There was another, crucial dimension of culling I wanted to examine as well: the impacts of shooting on elephant behavior.

I was ready to deal with complex issues again. I felt recharged by my sojourn on the Chobe's shores. At the same time, the Chobe had taught me that there is really no place so wild that it offers a total escape from the problems of a shrinking world.

Back in Zimbabwe, Mark Butcher introduced me to Hwange National Park authorities. They helped arrange for me to travel through remote sections of the reserve that were off-limits to tourists so that I could get an idea of how elephants used this part of their range. I supplied the Land Cruiser, the petrol, and the water. The park provided a veteran warden: Sergeant Sojayi Mlambo, who added a rifle and a radio to the expedition. He said it wouldn't be long before we were too far into the park's hinterlands for the radio to be of any use. Good. That sounded like the sort of place I wanted to be.

For our first day, we were still on the tourist route—except all the tourists had to be out of the park by dark, while we stayed on to sleep at Guavulala Pan. Four lions with cubs watched from the roadside as we first came into the area after nightfall. Sarge guided me to a little canvas tent stretched over a frame, from which a young man named Edward Tshuma emerged. Edward's job was to tend the water pump that kept this pan full long after it ordinarily would have begun to dry out.

Before bore holes and pumps were added, most of the area covered by Hwange was strictly wet season range for many spe-

cies. The pans dried out, and, as they did, herds moved northward toward permanent water pooled along the Gwayi River.
Some probably continued all the way north to the Zambezi
River and beyond into Zambia, then looped back down toward
the southern boundary of Hwange again once the rains began.

Barefoot and wearing a light cotton cloth wrapped around his
waist, Edward Tshuma blew a smoldering fire back to life outside the tent. As we hunched around the flames, he explained
that he was practicing to be a naturalist. By talking to passing
tourists and making careful notes, he had taught himself the
names of most of the local plants and developed a special interest
in identifying birds. Edward wished he had a field guide of his
own and, one day, maybe even binoculars. Instead, the park had
given him an axe to provide his own firewood while stationed
alone out here in the bush. It was also his only weapon for dealing with the lions, who had more or less laid claim to the place,
having had particular success hunting buffalo around the pan.
"They sleep sometimes at the edge of my tent," he sighed. "I
don't like it when they pull down the ropes."

"Very cheeky lions here," Sarge agreed. Their pug marks
were all over the broad stairs that led up to the watchtower overlooking the waterhole. Between the top of those stairs and the
platform where we unrolled our sleeping blankets to spend the
night, there was no Bite-You barrier. Sarge piled a duffel bag
atop two wicker chairs. This wouldn't have stopped a house cat,
but the idea was to provide a psychological boundary. Sure.

Every time we shone a flashlight on the ground around the
tower, lion eyes shone back. Several white rhinos were sipping
at the pan. Black rhinos used brushier habitats within this same
area and would come in to drink later. As the night wore on,
more and more elephants began to march in. As they sorted out
social concerns, giant screams and bellows rose above the sounds
of drinking and wading to puncture my dreams. In the relative
silence in between, Edward identified the thin, fluting nighttime
cries of geese, plovers, stilts, and teal. I could hear the lions moving around by the bottom of the stairs. Two or three times, I
heard the stair boards creak higher up.

"Lions?" I would whisper to Edward, who sat alert nearby with a blanket wrapped around his shoulders, expertly tuned into the night.

He would nod yes in a distracted way, then start, hold up a finger, and turn to me wide-eyed. "There. Do you hear it? That was—how do you say?—a pygmy goose!" I piled another chair at the top of the stairs. Not a restful night, but an informative one. Sometime in the middle of it, I tiptoed down the stairs to pee, swiveling my head constantly. I saw no movement close by, but when I looked up high, I saw the most amazing sight: the clouds had arranged a huge and perfect image of a running elephant, rendered in the style of Persia or India, with tapered legs and the crescent moon for its eye, charging white and silver through the sky.

The next day, Sarge and I quit traveling in early afternoon, pulling in to stay at the Mitswiri Pan, *mitswiri* being the local name for a big combretum tree common around waterholes. I used the remaining daylight hours to follow elephant spoor outward through the surrounding habitats. Deep, well-drained, ancient Kalahari sands underlie the greater part of southwestern Zimbabwe. They support tall, mixed forests that include Zimbabwe teak; mukwa (*Pterocarpus angolensis*), whose heartwood is golden and whose seed pods look like fried eggs dangling from the branches; various acacias; and *Brachystegia*, a pod-bearing tree that closely resembles acacia. Here and there, the sandy terrain has been eroded to form open, grassy swales or flats called *vleis*, seasonally saturated with water. Where soils are thin, rocky, or underlain by the carbonate deposits known as calcrete, scrub forests of mopane and terminalia take over.

Both the fine Kalahari sands and the dusty, white, calcrete soil make for excellent tracking. As with human fingerprints, the pattern of fissures and ridges left by the sole of a particular elephant is quite distinctive, once you became familiar with it. Younger animals have crisp designs, while older elephants show worn heels and smoother ridges. Elongated oval footprints generally indicate an adult male. The bull's rear leg often falls slightly to the side of the front leg, leaving a double print. Cows, by contrast, have round pads, and they tend to step more precisely in the same spot with both legs.

I was intrigued by the way some individuals left marks in the sand and dust with their trunks while strolling. Some made long, sinuous lines that suggested they were doing some tracking of their own—by scent. Other designs looked more like doodling. Striding alongside, Sarge showed me how the poachers here walked on their heels to mimic hoofprints in the loose sand. If wearing shoes, they might walk just on the toe instead, scuffing hard backward with each step, which left an impression almost indistinguishable from that of a fast-moving roan antelope or young buffalo. They also made use of the old trick of walking backward much of the time.

Nightfall at Mitswiri was announced by the roaring of lions. According to Sarge, the ones at this waterhole were as cheeky as those at Guavulala. "They will come right next to where you are sleeping," he shrugged, but went on to reassure me that they were not all that bad compared to the hyenas. Modern research has revised the hyena's reputation as a skulker and scavenger. Applying the formidable power of their jaws, designed for breaking open carcass bones, these animals can also be fierce, efficient pack hunters of live prey. As Sarge pointed out, occasionally a person sleeping in the open wakes up to find a hyena making off with part of his face. Another informative night in Bite-You land.

I heard a hyena from time to time, uttering its bizarre mix of cackles and meows. Still, it was the lions that shook the night, both with the males' calls and the concatenation of hooves that a fresh whiff of big cat caused to erupt from time to time around the waterhole. Trumpeting sounded far in the distance. I climbed up a tree and waited. Half an hour later, the first giants appeared.

Given the moonlight and the whitish sand and clay around the pan, I could make them out fairly well. While alert, and cautious of my scent, the elephants were not noticeably fearful of any other animals, and the contrast with the quivering wariness of the other herbivores coming in to drink was revealing. Even the big, surly buffalo were shying at moon shadows.

As far as most of the wild community was concerned, the big cats owned the waterholes. But elephants had solved the perennial Bite-You problem, which amounts to an evolutionary coup. Although nowhere near the top of the food chain, they had become all but invulnerable through size. The resulting dominion, the release from the necessity of having to look constantly over a shoulder, in a sense freed the species to develop other aspects of its existence, such as its social relationships and intelligence. To a far greater extent than heavily preyed-upon species, elephants can set their own agenda. At least, this is how it appears things work, from my human point of view. There is nothing like the African bush to help you appreciate just how much of a vulnerable animal's energy goes into staying alert.

At one point, I walked a ways toward the giants to see better and was met with a deep, elephant trumpet-growl from some dark patch of woods. It was a vocalization any species could understand. It meant: Back off—and don't make me tell you again. No problem. I'm on my way. Drifting off to sleep a couple of hundred feet farther removed from the waterhole, I thought again of what a good thing it is that elephants leave you alone as long as you don't bother them.

We started traveling at dawn and at midmorning came upon a solitary old bull drinking from a series of springs called Nehimba. He struck me as exceptionally long-legged—lanky; it seemed half his bulk was in his enormous neck, head, and trunk. Near a pool, he encountered a blacksmith plover. Characteristically, the bird raised its wings and threatened the bull, crying out in a piercing voice. Just as characteristically, the bull moved away, eight or nine tons of giant driven off by less than a pound of bird. While leaving, though, the old bull pranced a little bit, shaking his head, as if laughing to himself. Elephants often give that impression; it is what Joyce Poole called being silly. They seem to have an immense capacity for amusement and, I think, joy, not surprising in a life form supreme in its realm. It would be less anthropomorphic to say that the bull was merely exhibiting displacement behavior, releasing a bit of tension built up in response to the bird's threat. But what is the difference between this and many occasions that cause us to shrug and shake our heads, laughing to ourselves? In fact, that is exactly what I did when blacksmith plovers stalked forward yelling at me.

The waterholes were shrinking, drying out one by one. Sarge said the shallowest would be losing half their volume every week through evaporation. With adult elephants taking up to fifty gallons each in a drinking session, a herd can lower a small pan sharply in a single night. This being Zimbabwe's winter, the nights were still cool. But five more months of the dry season remained. Nights would soon grow hotter and hotter, and evaporation would continue around the clock until all but a few of the deepest pans and a few permanent springs and seeps were dry and the hard times began.

Since elephants must feed at least sixteen hours per day to obtain sufficient forage, that does not leave much time for traveling long distances to and from waterholes. Nor does it leave much time for waiting for a turn while other elephants sip from a slow-trickling seep. That was what would happen at Nehimba and also at Shakwanki and Shabi Shabi farther on. With the flow of water reduced to a trickle in seeps where only one elephant could drink at a time, some animals would begin to perish of thirst even as others sipped.

"You hear how elephants take care of their young and each other. Well, it was a different story back in the bad drought of '81," I would later hear from Forestry Commission warden Rich Aylwood, who was working in Hwange during the dry years. "Cows still wouldn't butt their own calves away, but other juveniles had tusk marks all over their rumps. Bulls shoved little orphans aside, and the matriarchs and other older females tusked the hell out of subordinates. You'd see turds made of solid sand from the elephants drinking deep in sandy seeps they'd dug down like pipes."

Shabi Shabi still held the wreckage of drought. Bones lay scattered everywhere. Strolling over to investigate one boulder-size skull, I almost stepped on a fat puff adder. I watched it disappear completely beneath the clumps of tough cynodon grass that had grown back thick and green around the drinking holes. Off to one side in the trees was an elephant graveyard—a shady grove heaped with jaws and long bones. Sarge told me it was a

collection left by park scientists studying the age and sex structure of elephants that had died in the drought of 1981—a year in
which even permanent seeps finally ran dry. A professor from an
American university came to Hwange to study the way the elephant bones were deposited on the landscape and scattered by
predators and scavengers. He hoped to relate such information
to finds of fossil mammoth and mastodon remains.

Moving ever farther south and west, Sarge and I began to
draw closer to Hwange's most remote reaches, bordering Botswana. The elephant herds were moving long distances each
day. We could not keep up with any one group on foot; the brush
was too thick and thorny for us to follow by car; and the giants
we encountered during the day were too nervous to let us get
close anyway. So we contented ourselves with tracking. Much
digging for the roots of grasses and shrubs was evident along
their trails. With the onset of winter, nutrients had been drawn
back from the leaves of most species to be stored underground;
the giants were searching for the plants' reserves. In places, the
woodlands had an autumn ambience, full of dry, golden foliage
that drifted downward onto the sands as wind gusted through.

The jeep track deteriorated into loose sand, and I burned up a
couple of fan belts and radiator hose sections working our way
through. At last we reached the Zimbabwe-Botswana boundary. Although much of the border was open, this segment was
marked by a veterinary fence made of steel posts and cable to
keep Hwange's buffalo confined. Cattle herds grazed just across
the way, centered around a permanent spring. We could see
where young elephants and their female relatives had failed to
cross the fence while older bulls paralleled the structure a ways
and then stepped over it.

More springs bubbled up on the Zimbabwe side. They were
beautiful oases—clear pools edged with slender, verdant reeds
and full of flowering lilies, jacanas, and fish. But instead of finding tracks from the sort of wildlife such water could support, we
found the tracks of poachers who crossed from Botswana to net
fish from the park's springs and snag a few buffalo or impala
while they were at it.

Sarge had been around when Botswana poachers were crossing into Hwange in large numbers, often taking along donkeys or mules to pack home the booty. Mark Butcher had been around then, too, and I recalled the story he had told me. It took place in 1981, just after the war for independence, when Zimbabwe was far from stable. The Fifth Brigade, comprised of members of the dominant Shona tribe, were rampaging through the countryside, wreaking vengeance on their old enemies, the Ndebele, cutting off men's lips and women's breasts. More people were killed during this civil unrest than during the struggle for independence.

"Poachers took advantage of our troubles and hit our wildlife big time," Butch said. "We trailed these guys deep into Hwange and found where they were camped. We snuck up and positioned ourselves. They were sitting around the fire throwing bones to tell the future. After one throw, they all stared and suddenly jumped up and started looking all around. It wasn't that any of us had made a false move. It was something they read in those bones that spooked them. Anyway, they finally quieted down.

"A little after that, we jumped them," Butch continued, "and we started in: Shaya! Shaya! Shaya!" (Shaya is a Zulu warrior's term for hit, bash, take down, kill. It is often accompanied by a slap of a forefinger against the palm of the opposite hand. Shaya! Smack! Shaya! Smack! Shaya! Smack!)

"I was chasing one down for a while. I finally caught up and drilled him. When I got back to the others, I found a great bloody cock-up had happened. One guy they had rounded up and got handcuffs on had broken away and grabbed a gun. They shot at him, and he shot back. And even with the manacles on, he managed to kill two of our guys. One of the shots at him actually hit his cuffs and busted them apart, just like out of a movie, and he shot a couple more guys. Four shots, four of our men —two rangers and two trackers—before they finally shaya-ed the bastard."

These days, the illegal killing of wildlife near Hwange's border is of a far lower intensity, more a matter of local herders grabbing food than commercial hunters taking meat and ivory.

After the poachers see fresh tire tracks along the border jeep road, they hustle over to shoot some game, knowing the park is not likely to patrol this far out again for a while. During the rainy season, the wardens cannot get here at all; but then neither can the poachers, for they sink knee-deep in the calcrete clay. Where elephants pass during this mud time, they leave tracks that become potholes the size of kegs and later harden in the sun to resemble fossil prints. It looks like brontosaurs went through.

Sarge and I began to lose count of days. The pans we visited had names such as Dzivannini, Lupanda, Luasha—Bushman names. After Hwange was set aside as a park in 1938, its borders took in a number of northern Bushmen. Focused around the permanent springs, they were among the few who had not been displaced from aboriginal lands by cattle herders. But then they found the park trying to move them out.

"Those are the days when they was pushing the Bushmen away," Sarge remembered. " 'No, no,' said the Bushmen, 'we want to stay and hunt.' The park said, 'You can not. We will kill meat for you—buffalo, elephant, anything. But you must go.' " The park rounded them up and moved them to headquarters, where most died or interbred with Bantu tribes. "These people, they don't know how to work, how to plow or grow crops. Only live here. We have some even now," Sarge added. "But they are bigger. Mixed. Sometimes I cut the spoor of a real Bushman out here. It looks like a child is walking. But it is a grown man."

We slept by springs with thorny thickets at our back to deter predators and awakened with crimson-breasted shrikes feeding in the spiked branches overhead. To walk on a cool winter morning in old Bushman territory at the edge of Zimbabwe, reading the story of the night as fresh sign in the dust, was a fine thing. But by afternoon all was heat and dryness again, and all the colors were washed out by the sun. And I was beginning to wonder why, in all our travels, we seldom saw elephants drinking at any waterholes before dusk and why those few we did see were almost always bulls.

A possible answer came at the pan called Josivannini. After we drove in, I began my usual scouting through the area, trailing footprints outward through thickets where the giants had been feeding on young acacia and terminalia. Sarge picked up cylindrical balls of fur from the side of one trail and asked if I could identify them. A small mammal? Dung from a predator that had been feasting on small mammals? He shook his head and made as if he were licking his arm. These were fur balls regurgitated by lions that had lain here in the shade grooming themselves. "Walk carefully," Sarge reminded.

I did, and in a while I came upon piles of bones. Massive piles of massive bones. It was another elephant graveyard. Like the one at Shabi Shabi, it consisted mostly of jaws collected by people to age the animals. But these were not from animals killed by drought. They were from elephants killed by culling teams during the late 1970s, Sarge informed me. Park staff had concentrated the animals by setting out salt licks near the pan and then shot them. Periodic culling had continued at other places throughout the park since that time.

When evening came to Josivannini, so did the first elephant— a bull—along with a solitary giraffe. They joined the roan antelope, buffalo, and kudu already there. Twilight deepened, and twenty elephants trooped up in an envelope of dust. Typically, the young ones soon went from dedicated sipping to showering to chasing off impala and trying to bluff buffalo while subadult males sloshed back and forth through the shallows in shoving contests.

In the gloaming, I noticed a dark line of trees on the brow of a hill above the pan. Why hadn't I noticed them before? Then I saw that the trees were moving. They were elephants—scores and scores of elephants. No, hundreds of elephants. It was as if the bones had reassembled, and the moonlight and haze had given them flesh. Behind the line of dark, massed bodies moved a single animal half again as tall as any other, a Goliath even among giants. How old was he? Fifty years? Sixty? More? God, I wish I could have seen him in the daylight; he was incredibly big. His span on Earth had surely bridged the era from the Stone Age technology of Bushmen's poison arrows to automatic rifles. What had he seen? What had he learned in that lifetime?

My mind held a more practical question as well: How much of the elephants' nocturnal behavior was a result of being hunted?

Elephants usually drink every day. But if they have to, females and young can go up to two days without drinking and a bull as long as three days. This being the cold season, the giants didn't need to spend a lot of time seeking water yet. They concentrated on feeding during the day and simply waited until night to get around to quenching their thirst. Or so Mark Butcher would later tell me. He may have been correct. Yet right next door along the Chobe River, elephants were arriving to drink all through the afternoon.

These Hwange animals were also extremely shy of people, compared to those in Chobe. Almost without exception, any elephants Sarge and I happened upon in the bush fled at once. That only the boldest class of animals, the big bulls, came in to drink in broad daylight seemed typical of a disturbed population as well. Past experience with poachers could account for such behavior. The fact that poachers did most of their work around waterholes could have further influenced elephants to stay away until dark. However, ranchers, safari guides, and biologists with whom I spoke later told me that they used to see elephants regularly in Hwange at all times of day. When? Before culling operations began.

🬀🬀🬀🬀🬀🬀🬀🬀🬀🬀🬀🬀

I am about to tread on sensitive ground, for Zimbabwe officials perceive culling as crucial to their ability to manage both elephants and the ecosystems upon which they and many other species depend. This would be a good place to emphasize that I lack lengthy enough experience with African elephants and their patterns of activity and behavior to really judge what is typical. Rowan Martin, head of Zimbabwe's wildlife and parks department and one of the foremost proponents of culling, told me that some temporary changes were to be expected after a round of shootings. But only temporary—he was adamant about that.

We discussed the findings of Richard Laws, who noted

groups of 1000 elephants acting like groups of ten as a result of harassment in East Africa, bunching up tightly and developing an aberrant leadership structure. Here in Zimbabwe, Rowan himself had seen small groups congregate into large groups as soon as they went outside Matusadona National Park, along the Zambezi escarpment, where they were subject to poaching and other disturbances. "Elephants know quite well where they are safe and where they are not. We did record that after culling, the elephants came to drink at waterholes only at night for a while," Rowan said. "But the herds returned to normal patterns within a matter of weeks or, at most, a few months." And physiological changes? "East Africa saw delayed puberty, an increased interval between births, poorer survival of young, and other negative impacts after culling. But we have seen no such deleterious effects here," he declared.

To some extent, the impacts of culling depend upon how efficiently the liquidation is carried out. Ideally, the cull takes a cross section of the population, so as not to skew its natural age and sex structure. A good way to do this is to remove entire family units, young and old alike. This also makes the most sense from the standpoint of keeping disruption of behavior to a minimum, insofar as dead elephants tell no tales. There must be no survivors, no wounded animals, not even badly frightened and emotionally shocked ones, to carry their fear away with them and spread it to others. The only exceptions made are for babies. Those old enough to survive without their mothers' milk, but young enough and small enough to be easily transported, may be salvaged. They are sold off to game farms, which in turn sell them to zoos, circuses, and the like.

Not long after returning from my travels with Sergeant Mlambo, I met Adrian Read, nicknamed Adie, at Hwange park headquarters. An athletic-looking man in his thirties, he ranched game, farmed crocodiles, and ran hunting safaris at the moment. But in the late 1970s and through much of the 1980s, Adie was a professional elephant terminator, culling giants for a contractor named Clem Coetzee. Since I had not been able to win permission to go along on a cull, and doubted I would in the near future, I listened closely to his description of the work.

"We got together a lot of trucks and went first to Nchebe, then to Hwange," he began, pronouncing the park's name the old Rhodesian/Afrikaaner way: Wankie. "Then we rotated our operations through the rest of the country. Hwange should hold 12,000 elephants. In 1980, it had 19,000 to 22,000. The idea was to take 4000 a year until we got them down to 12,000, and 1000 a year thereafter to take off the natural increase.

"We had one light airplane—a Super Cub. There were three hunters: a center, who is the boss man, and two flankers. Each guy had a radio for communicating with the others and with the scout plane. Each shooter had a gun bearer, too. We used .458 and .308 [*7.62 mm NATO caliber*] semiautomatics. The bearer carried a second weapon and spare ammo. It was his job to re-load while the hunter shot. Behind us came the trucks and 250 laborers for skinning and butchering.

"On a normal day, we were up at 5:00 A.M., and the pilot got up into the air soon after. If he saw a herd of more than forty, he called in, and we got ready to go to work. Less than that wasn't economical. Say the pilot saw fifty. Off we go before the day starts heating up. The pilot tells us the wind direction over the elephants. We stop our vehicles two kilometers away and walk in through the bush. Vultures learned to follow the plane, and we had to abort the mission now and again because the vultures were too thick to fly.

"The whole strategy was to get deployed so as to be able to take every single elephant. So the outlying ones have to go right off. The man in the center fires first, usually at one on the out-side. People seem to think we start with the matriarch so the oth-ers will stay around once she's down. No. Often we wouldn't see her until halfway through. But if you screw up or she gets your wind, she'll come charging, and you have to drop her quickly. The matriarch is always very big and very cheeky.

"With experienced guys, the actual killing part is incredibly quick. We got ninety-eight dead elephants in under a minute with three shooters once. If they don't bolt, you can do that. You have four rounds in the chamber. You fire three and give your gun to your bearer to reload—if you know what you're doing. Never all four. Otherwise, you turn and your bearer is gone, panicked, and you're left with an empty gun facing an elephant charge. You shoot only in the head. The animal is dead before it hits the ground. If it's running away, you have to hit the spine, then run around and shoot it in the head. Ninety percent of ours were shot in the brain."

I was still trying to imagine ninety-eight giants felled in less than sixty seconds. That was superb shooting, I told Adie. I had no idea such a thing was possible. It took scarcely longer than blowing them up with a bomb.

He elaborated. "You see, at the last second before you open up, you get the pilot to do a low-level pass and drive them toward you as you sprint in. This gives you the initial surprise. When things go right, the elephants mill. Total and utter confusion—they don't know what hit them. Just dust and shots and bodies falling down all over. We do most of the firing at just five to ten yards. Younger ones aren't keen on running away from the older ones. Our team left calves forty to fifty-five inches at the shoulder [*between about eight months and a year old*] to sell to game ranches. A lot of them went to the States.

"In the years I was culling, we got, oh, around 15,000 elephants." Roughly the number left in Kenya, I thought. "I can safely say that *one* wounded elephant got away, up around Lake Kariba. That's it. Now the strange part: If we went culling one day, we could go out the day after and shoot in the same area, because nearby elephants come over to investigate. No doubt about it, the message gets to other herds, even if you've killed every one in the first group. It's that infrasound. It has to be." Dead elephants may tell no tales, but dying ones apparently can, and over considerable distances.

"You go after a wounded calf, and even though the pilot hasn't seen another group anywhere close, the calf will run to the nearest herd. In fact, you see this sort of thing. . . ." He grabbed some paper and sketched the route of a fleeing baby elephant. The pencil started off racing aimlessly, headed more or less in the opposite direction from a large X signifying the closest live herd, ten kilometers distant. But gradually and unerringly, the pencil line arced around until it was headed straight toward that faraway herd. Infrasound. "If it got there," Adie said, "we'd often leave it alive."

So while only one wounded adult elephant got away out of 15,000, more than one live elephant did survive to perhaps pass along its experiences. "The Matetse Safari Area next to Hwange had 1500 elephants when we started culling in the park. A month later, it had 4000. Elephants definitely move out after culling. After the initial curiosity—that business of coming in to investigate a shooting site—they avoid culling areas over a long time. I think it also has something to do with elephants being more comfortable in an area with fresh elephant spoor, busted bushes, and so on. They act reluctant to venture into a range that has no smell or sign."

Rowan Martin had told me: "In culling whole clans, we were very scrupulous in some areas about removing all evidence. Not just the meat, hides, and ivory, but bones, stomachs, everything. Still, elephants came in from all over. We wondered, did they hear bullets? Smell something upwind? No, they came from every direction, 360 degrees. This was before Katie Payne's work. Now we understand about infrasonic communication. We began radio telemetry in association with culling. In some areas, we shot all except the radioed herds. We did not see any animals abandon their home range after culling." That seemed at odds with Adie's observation that herds did move out. On the other hand, when Rowan added, "Nor did they colonize empty niches right away," he perhaps confirmed Adie's impressions about herds avoiding areas that lack fresh sign.

In addition to the Zimbabwe reports of elephants coming in from all directions to investigate a killing grounds, we have an account by former Kenya warden George Adamson of elephants returning the disturbed bones and tusks of a deceased member of a herd to the place where it had originally died, as if there were something special about such a site. The thought recurs: So much death among animals so keenly aware of death.

About a century ago, Great White Hunter Gordon Cummings described an afternoon interlude as follows: "Having planted a bullet in the shoulder-bone of an elephant, and caused the agonised creature to lean for support against a tree, I proceeded to brew some coffee. Having refreshed myself, taking observations of the elephant's spasms and writhings between sips, I resolved to make experiments on vulnerable points, and approaching very near, I fired several bullets at different parts of his enormous skull. He only acknowledged the shots by salaam-like movement of his trunk, with the point of which he gently touched the wounds with a striking and peculiar action. . . . Aiming at the shoulder I fired six shots with the two-grooved rifle, which must have eventually proved mortal, after which I fired six shots at the same part with the Dutch six-pounder. Large tears now trickled down from his eyes, which he slowly shut and opened, his colossal frame quivered convulsively, and falling on his side he expired."

During culls made in Zimbabwe in 1984 and 1985, a sixty-five-year-old professor from Wyoming was given permission to spear wounded animals. He used flint-tipped Clovis points with chokecherry shafts such as Paleo-Indians carried in North America. He also tried out spears propelled with throwing sticks. Noting good penetration at twenty yards, he found that an elephant died within the hour if struck in a vital spot. The professor concluded that Clovis people could readily have brought down mammoths with the weapons of their era, reinforcing the theory that hunting by humans colonizing North America at the close of the Ice Ages combined with ecological change to bring on the extermination of mammoths and other megafauna. The very fact that this man conceived and carried out such an experiment—in the midst of other men busily expunging elephant families—gives you some interesting data about the lethal potential of our species.

"At last count, we have 23,500 elephants in Hwange, more than when I started culling," Adie pointed out. "The population has doubled in the last five years. That's too fast to be natural." The usual rate of increase among elephants is only about 3 percent annually, with a maximum of between 4 and 5 percent—the same as among humans in many tropical countries. "So a lot of the growth has been by inflow from other populations. The park plans some major culling again soon, and with its own teams.

"Park teams don't do it the way we did. They use more people. Now, having more people take part in a culling operation does not mean better or more efficient. The more you have, the higher the chance one will be shot in a crossfire in the confusion. That's why we stuck to three. Crossfire killed one of my team and wounded ten others during those years. Several more were stomped by elephants. I promise you, that was nothing compared to what you will see when the park takes over. Around 1985, a lot of people began leaving parks for other jobs. The wages were so low that they couldn't afford to stay. The culling planned for Hwange now will be done by a lot of inexperienced guys. You can count on more blood and more wounded elephants. It will be worse for tourism. Bad all around," Adie concluded.

Sergeant Mlambo was part of a park culling team during the late 1970s. "They told us to go for the lungs or just behind the eye," he said one night as we cooked *sadza*—corn meal, the local staple—over our fire in the bush. "The park rule is that if you wound an animal, you must follow it and kill it. So if you don't have a good shot, you just let it go, because if you hit it poorly, you will be tracking that animal all bloody day." The fact that men shot for the lungs means wounded animals must have escaped, since it takes a while for a lung-shot elephant to fall. Some hit in the chest area could survive their wounds altogether. The additional fact that men let elephants go when they didn't have a clear shot suggests many more survivors. This becomes an altogether messier story than that of hot-shot teams like Adrian Read's. And it suggests a much different conclusion than that culling causes only brief and limited change in elephant behavior. Especially when you consider the learning abilities and memory of this creature. After culling by professional teams took place in a part of Zimbabwe called Chizarira, elephants appeared to become badly frightened of airplanes, apparently associating them with the attacks.

This is not to argue that culling is unjustified—only that if you undertake it, you should be willing to accept the possibility that you may be creating an elephant population that becomes difficult to observe during daylight hours and no longer follows its natural routines. And if you are willing to create elephants that you rarely see, then you have to ask yourself just what it is you are preserving, especially in a park, since elephants always rank at or near the top of the list of animals tourists want to watch. Among the most popular locales in Hwange for visitors was a pan with a viewing platform not too many miles in from the park entrance. Elephants crowded into the place. They must have been doing so for as long as anyone could remember, for this waterhole's name is Nyamandhlodu, Bushman for Meat of the Elephant. A cull was carried out at this pan, and for years afterward no one ever saw an elephant there. Ever.

Sarge stuck a little spatula he had carved from a twig into the corn meal and gave it a final stir. Then he told me of how he grew up in awe of elephants, feeling that they were very powerful and that it was bad luck to kill them. His confession brought to mind Mark Butcher's description of a woman in his office—an urbanized, college-educated Ndebele woman—asking him with an embarrassed smile to please gather some elephant dung for her when he went on his next field trip. Being pregnant, she needed to make tea from it. She belonged to a clan whose totem is the elephant, and it was said that drinking elephant dung tea would help make her child strong. Most likely, there was nothing to this belief, she shrugged, but to ignore it would be unwise.

"I got used to killing them, but never in my heart," Sarge was saying. Slowly, almost unconsciously, he touched his chest with the side of the hand holding the mush-coated stick. "I still feel sorry for them." Another pause. "I hated it deep down."

Hwange ecologist Kathy Martin told me that many park employees felt that way. "It's only natural. They joined parks to save animals and enjoy nature. Then we tell them, hey, guys, your job this year is to shoot 4000 elephants for the long-term benefit of the environment." We spoke in Kathy's government quarters, continually shooing a house cat off the maps she had spread across the table. If this cat wasn't strutting through the middle of your work, it was in your lap, kneading your skin with its claws and sucking on your clothes. Its name, she informed me, was Piss Off.

The maps beneath the paws of her perfectly named puss, combined with aerial photographs, revealed areas around waterholes where elephants had reduced the percentage of certain plants. Of particular concern were Zimbabwe teak, becoming rarer throughout the rest of the country as a result of human-caused fires and excessive logging, and *Acacia erioloba*, known as camelthorn acacia.

The act of liquidating elephant families wholesale, slaughtering them faster than any poaching band, is so stunning and difficult to assimilate at an emotional level that the justification tends to be forgotten at times. Putting aside for the moment any possible long-term behavioral changes caused by culling, the argument for keeping elephants in balance with their habitat is a compelling one and needs to be examined carefully. So after a bite to eat, Kathy and I cleared the table of dishes and Piss Off and set out with her maps to survey the situation on the ground.

A great many plants that thrive in the Kalahari's miserly soils do so because they have the ability to fix nitrogen with the help of bacteria in their roots. The legume, or pea, family is particularly good at this. Camelthorn acacia is one of the largest among the tree-size legumes, and its seed pods represent some of the most concentrated protein in the plant kingdom. Better yet, the pods ripen and begin to fall from the tree during the dry season, just when other prime sources of nutrition are becoming more scarce. The giants hurry along the dropping-off process, either by grasping limbs with their trunks and shaking them or shoving up against the stout acacias with their tusks and foreheads to rock the trees. At times, the light-colored pods shower down through the branches and sunbeams and upon the elephants' backs like gold manna. While the elephants pick up pods with their trunks, baboons, kudu, impala, and common duikers come in behind them to scavenge any that were missed.

Drawing near the Dopi Pan, we found a band of big bulls under the acacias, alternately resting in the trees' shade and making them tremble to produce another rain of pods. The largest trees looked robust enough, but it was plain that the smaller ones had been smashed and greatly thinned out. Kathy said the cause was elephants stripping their bark for additional nutrients as they moved to and from the waterhole during the dry season—a scenario much the same as along the banks of the Chobe River. But once again the question was: What is normal? What is the vegetation around a heavily used waterhole supposed to look like?

Kathy pointed out that when elephants thin teak and acacia, more sunlight reaches the ground, resulting in more grass growth. More grass means that fires carry more readily, which opens the area further by knocking back woody shrubs. This phenomenon is part of the elephant's time-honored role in opening up woodlands and transforming segments of them to savanna. Zimbabwe is far enough from the equator that a secondary effect—frost—kicks in, accelerating the rate of change. The more open the area, the more subject invading woody plants are to leaf-killing cold. Thus, once a grassland develops, it is maintained by both fire and frost, and the woodland is lost.

How permanently? Good question. Kathy had documented the exact opposite effect in some places, too. She found elephants and herds of fellow grazers eating down the grass until there was no longer enough ground fuel to carry natural fires. As a result, woody brush was encroaching upon once-grassy vleis and other savanna openings. Was this a counterbalance or a double cause for concern?

Zimbabwe has chosen a density of 0.8 elephants per square kilometer (about two per square mile) as the maximum the land can support without damage. Beyond that magic number, culling is called for. Yet as Kathy explained it, the same number of elephants can affect different sites to different degrees. For example, in shallow soils underlain by calcrete or hard basalt, plants are not able to develop extensive root systems for storing water and nutrients. Most of their mass is therefore above ground and vulnerable to overuse. By contrast, as much as 80 biomass is below the surface in the deep Kalahari sands. "So what if an elephant breaks down a bush?" Kathy asked. "When four-fifths of it lies underground, it can regenerate easily."

The issue circles back to how much fluctuation is natural. More plant species than we realize may be adapted to periodic overuse, drought, fire, and other "catastrophes" that transform habitats. Put another way, perhaps the greatest diversity in a wildlife community is achieved when it is able to undergo drastic natural change, not when it is carefully sheltered.

Rowan Martin was well aware of the problem and told me, "Some of our colleagues ask, if you hold elephants at a constant level, aren't you fixing at stasis a dynamic ecosystem, locking it up in one stage of what should be a cyclical pattern? Unless you let ecosystems swing through dramatic ups and downs, you lose resiliency. Or do you? Should you manage tightly or allow build-ups and crashes? Is our job to fix things? Or manage for the process?" He was organizing an international symposium around those kinds of questions.

Rowan had more of them: "Are we caught up in an image of pristine Africa?" he inquired. "People elsewhere are fed so many images of wild Africa, they don't realize we hardly have a single truly pristine area left on the continent and certainly not in Zimbabwe. So we have to manage. But do we manage for what elephants need or what pleases people? I myself prefer a nice acacia forest with a few elephants over an elephant-blasted landscape, and I'm prepared to knock a few elephants on the head to achieve it. All life is an experiment. You set up management so you learn from it and keep modifying and tinkering."

Across the philosophical gulf stand those who would say that the goal is not to manage but to accept, appreciate, celebrate, revere, and, above all, simply let nature be. But are the workings of nature anywhere still far enough removed from our influence that we can just sit back and learn and let it be? Rowan was right about there being no truly pristine area left in Zimbabwe. Big as it is, Hwange National Park is nowhere near being an ecosystem complete unto itself. Before artificial waterholes and veterinary fences changed movement patterns, Hwange was merely a small part of an immense regional flow of moisture, nutrients, and migrating creatures. It supported very few elephants during the dry season. Now it hosts many thousands year-round. Hence, Rowan's question: "Aren't we mining out certain trees, grass, and mineral resources trying to keep permanent populations in places like Hwange?"

My question: What alternatives are there to holding elephants in reserves and periodically culling them? Contraception is one. With present technology, it would require the equivalent of culling teams with dart guns, tranquilizing females so that long-term birth control drugs could be implanted beneath their skin. This would be awfully time-consuming and awfully expensive for a developing nation to undertake, which is probably why no one in Zimbabwe seemed to be considering it. Of course, culling is difficult and costly, too, but it yields meat, hides, and ivory, which more than make up for the expense. At least, they used to. Zimbabwe has complained mightily that the end of profits from ivory sales has taken away a vital source of income used to fund other important wildlife management projects.

South Africa makes the same argument. In Kruger National Park, which is entirely fenced, managers cull to keep the elephant population stable at 6000 to 8000 and, prior to the ivory bans, plowed the money back into conservation. Culling is done with lethal drugs fired from dart guns by teams in helicopters. The chemical compounds used paralyze the animals so that they cease being able to breathe and essentially suffocate while wide awake. Even Zimbabwe biologists who strongly favor culling told me they found this technique distasteful. I wonder why they can't dart the animals to implant contraceptives instead.

South Africa has one other noteworthy elephant population that escaped extermination by Boer colonists. In the eastern Cape province, a small group of elephants holed up in a stretch of dense evergreen thicket called the Addo bush. Around the turn of the century, they still numbered around 120. Since they still emerged to raid fields from time to time, the local farmers and citrus growers called in professional hunter Major P. J. Pretorius to exterminate them. He spent eleven months trying and almost succeeded. By 1916, the Addo thickets sheltered no more than sixteen animals. Roads, railroad lines, and fences increasingly confined them even as the population bounced back a bit. Because they had no water in their evergreen refuge and little food, they had to keep raiding to live. And the locals kept trying to wipe them out.

Finally, the government had a change of heart. In 1931, Addo was declared a park. Eleven elephants were left. They still got nailed when they stepped outside the confines of their tiny refuge to eat and drink. From 1943 to 1953, eight calves were born and eight elephants were shot. In 1954, the government built an elephant-proof fence around 5440 acres, using cable strung along posts made of railway tracks. Confined within their refuge and provided with artificial water sources, the elephants increased. Yet as they did, they began to destroy the vegetation that had sheltered them for so long. The park extended the fence at considerable cost, incorporating an area of 19,800 acres. The population increased to 150 elephants.

However, 150 elephants remains well below a minimum viable population level. The Addo elephants are sometimes considered a different subspecies, or at least a separate ecotype, being distinctly small in stature with small tusks. They and another remnant group—this one a bare handful of animals—at Knysna are now more than 1000 miles from the next nearest elephant population, and completely cut off. If these elephants are not already genetically different from others, they soon will be as a result of their isolation and inbreeding. And yet this inadequate population of 150 elephants within its expanded reserve is once again destroying the vegetation, eating itself out of house and home.

Which brings us back to the serious problems of maintaining giants within reserves and the question of alternatives to culling. Fittingly, Zimbabwe, the most enthusiastic practitioner of culling, also offers one of the best ways out of the bind. It involves reestablishing large-scale migration patterns. This is done by expanding habitat through game ranching on private and communal, or tribal, lands around reserves. When property owners used to raise livestock, they rushed to erect fences between their acreage and parks and were quick to kill any wildlife that crossed through. Lately, they have been taking down their fences to allow more wildlife in since it is the stock they wish to raise now. As a result, Zimbabwe is one of the very few places in the world where wildlife range is actually increasing.

The situation around Hwange is a prime example, which is why I chose to focus upon this area. If enough communal lands join existing game ranches as wildlife areas here, elephants could regain their old dry-season migration route north from Hwange toward the Zambezi River on the border with Zambia. And as Hwange is already connected to good elephant range in Botswana, this could revitalize the workings of the original ecosystem on a vast scale, with Hwange once again serving primarily as seasonal range, no longer relied upon to function as permanent homeland for a confined population.

I went to spend more time under the tutelage of Mark Butcher. "Damn, boy, you're back on the very cutting edge of elephant conservation now," he pronounced. I couldn't hear him well, as he was lying beneath his ancient Land Cruiser, trying to repair a blown gasket. I soon discovered that this was usually when he talked about my great luck in being on the leading edge of elephant conservation—while we were broken down in one of his rigs.

It happened every time we went on a jolly runabout, and only in part because Butch thought nothing of driving along bumpy bush roads from before sunrise until well after dark. The other reasons were, first, that he never went anywhere slowly if he could help it, and, second, that most of the bush vehicles in Zimbabwe had already long since fallen apart and were patched together with scrap metal and blind optimism. Zimbabwe is one of those nations that manufactures very little itself but places forbiddingly high tariffs on imports of manufactured goods in order to keep capital from flooding out of the country. With duties, the average four-wheel-drive vehicle in Zimbabwe costs much more than a Mercedes luxury sedan in the United States, and parts are so scarce that most people who rely upon automobiles in the bush have learned to construct almost every moving piece from scratch.

One night, after we had crept along for hours in the darkness, whacking our way through brush with machetes to get the Land Cruiser back onto at least a game trail, hungry (our last meal had consisted of the meat of walnutlike seeds picked out of dry elephant dung), cold—I had been riding with some trackers in the open back of the vehicle under chilly skies for nearly sixteen hours on and off—and completely lost, I asked Butch if it might be possible for me to get the hell off the cutting edge of elephant conservation. He replied, "Not a chance. Once you're on, you stay on. It's a $%#@&*! toboggan ride to glory."

"We have 15 percent more wildlife range in Matabeleland North than we had a decade ago," he observed later, in a more serious vein. "Cattle are being moved out, wildlife moves in, and I can't say enough about what a pleasant change that is." What he meant is that cattle relentlessly graze and trample Zimbabwe's arid habitats to near-desert, lowering the fertility of the land until it cannot carry nearly as many creatures as before, domestic or wild. It is not that cows are inherently much worse than the native grazers. The problem is that, unless they are herded by nomadic pastoralists, cattle are restricted by fences from being able to migrate, and the usual densities at which their owners stock them amount to overcrowding. Consequently, cattle can only do what wild species do when they increase to high levels within a confined area: they hammer the environment. Since cattle need water more regularly than native stock does, they are particularly hard on vegetation around waterholes, streams, and lake shores. The kind of damage considered as justification for culling wildlife is something cattle cause as a matter of course.

As we passed the Gwayi River, Butch told me of floating along it twenty years earlier, fishing with his father; of how he could watch the lure sink down twenty feet deep in clear water. Today, the Gwayi is a foot or two deep in most places, and brown and thick, silted up as a result of overgrazing by cattle and intensive farming upstream.

The bird seen clambering up and down the towering necks of

giraffes or perched on the backs of buffalo and dozens of other kinds of large, hooved animals is an oxpecker. One of them eats hundreds of ticks per day off those wild hides. In many areas, ticks are so prevalent that cattle must be dipped in pesticide solutions every couple of weeks. This gets rid of the ticks, all right, but it also kills off populations of oxpeckers, which eat the poisoned ticks. The next thing you find is wildlife infested with the parasites—buffalo so laden that parts of their ears fall off, wildebeest racing aimlessly while shaking their heads, driven half-mad by the swollen ticks clinging inside their ear canal.

Another, more predictable effect of raising cattle is that their owners tend to wage constant war against predators, since the domesticated beasts have lost nearly all their own defenses. Wild hunting dogs have become extremely rare in Zimbabwe as a result of eradication programs to benefit livestock. A lot of ranchers kill baboons on sight, partly because they just don't like them but also because they occasionally bother stock. Butch told me of a rancher with land next to Hwange who once killed 107 lions in one year.

"He also shot elephants, zebra—anything that competed with his stock or was a possible source of disease," Butch said. "He thought wildlife wardens were in the enemy camp. Then the same guy saw the light and turned his ranch into a safari hunting area. He was one of the very first in the region."

This man's name is Buck DeVries. I met him at a little town along the road. Like half the people I met on the road in Zimbabwe, he offered me an elbow or wrist to shake, because he had so much grease on his hands from car repair. Buck was at work on a Land Cruiser more dilapidated than Butch's. People who raise livestock, regardless of their race or culture, are generally fairly conservative and resistant to change. Buck was no exception. Once he decided to make the move from cattle to game, he still had to deal with his neighbors. "Other ranchers—ah, that was the problem," he grunted, as he leaned under the hood to adjust a valve. "They were angry with me. Thought I was a traitor. One threatened to personally shoot me if his cattle got disease from my buffalo or kudu. We had broken fences, angry words at meetings, lawyers. . . . Aye, there were threats on my life then," he said.

Buck did not look to me like a man you would want to threaten to his face. A stocky, indestructible-looking Afrikaner, he had hands that could tighten a bolt on the car just about as snugly as a wrench could in someone else's hands. Hard work was something he embraced. Even so, it took a while to build up his new business.

"I used to do hunts for elephants; twenty-eight-day safaris, I'd lead, and I'd take my pay in weapons. For one hunt, I took a .44 magnum Smith & Wesson; for another, a repeating shotgun." But as the years went by, Buck started to farm a healthy profit from his hunting clients. In between safaris, he could always shoot abundant impala and other game to sell the meat.

I asked how many of those who formerly opposed him have since turned to game ranching.

"Every one of them. Every bloody one. Before, they wanted to kill me. Now, they've got big meetings all over the place to take the fences DOWN! Once you make money on it, it's automatic: you take good care of the game," he replied. "We lost 150, 160 head of cattle every year to lion. If we were still in cattle, we couldn't make any money at all. Especially not here so close by a park. I tell you, there's no comparison."

"Amazing how things have changed in twenty years, actually," added Buck's son, Penny, also working on the vehicle. "We've got photo safaris as well now, turning $100,000 Zimbabwe (around U.S. $40,000) per month. It's already more than we make from hunting safaris, I reckon. We've got all these new camps going up, and they're booked full already."

"Yop. Pictures make more for us than hunting now," Buck affirmed. "There's a very big demand for photo safaris. But the hunting, aye, it's the way to keep track of snares and poachers. You cover the ground the best way possible when you're hunting."

"Now we're thinking about ostrich farming, too," Penny said.

Another aspect of their business has been buying and selling baby elephants. Many an infant saved from culls on government land such as Hwange went to the DeVries ranch. "We were exporting elephants all over the world for a while," Buck informed me. "I'd bet 80 percent of the African elephants you'll find in the U.S. today came from my place here. We've had little babies raised in the house. You go under a car to fix it, the little bugger would come and lie down beside you." In Zimbabwe, even elephants get involved in auto mechanics. "A two-and-a-half-year-old elephant; we sell it for $6,000 Zimbabwe. Some get too big to fit into a crate. Those we just turn loose on the land and let them go off to join wild herds. And we end up with more elephants to hunt."

Near Buck's place is a ranch owned by Maxie and Deon Steffen, who switched over to game farming and safari work in the mid-1980s. Butch and I originally made our way to their spread because Butch knew they had a large garage with welding gear, and we needed serious equipment to salvage our car radiator. Maxie made us stay for lunch and served spicy strips of dried meat—jerky, or *biltong*, made from buffalo.

"A neighbor lost 147 cows since the start of the dry season," she said. "Crocs, wild dogs, cheetahs, lions, hyena. . . . Hard country on cows. With stock, you've also got the expense of hiring a full-time manager. And the cost to build and repair fences. And dip the cattle every two weeks in tick time. It's just so much easier with game, as well as more profitable. And more fun. We're not as tied to ranch management anymore. No handling, no veterinarian bills. You can't drive the game from pasture to pasture or between waterholes. You don't have to. The game looks after itself. We put out salt and water, and that's it. Well, except you have to do poaching patrols now and then. We had overgrazed the vlei with cattle. It came back in just four years. It's a nicer way of life now for me. We go for a drive in the evening, see kudu, wart hog, eland, maybe a waterbuck. I'd much rather see that than a bunch of cattle."

Maxie and Deon, who is the chief safari guide, offer hunts of fifteen, eighteen, or twenty-one days, mostly for "plains game," which is safari hunter talk for trophy antelope such as sable and roan, along with wildebeest, zebras, and the like. "For leopard, elephant, buffalo, we shoot on other ranches—sort of 'borrow' an animal from a neighbor. Then they can come bring clients on our place for plains game. We swap hunts," Maxie said. "A lot of game ranchers do that sort of thing now."

On the other hand, neighbors can be a problem if they take more than their share of animals. When their land lies between yours and a prime game reservoir such as a park, this can effectively cut off your supply. To counter the tendency of some owners to claim too much of a common resource, the wildlife department divided regions into intensive conservation areas, or ICAs. They then placed all the private landowners within each ICA on a board that sets quotas on how many of each hunted species may be taken (subject to approval by the wildlife department).

"It's enforced neighborliness," Butch smiled. "You put people's self-interest to work. They're going to police themselves, not because it's good for conservation but because if the other guy gets too greedy, it means money coming out of their pocket. The biggest obstacle is to get ranchers to appreciate how few trophy animals you can cull before you begin to change the natural age and sex structure. They're used to thinking cows: 'Well, I used to sell off 40 percent from my cattle herd every year without hurting it. I can take at least 10 percent of the elephants.' We set the harvest at about one-half to three-quarters of 1 percent of the sexually mature bull elephants. That's it, except for a few adult females here and there, and most hunters don't want a female anyway."

Three-quarters of 1 percent is not very many elephants. But then safari outfits generally charge anywhere from U.S. $750 to $1000 per day for a hunt, with a minimum of twenty-one days. On top of that, the government charges a trophy fee of U.S. $4500—and even more for the biggest tuskers. Most hunters who come after an elephant take plains game as well, if only for something to bag while they wait for their giant. And many are intent upon bagging a lion, leopard, and buffalo along with their elephant, for these together make up the much-venerated Big

Four. (It used to be the Big Five, but the fifth species, the rhino, is out of the equation, with both black and white rhinoceroses critically endangered.)

By the time a hunter adds trophy fees for the Big Four or plains game to the cost for an elephant, the price of a hunt is nearing U.S. $50,000. And that doesn't include air fare, other travel expenses, or tips to the guide and hunting camp attendants. Nor the U.S. $100 per day to a video camera operator, who has become a regular part of trophy safaris nowadays. Nor does it add in the cost of mounting the head, roughly another U.S. $5000 for an elephant. And more thousands for mounting any other trophies shot. Plus shipping charges to the hunter's home country.

Astonishing, the expense some people will bear to put a head on the wall. For that kind of money, you could save a lot of wildlife habitat, couldn't you? Yes, Butch would answer. That is precisely the point. Saving wildlife habitat is what we're doing by encouraging safari hunting. Those guys aren't going to donate the money to conservation. They want something; we give it to them. In fact, Butch himself oversees organized commercial shooting safaris on Forestry lands.

"Elephant safaris are 35 percent of my earnings for Forestry," Butch argued. "If I lost elephants, I'd lose that much in management funds. In practical terms, it would mean closing down one in three forests for want of manpower, vehicles, and equipment. And that would be a death sentence for those areas. Many of our communal lands are badly overpopulated. New generations are without a place of their own. They go to traditional game waterholes on forest lands and clear the woods for crops, bring in cattle, and start subsistence poaching. A lot of it is with snares, and a lot is with dogs to run down the game. Soon, crops fail because the soil is used up, and the cattle are in poor shape because of overgrazing. The people turn to commercial poaching. . . ."

On a poaching patrol through one forest reserve we visited in the Tjolotjo District, Butch's staff had come upon a new settlement in which the squatters had already established clearings and were just in the process of throwing up shacks. Butch kicked them out but said that if they had been much farther along, they might have been able to appeal to the government and win permission to convert that part of the forest to communal lands. Squatters' committees had been fairly successful at gaining state land that way, just as I had seen in Thailand. "They are young, landless families. What are they supposed to do? Hell, man, you or I would do the same in their circumstances. So what are we supposed to do as conservationists?" asked Butch.

Rancher Maxie Steffens had told me, "There are squatters everywhere. The government keeps opening new areas of forest and other state land for them to take off the pressure, but it doesn't last long. You put people in, they'll cut all the trees and graze it to dust. Then they'll say, 'Look at this crap land you gave us. We need more.' And they'll gradually take over the state land. One day, they'll get the private land, too. The government makes rumblings about breaking up private ranches every so often. That is our greatest fear." (In spring of 1992, with Zimbabwe in the grip of a devastating drought and its economy in a tailspin, President Mugabe, hoping to fend off growing political discontent, declared that half the privately owned ranches in the country would be confiscated and turned into communal lands.)

I had seen lands opened to communal settlement just a few years earlier. Maxie was right; they already looked like moonscapes. Dust and weeds and scattered flocks of grazing goats were all that was left of Kalahari forest once rich in game. And here was Butch, dispatching Forestry wardens to race through the bush, trying to spot squatters before they got too much of a toehold and repeated the process in a new stretch of forest. Clearly, this was not a prescription for long-term ecological stability. Instead, it was a classic people-versus-wildlife confrontation, even though both would share in the consequences of land abuse. Wildlife would be impoverished first. As the vitality of the support system drained away, the impoverishment of people would inevitably follow.

Before he rose in the bureaucracy to become head of the regional Forestry Commission's wildlife management arm, Butch spent a good deal of time leading antipoaching patrols. "Our high point man has shaya-ed nineteen poachers," he told me. "I sometimes arrested thirty or forty a month. One year, honest to God, I caught more than 350 poachers. Makes you wonder how many are really running around out there. About one in fifty elephants in the Zambezi Valley when I worked there bore signs of snares—inflamed and injured feet, ruined trunks, or at least scars on their feet or trunk. A lot of baby elephants die in snares.

"Conservation through the barrel of a gun—strong patrolling and enforcement—is fine if you combine it with good, full-time management," he said. "But it's still only a holding action. Rear-guard stuff. What happens as the population keeps increasing? You've just got more and more angry squatters. Most of the people in this country are communal farmers and herders who see elephants as dangerous pests and a hindrance to development. If they don't want elephants around, we won't have them in the future. If they do, we will. It's that simple. The question is how to help them understand the value of wildlife.

"You know, not very long ago, I'm out in this village, and eles have raided the fields, and I've got a grandma shrieking at me, 'Butch, my children and grandchildren are all going to starve and die because of your elephants.' She was casting witchcraft spells and cursing and warning of black magic. I've been yelled at and seen plenty of grief, but I tell you, man, my blood ran cold."

Not far from where that scene took place, we were backtracking elephants from fields of melons and sorghum, or millet, on communal land. We followed the trespassing elephants' spoor to water, where it intersected human spoor, which in turn led on to wells and gardens put in illegally by squatters on Forestry land. Soon, we were hiking by people who were trespassing openly on this government acreage. All we did was wave at them; it was too late to run anyone off.

Another day, I walked some distance along a dusty road and then down village trails to a tiny waterhole in an otherwise dry riverbed. I was seeking water for our rig's radiator, which had burst again. Upon leaving, I'd told Butch I thought it would be wonderful if, here on the cutting edge of elephant conservation, we saw elephants at least as often as the underside of vehicles. "Be fair now," he shot back. "We don't spend more than a third of our time being mechanics. The rest of the day, we're free to do whatever we like. Like hunt up parts." On my way back from the waterhole, I took a shortcut and ended up traipsing through fields with squashed melons all over them. I thought it looked like the work of elephants. I wasn't positive, though, because we were quite a ways from the nearest protected area. But as I neared a cluster of thatched huts, I saw unmistakable prints in the dirt.

George Nkube came out of his house and saw me studying the tracks. He directed my attention to others no more than forty-five feet from his front door. "They came in and took every melon," he said. "Then they ate a huge field of millet. They jump the fence and eat everything. We have to stay up all night screaming at them." Who? I asked. "Bulls. Big bulls. They step right over the fences and come wherever they please." The tracks confirmed it. Butch had told me that elephants were moving this way, headed north from Hwange toward the permanent pools of the Gwayi River, as in the old days. Females and young still had trouble negotiating the high, cable-strung veterinary fences designed to deter buffalo, but there were fewer fences than before. As for bulls, they roamed more or less freely throughout much of this region north of Hwange Park, expanding their range.

Dusk was settling over the dry countryside. George Nkube accompanied me along the path back toward Butch and the car. Across the sandy riverbed, drums started up. They were to frighten the elephants away for the night, George said. Farther on, he asked how many were in my family. One wife, two children, I replied. Oh. He tried to act impressed but failed. "For me, sixteen children, four wives," he announced, then returned to the subject of elephants. "They come in and wreck all our work. The government should control these marauders. Where is the help?"

Butch was waiting back under the car, blowing on a little fire built to speed up the drying of epoxy glue that we tried as a radiator patch. (We didn't think it would work, and it didn't.) After George left, Butch pointed out that the village and fields being raided were illegally put on Forestry land during 1983 and 1984. He didn't know what the right way was to deal with these particular squatters and their elephant problems. But he knew the best way to encourage a positive view of wildlife among local people: make it more profitable than anything else—more profitable than melons or millet, and more profitable than poaching.

In practical terms, the solution was to extend the safari program from private ranches and government lands to communal lands. This was not a simple step, for while private landholders had control over the wildlife within their property, the state retained ownership of the game on communal lands. However, the Ministry of Environment and Tourism could now delegate some authority over wildlife to a communal area, provided that its representatives came up with a sound plan for managing native animals.

This change in the law was prompted by advocates of a community action program called CAMPFIRE. Years ago, a Zimbabwean named Simon Metcalfe was seeking ways to funnel help toward rural communities in need of everything from medical clinics to better water supplies when he hit upon the idea of tapping the safari hunters who came to shoot in the area. According to Rob Monroe of the Zimbabwe Trust, an organization that assists rural development, the effort was somewhat patronizing at first. The safari outfits merely donated some money along with meat from the animals they took. But with the help of the Trust and guidance from the wildlife department, the CAMPFIRE concept evolved to put money directly in the hands of the locals in return for their participation in conservation. Instead of vanishing into the national treasury, revenues from hunting concessions stayed in each district. Now that they had the authority to negotiate directly with safari interests, it was to the locals' advantage to have good wildlife herds to offer.

"Now," Rob told me, "the local councils can say, 'Hey, if you want elephants, we've got them, but what will you do for us? Help with problem animals? How about handling international tourism contracts? We don't yet have the experience to market abroad. Show us how it's done.' Being responsible for wildlife, they have to learn to monitor populations, train scouts, and so forth. It's a big responsibility for communal areas, but there are also substantial profits to be made. And not just through safari hunting. You've got crocodile farming, photo safaris and lodges, birdwatching trips, you name it. The Zimbabwe Trust can help CAMPFIRE areas get capitalized. We give them money for vehicles and rangers to start off. Otherwise, the first few years' profits would be eaten up getting going, and people wouldn't be able to see the direct benefit of conserving wildlife."

In one ward of the Nyaminyami District in northern Zimbabwe, CAMPFIRE money from leasing just a couple of safari concessions helped build a hospital and put $200 Zimbabwe in the pockets of each household—in a country where the average annual income is only about twice that. "Lord, I wish I'd had a hundred reporters there when we handed out those checks," Rowan Martin told me. "This was a first in the history of Africa. We're decentralizing wildlife management to get the control and the revenues out there to the local level.

"I'd be surprised if we had 5000 elephants left here in Zimbabwe at the end of the last century," Rowan continued. "Now we've got 61,000 or so. Out of that, we killed 172 elephants for trophies this year—seventy-two from communal lands and the rest from state lands. And every one generated a minimum of U.S. $25,000. We're trying to handle what amounts to a burgeoning business in wildlife. We have guys buying and selling elephants, like in Asia. Elephant middlemen. We have a real growth rate of 39 percent per annum in the wildlife industry here. Within five years, it will be the biggest producer in the country. In fact, the minister of Agriculture is getting worried about cows. The irony is that cows yield the government minus seven dollars per square kilometer. They lose money all the way. It's a total subsidy.

"It was considered incompatible to have elephants and agriculture. Impossible, they said. Yet now we're seeing an increase of elephants in agricultural areas. This is because twenty years ago elephants were restricted to the periphery of the country, and now we're getting some back in the center as agricultural lands convert to wildlife ranching. People may also want elephants around to help keep brush from encroaching too heavily in cattle-grazing country." Especially as brushy cover is where tsetse flies thrive.

"An old man approached me and said a spirit medium came to him in a dream and told him the future is not in cattle; it's in wildlife. Of course, this was not long after we distributed that check for $200 Zimbabwe per household. A lot of local politicians from other wards and districts suddenly got interested, too."

🙂🙂🙂🙂🙂🙂🙂🙂🙂🙂🙂🙂

Rowan Martin and Rob Monroe are enthusiastic spokesmen for CAMPFIRE. Mark Butcher is perhaps even better, since he speaks from the front lines. I quoted these men at some length to give them a fair forum. I liked them. I liked the principle of local autonomy over wildlife. And I wanted badly to believe in some positive, workable way out of the worldwide elephant crisis. For all those reasons, I had to be careful and bear in mind that the emphasis on CAMPFIRE was partly propaganda, rather hastily cobbled together in response to the attacks on Zimbabwe's adamant pro-ivory, pro–elephant-hunting stance.

One moment, Zimbabwe was simply a great place for trophy hunters to shoot themselves a giant. The next moment, the Zimbabwe safari industry was a caring community of white people devoted to improving native communities while saving species. Zimbabwe had even flown some headmen from the Nyaminyami district to the CITES meeting in Lausanne, Switzerland, to sing the glories of CAMPFIRE. Many in the audience shared the impression that these men had been schooled in what to say. Some Zimbabwe broadsides gave the suggestion that CAMP-FIRE was an effective nationwide program. The fact was that

Nyaminyami was one of only two local communities that had subscribed to CAMPFIRE before I visited. Nine more were in the process, I was told, though it seemed the arrangement had been urged upon them so quickly that they were still unclear about the implications.

Still, any new program needs time to get up and running, and there was no denying the soundness of the concept. If you found safari hunting objectionable, you could console yourself with the hope that the communal areas would go the way of many private game ranches and gradually replace the quest for trophies with the quest for good photographs and similar natural history pursuits—nonconsumptive uses of wildlife, as the managers say.

So that I might see the responses of local people to CAMP-FIRE for myself, I was invited along on a kind of proselytizing safari in which Julian Trent and Alan Sparrow, both of the Zimbabwe Trust, joined Mark Butcher for a series of meetings with representatives from communal lands to outline the program. I was eager to join. I had gone one afternoon to speak with a headman in the Tjolotjo District, portions of which had recently adopted CAMPFIRE, but the most coherent thing he muttered was that I should come back when he was not so drunk.

The first stop for our group was at Sijarira, a safari lodge owned and operated by the Forestry Commission on the shores of Lake Kariba, one of the most beautiful settings in the nation. The camp was run by a hospitable wildlife specialist named Rich Aylwood. Like Mike Jones, a government ecologist I had met only days earlier, Rich got about on one good leg, having lost the other to a mine during the war for independence.

As we waited for men from the local Binga District to arrive, Alan Sparrow said, "We thought it would take generations to change local attitudes about wildlife. We assumed people were culturally attached to livestock and to the prestige of owning herds and so on. As it turns out, people get the idea overnight if they see revenue possibilities. It's the bureaucrats who are the obstacle. They are the most resistant to change, because they stand to lose their centralized power and authority as wildlife goes to the villages. The toughest job of all is to get decision-making powers down to the ward and family levels—to those most affected by wildlife."

The first to reach our retreat were Mr. J. P. Muleya, chairman of the Binga District council, and Isaac Zhou. (*Zhou* means elephant in Shona.) After another carload arrived and we made small talk over barbecue lunch, Rich, Alan, and Julian led the way to a display of skulls. They were of rhino, buffalo, and other beasts, and they were laid out alongside yards and yards of rusty coiled cable.

Here were the snares wardens had confiscated in the district. As an aside, Rich told me he had so many that he used them as reinforcement in the concrete poured for buildings here and at the Forestry crocodile farm next door. In a single snare line, he told the group, he had found a young male elephant, a kudu, a zebra, and a buffalo. All flyblown, all worthless as meat. Just dead. Useful to no one. The young bull didn't even have any tusks to speak of.

Alan whispered to me about seeing elephants with ruined trunks drink by kneeling to lap at the water and feed by kneeling to coil their stump around grass. Leaving me with this image of giants brought to their knees, he stepped forward and addressed the group. Taking over from Rich, Alan stood above the skulls and explained the value—per day—of such animals to a safari hunter. And the trophy fees. And other money that would be spent by trophy seekers. And how much of this could go straight back into the community.

Eyes that had been slightly glazed during introductory speechifying started to widen. "I'm saying this buffalo could have been taken by a hunter who would pay several thousand dollars," Alan reiterated. Eyes grew wider. "This kudu and zebra, thousands more for each one. And you can even have the meat! These hunters come all the way from across the seas and usually just want the head." Jaws dropped. "And this elephant bull, when he grew bigger, some hunters would pay 25,000 U.S. dollars to go after one." Strange sounds began to rise from the chests of the men from Binga. They had just been told that safari hunters would pay a minimum of fifty to a hundred years' worth of annual income in Zimbabwe to come and shoot an elephant and take back its head. It was a truly stupefying fact.

I heard the same spiel from Alan and Butch later on at a different Forestry safari camp not far from Hwange National Park. This time, a tall, straight-backed man with silver hair looked on, saying little, measuring much. It was Chief Hwange; the park had been created from part of his father's tribal land. Tapping a traditional carved staff of authority—often made of ivory— against his palm, he gave me his thoughts: "For a long time, the government told us that wildlife was their resource. But I see how live animals can be *our* resource. *Our* wealth. *Our* way to improve the standard of living without waiting for the government to decide things. From this point of view, a poacher is only stealing from us." He tapped his staff again, pondered, and continued: "All good things start with problems. If our forefathers guide me, my task now is to bring this message to the people."

That was what the representatives of Binga had said, if not quite so nobly: take the message that these animals have value for all and bring it down to the people. Down from the government, down from the bureaucrats, down from the politicians, and on to the people. These council members got the concept; no question about it. If some of them seemed even more interested in the Zimbabwe Trust's promise of a vehicle for their organization, that was understandable.

Joshua Munsaka, Siabuwa District chairman of the National Farmers Council, voiced his concern about crop damage from elephants. Butch countered that a farmer's share from safari hunting would far exceed the value of any patch of melons or bananas, and that CAMPFIRE money had been used elsewhere to compensate people for such losses. My impression was that selling CAMPFIRE was going to take repeated discussions of this sort, in part because the district people didn't quite believe that they were going to be given true autonomy over their wildlife resource. They had not enjoyed such a thing in recent memory. For that matter, although they could sell safari concessions under CAMPFIRE, they were still not allowed to hunt on their own lands themselves. Perhaps that right would come before long, once more trust was built on each side.

In the evening, Rich ran us out in a powerboat past hippos and crocs and goliath herons to Kangamani Island, where we saw three bulls feeding on the tall and tasty torpedo grass (*Panicum repens*) that flourishes along the lake shore. The bulls had swum out from the mainland. The distance is six-tenths of a mile; the swimming time for an elephant, about 2.5 to 3 hours, snorkeling along with eyes submerged and only the top of the head and the scent-seeking trunk showing above the surface.

Rich said elephants used to cross the Zambezi River at this point before the dam backed up the waters to form Lake Kariba. These days, the bulls were probably swimming to the island in order to escape safari hunting and perhaps poaching on the mainland. He had seen elephants swim easily for twenty-four hours at a stretch. Asian elephants have been reported swimming in the Ganges Delta for more like thirty-six straight hours. Another interesting fact is that the sight of big bulls on this island hide-out so inspired one American hunter that he tried to buy it from the government.

Hwange bulls are fairly long-legged with short, heavy tusks. These Zambezi bulls were markedly different, having shorter legs and comparatively long, thin tusks. This ecotype was more common across the lake on the Zambian shore and on into Zambia's Luangwa Valley, a tremendously rich wildlife area now depleted of elephants and rhinos by poachers.

In search of new booty, the Zambian poachers had moved on to Zimbabwe. They came across the lake in gangs as large as fifty to a hundred and then dispersed in smaller bands to make circuits as far south as Hwange, sometimes farther. They rendezvoused back at the lake shore to meet pickup boats. Not everyone made it at the appointed time. Zimbabwe fishermen had to haul their boats up and tie them to their houses at night to keep the Zambian stragglers from stealing them for return trips. Bandits pilfered one of Rich Aylwood's boats from right by the lodge.

"These Zambian rhino poachers are $%#@*&! bad news, man. We're shooting one out of every ten of the buggers, and still they keep coming," Butch marveled. Zimbabwe has lost

close to 1000 rhinos since 1985. The country has proudly
pointed out that it holds two-thirds of the black rhinos left in Africa. But two-thirds of all Africa's black rhinos comes to less
than a couple of thousand animals now. Two decades ago, Africa
had an estimated 65,000. No one seems able to stop the killing.
In 1992, Zimbabwe was forced to follow the lead of areas in Namibia and begin sawing off the horns of the last rhinos in the
hope that poachers will pass them by.

(In South Africa's Pilanesberg Game Reserve, tourists can go
on rhino safaris in which they pay for the privilege of bagging a
rhino with a tranquilizer dart. Scientists then insert a microchip
in the horn that enables customs officers to detect it if the animal
is killed and someone tries to smuggle the horn out of the country. Possibly, similar darting safaris will take place in the future
to saw off elephants' tusks, the way people now do in Southeast
Asia, or at least tag them with microchips.)

Sawing off rhino horns seems to me an admission that Zimbabwe cannot control poaching within its borders, despite its
insistence—and during the battle over whether to place the African elephant on Appendix I or II of CITES, Zimbabwe insisted loud and long—that it could. Nevertheless, Zimbabwe
wildlife managers say that they are dehorning rhinos only because they are prevented from going about conservation their
way. If the rhino hadn't been declared endangered and all trade
in horn stopped, Zimbabwe could sell a few rhino hunts and
raise enough money from sportsmen to save the rest, for there
are hunters who would pay almost any sum to shoot the fifth of
the Big Five. And if Zimbabwe could sell off its stocks of rhino
horns, taken from poachers and in dehorning operations, it
could raise enough money to buy even more protection. The
same goes for ivory, they say. Others are equally convinced that
to encourage any market, legal or otherwise, is to encourage
poaching. The debate rages on.

꒭꒭꒭꒭꒭꒭꒭꒭꒭꒭꒭꒭

During a discussion in Harare, Rowan Martin once presented
African conservation to me in pure dollars-and-cents terms,

drawing upon a comparative analysis that Kenya's Ian Parker had made of national parks and reserves throughout the continent. The current cost of absolute protection for wildlife appeared to run around U.S. $400 per acre per year, Rowan noted. If you could afford that, you could probably keep each and every species you wanted safe, no worries. South Africa spent such sums and had enviable results. Zimbabwe spent almost as much in some areas to counter heavy rhino poaching.

For U.S. $200 per acre, which is about what Zimbabwe was spending on the average, you had adequate protection of most species. If you dropped down to $100 per acre, you might still get acceptable results in general, but certain species prized by the bad guys would begin to disappear. And once you slipped below $100 per acre, you had no right to expect to save much beyond the most adaptable species. How much had countries such as Kenya and Tanzania been spending in U.S. dollars per acre to protect their reserves during their era of heaviest poaching? Less than $10. This was the rule rather than the exception in Africa.

Rowan's point was clear: All the rhetoric about the value of preserving nature, all the poetry, all the moralizing and appeals to people's better impulses that can be mustered, won't do the job. If you want wildlife, you have to pay for it, like anything else. There is no alternative in the real world of modern Africa.

For a long time, Zimbabwe's excellent park system reflected a high investment in protection by the government. Lately, funding had been cut way back as Zimbabwe's economy struggled, and the results were beginning to show, especially in the national parks. Wardens such as Sergeant Mlambo told me they barely made enough to feed their families while they were off on patrol. Many seasoned veterans left for the private sector.

In Mark Butcher's opinion, these were further arguments for having wildlife generate its own income through safaris and CAMPFIRE programs. His Forestry Commission, a peristatal organization, was currently able to spend three or four times as much as the parks department per acre of reserve.

Yet parks were one of the prime foreign-currency earners in the nation. The problem, as usual, was that the income was sucked away into the bottomless hole of the central government. "We'd be the richest government agency of all if we got to keep the revenue parks generate," Kathy Martin said. "Instead, we get about six cents of every dollar we earn. We're having to rely on private donations to buy enough gas to keep pumping water at certain drinking holes in Hwange."

Zimbabwe's CAMPFIRE program holds tremendous promise, but it is no panacea. After all, most of the rhino and elephant poachers come not from Zimbabwe's communal lands but from Zambia, Botswana, and Mozambique. Perhaps those countries need community wildlife programs of their own. In fact, Zambia already has them, but they don't seem to have slowed down the flow of poachers to Zimbabwe. Curiously, Zambia is one of the countries joining Zimbabwe in its petition to get the elephant removed from Appendix I so that ivory can be sold again.

None of this undermines the basic premise of CAMPFIRE. As Butch said, "I dunno if it will work completely or not. But we ought to give it a bash."

The one thing I had not done was actually go on an elephant hunting safari. But I was about to. Through the auspices of National Geographic, I had arranged earlier to accompany some Americans who planned to go after trophy animals with Butch. Now the time had arrived to get down to stalking and shooting.

So far, all I had heard were the stories of the guides I had met at gatherings here and there. The tales they told one another were not of derring-do but of clients who gut-shot their prey, condemning it to a slower, painful death so as not to take a chance on ruining the head or cape (forequarters) for mounting by the taxidermist. There was the tale of an underworld figure from Chicago on safari in the bush, accompanied by his bodyguards, who wore shiny black shoes and carried revolvers under their shiny suit coats. ("Little snub-nosed .38 specials! What were they going to stop with those pop-guns?") Tales of wealthy Arabs arriving with an entourage of bodyguards plus imported hookers.

My favorite was a tale from back home of a man who offered exotic game safaris in Texas—the kind where the client drives in to a fenced ranch pasture and shoots a trophy. The man imported five leopards from Zimbabwe and presold hunts on all of them with little trouble. Unfortunately, the last leopard died before the client arrived to hunt it. The game rancher put the leopard in a freezer and then, just before the shooter showed up, stuck the frozen cat high in a tree. The client blasted it, the body fell to the ground. Quickly, the rancher started in with a prepared patter about how the cat was wounded and vicious and the hunter must not approach for any reason. Heedless, the client crept forward to finish the job, only to find his prey not only dead but so stiff that it had all four legs sticking straight up into the air.

The American hunters I rendezvoused with at the Amandundamella forestry safari camp in the Tjolotjo area were very pleasant and mannerly folks. They comprised two families, and the most enthusiastic hunter in the group was one of the women. They were Texans. They were in the oil business. They were dressed in brand-new safari outfits from head to boot, even though they did this sort of thing all the time. One of the men spent at least four months of every year traveling the world to hunt game, from Mongolian sheep to little dik-diks. He had already shot eleven elephants and now wanted a Hwange-type bull. He had a snarling pride of eight lions mounted in his house and wanted more.

Butch intended to get him a lion right off and win points with some communal people at the same time: just the day before, several herders had come to him complaining of a male lion that was clawing their herds every night. By the same token, Butch hoped to use the elephant safari to take out a couple of bulls that had been causing more than their share of problems in fields.

To warm up, the Texans started shooting plains game on a vlei just downhill from camp. In the morning, after a breakfast served by the large native staff, the hunters would be driven off, riding on padded seats high in the back of two specially equipped and freshly scrubbed vehicles. Soon, we would hear the guns booming. Then the natives would appear hauling a carcass from a truck to the butcher shed to be hung and processed. The Texans would return for meals, as spotless and perfectly creased as ever, accepting the cool drinks proffered along with congratulations as they stepped down from the vehicle. In the evening, they would regale us with tales of the day's pursuit and other safaris in exotic lands. Sometimes, they went a little misty-eyed—though it could have been an effect of the after-dinner brandy—as they spoke of the hunt as a timeless part of human-kind and of how nonhunters would never know the deep and an-cient joy of the stalk, the sweat and toil, the feel of warm blood on the hands. The staff would set fresh drinks on fresh linen nap-kins, and the stories of timeless, savage union between hunter and prey would continue into the night.

You see? I can't write objectively about the situation, and that is not right. These were genuinely decent folks and probably more open-minded than I. I had kidded myself into thinking I could make an unbiased report. I really believed I could when I spoke to the Texans back in the States and tried to convince them to let me join in. But I could quickly tell that it wasn't going to work. I now felt that if I carried on with them through the plains game warm-up all the way to the elephant shoot, I would be be-traying their good will and doing both them and National Geo-graphic a grave disservice. Nothing fair to the hunters was going to come of it; my prejudices were too deep.

I grinned my way through a few more meals, cocktails, and safari tales; grinned my way through the jokes of the guides in the bunkhouse, who were a good, hospitable bunch, too. June Farquhar, the camp manager, was a notorious animal lover who kept a tame kudu on the grounds. She took a lot of kidding from the guides, but they were really trying to take some of the sting out of the proceedings by exaggerating their barbarity. "Murder Day today, eh, June? We're going to smoke 'em out there, blow the little furry bastards to hell, and make the vleis run with blood so we can get on to the elephants." June grinned. I grinned. My mouth was getting tired.

In the end, I made up a polite reason for excusing myself from the hunt early. I spoke with Butch and expressed my moral di-lemma about staying on. I could see he was disheartened. Yet he himself had told me that when he first started, he had no use for the safari business and thought it a lot of overblown nonsense. His view had evolved since then. "Moral niceties are secondary. I'm sorry. This is Africa," Butch told me. "People are hungry for land and meat. And where are all these lovely animal lovers when we've got poachers slipping by in the night and farmers suffering from malnutrition and cows beating hell out of the land. If they don't like what we're doing, for God's sake come out and show us what will work. We know this does. All the world sees conservation as merely limiting the damage. Here is Zimbabwe actually increasing animal habitat."

I said I was more convinced than ever of the need to make conservation economically viable to local people, and he had shown me a sound, pragmatic way to go about it. My problem was personal. I still could not accept the idea that the best scheme we could come up with for protecting beings such as elephants was to let wealthy foreigners come and knock them down to add to their collections.

I had been two years on the elephant trail, and now I was going home. My work was not finished—far from it. I was done with the field part of it, though, for I felt I had seen and heard all I could possibly absorb. From here on, my job was not to gather more information but to try and interpret what I had already learned about the fate of elephants. Then I needed to summarize what that told us about the fate of nature as a whole.

A FUTURE

🝔🝔🝔🝔 YEAR AFTER YEAR through the 1970s and 1980s, elephant herds were gunned down at a pace not seen since the bison massacre on America's frontier. And, year after year, opponents of a ban on ivory argued that such an action would only make elephant tusks more valuable and lead to even more illegal killing. They were mistaken. As soon as CITES listed the African elephant on Appendix I of the Endangered Species List in 1990, prohibiting international trade in tusks, the market for them crashed. It has remained relatively minor ever since. Curtailed demand has kept the price of ivory down, which has in turn curtailed poaching.

Not that the whole bloody business has ceased. Though tusks bring but a fraction of their former price, they are still worth several months' wages to rural people in quite a few nations. According to various sources, the international black market for ivory is increasingly dominated by the same criminal syndicates running drugs and other contraband. They have the networks in place; they move whatever is profitable.

Millions of pounds of mammoth and mastodon ivory have been prized from the ground over the years. They can be legally traded, and some poached elephant ivory is being passed off as having come from fossil tusks. Fortunately, scientists at the National Fish and Wildlife Forensics Laboratory in Ashland, Oregon, recently discovered a method to distinguish ancient tusks from modern ones. Using a scanning electron microscope, they focus on the tooth's characteristic crosshatched patterns, called Schreger lines. These are formed by tiny dentinal tubules, which turn out to be twice as dense in mammoths and mastodons as in modern elephants. As a result, the Schreger lines meet at angles of less than 90 degrees in the bygone species but more than 110 degrees in existing elephants, a minor but unmistakable difference. Forensic techniques can also distinguish proboscidean ivory from that of hippos, wart hogs, and walruses. Conservationists hope that advances in chemical "fingerprinting" techniques will soon enable specialists to identify which particular elephant population a tusk came from, on the basis of DNA from tissues coating the base of the tooth.

In addition to low-level ivory poaching, elephants continue to be subject to poaching for meat. Many end up killed or injured in traps and snares that poachers set to catch other creatures. Perhaps even more are purposefully killed or injured as they come into conflict with expanding human settlements. These kinds of losses are widespread but extremely difficult for officials to control. I know of a country that is comparatively uncrowded and prosperous, with a high level of education and concern for resources, and even there the number of game animals poached each year equals or exceeds the number taken lawfully by hunters. This country is the United States. For that matter, it has an ivory debacle of its own. Under the guise of subsistence hunting, Native American poachers, in collusion with dealers, have lately been slaughtering walruses by the thousands for their tusks.

At the 1992 meeting of CITES held in Kyoto, Japan, in mid-March, five southern African countries—Zimbabwe, South Africa, Botswana, Malawi, and Namibia—lobbied to downlist the African elephant from Appendix I to Appendix II, changing its status from endangered to threatened. Although they agreed not to resume trade in ivory in the near future, they said they wanted to sell hides and meat.

Only two other nations among CITES' 112 members, Japan and Switzerland, supported downlisting. Once it became obvious that their proposal would be soundly rejected, the southern African block withdrew it. But they did not agree to abide by the will of the majority. Instead they left threatening to establish trade in elephant products—including ivory—among themselves and the more than fifty nations that are not signatories to CITES and do not abide by international regulations on commerce in wildlife.

Such a move could undercut the current ban, greatly damage CITES and all species it attempts to protect, revive the ivory poaching frenzy, put African elephants back in free-fall toward oblivion, and add heavily to pressures upon the already seriously endangered Asian elephant. It seems sad that the fate of the elephant should hinge on something so arbitrary as human spitefulness, but that is how matters stand at this stage of history. Rather than take it as cause for despair, we might seize the opportunity to overhaul the way we deal with our world's living resources.

🜲🜲🜲🜲🜲🜲🜲🜲🜲🜲🜲🜲

My *National Geographic* assignment to report on elephants was sparked by the ivory holocaust sweeping Africa. Yet one of the first things I learned was that the fever for tusks involved Asian elephants as well and to a greater extent than many people realized. And the demand driving the whole crisis emanated from still different portions of the globe, where consumers had a surfeit of disposable income—Japan, Europe, and the United States. The next thing I learned was that, despite the enormity of the international ivory trade, and despite all the controversy, political maneuverings, and publicity keeping it company, this was not really the gravest threat to the elephants' future. The ultimate threat comes from the explosive growth of the human populace.

Both *Loxodonta africana* and *Elephas maximus* are already running out of living space among 5-plus billion of us. Where are they, with their huge needs, to fit as humanity increases to a projected 10 billion to 12 billion within the next half-century? Before I started traveling so extensively in tropical countries, the population bomb had been a largely abstract concept to me. It quickly became the overwhelming reality of my existence, as it was for virtually every other creature I encountered. The ivory ban promises to be only a temporary reprieve in the struggle of the last true giants that stride the land to keep a home on this planet.

The problem is not just that elephant habitat is shrinking in terms of absolute size. It is being fragmented at the same time, shattered into discontinuous shards. Conservation biologists have a particularly descriptive term for areas where development cuts off one portion of habitat from another; they call them fault lines or fault zones. For example, when clearing for farmland creates fault zones that divide a solid expanse of elephant range into several separate chunks, the actual habitat available might only be reduced by, say, a quarter. Yet if none of the resulting chunks is large enough in and of itself to sustain an elephant population year-round, the population could eventually be lost completely. This is the actual case far more often than not.

Fragmentation also has serious consequences for the other species living in elephant range. To fully understand why, we need to turn to the realm of ecological theory known as island biogeography. I am going to draw upon "The Biodiversity Challenge," a special report I wrote for Defenders of Wildlife, for help in outlining this complex subject:

"It only makes sense that large geographical areas should hold more animals than small ones. But why will the larger areas also hold more *kinds* of animals? Scientists first recognized a correlation between species richness and area early in this century. Then, during the 1960's, ecologists studying the biota of islands developed a set of principles relating the size and isolation of areas to the number of species the areas can support over a period of time. The findings most relevant to conservation as a whole come from the study of what are called land-bridge islands that used to be attached to the mainland before being cut off by the sea.

"The longer an island has been isolated, the less its flora and fauna will have in common with communities on the mainland.

Many of the island's original species will have gone extinct, while many of the survivors will have evolved into uniquely adapted forms. Over time, the biota of the smaller islands becomes especially skewed, with a marked drop in overall biodiversity. Such areas simply cannot hold enough members of certain species, especially the larger animals, to maintain a stable gene pool. Small, insular populations lack the genetic flexibility to cope with changes in the environment, and their vulnerability worsens as undesirable traits accumulate through inbreeding. Sooner or later the result is extinction. The loss of each species ripples through the community, further destabilizing the balance among survivors and often triggering more extinctions.

"If you compare a particular island to one that is generally similar but only a tenth as large, the smaller island may be expected to hold only about half as many species, and often far fewer. Now, let's turn to a habitat slated for development on the mainland. Suppose a tenth of the original area is slated to be set aside in a preserve. That may be a fairly generous percentage in many people's minds, especially considering that just five percent of the lower 48 states as a whole lies within protected areas. They might assume that this preserve—this island within a sea of disturbance—ought to be more than enough to maintain a representative sample of all the community's original inhabitants. They might be right for a few years. Then every year afterward, they would be more and more wrong. . . .

"The main lesson of island biogeography is this: We cannot tuck species away in little preserves as if we were storing pieces in a museum, then come back a century later and expect to find them all still there. The essence of life is change. Organisms are constantly growing, interacting, adapting, evolving. Their numbers and distribution across the landscape fluctuate in cycles linked to climatic patterns and to other, less understood rhythms. They are defined as much by their place in food webs and nutrient flows as by their own physical traits or any current geographic location. Many alter their range and behavior under different conditions. Some assume entirely new behaviors through learning. In short, an ecosystem is not a collection of plants and animals. It is a seamless swirl of communities and processes. If you don't save the processes, you won't save the parts. So if you're going to create a preserve, you had better make it a big one. . . .

"The plain fact is that most of our existing preserves have the same problem as fragments of habitat elsewhere . . . : they are too small and isolated to guarantee the long-term survival of many of their wild residents. Few, if any . . . are big enough to sustain species with very large home-range requirements. . . ."

Almost none are big enough to sustain a minimum viable population of elephants. Moreover, Asian elephants, African savanna elephants, and African forest elephants are all keystone animals, meaning that they strongly shape the communities they inhabit. Once such giants cease to play their usual ecological role, the loss of species diversity that occurs over time in small, isolated islands of habitat can be all the more profound.

<hr>

From the outset, I felt that questions about the survival of elephants are part of a greater question concerning whether or not nature itself will endure. Well? Will it? After following elephants all over the world, what did I decide? I think nature will endure as a collection of individual plant and animal species. But, as I pointed out, ecosystems are really much more than that. Nature is a superstructure of communities and processes from which issues a flow of wonder and possibilities. That flow, creation, the very nature of nature, will be greatly diminished before long, I fear. I do not see how it can continue as we have known it without big, diverse stretches of wildlands and linkages between them—the very things elephants need to survive.

The metaphor of the canary in the coal mine may be terribly overworked, but try thinking of elephants in that context. If a trumpeting, five-ton canary cannot hold our attention, what can? The giants are an excellent indicator of the dimensions of the natural world we are going to be able to save. How large and varied? How strong and healthy and interconnected? Where will there be places that cannot merely preserve the likes of elephants, peacocks, orangutans, and buffalo but preserve that magnitude of evolutionary potential? Such beings were not fashioned by small, hemmed-in, or simplified ecosystems, and they will not long be maintained by them.

Elephants also tell us that the diversity of indigenous human cultures is tied to natural diversity. It is no coincidence that my travels to prime elephant range took me to the homeland of pygmies and Bushmen in Africa, Kurubas in India, Negritos in Malaysia, and other aboriginal groups. They are part of the last untamed ecosystems. You may not agree with Thoreau's famous dictum that in wildness lies the salvation of the world, but it certainly represents the salvation of the world of some peoples. As the final grand tracts that sustain elephants go, so go native human societies and their knowledge of how to live on the earth. So go those alternatives to modern mass culture and the large-scale industrial development that serves it.

In his book *The End of Nature*, Bill McKibben makes the case that once our activities begin to influence global temperature, ozone concentrations, weather patterns, and so on, all environments become, to some extent, artificial; to speak of the natural world as a realm distinct from modern human culture is mere nostalgia. I agree, but for somewhat different reasons. Even if all the indications of global warming and ozone loss prove to be normal fluctuations and nothing to be alarmed about, I would argue that the end of nature as we have known and understood it is indeed at hand, because the evolutionary process can no longer operate in the fashion that produced the past and present diversity of life on Earth.

Let me describe the population bomb in a slightly different way. It took more than a million years for human numbers to add up to 1 billion. That mark was reached around the year A.D. 1800, two centuries ago. The second billion was added during just the next 130 years. Barely thirty years later, the third billion had arrived. Fifteen years later, the total was 4 billion. We reached our current 5 billion in another dozen years.

Twelve years, compared to more than a million years for the first billion people. Plain enough? For most large species throughout the planet, the primary forces influencing how many there will be and where they will be found are now those generated by humans: global deforestation, replacement of native flora with crops, replacement of native fauna with livestock, fragmentation of intact ecosystems, hunting, trapping, trade in wildlife and its products—and, occasionally, the setting aside of reserves and other protected areas.

I plainly saw the end of self-sufficient nature in Asia. I believe it heralds the fate of Africa, whose human population is surging while intact wildlife communities become ever smaller and farther apart. The old vitalizing flow of wildness from one area to the next is being choked off. As if to underscore that fact, both Namibia and South Africa already have game-proof fencing completely around wildlife reserves, and Kenya's government has called for the fencing of all that country's major reserves.

I found plenty of reasons to be discouraged about the prospects for conserving the earth's wild heritage. But then who among the observers of nature hasn't lately? Eco-woe and gloom are cheap. The important question is: What are the solutions? What did I learn of those?

I learned the value of the strategies offered by conservation biology to counter fragmentation. Step one: where possible, protect areas of landscape dimensions—huge expanses on the order of an entire plateau, or all the lands drained by a particular river system from high elevations to low bottomlands. Examples of well-planned reserves include the vast Serengeti Plains, with portions in both Kenya and Tanzania, and the Nilgiri ecosystem, involving three different states in India. Step two: design reserves so that a fully protected core area is surrounded by buffer zones in which the needs of wildlife can be integrated with increasing levels of human activities. This is the model favored for biosphere reserves, established under the United Nations' Man and the Biosphere Program, for which the Nilgiri area can again serve as an example. Step three: build in connectivity by also setting aside lands that lead from one protected, buffered landscape to the next, thereby minimizing the island effect.

Fragmentation of habitat has its counterpart in fragmentation of resource management. Responsibilities are divided among a welter of agencies and organizations with competing sets of goals, sometimes in different nations that don't get along very well. Building linkages between wild tracts of land is going to require better linkages between groups of people. The goal is positive; the potential, tremendous. But the practicality of it all is doubtful.

During the course of my travels, the percentage of elephant habitats unbalanced by serious civil unrest, if not outright war, was startling. I kept wondering: How can we hope to get along with other species when we are doing so poorly at getting along with one another? In fact, much of the threat posed to wildlife by our exploding population has to do with the political instability that overcrowding and resource scarcity engender. A fiery instant of upheaval within a nation can unravel all the carefully laid schemes for long-term protection of nature. How many nations have gone a century without at least one such upheaval? How many have gone ten centuries?

Perhaps Thoreau's dictum should be revised to say that in tolerance lies the salvation of the world. Humankind does seem to be making progress in that respect, albeit slow and fitful progress. There is still slavery and subjugation of minorities, tyrannies and torments of every kind. But there is not as much as there used to be. And the fact that the most widely suppressed group of all, women, are assuming a greater role than ever before in governing surely ought to improve the prospects for peace. An odd thought arises: Won't egalitarianism eventually lead to more cultural uniformity rather than cultural diversity? Not necessarily. Not if we follow the example of nature, whose great achievement has been to create wholeness and stability out of infinite variety.

I'd rather stick to known facts about elephants. I'm uncomfortable drawing conclusions about their fate in relation to human society. My travels taught me that I couldn't hide from the subject, though. I learned that one of the serious failures of conservation in the past has been its tendency to exclude local human communities and their aspirations from schemes to protect wildlife communities. As long as people feel conservation is being imposed upon them from above, a country's preserves may last no longer than the current government's power. If, by contrast, those people have a direct interest in saving natural habitat—perhaps for tourist revenue, but maybe just to ensure a reliable source of water for irrigation and wood for cooking fuel—the resources within a reserve have a far better chance of weathering political flux.

This brings me to a final problem and possible solution in conservation. To save species in the coming years is going to require an exceptional effort. I do not really believe people are going to put forth that effort because they are moved by intellectual concepts such as biodiversity. Nor do I see any assurance that practical reasons to protect nature over the long term can always compete with the short-term profits to be made by pillaging it.

A deeply held moral conviction can be a stronger motivator than either scientific knowledge or riches. However, the conservation movement lacks a common philosophy to clarify our relationship with fellow creatures. What *is* the right way to treat beings such as elephants? What is their proper share of land and resources? Why bother to keep them around in the first place? It depends upon whom you ask.

We have relied upon animals for survival throughout our own evolution as a species. Mostly, we hunted them for food. Later, we developed ways to domesticate some to have them closer at hand when we got hungry. This was neither good nor bad, only a condition of our existence. But because of our capacity for empathy, we did wonder at times whether it was good or bad. We wonder still.

We cannot help but recognize commonality between ourselves and other species, especially the more intelligent and expressive ones. Yet large segments of society subscribe to moral and philosophical systems that emphatically distance ourselves from other creatures. They are beasts, one and all, say the believers; humans are an altogether different and superior kind of being.

What we have done is to fashion a big moral loophole for ourselves so that we can continue to exploit other beings without guilt and confusion. At least, that's how it seems. Consider the way we also demean human enemies and competitors as being far less worthy than ourselves—dirty where we are clean, stupid where we are clever, savage where we are refined, and so forth. Such belittling is not a conscious trick so much as a pattern of rationalization that has emerged over time, like other codes of belief. It helped us get on with our affairs and attain dominion.

Today, our challenge is less to subdue other species than to hang on to those that remain. Yet we continue to assume that the barriers we fabricated between us and animals have some counterpart in reality. The facts insist otherwise. No obvious differences distinguish our glands, nerves, or muscles from those of most other mammals. They're made of the same stuff; they work the same way. No great gulf divides the sort of emotions and social relationships displayed by other species from those that characterize us. Nor do we seem to be nearly as far removed from other mammals in the matter of mental faculties as we once believed.

If I learned anything from my time among the elephants, it is the extent to which we are kin. The warmth of their families makes me feel warm. Their capacity for delight gives me joy. Their ability to learn and understand things is a continuing revelation for me. If a person can't see these qualities when looking at elephants, it can only be because he or she doesn't want to.

If a continuum exists between us and such beings in terms of anatomy, physiology, social behavior, and intelligence, it follows that there should be some continuum of moral standards. Shouldn't there? This is not to argue, as some animal rights advocates do, that identical standards should apply to all species.

But placing wild creatures in an entirely separate moral sphere cannot really be justified either, except by expediency.

I want to believe that we will ultimately save elephants and that we will do it because we acknowledge and accept their commonality with us. The moral progression that is gradually taking us beyond the old patterns of arrogance, prejudice, and subjugation of our fellow humans will come to include other species to an ever larger degree. I wouldn't be surprised if elephants, closely and clearly observed, help show the way.

SELECTED BIBLIOGRAPHY

Amin, Mohamed, and Ian Parker. 1983. *Ivory Crisis*. London: Chatto & Windus.

Beard, Peter H. 1988. *The End of the Game*. San Francisco: Chronicle Books.

Bell, W. D. M. 1923. *The Wanderings of an Elephant Hunter*. Suffolk: Neville Spearman.

Bosman, Paul, and Anthony Hall-Martin. 1986. *Elephants of Africa*. Cape Town: Struikhof Publishers.

Carrington, Richard. 1958. *Elephants*. London: Chatto & Windus.

Chadwick, Douglas H. 1991. Introduction to *Landscape Linkages and Biodiversity*. Edited by Wendy E. Hudson. Washington, D.C.: Island Press.

———. 1991. "Elephants: Out of time, out of space." *National Geographic* 179 (5): 2–49.

Cumming, D. H. M., R. F. DuToit, and S. N. Stuart. *African Elephants and Rhinos: Status Survey and Conservation Action Plan*. Gland: IUCN/SSC African Elephant and Rhino Specialist Group.

Douglas-Hamilton, Iain. 1987. "African elephants: Population trends and their causes." *Oryx* 21 (1): 11–24.

Douglas-Hamilton, Iain and Oria. 1975. *Among the Elephants*. London: Collins & Harvill Press.

Freeman, Dan. 1981. *Elephants, the Vanishing Giants*. New York: G. P. Putnam's Sons.

Gale, U. Toke. 1974. *Burmese Timber Elephant*. Singapore: Toppan Printing Co.

Hunter, J. A. 1952. *Hunter*. London: Hamish Hamilton.

Khan, Mohammed Khan bin Momin. 1988. *The Status, Distribution, and Conservation of Elephant in Peninsular Malaysia*. Kuala Lumpur: Dept. of Wildlife and National Parks.

Kunkel, Reinhard. 1989. *Elephants*. New York: Harry N. Abrams.

Kunz, George F. 1916. *Ivory and the Elephant; in Art, Archaeology and Science*. New York: Doubleday, Page & Co.

Laws, Richard M., I. S. C. Parker, and R. C. B. Johnstone. 1975. *Elephants and their Habitats: The Ecology of Elephants in Northern Bunyora, Uganda*. Oxford: Clarendon Press.

Lewis, George W. "Slim." 1955. *Elephant Tramp*. London: Peter Davies.

MacArthur, R. H., and E. O. Wilson. 1967. *The Theory of Island Biogeography*. Princeton: Princeton University Press.

Martin, Esmond Bradley. 1981. *The Japanese Ivory Industry*. Gland: World Wildlife Fund-Japan and IUCN.

Martin, R. B., G. C. Craig, and V. R. Booth, eds. 1989. *Elephant Management in Zimbabwe*. Harare: Dept. of National Parks and Wildlife Management.

Matthiessen, Peter. 1991. *African Silences*. New York: Random House.

Milliken, Tom. 1989. *The Japanese Ivory Trade: Tradition, CITES, and the Elusive Search for Sustainable Utilization*. Tokyo: World Wildlife Fund/TRAFFIC-Japan.

Moss, Cynthia. 1975. *Portraits in the Wild: Behavior Studies of East African Mammals*. Boston: Houghton Mifflin.

―――. 1989. *Elephant Memories*. New York: Fawcett.

Moss, Cynthia, and Joyce Poole. 1988. "Relationships and social structure of African elephants." In *Primate Social Relationships, An Integrated Approach*. Edited by R. A. Hinde. Oxford: Blackwell.

Pal, Pradtapaditya. 1981. *Elephants and Ivories*. Los Angeles: Los Angeles County Museum of Art.

Payne, Katharine B. 1989. "Elephant talk." *National Geographic* 176 (2): 264–77.

Payne, Katharine B., William R. Langbauer, Jr., and Elizabeth M. Thomas. 1986. "Infrasonic calls of the Asian elephant (*Elephas maximus*)." *Behavioral Ecology and Sociobiology* 18 (4): 297–301.

Poole, Joyce. 1989. "Mate guarding, reproductive success, and female choice in African elephants." *Animal Behavior* 829 (1).

Rensch, Bernhard. 1957. "The intelligence of elephants." *Scientific American* 196 (2): 44–9.

Santiapillai, Charles. 1987. *Action Plan for Asian Elephant Conservation*. Bogor: World Wildlife Fund-Indonesia.

Scullard, H. H. 1974. *The Elephant in the Greek and Roman World*. London: Thames & Hudson.

Shaffer, M. L. 1981. "Minimum population sizes for species conservation." *Bioscience* 31: 131–4.

Sillar, F. C., and R. M. Meyler. 1968. *Elephants Ancient and Modern.* London: Studio Vista.

Sukumar, R. 1989. *The Asian Elephant: Ecology and Management.* New York: Cambridge University Press.

Williams, Heathcote. 1989. *Sacred Elephant.* London: Jonathan Cape Ltd.

Williams, J. H. 1950. *Elephant Bill.* London: Rupert Hart-Davis.

———. 1953. *Bandoola.* London: Rupert Hart-Davis.

Wilson, Derek, and Peter Ayerst. 1976. *White Gold.* London: Heinemann.

Wilson, E. O., ed. 1988. *Biodiversity.* Washington, D.C.: National Academy Press.

Woodhouse, Charles Platten. 1976. *Ivories.* London: David & Charles.

Wylie, Hugh. 1988. *The Gould Collection of Netsuke.* Royal Ontario Museum.